THE BEST LAND UNDER HEAVEN

LIVERIGHT PUBLISHING CORPORATION

A Division of W. W. Norton & Company

Independent Publishers Since 1923

NEW YORK | LONDON

THE BEST LAND
UNDER HEAVEN

THE DONNER PARTY IN THE
AGE OF MANIFEST DESTINY

MICHAEL WALLIS

Copyright © 2017 by Michael Wallis

All rights reserved
Printed in the United States of America
First Edition

For information about permission to reproduce selections from this book,
write to Permissions, Liveright Publishing Corporation, a division of
W. W. Norton & Company, Inc., 500 Fifth Avenue, New York, NY 10110

For information about special discounts for bulk purchases, please contact
W. W. Norton Special Sales at specialsales@wwnorton.com or 800-233-4830

Manufacturing by LSC Communications, Harrisonburg, VA
Book design by Marysarah Quinn
Production manager: Anna Oler

Library of Congress Cataloging-in-Publication Data

Names: Wallis, Michael, 1945– author.
Title: The best land under heaven : the Donner Party in the age of Manifest
Destiny / Michael Wallis.
Other titles: Donner Party in the age of Manifest Destiny
Description: New York : Liveright Publishing Corporation, a division of
W. W. Norton & Company, [2017] | Includes bibliographical references and index.
Identifiers: LCCN 2017012937 | ISBN 9780871407696 (hardcover)
Subjects: LCSH: Donner Party. | Pioneers—California—History—19th century.
| Pioneers—West (U.S.)—History—19th century. | Overland journeys to the
Pacific. | Frontier and pioneer life—West (U.S.) | Sierra Nevada (Calif. and
Nev.)—History—19th century.
Classification: LCC F868.N5 W36 2017 | DDC 978/.02—dc23
LC record available at https://lccn.loc.gov/2017012937

Liveright Publishing Corporation
500 Fifth Avenue, New York, N.Y. 10110
www.wwnorton.com

W. W. Norton & Company Ltd.
15 Carlisle Street, London W1D 3BS

1 2 3 4 5 6 7 8 9 0

FOR SUZANNE,

MY LOVER, PARTNER,
AND COMPANION
ON EVERY TRAIL

CONTENTS

AUTHOR'S NOTE | xiii

INTRODUCTION: 1846 | xv

PROLOGUE: Donner Lake, June 6, 1918 | xix

ONE: CALL OF THE WEST

1. A Migrating People | 5

2. The Best Land Under Heaven | 8

3. Gray Gold | 16

4. Snake Heads | 22

5. California Dreaming | 27

6. The Bold Plunge | 33

7. Wagons Ho! April 1846 | 39

8. Farewell, April 14–15, 1846 | 42

9. Independence Bound, April 15–May 10, 1846 | 48

TWO: THE JOURNEY

10. Queen City of the Trails, May 10–12, 1846 | 55

11. Indian Country, May 12–18, 1846 | 60

12. Soldier Creek, May 19, 1846 | 65

13. The Others, May 20, 1846 | 70

14. People of the South Wind, May 21–24, 1846 | 75

15. Alcove Spring, May 25–29, 1846 | 82

16. The Rhetoric of Fear, May 30–June 2, 1846 | 89

17. Ebb and Flow, June 3–7, 1846 | 95

18. On the Platte, June 8–10, 1846 | 100

19. Life Goes On, June 10–15, 1846 | 103

20. A Letter from Tamzene Donner, June 16, 1846 | 112

THREE: THE PROMISED LAND

21. Change of Command, June 16–19, 1846 | 117

22. Chasing Mirages, June 19–25, 1846 | 122

23. Sage Advice, June 26–27, 1846 | 126

24. A Sense of Urgency, June 28–July 12, 1846 | 133

25. Parting of the Ways, July 13–19, 1846 | 141

26. The Donner Party, July 20–28, 1846 | 147

27. Betrayed, July 28–31, 1846 | 150

28. The Hastings Cutoff, August 1–22, 1846 | 157

29. The Fearful Long Drive, August 23–September 10, 1846 | 164

30. Race against Time, September 11–October 4, 1846 | 175

31. Blood Rage, October 5–20, 1846 | 181

32. Perseverance, October 21–30, 1846 | 194

FOUR: OUT OF TIME

33. Snowbound, November 1846 | 205

34. Desperate Times, Desperate Measures,
November–December 1846 | 217

35. The Forlorn Hope, December 1846 | 230

36. Camp of Death, December 1846 | 240

37. The Starving Time, January 1847 | 250

38. In Dire Straits, January–February 1847 | 262

39. Man on a Mission, January–February 1847 | 269

40. To the Rescue, February 1847 | 278

41. The First Relief | 282

42. The Second Relief | 292

43. The Third Relief | 339

44. The Fourth Relief | 351

Aftermath | 355

APPENDIX 1: DONNER PARTY MEMBERS AND AFFILIATION WITH GROUP | 359
APPENDIX 2: RELIEF TEAMS AND DONNER PARTY SURVIVORS/DEATHS | 371
ACKNOWLEDGMENTS | 375
NOTES | 379
BIBLIOGRAPHY | 427
INDEX | 437

AUTHOR'S NOTE

THIS IS THE story of a large cast of disparate characters whose lives intertwine in pursuit of a single action—the opening of the American West. Much of their quest is revealed through quotations and paraphrase of their own letters and journals.

In telling the story of the Donner Party, many families and individuals emerge throughout the chapters. Not all those characters started with the Donner and Reed families and their hired hands and servants who comprised the original wagon caravan that departed from Springfield, Illinois. To help the reader, I have included a complete list of all members of the Donner Party and a route map.

I have also selected several major figures that had a significant role in the Donner Party drama. The voices and actions of those central characters, along with many secondary characters, are interwoven throughout the book. Although most accounts of the Donner Party portray the members' actions as either heroic or villainous, it can be argued that there were no shades of black and white, but only gray.

The canvas for this story stretches westward from the dark topsoil of Illinois across prairies, deserts, and mountains to the foothills of the high Sierras flanking the midsection of California.

This is the story of individuals and families . . . who they were and how they lived. It is the important and neglected "backstory" of these pilgrims of Manifest Destiny.

INTRODUCTION

1846

By the 1840s—despite the bounty harvested from the fertile Illinois soil—restlessness crept across the land. Mindful of the severe cholera epidemics and the lingering consequences of the financial panic of 1837, some farmers, like so many more to come, were inspired also by the promise of a richer life. They had heard the call that swept across the nation as fast as prairie fire, clearly expressing the widely held belief that the United States had a mission to expand, to spread its form of government and way of life across the continent.

The catch phrase "Manifest Destiny" gave the movement a name. John L. O'Sullivan, a New York publisher, coined this rallying cry in an editorial in the July-August 1845 issue of the *Democratic Review* when he proclaimed that it was "by the right of our manifest destiny to overspread and to possess the whole of the continent which Providence has given us for the development of the great experiment of liberty. . . ."

On April 15, 1846, some of the early foot soldiers of Manifest Destiny—a band of emigrants that came to be known in American history as the Donner Party—departed Springfield, Illinois, headed for the Mexican province of Alta California. The America they were leaving behind was a nation of some 20 million people, including Indians and others held in bondage as slaves. Plantations and farms still predominated, but the surge of cities, the stirring of industry, and the rush of transportation and commerce marked the times. There was no holding back America in 1846.

Historian Bernard DeVoto later called 1846 "the year of decision." Not all the decisions proved wise. America was evolving from a struggling new nation into an international force. Only the year before, the sovereign nation of Texas had been annexed and become a slave state. But America wanted more—present-day California, Arizona, New Mexico, Nevada, and Utah. So the nation, led by the bellicose and land-hungry President James K. Polk—known to be "single-minded and fanatical" about acquiring the West—went to war with Mexico. Before the war ended, the United States had lost two thousand men in action and twelve thousand more to disease—but in return, it got all that land.

Some political leaders, such as Abraham Lincoln, the new Whig congressman from Illinois, believed the content of the country's national character had changed—for the worse. But some of Lincoln's acquaintances in Springfield did not share those feelings. As more than a million starving refugees from Ireland's potato famine came to America, thousands of Americans were eager to become part of what they thought would be a grand adventure.

The Donner Party's collective dream, however, tragically morphed into a collective nightmare. Poor timing, terrible advice, and even worse weather meant that only about half of those who started the journey reached their final destination. After becoming snowbound in the Sierra Nevada Mountains near the border of present Nevada and California, the party ran out of food and resorted to feeding off the flesh of their dead companions and family members. It is this aspect of the Donner Party story that makes it grotesquely fascinating and one of the most haunting to come out of the settlement of the West.

In an effort to remove the stigma and shame of cannibalism, published accounts of the Donner Party from members who were children at the time of the tragedy largely avoided or played down the consumption of human remains as a means of survival. Other books and writings chronicling the Donner Party's journey focus on the "unspeakable horrors" experienced in the icy passes of the Sierras.

Kristin Johnson, a highly regarded scholar who served as historian for the Donner Party Archaeology Project, explains, "As it stands . . . none of the currently available histories of the Donner Party was written by a trained historian, and each suffers from its author's lack of objectivity, unfamiliarity with standards of historical scholarship, literary inclinations, or a combination of these factors." In addition, as Johnson and others point out, much new and reliable information has surfaced since the latest books about the subject were published.

The story of the Donner Party is a long and complex account of how a group of people from varied backgrounds, stratified in age, wealth, education, and ethnicity, followed their different dreams. Out of necessity, they were made to unite and battle against the unknown—weather, nature, and finally life and death. Their story has come to symbolize the Great American Dream gone awry. The Donner Party's fate highlighted the ambitiousness, folly, recklessness, and ruthlessness that marked the great expansionist westward movement. The party becomes a microcosm of the United States which, while busily consuming other nations (Mexico and Indian tribes) that stood in the way of westward migration, had the potential to consume itself. This Gothic tale of cannibalism draws a real parallel between individuals consuming flesh and the desire of a country to consume the continent.

Some members of this party of trail-weary pioneers became victims of their own greed. Their story is a frightening reminder of what could be. Were it not for a few wrong turns, bad directions, and fierce winter storms, the Donner Party would have been an unremarkable wagon train. But as it happened, it became a cautionary tale of Manifest Destiny and an unforgettable calamity.

Personal motives of the emigrants varied. Some planned to build permanent homes or farms, but others hoped to make or enhance their fortunes and return east. A few of the younger single men saw the journey into the unknown as the adventure of a lifetime. The bulk of the Donner Party, however, was composed of people who left the country of their fathers to dwell in the land they sincerely believed their children were destined to inherit. They were vivid examples of those who live in the future and make their country as they go along. They found that in pursuing what came to be known as the American dream, nightmares are sometimes the consequence.

On June 6, 1918, the Pioneer Monument was dedicated at Donner Lake, originally Truckee Lake, in California. Atop a twenty-two-foot-high pedestal—the same height as the snow in the winter of 1846–1847—stands an eighteen-ton bronze depicting a pioneer family in honor of all those who ventured across the plains to settle in California.

(Courtesy of the Norm Sayler Collection at the Donner Summit Historical Society)

Pictured at the dedication of the Pioneer Movement are three women survivors of the Donner Party and two governors: Nevada Governor Emmet D. Boyle, Martha Jane (Patty) Reed Lewis, Eliza P. Donner Houghton, Frances Donner Wilder, and California Governor W. D. Stephens. More than five thousand glass vials containing splinters of wood from the Breen family cabin were sold as souvenirs to help fund the monument.

(Courtesy of the Norm Sayler Collection at the Donner Summit Historical Society)

DONNER LAKE

JUNE 6, 1918

On an unseasonably hot Thursday morning below the crest of the Sierra Nevadas, just west of Truckee, California, in a valley sculpted by ancient glaciers, a crowd of thirty-five hundred people gathers for a ceremony to unveil a towering granite monument.

The eighteen-ton bronze statue depicts a pioneer family facing the mountain that needed to be crossed before striding boldly into the future. It sits atop a twenty-two-foot-tall pedestal—the same height as those winter snows of 1846–1847 that came as silently as a serial killer. On this very ground once stood one of the cabins that sheltered some of the trapped emigrants of what came to be commonly called the Donner-Reed Party.

The day before, many of those in attendance were treated to a trout banquet and rides around nearby Donner Lake in one of three steamers. Although it was not stated in newspaper reports, many believe this event will help restore the names and reputations of both those who perished and those who survived that terrible winter siege more than seventy years before.

The audience of dignitaries, area residents, reporters, and visitors from afar now waits for the unveiling of the monument dedicated to "The Pioneers Who Crossed the Plains to Settle in California." There is band music provided by the Native Sons of the Golden West, followed by speeches from the governors of California and Nevada. Then the onlookers erupt in thunderous applause and cheers when two young girls dressed in white pull the drape off the grand bronze statue.

Below the monument, standing with the notables, are special guests of honor—three old women wearing their Sunday best. Martha (Patty) Reed Lewis and sisters Eliza Donner Houghton and Frances Donner Wilder are survivors. Seventy years before, they were little girls fighting to stay alive. Frozen and famished, they huddled together day after day, week after week, for long hard months while the snow kept coming and almost all hope was gone. They were here when there was no more game, no more oxen or horses to eat. They were here when they and their families devoured mice and chewed on boiled hides and pinecones. Then they ate their pet dogs. Finally, they watched as others cut flesh from the dead and ate members of their families and their friends.

Now they are back, representing the eight remaining survivors from that horrific time. They gaze far beyond the crowd before them. They look out to where lodgepole pine and white fir poke out of the smooth rock outcrops and the granite bedrock exposed by erosion and time. They see the meadows where buttons, spoons, coins, and bits of bone remain deep in the earth. They do not cry. All their tears are gone, used up over the years while they grew into women and married and had children and then grandchildren. They learned to listen to the ghosts.

As the crowd cheers and photographers record the scene, Frances slides her hand into the pocket of her coat. She feels the crackers and bits of peppermint. She has always carried morsels of food since the day she was rescued from this place so many years ago. She squeezes the hard candy tight in her fist, and she smiles.

ONE

CALL OF THE WEST

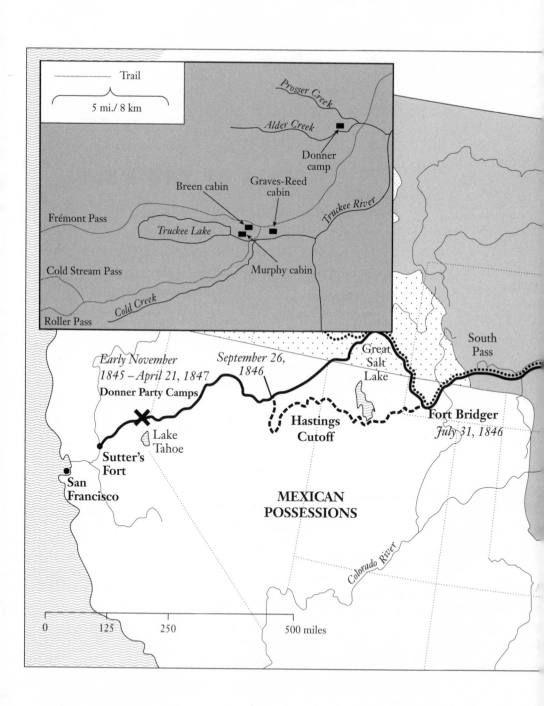

Trail

5 mi./ 8 km

Prosser Creek

Alder Creek

Donner
camp

Breen cabin

Graves-Reed
cabin

Truckee River

Frémont Pass

Truckee Lake

Cold Stream Pass

Murphy cabin

Cold Creek

Roller Pass

South
Pass

*Early November
1845 – April 21, 1847*
Donner Party Camps

*September 26,
1846*

Great
Salt
Lake

✕

Lake
Tahoe

**Hastings
Cutoff**

Fort Bridger
July 31, 1846

**Sutter's
Fort**

**San
Francisco**

**MEXICAN
POSSESSIONS**

Colorado River

0   125   250   500 miles

THE DONNER PARTY ROUTE

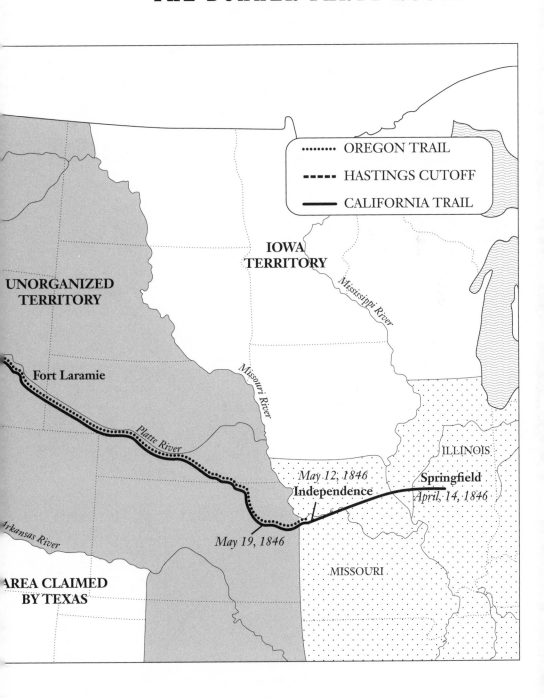

OREGON TRAIL
HASTINGS CUTOFF
CALIFORNIA TRAIL

IOWA TERRITORY

Mississippi River

UNORGANIZED TERRITORY

Fort Laramie

Missouri River

Platte River

ILLINOIS

May 12, 1846
Independence

Springfield
April, 14, 1846

Arkansas River

May 19, 1846

MISSOURI

AREA CLAIMED BY TEXAS

1. A MIGRATING PEOPLE

IT WAS ALWAYS all about the land for brothers George and Jacob Donner, just as it was for the Donners before them. For them, land was money. The Donners were sons of the soil—born to till the earth. They understood crops and cultivation and recognized that those willing to work the land could make egalitarian dreams come true. The Donners were dreamers. All their lives, they dreamed of taming wild land, cultivating crops, and profiting from abundant harvests. Determination was in their blood.

George and Jacob's father, George Donner Sr., was born in 1752 in Lancaster County, Pennsylvania, to German immigrant parents who eventually moved to the colony of North Carolina. When war erupted in 1775, George and two of his brothers fought for American independence.[1] By the time the conflict ended in 1783, the Donner brothers had resumed farming their own lands in nearby Surry County. George Sr. returned home from the militia toting a three-pound cannonball, a keepsake of battle that became a prized family relic.[2]

George was pleased to be back with his wife, Mary Margaret Huff, a native North Carolinian, and reacquaint himself with their first child, Ann Mary.[3] Seven more children followed in rapid succession—Lydia, Elizabeth, George Jr., Tobias, Jacob, Susannah, and John. Like other children of the frontier, George and Mary's brood quickly learned that hard work was a virtue and was essential to their survival. There was always something that needed to be done. This was true not only at planting and harvest times but even in the worst winters. Cooking fires required fuel, fresh game had to be hunted, and work animals needed tending despite deep snowfalls, icy rain, and nights so cold that pails of water froze by the fire. As the oldest son, George Jr. naturally assumed the role of leader and led the other boys on squirrel shoots and forages for sweet wild grapes and fat hickory nuts.[4]

The Donners worked their various farms throughout the 1790s, but by 1795, some began to get itchy feet. At least one of the Donners had already left North Carolina and followed the trail of the adventurous Daniel Boone, moving farther west.[5] Finally, in 1799, George Sr. felt the irresistible urge to uproot his family and seek new land. He sold off his Stokes County property except for a quarter acre reserved as a burial plot for his parents and other family members.[6]

Speculators and promoters claimed the land in Kentucky to be the most fertile in North America and probably the world. Sometime during the early 1800s, George Sr. and Mary Donner, along with family members including George Jr. and Jacob, joined the many other emigrants from North Carolina and Virginia who were moving to Kentucky. Like Donner, most of them had fought in the Revolutionary War and were enticed by the promise of free land for veterans.

The Donners came by the most direct route—due west through the Cumberland Gap of the Appalachian Mountains, across the corner of Tennessee, and then on the popular Wilderness Road into Kentucky. The Donners settled on farmland just south of Lexington, where black loam yielded great harvests of hemp and other cash crops. The Donner children developed an appreciation of fine horse stock as they grew into adulthood. Donner daughters looked for suitable husbands, while some of the sons sought out willing young women ready to become farmers' wives.

On December 12, 1809, George Jr. wed a young local woman, Susannah Holloway. Like most girls of her time, Susannah had had little formal schooling, but she could hand-pull stalks of flax and could hoe corn as well as any field hand. By the time of her marriage, Susannah had already given birth to their first child, Mary, or Polly.[7] George Jr. and Susannah settled into married life. During the next ten years, they had five more children —William, Sarah, Lydia, Elizabeth, and Susannah.

. . .

AS THE VARIOUS branches of the Donner family grew, George Sr. and his sons acquired more land. However, they were ready to move on once again—to neighboring Indiana. After the War of 1812, thousands of Kentuckians, many collecting land bonuses for military service, crossed the Ohio River into southern Indiana.[8] In 1818, just two years after Indiana became a state, the federal government purchased almost all the Delaware and Miami tribal lands in central Indiana. Known as the New Purchase, this huge tract of land was opened for legal settlement in 1821.[9]

By April of that year, the various Donner families—including George Sr. and three of his sons, George Jr., Jacob, and Tobias—had settled in Fugate Township in the northeastern part of Decatur County, where they purchased two eighty-acre tracts of land for $1.25 an acre. Just after the move, Susannah Holloway Donner, his wife and the mother of his six children, died.[10] George's mother, sisters, and sisters-in-law helped care for his children while he farmed the land.

Like many other families of that time, the Donners were always ready to pull up stakes. Their incentive was not lack of economic success. They simply wished to leave what was perceived as depleted land for more fertile ground. Poor farmers could not afford to leave their land, but the Donners could move, and they did just that.

They were of solid and practical German stock, but they also had a touch of the gambler in their blood.

2. THE BEST LAND UNDER HEAVEN

LONG BEFORE THE COMING of any white settlers, virgin prairie stretched uninterrupted across what would become Illinois. The prairie yielded abundant stands of waving bluestem grass as tall as a man on horseback.

At first, nineteenth-century settlers shunned what they called the "much dreaded prairies." Because no trees grew, the newcomers believed prairie soil to be infertile. Instead, they built their cabins in wooded areas where they painstakingly cleared and cultivated the land. Finally, they discovered that the darker soil beneath the prairie grasses was more fertile than the soil under the timber along streams.[1] Illinois topsoil contained just the right amount of organic matter, mineral nutrients, and other ingredients to make it some of the most productive cropland in the world. No manure was needed to fertilize the rich black mold.

A growing number of settlers cast their eyes on Illinois soon after statehood in 1818. Land back east was no longer at a premium. Throughout the 1820s and 1830s, hard-sell hyperbole and the ease of purchasing rich tillable land from the federal government fueled waves of American migration, including sizable numbers of New Englanders.

Among those who caught a whiff of that fecund soil were brothers George and Jacob Donner and other family members, including their father. George Sr. once more ventured west. He bought eighty-acre parcels of Illinois farmland from the federal government as early as 1825, and some of the Donners soon followed suit.[2] It was the old soldier's final move, but not the last for two of his sons and others of the rambling Donner flock.

By 1828, George Jr. and his six children were established in San-gamon County, Illinois, along with his brother Jacob and sister Susannah Donner Organ, her husband, Micajah, and their five chil-dren. Another Donner brother, Tobias, and his family also came but eventually moved on to farm elsewhere in Illinois.

The Donners liked what they found. The Sangamon River formed a large arc through central Illinois. Its name came from a Potawatomi Indian word *Sain-guee-mon* (pronounced "sang-ga-mun"), translated loosely as "Where there is plenty to eat."[3] It was a fitting name. The Sangamon watered the farmlands, and in the winter, ice was cut from the river and stored for summer use. The nearby stands of massive old-growth oak and walnut provided fuel and lumber for building homes and businesses in nearby Springfield, which by 1837 had been chosen as the state capital.

It did not take long for George Jr. to find a Sangamon County wife. On January 10, 1829, he wed Mary Blue Tenant, a childless widow. Their daughter Elitha Cumi Donner was born in 1832, fol-lowed by Leanna Charity in 1834. By that time, some of the off-spring from George's first marriage were on their own, including his only son, William Donner, who had married Elizabeth Hunter in 1832. Then in 1835, George's younger brother, Jacob Donner, ter-minated his bachelorhood by marrying George's sister-in-law Eliza-beth (Betsy) Blue Hook, a divorced woman with two young sons, Solomon and William Hook. Jacob and Elizabeth had five of their own children—George, born in 1837, followed by Mary, Isaac, Sam-uel, and Lewis.[4]

The Donners soon learned that "prairie breaking," as it was called, was not an easy chore. Simple wooden plows could not penetrate the sod, so enterprising farmers used enormous prairie-breaking plows that required as many as eight pairs of oxen to pull.[5] Even then, thick earth clung to the wooden and cast-iron plows, which meant farmers had to repeatedly stop plowing to clean off the soil. The Donners persisted, and farming technology improved, thanks to innovators such as John Deere, a Vermont blacksmith who invented a steel plow that easily cut through the roots of the most stubborn prairie grasses.[6]

The soil that oozed between the barefoot Donner children's toes was indispensable to those who worked the land. The aroma of earth was the promise that they would live another day.

Regrettably, that promise of long life did not extend to all the Donners. Mary Blue Donner, George's second wife and the mother of his two youngest children, suddenly died in 1837 at age thirty-seven. That same year, a national financial crisis—the Panic of 1837—touched off a major recession that rocked Springfield's economy. The combination of his wife's death, the economic dilemma, and that Donner urge to move resulted in George's decision to take a leave of absence from Sangamon County.

In 1838, George Jr., his two little girls, and his grown son William and family packed up and asked relatives to mind their farms. George's brother Jacob and his family joined them. Together, they formed a wagon caravan and headed south to the brand-new Lone Star Republic of Texas. George had heard tales about the offers of land in Texas and decided to have a look.

The Donners acquired land about fifty miles south of Houston, not far from the Gulf of Mexico.[7] They had doubts about the move from the start. Besides finding that the marshy land was not as fertile as prairie soil, the Donners had to deal with snakes and alligators, swarms of mosquitoes, a generally inhospitable climate, and the threat of hepatitis and dysentery.

They also had to be aware of the Karankawa Indians who—even though their numbers had been reduced greatly through conflicts with American colonists—still resided in the coastal region. They were reputed to be cannibals who practiced a ceremonial ritual that included eating bits and pieces of the flesh of their dead and dying enemies.[8] Privateer and slave trader Jean Lafitte called them the "demons of hell."

Shortly after planting their first crop, the Donners realized the move to Texas had been a mistake. About the only good thing that happened during their brief stay was the birth of William and Elizabeth's third child, a healthy boy named George T. Donner after his grandfather.[9] The Donners did not plant a second crop. By 1839, after less than a year's absence, they were safely home with the rest of the family in Sangamon County and once again farming their land on German Prairie in Clear Lake Township.[10]

Soon afterward, George Donner rode out to visit his sisters, Lydia and Susannah, at their homes on nearby Sugar Creek. According to Donner family lore, along the way, George happened upon a diminutive woman and a flock of youngsters standing waist deep in the grasses and blooms of a meadow. He dismounted, swept off his hat, and introduced himself. It was the first time he had set eyes on Tamzene Eustis Dozier. She was simply dressed but elegant with her wide-brimmed hat and gloves. George could see that this was no country girl. She was a lady.[11]

He was apparently taken with her dark hair, gray-blue eyes, and trim figure. Barely five feet tall, Tamzene shook George's large calloused paw. She felt at ease with the bearded and broad-shouldered farmer who was once described as "a large fine-looking man, fully six feet in height, with merry black eyes, and the blackest of hair, lined with an occasional silver thread."[12]

Tamzene explained that she was the schoolmarm at Sugar Creek, leading her students on a botany field trip. They were searching the meadows, thickets, and creek banks for red clover, goldenrod, switch grass, prairie mimosa, and other local plant specimens. That first encounter with Tamzene lasted only a few minutes, but George knew it was not going to be their last meeting. So did Tamzene.

Although she was petite and refined, Tamzene—thirty-seven years old when she met the much older George Donner—was also a determined and resilient woman. Born in 1801 in Newburyport, Massachusetts, she was the youngest child of wealthy mariner William Eustis and his wife, Tamesin. They named their daughter Tamesin after her mother, who died before the girl's seventh birthday. Ultimately, she chose the spelling Tamzene, a version of Thomasine, the feminine form of Thomas.[13]

Tamzene's widowed father later wed Hannah Coggswell, a loving stepmother who encouraged the little girl to pursue her dreams.[14] Like her older siblings, Tamzene was well educated. Always a voracious reader, she also wrote poetry, spoke French, and was schooled in art, philosophy, and mathematics. Her favorite subject was botany, and she put her artistic skills to good use making drawings of the plants and flowers she studied.

After receiving her teacher's certificate, Tamzene accepted a post at a school in Maine. Meager wages and her growing desire to leave the Northeast soon caused Tamzene to grow restless. She took a teaching position at an academy in Elizabeth City, North Carolina, a seaport at the narrows of the Pasquotank River. This meant a major upheaval in her life, but once she made up her mind to move even farther from home, Tamzene was comfortable with her decision.

"I do not regret nor shall I the fatigue expense nor embarrassment to which I have subjected myself," Tamzene wrote in 1824 to her older sister Elizabeth (Betsey) Eustis Poor in Massachusetts. "My heart is big with hope & impatient with desire. There is one impression, however, which rises above this huge chaos and presses itself upon my notice [to leave]. It is that the hand of God is remarkably visible in directing my steps. So fully aware am I that he will guide me, that I feel not the least hesitation in proceeding."[15]

By 1829, Tamzene, content with teaching and presiding over the Female Department at the academy, was fast approaching thirty and still single at a time when most women had married by age twenty. Soon, however, she met Tully B. Dozier, a farmer described as "a young man of education and good family." They married on Christmas Eve 1829 in Camden County, North Carolina.[16]

"I do not intend to boast of my husband," Tamzene wrote to her sister Elizabeth, "but I find him one of the best of men—affectionate, industrious and possessed of an upright heart, these are requisite to make life pass on smoothly."

Although Dozier was said to be "not a man of means," the newlyweds lived comfortably on his farming operation and Tamzene's teaching salary. Within two years, they were the parents of a baby boy whom Tamzene lovingly described as bearing no resemblance to her family but "a true copy of his father."[17]

In the same letter to her sister, dated June 28, 1831, Tamzene noted that her son "has been very sick, and for a few days we feared we should lose him but at this time he is in fine health and sitting upon the table as I write. He at one time scolds me for the inkstand and another knocks my knuckles with a spoon." Tamzene also fretted about her husband's well-being. "I have had excellent health since I saw you, but Mr. Dozier has twice been reduced very low since we married. His precarious health and our strong dislike to slavery has caused us to determine upon removing to some western state. But not until next year."[18]

That move never took place. Tragedy brought on by an influenza epidemic intervened, changing Tamzene's seemingly idyllic life. "My sister I send you these pieces of letters that you may know that I often wrote to you even if I did not send," Tamzene wrote on January 26, 1832, in a letter appended to another, unmailed, from the previous year. "I have lost that little boy I loved so well. He died on the 28th of September. I have lost my husband who made so large a share of my happiness. He died the 24th of December. I prematurely had a daughter, which died on the 18th of November. I have broken up housekeeping and intend to commence school in February. O, my sister, weep with me if you have tears to spare."[19]

For whatever reason, there was no immediate reply from her sister. When Elizabeth finally did write, Tamzene found the letter disappointingly brief and less than comforting. In July 1833, Tamzene sent a prickly response. "I received the scrap you sent me and read it over again to see if I could not make more of it; but twenty lines it was and with all my ingenuity I could not make myself believe it was a well filled sheet. But sister, I will do as you like to be done by. See how close my lines are together, how small my hand, and how many words I put in one line; and say does it not please you? And will you not smile to see my name at the last end of the third page? Well, so should I like to have you write—so pleased should I be, and so would I smile seeing no blank space in your letter. You cannot realize the delight I feel at the very sight of 'Mrs. Tamsen Dozier' with a Newburyport postmark. And may you never know, for to feel it must be purchased as too dear a rate."[20]

Lonely and melancholy, Tamzene turned to her love of nature and, as always, her writing. "Tis morning and nature is lovely indeed. I rise very early and I cannot describe my feelings on viewing the dewy southern landscape. It seems my feelings struggle for vent and rushing to my pen (they) are lost for want of words in which to clothe them. Why was I made with eye and heart to enjoy these delights? To overcome all unamiable feelings—to participate in the joys and sufferings of others, to trace every incident in life to a Supreme power and realize that it is also the expression of goodness."[21]

Once her husband's estate was settled, Tamzene reconciled with her sister and returned to the home of her father and stepmother in Massachusetts. She remained there until 1836, when her older brother William, who recently had lost his wife, asked Tamzene to move to his home in Auburn, Illinois, near Springfield, to tutor his two children. Tamzene jumped at the chance. She proved to be so successful that she was soon asked to teach in the local school.

Dealing with a bunch of unruly farm boys was a far cry from teaching young ladies at a fancy academy, but Tamzene was up to the challenge. One of her male students later recalled the moment when Tamzene first entered the classroom. "I looked at her quiet face and diminutive form, and thought how easy it would be for me to pick up two or three such little bodies as she and set them outside the door." The youngster quickly changed his tune once Tamzene took charge. "Her pluck had won our admiration and her quiet dignity held our respect, and we boys ceased to wonder at the ease with which she overturned our plans and made us eager to adopt hers; for no teacher ever taught on Sugar Creek who won the affections and ruled pupils more easily than she. She expected us to come right up to the mark; but if we got into trouble she was always ready to help us out, and she could do it in the quickest way imaginable."[22]

Her students' favorite activity was the frequent field trips she organized to collect plant specimens. And after three successful years of what the boys called "land-looking" and the girls called "botanizing," it was that excursion in 1839 that led to Tamzene's first encounter with George Donner.

George wasted no time. He accelerated the courting process and made every effort to win over the comely schoolteacher. Fortunately for the lovestruck farmer, Tamzene had overcome her sorrow and was ready to have another try at marriage. George was almost thirty years older than Tamzene, but he was a prosperous landowner in good health and was well liked and admired in the community, where folks often called him "Uncle George."

On May 24, 1839, George Donner Jr. wed Tamzene Eustis Dozier in a quiet ceremony attended by family and friends. Tamzene became a caring mother to George's two youngest daughters, who were still at home. In quick succession, three more daughters were born—Frances Eustis in 1840, Georgia Ann in 1841, and Eliza Poor in 1843. George built an elegant stone house for his doting wife and five daughters. Tamzene entertained friends, wrote verse for the local newspaper, and delighted in watching her husband's bees gather nectar from the fields of wildflowers.

"I find my husband a kind friend, who does all in his power to promote my happiness and I have as fair prospect for a pleasant old age as anyone," Tamzene wrote to her sister in 1840. "Mr. Donner was born at the south, in N. Carolina, at eighteen he went to Kentucky, then to Indiana, then to Ill. And a few years ago to Texas. But his rovings, he says, are over; he finds no place so much to his mind as this."[23]

3. GRAY GOLD

THE CHEAP AND FERTILE cropland that attracted the Donners was not the only thing that drew settlers to Illinois. Another major lure was lead. The high demand for this important mineral after the War of 1812 brought large numbers of miners into the Indian lands of northwestern Illinois, which at the time was considered the richest lead-bearing region in the world.

One of those who joined the rush for what became known as "Gray Gold" was an eager young immigrant named James Frazier Reed. By most accounts, his family name was originally Reednoski (sometimes spelled Rynowski) until the late 1700s.[1] That was when Reed's ancestors—purportedly of noble Polish birth—chose exile rather than submission after Poland was divided among its powerful neighbors of Russia, Prussia, and Austria. After fleeing the upheaval in their homeland, the Reednoskis became the Reeds when they moved to Ireland. They established themselves in County Armagh, one of six counties that formed Northern Ireland on the northeastern side of the island, where James Reed was born on November 14, 1800. His mother, Martha Frazier Reed, gave him the middle name Frazier to honor her lineage from the illustrious Clan Frazier of Scottish history.[2]

Reed was just a young boy when his father died. He and his mother then moved to America. They resided in Philadelphia for a short time before settling in Virginia, where other members of the Scots-Irish Frazier family had lived for many years after escaping the tyranny of the British crown. James attended school until he was about eight or nine years of age, old enough "to be of service to himself." Then he moved in with the family of James Anderson Frazier, a maternal uncle, who employed him in a general-merchandise store.[3] By the time he turned twenty, Reed was ready to go out on his own. Like so many others, he had heard stories of the lead bonanza in Illinois and Wisconsin, and he was eager to earn more than clerk's wages. He bid his mother and the other Fraziers farewell and headed west.

Reed moved to Galena, a remote outpost surrounded by Indians and wilderness that was fast becoming a mining epicenter because of the very stuff that gave the town its name—*galena*, the Latin word for lead ore.[4] Carved into a steep, rocky hillside on the Fever River (later named the Galena River), a tributary of the nearby Mississippi, the village was growing into a hub of commerce as men flocked there on steamboats and packets to work the mines. In 1825, the busy river port was larger than Chicago, and only three years later, it exploded to more than ten thousand residents, including transient miners.

Miners such as James Reed, who lived too far from home and had no place to go when winter set in and the steamboats and teams of oxen returned south, had to gut it out in hillside caves or huts. Wintry weather resulted in outbreaks of "cabin fever" that could be soothed by visiting gambling dens and saloons, known as "lighthouses."[5] Liquor flowed freely, and in the back rooms, patrons placed heavy bets at cockfights and wolf fights. Brawls were sometimes settled by "stone duels." Men would stand next to a pile of river rocks and throw stones at each other until one of them was struck "unconscious or dead." Females were said to be "as rare in the diggings as snakes upon the Emerald Isle," so bachelor miners did their own cooking and washing and often sought the services of soiled doves plying their timeless trade.[6]

Besides frequent mining accidents, diseases such as milk sickness, dysentery, pneumonia, and malaria—known at the time as "the fever and ague"—also took a toll.

Although life in a rowdy mining town was a far cry from genteel Virginia, Reed prospered in Galena. It is unknown whether he spent the whole time digging with a pickax by the light of a tallow candle deep in the earth or worked his way into a management post, but after several years, he accumulated a grubstake that allowed him to put his money to good use elsewhere. In 1831, Reed moved south to

Sangamon County, where he eventually entered into several business ventures. He had barely landed in Springfield when he was summoned to take up arms.

In the spring of 1832, a short-lived conflict known as the Black
Hawk War erupted in Illinois and Wisconsin. Black Hawk, a Sauk
war leader, rallied a confederacy of Indians enraged with farmers
who plowed up sacred burial grounds and planted corn on ancestral
land. The Indians had lost the land in a treaty that they considered
invalid. Inevitably, violence broke out between the white settlers and
the Indians.[7] Many settlers abandoned their homes and sought shelter in larger towns or at army posts.

A call went out for volunteers to curb the rebellious Indians. All
white males between the ages of eighteen and forty-five were obli-
gated to enlist at once in the state militia. Reed joined a scouting unit
of mounted volunteers known as the "Spy Company," led by Captain
Jacob M. Early, a Springfield physician who also served as regimental
surgeon.[8] Besides Reed, others on the company's rolls included James
Clyman, a veteran of the War of 1812 who spent years as a mountain man and guide in the far West; Stephen A. Douglas, a rising
star in Illinois politics known as the "Little Giant"; Robert Anderson, a spirited West Pointer who thirty years later commanded Fort
Sumter, site of the start of the Civil War; and a gangly storekeeper
and fledgling politician named Abraham Lincoln. Like the Donners, Lincoln had come to Illinois by way of Kentucky and Indiana,
and like his messmate James Reed, Lincoln had moved to Sangamon
County recently.[9]

Captain Early's outfit saw no real military action during its few
weeks of service other than retrieving and burying the bodies of several other militiamen. "I remember just how those men looked as we
rode up the little hill where their camp was," Lincoln later wrote.
"The red light of the morning sun was streaming upon them as they
lay towards us on the ground. And every man had a round red spot on
top of his head, about as big as a dollar where the redskins had taken
his scalp. It was frightful, but it was grotesque, and the red sunlight
seemed to paint everything all over."[10]

Early's company of mounted volunteers mustered out of service on July 10, 1832, on the White Water River in Wisconsin.[11] Lincoln and Reed's soldiering days were over, but definitely not their relationship.

A natural-born entrepreneur, Reed became involved in a variety of pursuits, including a general-merchandise store that he opened in 1832 that provided enough income for him to purchase a farm.[12] The next year, Reed opened a starch factory just northeast of Springfield at German Prairie, where the Donners resided and farmed.[13]

Commercial starch had not made its way into many households on the Illinois frontier. Until starch came along, cooked gluten paste was used to make men's shirt collars rigid and give body to the voluminous petticoats in vogue with the ladies. Starch was a logical product because so many area farmers, such as the Donners, grew corn and wheat. To solicit farmers and at the same time offer an alternative method of payment to parties who owed him money from various business ventures, Reed placed notices in the Springfield newspaper. He also offered to sell livestock, farm implements, or other goods, including "three yoke of well broke Oxen in good order, and one stout wagon with chains," in exchange for cash or wheat.

Generally, Reed was well liked by his business associates and friends and was described as bright and energetic. However, even those close to him thought he often came off as overbearing or, as some put it, aristocratic, perhaps because of his noble Polish blood.[14]

Among those closest to the young man were members of the Keyes family who, like Reed, had come to Illinois from Virginia. Humphrey Keyes had been a substantial landowner near the Shenandoah River in Virginia with a working plantation and a few slaves when his first wife died, leaving him with five children. He married Sarah Handley in 1803, and the couple had six more children.[15] Keyes's son James opened a tailor shop close to the town square. That is where he probably met Reed. They became especially close friends, and by the time Humphrey Keyes passed away in 1833, Reed had become engaged to Elizabeth Keyes, one of James's younger sisters. The wedding, however, never took place.

Tragically, Elizabeth died in a cholera epidemic that struck much of the nation that summer of 1833.[16] There was no known prevention or cure for what some people called "the ghost on the stairs." Without knowing the exact cause of the disease, doctors were not sure how to treat it beyond bleeding those afflicted.

The pestilence soon became a pandemic. Thousands succumbed on the Illinois frontier. The "destroying angel" not only took the life of young Elizabeth Keyes but also struck the family a second blow by claiming her brother-in-law, Lloyd Carter Backenstoe, a twenty-three-year-old tailor who worked in James Keyes's shop. Backenstoe left behind a widow, Margret Wilson Keyes Backenstoe, and a one-year-old daughter, Virginia Elizabeth.[17]

Born in 1814, Margret—two years older than her sister Elizabeth Keyes—had little time for grief. Apparently neither did Reed. Margret was struggling with illness herself when she gave her dead sister's fiancé permission to come courting. She was, of course, well acquainted with Reed, a frequent visitor sporting a well-groomed beard and wearing handsome suits tailored by her brother. Reed married Margret on a crisp October evening in 1835 after a rather brief engagement. Margret was in such poor health that the wedding ceremony took place with the bride lying in bed and the groom standing beside her holding her hand.[18]

Reed was appointed legal guardian of his stepdaughter in 1836. Although he never formally adopted Virginia, she used his surname, and a strong bond quickly developed between them. Many people who knew the family recalled that the girl was always treated as if she were Reed's own child. When she was a grown woman, Virginia declared that Reed was "the most loving and indulgent step-father that ever lived."[19]

During the eight years following their marriage, James and Margret added to their family. Martha Jane Reed, whom everyone called Patty, was born in 1838, followed by James Frazier Reed Jr. in 1841 and Thomas Keyes Reed in 1843. Their widowed grandmother, Sarah Handley Keyes, also joined the Reed household and helped Margret, who was prone to migraines, with the children.[20]

By most accounts, James Reed—a prosperous businessman, happily married with a brood of youngsters—appeared to be in an enviable position. His various enterprises, including a mercantile store, a starch factory, and real-estate investments, were profitable and allowed him to explore new commercial pursuits. So Reed did not hesitate when he was offered yet another opportunity. It came from John Taylor, a pioneer merchant and land speculator, who platted a new settlement on the Sangamon River, just a few miles from Springfield.

By 1837, talk of bringing a railroad to Illinois had turned to action. That year, the legislature, which included Reed's friend Abraham Lincoln, passed the Internal Improvements Act, which funded a network of train lines, starting with the Northern Cross Railroad, originally planned to run across Illinois from Quincy to the Indiana line.[21]

A contract to construct the rail line between Springfield and the Sangamon was awarded to James Reed. Timber would have to be cut to furnish the ties for the railroad. Plans called for the rail line to pass through Taylor's proposed village site, where he was selling lots for businesses and homes. It was also where Reed had constructed a large mill on the river that would produce the railroad ties.[22] As early as 1835, Reed was paying "a liberal price" for the hundreds of mulberry posts being hauled to his starch mill, where he had assembled a sizable stock of timber.[23]

All that was needed was to choose a proper name for the settlement. Only one name was put forward. It honored the man whose mill employed many men and gave the place a purpose.

They called it Jamestown.

4. SNAKE HEADS

LIFE WAS SWEET as pie for James and Margret Reed for a while. They had a comfortable home in Jamestown, shortened to "Jimtown" by the locals, with plenty of room for Margret's widowed mother, Sarah Keyes, young Virginia, and the four other children who were born in the next several years.

At Reed's mill on the Sangamon River, he stopped producing starch and hired more workers to help turn out wooden ties for the railroad that was being ballyhooed as the first one to operate in "the entire area west of the Allegheny Mountains and north of the Ohio River."[1] Surveying began in 1837 on the first segment of the Northern Cross track linking Meredosia, a tiny town on the east bank of the Illinois River, to the new capital of Springfield, fifty-nine miles away.[2] Although the Panic of 1837 quickly put an end to funding for the Internal Improvement System, political and business leaders remained optimistic that at least this part of the ambitious railroad network appeared to be a certainty.

Grading the right-of-way took all winter. By spring 1838, the construction crews were ready to lay track, but a shortage of materials stymied railroad workers all summer. Iron for the rails had to be shipped from New Orleans to St. Louis and then up the Mississippi and Illinois Rivers to Meredosia. Only eight miles of track had been completed by early November.[3]

Because of the prolonged national economic collapse that ravaged the credit of the Illinois state government and greatly reduced the value of its bonds, work on that section of the railroad line continued slowly for the next four years. The first train finally steamed into Springfield on February 15, 1842. Hundreds of curious people congregated to get a look at the huge iron machine that some people claimed would replace oxen and horses. When the snorting locomotive belched thick clouds of smoke as it rolled noisily into town, many of the gawkers and most of the horses panicked and bolted for cover.[4]

Order was quickly restored, and the public eagerly lined up when the Northern Cross began to make three weekly trips between Springfield and Meredosia. One excursion of thirty stalwart Springfield citizens, which included Abraham Lincoln's future wife, Mary Todd, a brass band, and a cargo of 205 barrels of flour, took the train westward only a little more than thirty miles to Jacksonville for a celebration.[5]

It cost just twenty cents to ship a barrel of flour to the Illinois River. Passengers paid $2.50 for a train ride that took two hours ten minutes one way—if there were no delays, which became more frequent.[6] It was not long before farmers such as the Donners complained that the state-owned railroad was inadequate and inefficient for transporting their products to the best markets.

Traveling by train also could be dangerous and sometimes lethal. Accidents and derailments were not uncommon. Farmers were known to steal rails for use as sled runners and to pull up James Reed's ties for building material. Rails at that time were straps of iron nailed to oak runners, or stringers. Such rails were inexpensive but prone to failure. The constant pounding of the wheels worked the spikes loose. Consequently the iron strap would separate from the wooden base, curl upward, and shoot right through the wooden floors of the coaches, sometimes injuring or even killing a passenger or crewman.[7]

Railroaders dubbed the curls of deadly steel "snake heads." Trusted workers called "snake spikers" were assigned to patrol a certain section of track with a sledgehammer and leather bag of new spikes. If they spied a snake head, they hammered it down flat to the stringer again.[8] In spite of their effort, the snake spikers could not always keep up.

As a result of all the problems, James Reed witnessed his holdings steadily shrinking. Early on in the struggle to build the Northern

Cross, he wisely decided to diversify. He partnered with John R. Weber, a skilled cabinetmaker, and they expanded the Jimtown mill.[9]

Besides producing railroad ties, Reed and Weber manufactured cabinet furniture, mahogany chairs, and ornamental fencing. They even made venetian blinds and sold them "at lower rates than they are imported from abroad."[10] The two men advertised quality craftsmanship and low prices. Cash customers were preferred, but Reed and Weber also gladly accepted "cattle, hogs, wheat, corn, potatoes, bacon, lard, butter, eggs, &c, taken in exchange for work."[11]

The mill hummed along at a steady pace for a few years until 1841, when Weber lost his left hand in a buzz-saw accident. Fortunately for Weber, he was right-handed and soon found work as a copyist recording state land records.[12] Regrettably, Reed was now without a partner who possessed most of the woodworking expertise, but he did not give up. Instead, he placed advertisements seeking a sawyer, timber choppers, oxen driver, and workers to operate the wood turner and lathe.[13] The railroad still needed ties, but ultimately the Northern Cross was doomed.

Not yet ready to surrender, land speculator John Taylor looked for a solution. His sale of lots in Jamestown was far below what had been projected. In 1843, Taylor tried to boost his landholdings and keep railroad momentum going by leasing the entire Northern Cross operation from the state.[14] The tracks and trains were in such poor condition, however, that the locomotive speed was only six miles an hour, down from its average of fifteen the year before. Frequently, mules and oxen had to pull trains when locomotives failed, forcing an embarrassed Taylor, as one observer noted, to watch as "the stagecoaches dashed by in a cloud of dust."[15] To alleviate this problem, different schemes were tried. None of them worked.

By 1845, even the optimistic James Reed had to admit that the Northern Cross rail system was a total disaster. The state continued to run the deteriorating line until 1847, when it was auctioned to a private party for $21,000, or approximately 2.5 percent of its original cost. It eventually became part of the Wabash Railroad system.[16]

With the closing of the railroad, Jamestown fell on harder times.

John Taylor was unable to pay the property taxes on the town. The land was sold at a tax sale.[17] Reed tried to keep his mill going by grinding corn and wheat into superfine flour and meal, but it did not provide enough income to relieve his growing debt.

When his prospects began to sour, Reed turned to an old and trusted friend for counsel—Abraham Lincoln. This comrade from the Black Hawk War had made quite a name for himself in Springfield from his first major trial, a sensational murder case. The victim was Dr. Jacob Early, physician, Methodist preacher, and former commanding officer of Lincoln and Reed in the Black Hawk War.[18] Lincoln's political affiliation was with the Whig Party, forerunner of the Republican Party, and Early was a staunch Democrat.

Lincoln, who knew five of the jurors and was well acquainted with the defendant, victim, and witnesses, was selected to give the defense summation. Stephen A. Douglas, one of Lincoln's chief political and personal rivals, led the prosecution team. It appeared to be an easy case to prosecute. Four state witnesses—James Reed, John Roberts, and James and Henry Spottswood—gave depositions.[19] Despite the overwhelming evidence, Lincoln's final argument (which unfortunately did not survive) maintained that the defendant, Henry B. Truett, had acted in self-defense. The trial lasted three days, and the jurors were out just one hour forty minutes before surprising everyone by returning a verdict of not guilty.[20]

Reed's respect for Lincoln's legal skills not only grew, but so did their friendship. Less than a year after the trial, Reed, one of the executors of the Early estate, engaged Lincoln to petition the Sangamon County Circuit Court to sell off land to settle the estate.[21] Lincoln provided assistance to Reed throughout the early 1840s. No doubt Lincoln gave advice in 1845 when Reed accepted the post of U.S. pension agent for Springfield, dispensing government funds to military veterans. He kept the job less than a year.[22] The income helped Reed to pay off some of his debts, but it was too little and much too late. Out of desperation, Reed mortgaged the mill, along with some other real estate he owned, to the Sangamon County school commissioner for $1,000. Although he faced complete financial ruin, Reed could still rely on Lincoln's legal skills and count on the support of Margret and his children.

More than ever, Reed had to remember the motto that had seen him through ever since he grubbed out a living in the lead mines at Galena—"Persevere."[23]

5. CALIFORNIA DREAMING

THE YEAR 1846 became the pivotal "year of decision," as decreed by historian Bernard DeVoto, when an increasing number of people made up their minds about when and where to go.[1]

By 1845, the Reeds and the Donners, like countless other Americans, generally accepted the idea that God had bestowed on the United States the right to grow and prosper by advancing the frontier westward. The phrase "Manifest Destiny" came from John L. O'Sullivan, editor of the *United States Magazine and Democratic Review*. He urged the annexation of Texas and total control of Oregon Territory, where there was an ongoing boundary dispute with Great Britain. Manifest Destiny became the nation's watchword.[2] The federal government encouraged residents in the East to move across the Mississippi River. There awaited rich natural resources, vast farmlands and rangelands, boundless timber forests, and untapped mineral riches.

This spawned the systematic penetration of the Great Plains first by overland trade, then by yeoman farmers, a movement that fulfilled the dreams of Thomas Jefferson and was said to please almighty God. It galvanized proponents of expansionism and proslavery southern planters eager to expand their domain.

Many of them got their marching orders directly from the pulpit. These were the latter days of religious fervor caused by the Second Great Awakening, a Protestant revival movement in the first half of the nineteenth century. Powerful spiritual figures, such as the evangelical theologian Lyman Beecher, reasserted the claim that America was chosen by the Almighty and was "destined to lead the way in the moral and political emancipation of the world."[3]

Certainly, not all Americans endorsed the idea of a divine mandate. William Ellery Channing, the foremost Unitarian theologian in the United States, wrote to Senator Henry Clay of Kentucky in 1837. "We boast of our rapid growth, forgetting that, throughout nature, noble growths are slow . . . the Indians have melted before the white man, and the mixed, degraded race of Mexico must melt before the Anglo-Saxon. . . . We talk of accomplishing our destiny. So did the late conqueror of Europe (Napoleon)."[4]

Channing's warning would go unheeded. The entwining of religion with the ideology of Manifest Destiny served as a creation myth for the country. It soon became so ingrained in the national consciousness that many Americans still accept it to this day. The belief that God intended for the continent to be under the control of Christian European-Americans became official U.S. government policy. It helped to fuel incentive to take the land from those who were considered inferior to white Americans—indigenous tribal people characterized as savages and Mexicans, who were described as backward. In short, Manifest Destiny became a convenient way to colonize the rest of the continent "from sea to shining sea" and exterminate anyone who got in the way.

Although scars from the Panic of 1837 remained, the restlessness sparked by Manifest Destiny resonated in Illinois, but not everyone in the state was ready to look elsewhere for greener pastures.

Brothers George and Jacob Donner were practical businessmen concerned with the success or failure of their own operation. The same held true for James Reed, a classic capitalist in every sense. In Sangamon County, Illinois, James Reed's family had expanded to five children just before New Year's 1845, when Margret gave birth to Gershom Francis, named after one of her brothers.[5] Besides being another mouth to feed, the newborn son was sickly. Even with help from Margret's mother, Sarah Keyes, and the Reeds' eldest daughter, Virginia, the added stress caused a sharp increase in Margret's debilitating migraines.

Reed became convinced that a fresh start was in order. He cast his eyes westward. Whether or not Abraham Lincoln fully concurred with his friend and client, he understood the attraction. Both Lincoln and Reed had received firsthand reports from family members who had made the long trek to the Pacific in 1845.

William Levi Todd, nephew of Lincoln's wife, Mary Todd, and Robert Caden Keyes, one of Margret Reed's brothers, joined a wagon train that left Springfield in April 1845 bound for what was then called the Oregon Country.[6] Reed and others in Springfield anxiously awaited news from the caravan. A detailed account written in June 1845 by caravan organizer William Brown Ide appeared in a Springfield newspaper two months later.[7] By then, the caravan was at Fort Laramie, more than a thousand miles west of Springfield.

The caravan camped at Fort Hall, in present-day Idaho, to replenish supplies and trade for fresh horses with some Snake Indians. While at the fort, they were approached by Caleb Greenwood, a grizzled fur trapper and trail guide thought to be well over eighty years old, and his three half-Indian sons from a Crow wife.[8] Greenwood was a "squaw man," a white man who had "gone Injun" by marrying into a tribe and adopting its traditions.[9]

Dressed in buckskins and sporting long whiskers, "Old Greenwood" met with the emigrants, hoping to persuade them to head to Alta California, then a province of Mexico, instead of to Oregon. Greenwood—described by one of his detractors as "an old mountaineer, well stocked with falsehoods"—had a vested interest in diverting wagon caravans to California.[10] Hired as a recruiting agent, his main task was to convince any settlers he encountered to move to Sutter's Fort.

A Swiss expatriate, the ambitious but land-poor John Sutter vigorously encouraged American migration to his personal empire, which lay at the terminus of the main westward trail. Sutter frequently dispatched some of his Indian vaqueros, little more than slaves, to assist emigrant parties that were in trouble and needed provisions. Once they arrived at his compound, Sutter sold parcels of land to any newcomers willing to make a go of it.[11]

After the party listened to Greenwood's convincing spiel, a heated debate almost became violent, but the question was put to a vote.

Most of the emigrants, including Ide, Todd, and Keyes, opted for California.[12] With Greenwood and his three sons in the lead, a company of about one hundred struck out for the Sierra Nevadas and the Sacramento Valley and Captain Sutter's colony on the other side of the summit. When the caravan began the ascent of the Sierras, they broke into small groups, each one determined to find its own way to the summit and down the western slope. Little by little, the various parties finally straggled into Sutter's Fort, with far fewer cattle left from the huge herd that had started the journey. The going had been difficult, but they were all thankful that they had made the mountain crossing before the first snowfall.

Young William Todd and the Ide family were among those who took Sutter up on his generous—and somewhat self-serving—offer of assistance. They remained in the area long enough to get their bearings. Robert Keyes, however, took another path and soon made his way with a pack train to Monterey, a major seaport on the sloping Pacific coast and the provincial capital of Alta California.[13] Keyes soon discovered that Monterey was far too exotic for his tastes. In a letter to James Reed in late October 1845,[14] Keyes had nothing good to say about the land in California and made even worse comments about the people. He stated that he would head north to Oregon, where he had planned to go in the first place.

Keyes's report did not deter James Reed, who believed that he could start anew in California and that the climate would be healthier for his frail wife. Once the urge to move to the far West became firmly planted in his mind, he quickly found others ready to join him—George and Jacob Donner. The Reeds were not close friends of the Donners, but they were acquainted through business dealings at Reed's Jimtown mill and a common interest in community affairs. The Donner brothers also had caught the California fever.

Much to the surprise of Tamzene Donner, who had been convinced that her restless husband would never again contemplate moving, George and his younger brother could not resist the siren call of new land. On September 24, 1845, George Donner placed a notice in the newspaper advising "A Good Farm for Sale." He was ready to part with 240 acres, including eighty acres of timber, a productive orchard, a farmhouse with two brick chimneys, and a first-rate water well.[15] Jacob Donner, inclined to take his orders from George, followed suit.

Tamzene Donner, although perfectly content where she was, understood her husband and his restless nature. She quickly adjusted to the notion of leaving her comfortable home, where she entertained family and friends with weekly readings from her library and periodicals. She was fully prepared to leave her gardens and the fields of prairie blossoms and grasses she loved to collect. She knew there would be even more new discoveries in the Eden that waited. First and foremost, she loved her husband and children more than her own breath and wanted only the best for them. Once they were settled in California, Tamzene decided, she could establish a school for girls and resume her passion for teaching.

For James Reed, it was a last chance because there was nowhere else left to go. But even Reed's capacity to persevere was constantly put to the test. On December 10, 1845, his youngest child, Gershom Francis, succumbed to the illness that had plagued him since birth.[16] He was only eleven months twelve days old. His passing brought on the "sick headaches" that incapacitated his frail mother. Margret remained inconsolable for weeks, yet she ultimately came to bear the thought of leaving her child behind in the cold earth because he was laid to rest beside his grandfather, Humphrey Keyes. Many years later, an inscription was chiseled into the boy's tombstone—TOUCH NOT MY LITTLE GRAVE, MAMA IS FAR AWAY.

Besides the specter of death, uninvited visitors came calling at the Reed household. Most of them were debt collectors. Even a cousin in Virginia, where Reed had grown up, called in a promissory note. There is no record of whether Reed responded.

Reed's attitude did not help matters. Always in a stylish suit and riding a fine horse even when he was on the financial ropes, Reed showed a self-confidence that was taken as arrogance. However, those who knew him best recalled that Reed "was more high-handed than high and mighty."[17]

By early 1846, the list of creditors and others seeking recompense from Reed could have stretched from the Springfield public square to the nearby capitol. The final blow came in March 1846 when the circuit court ruled in favor of William Butler in his suit for the $1,000 that Reed had borrowed but could not repay.[18] Reed's land, including the mill, faced immediate foreclosure. Reed was declared insolvent.

Reed had become a "plunger," the name for the most reckless bettors or speculators. As an inventory of all his property and goods and a final list of his creditors were being drawn up for a public sale, Reed stepped up his own preparations for what would become the biggest gamble of his life.

6. THE BOLD PLUNGE

THROUGHOUT THE WINTER and early spring of 1846, the Reeds and Donners readied themselves for the long trek from Springfield to California. Like foot soldiers of Manifest Destiny, they were convinced that the lands on the far side of the continent were theirs for the taking. Now they had to erase the past and plunge into the future.

James Reed and the Donner brothers sought solid practical advice about the new land and tips for negotiating the long trail. Letters from those who had already moved west were printed in local newspapers. The correspondence and other bits of trail wisdom were shared at community meetings and church services. The Donners' church was Prairie Christian Church, a short way north of what some folks called George Donner's "plantation."[1] It was well known that Tamzene used every ploy to get George to go to church, with little or no avail. Her husband's obstinacy on the Sabbath, however, did not stop Tamzene from visiting with other parishioners and learning all she could about the approaching journey. The same was true of Jacob and Betsy Donner. They regularly attended services, and in the spring of 1846, they were given letters of introduction from the preacher to use in California.[2]

Reed also took advantage of his ecclesiastical connections. His family worshipped at the First Episcopal Methodist Church in Springfield, where Reed was on the board of trustees.[3] Reed became a Freemason in 1839 and was initiated into Springfield Lodge No. 4, A.F. & A.M. As a brother of the "Mystic Tie," he forged important social, political, and business relationships with the network of Masonic brethren.[4]

One of Reed's chief sources of knowledge was James M. Maxey, a Masonic brother who had left Springfield to run a general store in Independence, Missouri, a primary departure point for wagon caravans. Because Independence was an eastern terminal for the Santa Fe Trail and the California-Oregon Trail, Maxey dealt with customers who told him of their experiences.

During their correspondence in 1845, Maxey was still uncertain which westbound route Reed planned to use and offered advice about all the routes, including tips about smuggling trade goods if Reed chose the Santa Fe Trail. If Reed intended to go to California, Maxey advised taking "a good family ox waggon" and an ample supply of muslin and calico cloth, ribbons, and beads to use as trade goods with Indians and for staples at various forts along the way.[5] Maxey also told Reed he could get many supplies from his store in Independence for better prices than in Springfield. He stressed the importance of getting the largest oxen available to pull the wagons, as well as a good gun and a fleet horse for hunting buffalo.

In a letter on March 9, 1846, Maxey was more specific about weaponry. He suggested that Reed gather up as many "U.S. Yawgers as you can get."[6] Variously misspelled, "yauger" was one of several nicknames for the U.S. Model 1841, a .54-caliber weapon manufactured at Harper's Ferry, Virginia, and the first regulation muzzle-loading percussion rifle issued to federal troops.

From the same letter, Reed learned that a large company of emigrants would depart Independence in about mid-May. Maxey urged Reed to make sure the wagon caravan from Springfield arrived in Independence as early as possible to let the livestock rest and to be sure all wagons were amply provisioned—preferably from his store.

Reed and the Donners compared notes and pored over a wide variety of reference books, guides, and maps. A major source was one of the most important works on the opening of the West—the firsthand accounts of the 1842 and 1843 exploratory expeditions of the daring John C. Frémont.

Despite being born the illegitimate son of a Virginia socialite, Frémont, with his dashing good looks and ability to forge strategic connections, went far. In 1838, as a newly commissioned army officer, he showed his skill at surveying and mapmaking, while wooing Jessie Benton, the teenaged daughter of Thomas Hart Benton. Benton was the Missouri powerhouse in the U.S. Senate for thirty years and a champion of Manifest Destiny.[7] "It would seem that the white race alone has received the divine command, to subdue and replenish the earth," Benton said in an 1846 speech to Congress.[8]

Although he initially opposed his daughter's marriage to the rash Frémont, Benton quickly recognized the bold young man's potential. Benton rushed through congressional appropriations to fund his new protégé's survey expeditions of the Oregon Trail, Oregon Territory, and the Great Basin and Sierra mountains of California. Frémont's journals—filled with detailed notes about finding potable water, where grazing grass was abundant, and information about various Indian tribes and the forts—were edited and enhanced in collaboration with his wife and published with great fanfare by Congress in 1845. Frémont became a national hero and charismatic symbol of Manifest Destiny. Those who read of his exploits considered him one of the nation's best explorers, and the press dubbed him "The Great Pathfinder."[9]

Frémont's tome, *Report of the Exploring Expedition to the Rocky Mountains in the Year 1842, and to Oregon and North California in the Years 1843–44*, was quickly published by various publishers in many editions, making it more widely read than any other account of the American West prior to the gold rush.

Frémont's vivid descriptions of fauna and flora intrigued Tamzene Donner. She packed botanical references, notebooks, and containers for plant samples. "My mother was energetic in all these preparations," her daughter Eliza wrote many years later, "but her special province was to make and otherwise get in readiness a bountiful supply of clothes. She also superintended the purchase of materials for women's handiwork, apparatus for preserving botanical specimens, water colors and oil paints, books and school supplies; these latter being selected for use in the young ladies' seminary which she hoped to establish in California."[10]

Frémont's text noted the harrowing winter of 1843–1844, when his expedition trudged through the deep Sierra snow along the

Truckee River before descending the western slope and arriving at Sutter's Fort. Although none of his men perished, more than half of their horses and mules died. The members of the party ate the flesh of the dead animals and, on the advice of local Indians, consumed acorns, pine nuts, grasses, and wild onions. One of Frémont's 1843 entries read, "We had tonight an extraordinary dinner—pea soup, mule, and dog."[11]

In addition to the Frémont book, the Donners and Reed relied heavily on another bestseller—the *Emigrant's Guide to Oregon and California*, written by a young real-estate promoter named Lansford W. Hastings and published in 1845. The Ohio native had financial and political interests in Alta California. Historian Bernard DeVoto characterized Hastings as "a young man on the make . . . who wrote a book without knowing what he was talking about."

Hastings, who was only twenty-three when he went west in 1842, idealized the American settlers as hardworking and honest and with few faults. Indians and Mexicans, on the other hand, were depicted as stupid, lazy, and dishonest. His book had little value as an overland travel planner. It mostly promoted the land and climate of California and the Oregon coast. Even though it did not provide much practical information, Hastings's guide motivated the Donners and Reed. A well-thumbed copy of the book was tucked into a saddlebag.

Finally in March 1846, George Donner sold his property that had been on the market for many months. He deeded shares of his land to his grown children and reserved 110 acres near the homestead for his five younger children in case they ever decided to return to Illinois.[12]

On March 26, 1846, an advertisement was published in the *Sangamo Journal*:

WESTWARD HO!
FOR OREGON AND CALIFORNIA!

Who wants to go to California without costing them anything? As many as eight young men, of good character, who can drive an ox team, will be accommodated by gentlemen who will leave this vicinity about the first of April. Come

boys! You can have as much land as you want without costing you any thing. The government of California gives large
tracts of land to persons who have to move there. The first
suitable persons who apply will be engaged.

The emigrants who intend moving to Oregon or California this spring from the adjoining counties, would do well to
be in this place about the first of next month. Are there not a
number from Decatur, Macon county, going?

G. DONNER and others.

Springfield, March 18, 1846[13]

Despite the advertisement's bold headline, the Donners were
not overwhelmed with job applicants. The work of teamsters—best
known as bullwhackers—was never ending. The main task was to
make sure the caravan stayed on course. Like most of the people in
the party, with the exception of the elderly or infirm, teamsters did
not ride in wagons. They walked alongside, cracking bullwhips to
keep the yoked oxen moving forward. They made camp every evening to feed, water, and rest themselves and their beasts and carried
out any other tasks their employers asked them to do.[14]

Those who dared to sign on were mainly young single men eager
for adventure and new prospects. It was helpful if they were resolute
and as stubborn as a mule, although—as almost every trail guidebook pointed out—the best animals for pulling a wagon across half
the continent were oxen. Mules were strong and could go faster, but
they also were willful and cantankerous. Draft horses could not live
off prairie grasses along the trail, but oxen could eat grass as well as
sagebrush and most other vegetation. Traders and others familiar
with the trail preferred oxen from Illinois or Missouri because they
were known to be more adaptable to trail forage.[15] Oxen were slow,
averaging twelve to fifteen miles on a good day, but they were less
likely to run off. Oxen also cost less than mules and horses. In 1846,
for one pair of oxen, known as a yoke, the Donners and Reed forked
out the going rate of $25.

The Donner brothers and Reed had three wagons apiece, all

pulled by teams of stout Illinois oxen. The wagons were crammed with provisions, household furniture and goods, books, clothing, and all the essentials a family needed. Many years later, Eliza Donner, at the time of the journey a girl of three, recalled memories of the preparations: "Strong, commodious emigrant wagons were constructed. . . . The oxen to draw them were hardy, well trained, and rapid walkers. Three extra yoke were provided for emergencies. Cows were selected to furnish milk along the way. A few young beef cattle, five saddle horses, and a good watchdog completed the list of livestock."[16]

The most extravagant and largest of the wagons was one that the Reed family provided for Grandma Keyes, by then an invalid mostly confined to bed. She steadfastly refused to listen to family pleas for her to stay in Springfield because she could not bear to be separated from her daughter and wished to rendezvous with her son Robert, who had moved west the year before. The entrance to the two-story wagon was on the side like a stagecoach door. Although Hastings's guidebook cautioned against bringing heavy items that could bog down a wagon, Reed installed an iron cookstove with a vent pipe running through the top of the wagon, spring-cushioned seats, and comfortable bunks for the second level.

In her 1891 memoir, Virginia Reed Murphy, the Reeds' oldest daughter, who was twelve when her family left Illinois, dubbed the wagon the "Pioneer Prairie Palace."[17] The fancy arklike vehicle—which the Reeds simply called the "family wagon"—drew some snickers and wisecracks from some of the other members of the party. No one had seen anything like it.

For weeks leading up to their departure, the Donners and Reeds were feted at farewell dinners by friends and loved ones. By early April, all the teamsters had been hired, the wagons were almost loaded, and last wills and testaments were signed, sealed, and delivered. Reed still faced some legal challenges in regard to his insolvency, but he was more committed than ever to starting anew far away. Much like his excited children, he could hardly wait.

7. WAGONS HO!

APRIL 1846

In April 1846, there was still a chill in the morning air, but for the Donner and Reed families, California fever burned high. Like one of his blooded stallions, James Reed was chafing at the bit. His eagerness to get the wagon train rolling out of Springfield was surpassed only by his anxiety. Reed, at least on paper, was dead broke. A "Tax Sale Notice" had been published in the *Sangamo Journal* listing the Reed property, including four lots in Springfield, to be sold on July 28, 1846, at a public auction to pay the back taxes he owed.[1] In a last-ditch effort to satisfy his creditors, Reed, with ample help from lawyer Abraham Lincoln, drafted a list of those to whom he owed money and how much, as well as an inventory of his goods, chattel, real-estate holdings, and credits.

Bankruptcy papers were filed in probate court, and William Lavely, a justice of the peace, was assigned to oversee the public sale. Thankfully, Reed persuaded Lavely, a brother Mason, to exempt from insolvency three hundred pounds of bacon and two barrels of pickled pork.[2] The generous supply of meat was loaded quickly onto a waiting wagon, and Reed signed the bankruptcy papers. They were dated April 13, 1846, just one day before the emigrant party took its leave.

Reed was cutting it close, but he was always ready to gamble if the stakes were high enough. The overland expedition to California required substantial capital to outfit the wagons, purchase oxen teams, buy supplies, and hire teamsters. Although he was bankrupt in the eyes of the court, Reed managed to hide some fine wines and brandies and some cash. He was confident that once he was in California, he would regain his wealth if only he could persevere.

Reed still had to hedge his bets. Besides settling his financial predicament, he also looked for ways to ensure a warm reception and smooth transition in California. He wanted to be recognized as a gentleman of good standing. Having attained the high rank of Royal Arch Mason, he carefully packed all his Masonic regalia and badges of distinction, including the fraternal apron, collar, sash, and gloves.[3] Reed also petitioned members of the Illinois congressional delegation to help him win an appointment as "Sub Indian agent west of the Rocky mountains." He even indicated a willingness to at least visit the exotic Sandwich Islands, which later became known as the Hawaiian Islands.[4]

At the last minute, Reed also sought a letter of introduction from Illinois Governor Thomas Ford. The predated testimonial, on April 15, 1846, was delivered to Reed just before his departure. It vouched for Reed's "correct and gentlemanly deportment as a citizen and . . . his very efficient and businesslike habits as a man. . . ."[5]

Reed placed the letter in a small carpetbag, along with some family heirlooms and other valuable papers, such as the muster rolls for Captain Jacob M. Early's company of mounted volunteers during the Black Hawk War of 1832. Each of the four documents had the name of Private Abraham Lincoln listed, and in one instance, Reed's name appeared just beneath Lincoln's.[6]

The only letter of introduction any of the Donners carried was from the Jacob Donner family's country preacher. In contrast to Reed, the Donners had a substantial amount of surplus cash squirreled away. As Eliza Donner later explained, "A liberal sum of money for meeting incidental expenses and replenishing supplies on the journey, if need be, was stored in the compartments of two buckskin girdles, to be worn in concealment on the person. An additional sum of ten thousand dollars, cash, was stitched between the folds of a quilt for safe transportation. This was a large amount for those days, and few knew that my parents were carrying it with them."[7]

In the final days before leaving, the Donners and Reeds rechecked their inventory of staples and supplies. The list included "two hundred pounds of flour for each person ten or older and one hundred pounds for each younger child; fifteen pounds of coffee, and the same quantity of sugar, for each person; one hundred pounds of bacon for persons over ten, and half that quantity for those under that age; fifty pounds, each, of salt and rice, for every mess; five pounds of pepper, and from three to five bushels of corn meal, for each mess; fifty pounds of fruit, dried apples and peaches; a good tent, to accommodate five to eight persons; and last, yet most important a good rifle or heavy shot gun with five pounds of powder and twelve pounds of lead, of fifteen pounds of shot, to each man."[8]

Much of what they packed would not be used until they had reached California, including farm implements, seeds, furniture, and other supplies. Both Tamzene Donner and the Reeds also brought a substantial number of books. "Knowing that books were scarce in a new country, we also took a good library of standard works," explained Virginia Reed. "Certainly no family ever started across the plains with more provisions or a better outfit for the journey."[9]

For bartering with Indians, the Donners and Reeds brought bolts of inexpensive cotton prints, blue calico, yellow and red flannels, ribbon, bright-bordered handkerchiefs, glass bead necklaces, brass finger rings, and pocket mirrors. To use when negotiating for land grants with Mexicans, they packed much finer fabrics such as bolts of muslin, silk, satin, and velvet.[10] Although there were efforts to lighten the load—such as George Donner leaving behind his father's treasured cannonball for safekeeping—all the wagons were jam-packed.

"Our clothing was packed—not in Saratoga trunks—but in strong canvas bags plainly marked," wrote Virginia Reed. "Some of mama's young friends added a looking glass, hung directly opposite the door [of the large Reed wagon], in order, as they said, that my mother might not forget to keep her good looks."[11]

Finally, the nine wagons were loaded and the families of James Reed, George Donner, Jacob Donner, and their hired hands were ready to leave Springfield.

8. FAREWELL

The exodus from Illinois began before dawn on April 14, 1846.[1] The heavy wooden wheels gradually turned as the oxen strained to pull the laden wagons. It became clear from the beginning that the overland journey to California was not suited to anyone in a hurry. The learning curve for travelers was steep, and the pace would mostly be slow and laborious. Although most of the Donners and Reeds were eager to start, once the wagons were loaded and moving, it took almost two days to get out of town.

The nucleus of what came to be called the Donner Party centered on the Donners and Reeds and their employees.[2] The George Donner family participants consisted of George, aged sixty; his wife, Tamzene, forty-four; their three children—Frances, six, Georgia, four, and Eliza, three; and George's two daughters from his second marriage—Elitha Cumi, fourteen, and Leanna, twelve.

Traveling with Jacob (Jake) Donner, aged fifty-six, were his wife Betsy, forty-five; their five children, George, nine, Mary, seven, Isaac, five, Samuel, four, and Lewis, three; and Betsy's two sons from a previous marriage, Solomon Hook, fourteen, and William Hook, thirteen.

Hired as teamsters to help with the Donner brothers' wagons were Noah James, sixteen, a cousin of William H. Herndon (Abraham Lincoln's last law partner and biographer); Samuel Shoemaker, twenty-five, thought to be an Ohio native; John Denton, twenty-eight, a gunsmith and native of Sheffield, England, who had become friendly with the Donners during his four years in Springfield; and Hiram Owens Miller, twenty-nine, a Kentuckian with blacksmithing skills and a friend of James Reed who worked for the Donners.

The Reed contingency was comprised of James Reed, forty-six; his wife, Margret, thirty-two; and their three children, Martha (Patty), eight, James Jr., five, and Thomas, three; Margret's daughter from a previous marriage, Virginia, twelve; and Margret's mother, Sarah Keyes, seventy.

Accompanying the Reeds were five employees, including two siblings: Eliza Williams, thirty-one, a deaf woman who had worked for the Reeds for several years and was described by a family member as "a first class cook"; and Baylis Williams, twenty-five, Eliza's half brother, an albino who, because of his condition, would sleep inside a wagon during daylight and tend to the livestock and campfires at night. Reed also hired teamsters: Milford (Milt) Elliott, twenty-eight, a Kentuckian who had worked at Reed's mill in Jamestown for several years and was so well acquainted with the family that he often called Margret Reed "Ma," even though she was only four years his senior; Walter Herron, twenty-seven, a native of Virginia; and James Smith, twenty-five.

"Never can I forget the morning when we bade farewell to kindred and friends," recalled Virginia Reed. "The Donners were there, having driven in the evening before with their families, so we might get an early start. Grandma Keyes was carried out of the house and placed in the wagon on a large feather bed, propped up with pillows. Her sons implored her to remain and end her days with them, but she could not be separated from her only daughter. We were surrounded by loved ones, and there stood my little schoolmates who had come to kiss me good-by. My father with tears in his eyes tried to smile as one friend after another grasped his hand in a last farewell. Mama was overcome with grief. At last we were all in the wagons, the drivers cracked their whips, the oxen moved slowly forward and the long journey had begun."[3]

When she was an old woman with a lifetime of memories, Virginia could still see her "little black-eyed sister Patty, clutching her cherished wooden doll as she held up the wagon cover so Grandma

Keyes, tucked in the feather bed, could have a last look at the family home. We were full of hope and did not dream of sorrow."[4]

At the George Donner place, the children were all scrubbed and dressed in new traveling clothes made of sturdy homespun linsey-woolsey cloth. Three big wagons covered with white canvas stood in the yard. Feed boxes were attached to the back of one wagon for Fanny and Margaret, the Donners' favorite saddle horses.

"Early in the day, the first two wagons started, each drawn by three yoke of powerful oxen, whose great moist eyes looked as though they too had parting tears to shed," wrote Eliza Donner. "The loose cattle quickly followed, but it was well on toward noon before the family wagon was ready. Then came a pause fraught with anguish to the dear ones gathered about the homestead to say farewell. Each tried to be courageous, but no one was so brave as father when he bade good-bye to his friends, to his children, and to his children's children. I sat beside my mother with my hand clasped in hers, as we slowly moved away from that quaint old house on its grassy knoll, from the orchard, the corn land, and the meadow; as we passed through the last set of bars, her clasp tightened, and I, glancing up, saw tears in her eyes and sorrow in her face. I grieved at her pain, and in sympathy nestled closer to her side and sat so quiet that I soon fell asleep."[5]

The wagons rolled into Springfield, where some of the party briefly paused to bid farewell to friends gathered at the public square, not far from the State House.[6]

Reed had tried his best to convince his friend Abraham Lincoln to pack up his family and join the wagon train. Seventy-three years later, based on a reporter's interview with Patty Reed, who was only eight years old when her family left Springfield, a California newspaper declared, "Abraham Lincoln had half a notion to come to California with the Donner Party."[7]

Early on, Lincoln had an abiding interest in Oregon and California and often expressed a desire to visit both. In 1849, Lincoln turned down a patronage appointment as Oregon's territorial governor. Mary Todd Lincoln was not keen on moving to Oregon Territory at that time, just as in 1846, when she had opposed leaving the United

States for the unknown in California. The ambitious Lincoln, only a few months away from being elected to his single term in the U.S. Congress in August 1846, also knew such a move would effectively end his political career.[8]

Reed had hoped his old friend would amble down the third floor of the Tinsley Building to say farewell, but Lincoln was not there. He was on his horse "Old Tom," traveling the rough roads and prairie trails of the fifteen counties of the Eighth Judicial Circuit. Mary Todd Lincoln, however, joined the crowd to give her good wishes to the Reeds and offer an apology for her husband's absence.

It was late afternoon by the time the handshaking, hugging, and tearful farewells were over. The caravan made it only as far as the western outskirts of town before halting and setting up camp for the night. The site was a grove on a wooded hill near the two-story brick residence of Thomas Mather, a prominent civic leader and one of the proponents of rail transportation who, in 1849, would take over and rename Reed's ill-fated Northern Cross railroad company.[9] Many early settlers had been drawn to the area and had built cabins on the edge of the Town Branch of Spring Creek. It also became a popular meeting place for public gatherings and political rallies.

Kindling was collected, water was fetched from the creek, and the teamsters tended to the livestock. None of those on the hill could have even guessed that their first campsite of the trip would one day be the location of a new state capitol.[10]

"Mr. Reed and family, and my uncle Jacob and family, with their traveling companions and cattle, were already settled there," wrote Eliza Donner. "Under father's direction, our own encampment was soon accomplished. By nightfall, the duties of the day were ended, and the members of our party gathered around one fire to spend a social hour."[11]

As supper was being prepared, the hired hands sniffed around each other, much like hounds sizing up the pack, and children from the various families began to get better acquainted. Suddenly a party of eight horsemen galloped into the camp. The riders quickly dismounted from their panting steeds and walked from the shadows into the flickering firelight, shouting their hurrahs. They were members of the Springfield reading society and had come to hold one last visit with their own Tamzene Donner and all the others. Among the surprise guests were brothers Simeon and Allen Francis, close friends of Lincoln and publishers of the *Sangamo Journal* (later the *Illinois State Journal*).[12]

Simeon's mission was to convince Tamzene to serve as a correspondent and send letters back home to be published in the newspaper. She promised to do so, much to the delight of everyone. Bottles of brandy and other spirits were passed around, but several were tucked away for safekeeping until the Fourth of July. On that auspicious date, the Reeds and Donners promised that no matter where they were on the trail, they would turn east to face Springfield at high noon. At the same time, their friends back home would come to this hill and face west. Miles apart, all would then lift their glasses in a toast.[13] Promises made, the visitors from the reading society joined the travelers for the evening.

"They piled more wood on the blazing fire, making it a beacon light to those who were watching from afar," noted Eliza Donner. "They sang songs, told tales, and for the time being drove homesickness from our hearts. Then they rode away in the moonlight, and our past was a sweet memory, our future a beautiful dream."[14]

Early the next morning, before everyone began to stir except for Baylis Williams tending the fire, Margret Reed slipped out of the campsite. Not far away was the Old City Graveyard, Springfield's earliest burial site, and just to the west the newly opened Hutchinson Cemetery, the first private burial ground.[15] Margret made her way through the damp grass to the old burial ground, where members of her family were interred. She stood at the grave of her beloved father and the grave of Gershom Francis Reed, her little boy who had died before his first birthday.[16] Margret must have memorized the moment, not certain if she would ever be there again.

She then rejoined the others and was packed and ready to go before the dew had dried. This was a good omen, for as the time-honored proverb put it: "When dew is on the grass, rain will never come to pass." The Donner-Reed Party struck out on the Jackson-ville Road, confident that at least on this day, there would be no rain to make their route a muddy quagmire.

Besides the families and hired hands, three other people accompanied the wagon caravan on the first leg of the trip. Gershom and James Keyes, concerned about their ailing mother, Sarah Keyes, rode with the party for several days. William Donner, George's grown son from his marriage to Susannah Holloway, helped drive the cattle and stayed with the wagon train all the way to Independence, Missouri.

"The family wagon was drawn by four yoke of oxen, large Durham steers at the wheel," wrote Virginia Reed. "The other wagons were drawn by three yoke each. We had saddle horses and cows, and last but not least my pony. He was a beauty and his name was Billy. I can scarcely remember when I was taught to sit a horse. I only know that when a child of seven I was the proud owner of a pony and used to go riding with papa. That was the chief pleasure to which I looked forward in crossing the plains, to ride my pony every day."[17]

Headed west on the Jacksonville Road on her cream-colored pony, Virginia rode beside her father, mounted on his handsome gray racing mare, Glaucus, named from Greek mythology. The ancient tale held that Glaucus was a nobleman who fed his team of spirited chariot mares human flesh, believing that this made them swifter and bolder, only to have the horses turn on him when his chariot upended and eat him alive.[18] Only later in 1846 would the irony of the name of Reed's horse become apparent.

9. INDEPENDENCE BOUND

James Reed and the Donner brothers estimated that it would take their nine-wagon caravan at least three weeks to reach Independence, Missouri. There they planned to replenish their supplies and join with a larger wagon train bound for California, a journey of four to six months.

Members of the Donner-Reed Party did not necessarily think of themselves as "pioneers." They thought of themselves as movers aspiring to become settlers in a foreign land that they hoped would soon become part of the United States.[1] Ultimately, because of what would come to pass during their trek, the Donner-Reed Party became a prominent symbol of America's Manifest Destiny.

The story of their travels still arguably remains the most well known and best documented of all western emigration narratives. Yet ironically, the first leg of the journey—from Springfield to Independence—was not mentioned in any of the travelers' surviving diaries or correspondence. Consequently, no description or reference to the first weeks of the trip was included in the many books and memoirs that were published. Perhaps, as some historians have theorized, the travelers found the Illinois and Missouri countryside so familiar that they decided the trip did not officially begin until they reached Independence, perched on the edge of the United States and the eastern terminus of several emigrant trails. For them, the bustling trail town of Independence was the true starting point.

"Nothing of much interest happened until we reached what is now Kansas," was how Virginia Reed remembered the first few weeks of the trip.[2]

Tragically, except for a few letters, the writings of Tamzene Donner did not survive. She was the one person from the party who most likely recorded her daily observations of the western Illinois and Missouri portion of the journey. A long-rumored "lost journal" kept by Tamzene that has never been found remains a kind of unattainable Holy Grail for some history scholars and others who consider Tamzene a true heroine as a woman of education, a teacher, linguist, and botanist.[3]

One Donner family history described Tamzene as "joyous with her school-teacher instincts for she had prepared a portion of a manuscript which she planned to continue upon the way, doing her sketches of rare botanical species, and to finish this in California thus creating a new comparison of species, and to have the book published when completed. Day after day she added to the number of sketches and wrote many notes that would be used in the text."[4]

As she had promised—and thanks to obliging eastbound travelers who were willing to help fellow voyagers by delivering their mail to the nearest post office—Tamzene faithfully sent Springfield newspaper publisher Allen Francis her dispatches from the trail. Unfortunately, when Francis became U.S. consul and moved to Canada, hungry mice breached the storage boxes and soon destroyed untold numbers of pages of Tamzene's manuscript, verse, and letters.[5]

Shortly after the Donner-Reed Party departed, William Todd wrote a letter from California that did survive. A nephew of Mary Todd Lincoln, the young man had left Springfield the year before along with one of Margret Reed's brothers. Todd described some of the hardships he had endured on the journey and included some pointed advice for others who might be contemplating the trip.[6] Todd wrote, "If there are any persons in Sangamon who speak of crossing the rocky mountains [sic] to this country, tell them my advice is, to stay home."

Todd's letter, written on April 17, 1846, did not find its way back to Illinois for several months and was not published in the *Sangamo Journal* until August 13. By that time, the Donner-Reed wagon train was past the point of no return. They were oblivious to Todd's concerns during the last days of April as their wagons lumbered down the Jacksonville Road across the Illinois prairie.

"Milt Elliott, a knight of the whip, drove our family wagon," wrote Virginia Reed. "He had worked for years in my father's large saw-mill on the Sangamon River. The first bridge we came to, Milt had to stop the wagon and let us out. I remember that I called to him to be sure to make the oxen hit the bridge, and not to forget that grandma was in the wagon. How he laughed at the idea of the oxen missing the bridge! I soon found that Milt with his 'whoa,' 'haw,' and 'gee,' could make the oxen do just as he pleased."[7]

For a few days, the wagon train's route was the same path used by more than eight hundred Potawatomi Indians in 1838 when the federal government forcibly removed them from Indiana to reservation land in Kansas.[8] The Indian Removal Act of 1830—part of the legacy of President Andrew Jackson—resulted in thousands of Indians from several tribes being uprooted from their homelands. Forty-one Potawatomis, mostly children, died from disease and accidents during the grueling ten-week trip on the 660-mile Potawatomi Trail of Death.

Forging ahead into the prairie country of Morgan County, the next logical stopping point for the Donner-Reed Party was Jacksonville, an early contender for the state capital, named in honor of Andrew Jackson. The Donner-Reed Party passed through the public square. They more than likely spent a quiet night before continuing their journey beneath a canopy of elms and maples. The wagons slowly paraded by stately brick homes, the campus of Illinois College (founded by New England abolitionists in 1829), and the newly opened State School for the Deaf and Dumb.

West of Jacksonville, instead of staying on the Potawatomi Trail of Death, the Donner-Reed caravan took a southwesterly path. Ahead was Winchester, and then the route traversed rolling hills along the valley of the Illinois River. Until then, the wagon train had encountered only creeks that could be crossed on bridges or, most of the time, by simply fording shallow streams. The Illinois River—a principal tributary of the Mississippi—was the first major river crossing for the party. They ferried across the Illinois to the village of Florence, where a long line of wagons and horsemen waited to cross. It probably took a few hours for the Donner-Reed party to shuttle their wagons and animals across the river and resume travel up a gravel road that wound through outcrops of limestone.

The trail gradually moved to the northwest past the village of Barry through wooded hill country before descending to the broad valley of Hadley Creek. Just beyond Kinderhook, the last village the caravan would encounter before leaving Illinois, the wagons moved across the bottomlands of the Mississippi, the longest river in North America. Beyond the stands of cottonwoods and willows was a ferry landing, and across the wide river on the west bank, they could see Hannibal, Missouri.[9]

"We crossed the Mississippi at Hannibal," Virginia Reed wrote almost thirty-four years later in one of the few references to the first part of her family's journey. Fortunately, before they made the formidable crossing at Hannibal, two improved steam ferries joined the old hand-propelled flatboat ferry operated by Theophilus Stone. It took the better part of a day to load and unload the ferry and make several round trips across the river.[10] Once the Donner-Reed Party was safely across the river, the group set out for Independence, on the opposite side of Missouri.

By the first days of May, the emigrants had become accustomed to the daily routine. They were ready to get beyond the familiar rolling prairie and river hills. They pushed hard across Missouri, stopping to rest at small settlements. From about the midpoint of the state, the villages were strung out just north of the winding Missouri River on its way to a rendezvous with the Mississippi near St. Louis.

For most of the way, the party again followed the same path that Potawatomis had used in 1838. The Donner-Reed Party crossed the Missouri River at Lexington, the largest city west of St. Louis throughout the 1830s and 1840s. Lexington was a major shipping point that supported many prosperous merchants, thanks to the farmers who raised tobacco and hemp, used for making rope and burlap to wrap bales of cotton picked by large slave forces.

The route west from Lexington followed the old Santa Fe Trail, pioneered by trader William Becknell in 1821. The trail's first starting point was east of Lexington at Franklin, Missouri, on the banks of the Missouri River. This was the preferred route for many early traders and emigrant wagon trains. With May coming into bloom, the Donner-Reed Party must have become more excited as the trail drew closer to Independence—the westernmost city of the United States, the edge of the frontier.

TWO

THE JOURNEY

10. QUEEN CITY OF THE TRAILS

MAY 10–12, 1846

On May 10, 1846, the Donner-Reed wagons rolled into the bustling
Jackson County seat of Independence, Missouri. It was a Sabbath,
and no doubt, prayers of thanksgiving were raised. At last, after
twenty-five days of travel, they had arrived at the place where they
believed their grand adventure would start.

Beginning with the Lewis and Clark Expedition in 1804, Missouri played a key role in westward expansion. Fur trappers and traders helped St. Louis become known as the "Gateway to the West."
St. Charles, St. Joseph, and Westport—later part of Kansas City—
also became popular starting points for emigrants who settled the
great expanse between Missouri and the Pacific. Yet Independence
deserved special credit for Missouri having earned its distinctive
moniker, "Mother of the West."[1]

It was a matter of geography. Founded in 1827 a few miles from
the south bank of the Missouri River at the farthest point where
steamboats could navigate, Independence became the epicenter of
western migration. Typically, wagon trains did not leave until about
the middle of May, when there was enough green grass to provide
pasturage for draft animals. The original townsite was the eastern
terminus for three principal trails—the Santa Fe, Oregon, and California. That was why Independence had a sobriquet all its own—
"Queen City of the Trails."

Chief among the caravan's supporters was James Maxey, Reed's
Masonic brother, who ran a general store in Independence. Maxey
and his business partner, William S. Stone, were delighted to sell

fresh goods to familiar faces. Reed later noted that Maxey and Stone "treated us like as if we ware Brothers."[2]

When the wagon caravans reached Independence's public square, the emigrants were astounded by what they beheld. They were assaulted by the smells of toiling men and overworked beasts, fresh manure, tobacco and wood smoke, and many exotic aromas they could not place. The dirt streets teemed with people speaking a cacophony of languages, accents, and dialects—Spanish, German, Italian, and various Indian languages, including Osage, Kaw, Choctaw, and Chickasaw.

"The town of Independence was at this time a great Babel upon the border of the wilderness," was how emigrant Jessy Quinn Thornton described Independence in May 1846.[3] Thornton and his wife were eager to leave the United States and move to what was soon to become Oregon Territory. He had been practicing law and editing a newspaper in Palmyra, Missouri. Because of their staunch abolitionist views, Thornton and his wife left proslavery Missouri in 1841 and moved across the Mississippi to Quincy, Illinois, where he continued his work as a lawyer. Thornton corresponded regularly with influential newspaper editor Horace Greeley and maintained a close friendship with Senator Thomas Hart Benton and with Stephen A. Douglas, former comrade and political rival of Abraham Lincoln.[4]

On April 18, 1846, just a few days after the Donner-Reed Party left Springfield, Thornton and his infirm wife set out for Independence with their noble greyhound, Prince Darco, and two young hired men to handle their wagon.

"Most of the emigrants had already departed," Thornton wrote in his trail diary. "Some were assembled at Indian Creek; a few were still in this place not yet prepared to depart. Among these, I became acquainted with Messrs. James F. Reed, George Donner, and Jacob Donner, together with their wives and families, all from the neighborhood of Springfield, Illinois, and all of whom proposed to go to California."[5]

Thornton told the Donner brothers and Reed that he was waiting for a few other emigrants to arrive and expected to move on within the hour. He also urged them to get going as soon as possible and join his party on the trail, where an even larger caravan awaited them on the Kaw (Kansas) River. Thornton's advice made good sense; they agreed that they would all meet again soon. Then the Donner and Reed families continued their inspection of Independence.

The panorama was nothing like they had ever seen on the public square in Springfield. Besides the many emigrant wagon trains, several sizable trading caravans from Chihuahua, Mexico, had just arrived after forty-six days on the Santa Fe Trail.[6] After three weeks on the trail, the Donner and Reed children were especially excited.

Among those in Independence who took notice of the Donner-Reed Party's arrival was Francis Parkman. A twenty-three-year-old Harvard law graduate from a wealthy Boston family, Parkman was starting a two-month adventure that he described as "a tour of curiosity and amusement to the Rocky Mountains."[7] Destined to become one of the nation's preeminent historians as a result of his experiences in the American West, Parkman published in 1849 *The Oregon Trail: Sketches of Prairie and Rocky Mountain Life*. This book—despite its misleading title, since Parkman's excursion took him along only the first third of the Oregon Trail—inspired many people to move westward and had a profound impact on generations of readers.

The clamor of the town square was enough to give Margret Reed one of her crippling migraines. Fortunately, the party's campsite was not far away at the public spring on the east side of Independence. For as long as anyone could remember, the many springs in this area had provided potable water for roaming bands of Indians and any travelers who dared to venture into the land.

On May 11, Tamzene Donner took a break from her camp chores to write her sister, Elizabeth Poor, in Newburyport, Massachusetts.[8]

> My dear sister
> I commenced writing to you some months ago but the letter was laid aside to be finished the next day & was never touched. A nice sheet of pink letter paper was taken out & has got so much soiled that it cannot be written upon & now

in the midst of preparation for starting across the mountains I am seated on the grass in the midst of the tent to say a few words to my dearest only sister. One would suppose that I loved her but little or I should have not neglected her so long, but I have heard from you by Mr Greenleaf & and every month have intended to write. My three daughters are round me one at my side trying to sew Georgeanna fixing herself up an old indiarubber cap & Eliza Poor knocking on my paper asking me ever so many questions. They often talk to me of Aunty Poor. I can give you no idea of the hurry of this place at this time. It is supposed there be 7000 waggons start from this place, this season [?] We go to California, to the bay of Francisco. It is a four months trip. We have three waggons furnished with food & clothing &c. Drawn by three yoke of oxen each. We take cows along & milk them & have some butter though not as much as we would like. I am willing to go & have no doubt it will be an advantage to our children & to us. I came here last evening and start tomorrow morning on the long journey. Wm's family was well when I left Springfield a month ago. He will write to you soon as he finds another home. He says he has received no answer to his last two letters, is about to start to Wisconsin as he considers Illinois unhealthy.

> Farewell, my sister, you shall hear
> From me as soon as I have an oppertunity,
> Love to Mr. Poor, the children & all friends. Farewell
> T. E. Donner

The following day, Margret Reed rested in a tent with the family dog, Cash, while her mother, Sarah Keyes, napped in the comfortable feather bed in the family wagon. Meanwhile, James Reed drafted a formal agreement with a few stipulations, contracting the services of teamster Milt Elliott for $8 per month. Gershom Keyes signed the document as a witness.[9]

By sunrise on May 12, the Donner-Reed camp was stirring.

Gershom Keyes bid his ailing mother and sister farewell. He and George Donner's son, William, had ridden with the company all the way from Springfield, but now it was almost time for them to go home. They would ride with the wagons a ways and then head east to Illinois. The departure from Independence was emblazoned in the memories of many members of the party.

"As we drove up Main Street, delayed emigrants waved us a light-hearted good-bye," recalled Eliza Donner. "And as we approached the building of the American Tract Society, its agent came to our wagons and put into the hand of each child a New Testament, and gave to each adult a Bible, and also tracts to distribute among the heathen in the benighted land to which we were going. Near the outskirts of town we parted from William Donner, took a last look at Independence, turned our backs to the morning sun, and became pioneers indeed to the far West."[10]

11. INDIAN COUNTRY

The Donner-Reed Party's nine wagons and herds of livestock took to the Santa Fe Trail. This pathway out of Independence would be their route for a few days until they reached the junction where the emigrant trail winding its way to Oregon and California split off to the northwest and the lumbering merchant wagons continued southwest to Santa Fe and distant Chihuahua in Mexico.

The trail was easy enough to follow. The hooves of thousands of oxen, mules, and horses and the steel-rimmed wheels of heavy wagons had carved grooves into the soft earth. Over time, the ruts had deepened into swales from the steady parade departing and arriving in Missouri.[1]

The going proved to be slow that month. Torrential rains turned the trail into a quagmire of thick, sticky mud that clung to wagon wheels and bogged down animals. Soon, all the oxen and cattle were struggling to move in the mess. The saddle horses, including James Reed's fancy mount, Glaucus, had mud up to their hocks, and their tails were caked with muck.

Eighteen to twenty miles a day over prairie was an exceptional day's travel for wagon trains, but eight to twelve miles was considered quite acceptable. Yet according to the initial diary notation of Hiram Miller, a Donner teamster and a friend of Reed's, by the end of the party's first day out, they had managed to go only four miles before stopping for the night.[2]

Early the next morning, despite more bad weather, the company pushed on and fared much better. By evening, they were huddled over cooking fires to dry their clothing. Hiram Miller scribbled,

"May 13 next day travelled about 16 miles in the rain, bad roads and rainy night."

Unknown to the weary travelers, that very day, the United States Congress—acting in the spirit of Manifest Destiny and fueled by President James Polk's cries for more American expansionism in the wake of Texas joining the Union—declared war on the Republic of Mexico. Before the Donner-Reed Party left home, Mexico had broken off diplomatic relations with the United States. On April 23, Mexico declared war on the United States, vowing to defend its territories under attack, but without taking the offensive. Tensions heightened even more as Polk sent troops under General Zachary Taylor south of the Rio Grande while the Mexican army moved northward. By early May, battles had been fought and blood had been shed on both sides.[3] Although the members of the Donner-Reed Party did not learn of the war immediately, they knew it was inevitable.

On May 15, the party made it to a well-used campground on Hart Grove Creek, not far from where it emptied into the Big Blue River. Named for a pioneer family, Hart Grove was often misspelled, as Miller did in his diary: "May 14–15 camped at Heart Grove in Jackson County near the Indian line twenty two miles from Independence on the Big Blue."

After two nights' rest, the company made its way to the wagon crossing of the Big Blue, where the swales leading to the stream's edge were deep and muddy.[4] Fording a stream could be a challenge. A wagon could overturn or get stuck, and animals could be swept away or axles broken. Less than a week before, a wagon from another party had capsized in the high water. When the Donner and Reed wagons approached the river, the teamsters cracked their long whips to quicken the pace of the oxen teams to get up the steep hill on the other side.

After four days' travel, the Donner-Reed Party had only one more stop to make in Missouri—the hamlet called Little Santa Fe. Once the site of an Indian village, the spot became popular soon after the Santa Fe Trail opened in the early 1820s because of the abundance of grass and water and a well-stocked log tavern.[5] Little Santa Fe was the last chance for many miles to get a wheel fixed by a blacksmith, replenish the buckets of "dope" (axle grease), and—most important—purchase whiskey.

On May 16, only a few miles beyond Little Santa Fe, the Donner-Reed Party was on the brink of leaving the United States. Soon they crossed an invisible border and entered present-day Kansas, part of a vast expanse that the U.S. government had designated as the Permanent Indian Frontier, also known as Indian Territory. The creation of a separate homeland—in essence, one gigantic reservation—for all tribal people was considered the best solution for dealing with what for many years was known as the "Indian problem."

In 1825, Secretary of War James Barbour explained the federal government's rationale for the establishment of Indian Territory: "The principal recommendation of this plan, next to the advantages to be gained to ourselves, is that the future residence of these people will forever be undisturbed . . . and being exclusively under the control of the United States, . . . that it shall be theirs forever. . . ."[6] Of course, the operative phrase in Barbour's explanation was "the advantages to be gained to ourselves."

The region chosen for this vast Indian holding pen was the "Great American Desert," a flat, treeless, arid land considered totally unfit for white American settlement and any kind of cultivation.[7] Much like the bogus tales that the Illinois prairie was unsuitable for agriculture, it eventually became clear that the negative image of Indian Country land was pure myth. Politicians and business leaders in New England, fearful that westward expansion would diminish their region, perpetuated much of that myth. Ironically, much of the land the Donner-Reed wagons rolled over eventually became productive agricultural land called the Great Plains. In 1846, however, the prairie—and streams and mountains ahead—were nothing but obstacles on the route to California.

Tamzene Donner was delighted with the wildflowers and the budding shrubs and brush along the trail. She collected botanical specimens at every stop or had her husband, George, and other riders help with the gathering. Tamzene and George's young daughter

Eliza had idyllic memories of the party's time in Indian Country and wrote about it as an adult but from the perspective of a small child:

> During our first few days in the Territory of Kansas we passed over good roads, and through fields of May blossoms musical with the hum of bees and the songs of birds. Some of the party rode horseback; others walked in advance of the train; but each father drove his own family team. We little folk sat in the wagons with our dolls, watching the huge white-covered 'prairie schooners' coming from Santa Fe to Independence for merchandise. . . . We overtook similar wagons, heavily laden with goods bound for Santa Fe. Most of the drivers were shrewd; all of them civil. They were of various nationalities; some comfortably clad, others in tatters, and a few in picturesque threadbare costumes of Spanish finery. Those hard wayfarers gave us much valuable information regarding the route before us, and the Indian tribes we should encounter. We were now averaging a distance of about two and a half miles an hour, and encamping nights where fuel and water could be obtained.[8]

On May 16, the party spent their first night in Indian Country at Lone Elm, where there was a spring, and the grass was as high as a man's waist. Over the years, thousands of traders, soldiers, missionaries, hunters, opportunists, and pioneer pilgrims had camped there, including the young Kit Carson, William Becknell, James C. Frémont, and Francis Parkman. Although the site originally was known as Round Grove, by the time the Donner-Reed Party stopped, so many campers had felled the trees for firewood that only a single elm was still standing. The name Lone Elm endured even after that last remaining tree had been cut down and used for kindling.[9]

The following day, May 17, the party reached the fork in the road where the trails parted. The road to Santa Fe continued to the left, and the Oregon and California Trails veered to the right in a westerly direction. At the junction, a crude signpost read "Road to Oregon," unostentatiously marking perhaps one of the most important inter-sections in the American West.

Ever since the Donner-Reed Party had left Independence, they had been intent on catching up with the larger wagon train they had been told about by J. Quinn Thornton, who often went by Jessy, the lawyer from Quincy, Illinois, heading west with his infirm wife and their greyhound. Reed and the Donner brothers believed in strength in numbers, especially on the trail.

The Donner-Reed emigrants left their camp on the Wakarusa River before first light and pushed on, barely stopping at twelve to "noon it" (have lunch). On the evening of May 18, the camp was buzzing with excitement. The larger caravan was close. All they had to do was get across the Kaw River.

12. SOLDIER CREEK

Newspapers across the nation were filled with reports of the war with the Republic of Mexico—mostly vainglorious accounts of battles and of the many volunteer regiments being formed across the country. Some war news was intended to be humorous, such as an item laced with sarcasm in the *New Orleans Picayune* that told of an unusually large number of persons seen on the city streets with their arms in slings. "Can it be," the newspaper asked, "that the *drafting* has anything to do with it?"[1] Amazingly, the slings quickly disappeared when rumors of military conscription were quelled.

Early in the war with Mexico, a draft was threatened in Louisiana and Texas, but it never materialized. When hostilities broke out in May 1846, the United States Army numbered only eight thousand. Soon—despite strong opposition to the war from Abraham Lincoln and other notable Whigs—more than seventy thousand volunteers had joined the ranks in an immense wave of nationalism. Thousands more enlisted in the regular army. There were reports that in some places, so many men flocked to the recruiting stations that large numbers were turned away.

Meanwhile, the U.S. Congress approved an act to establish military posts as protection from Indians along the road between Independence and the Oregon Country,[2] the road the Donner-Reed Party was traveling.

One of the more apprehensive emigrants was young Virginia Reed. Back in Springfield as the Reeds prepared for the journey, Virginia had spent many winter nights listening to her grandmother, Sarah Keyes, tell Indian stories. "She had an aunt who had been taken prisoner by the savages in the early settlement of Virginia and Kentucky and had remained a captive in their hands five years before she made her escape," Virginia later wrote.

> I was fond of these stories and evening after evening would go into grandma's room, sitting with my back close against the wall so that no warrior could slip behind me with a tomahawk. I would coax her to tell me more about her aunt, and would sit listening to this recital of the fearful deeds of the savages, until it seemed to me that everything in the room, from the high old-fashioned bed posts down to the shovel and tongs in the chimney corner, was transformed into the dusky tribe in paint and feathers, all ready for the war dance. So when I was told that we were going to California and would have to pass through a region peopled by Indians, you can imagine how I felt.[3]

As it turned out, Virginia's worst fear became real on that May 19 when they encountered Indians on the trail. The meeting was early in the day as the wagons and herds reached the banks of the Kaw River. Virginia, riding her pony, Billy, bristled when she saw them, even though none was in war paint or brandishing a weapon.

"The first Indians we met were Caws [Kaw or Kanza] who kept the ferry, and had to take us over the Caw River," she wrote. "I watched them closely, hardly daring to draw my breath, and feeling sure they would sink the boat in the middle of the stream, and was very thankful when I found they were not like grandma's Indians."[4]

Although Virginia identified the Indians at the ferry crossing as "Caws," others said they were either "French-Indians," Shawnees, or, in the words of a traveler who made the same crossing just a day before the Donner-Reed Party, "two half-breed Indians."[5] Virginia and the others were not concerned about tribal affiliation. As was the case with most white travelers, despite the diversity of the hundreds of tribes, all Indians were alike and were considered "savages" to be approached with caution.

The crossing of the Kaw—which ran full from the spring rains—took some time. The livestock and horses had to swim the river while two flatboats were pushed with long poles. Each boat could take only two wagons at a time, at one dollar per wagon. Once all the wagons and animals were on the north bank, the travelers continued for five miles until they reached Soldier Creek.[6]

At last, the Donner-Reed Party had caught up with the much larger caravan. From that day forward, even though the nucleus of Donners and Reeds and most of their entourage would remain intact, the party would never be the same. The numbers would ebb and flow, with some people dropping out and others joining along the trail.

The Donners and Reeds became part of the Russell Party, named for William Henry Russell, a flamboyant and affable lawyer and politician who had acquired the courtesy title of "Colonel" in Kentucky, where he was born in 1802.[7]

William Henry Russell practiced law, served a hitch in the Kentucky legislature, and wed a Baltimore belle, Zanette Freeland.[8] Early on, Henry Clay, the skilled orator and statesman who represented Kentucky in the U.S. Senate and House of Representatives, befriended Russell, who served as Clay's secretary for a time. Their families also became quite close.

The relationship with Clay produced Russell's curious nickname—"Owl." According to a popular campfire story, one evening Russell was stalking game deep in the woods when he heard a chorus of owls hooting and took their "Who" as a question posed to him. Immediately Russell thundered back, "Why, it is I, Colonel William Henry Russell of Kentucky, a bosom friend of Henry Clay."[9] From then on, most people called him Owl Russell. The moniker stuck after he moved with his family and fourteen slaves in 1831 to Fulton, Missouri. In 1841, President William Henry Harrison appointed Russell U.S. marshal of the District of Missouri, a vast territory that included Indian Country.[10]

Russell yearned to see the much ballyhooed California. In May 1846, he assembled a caravan in Independence. At Soldier Creek, Russell again faced the task of making sure the party that showed up

was a good fit. Before being officially accepted into his larger caravan, the new arrivals had to pass muster. It was standard procedure
for wagon-train captains to weed out potential troublemakers.

Already that morning, several other travelers had tried to join and
had been rejected. The day before, a party headed by the Reverend
James G. T. Dunleavy, a Methodist preacher, was expelled from the
Russell wagon train. The excuse given was that Dunleavy's especially
large herd of livestock had slowed down everyone on the trail.

With the Dunleavy group was Thomas H. Jefferson, a largely
unheralded cartographer who later created what historian Dale L.
Morgan called "one of the great American maps, an extraordinary
original production which will always have a special place in the car-
tography of the West, and which adds up to a trail document of high
importance."[11] But in 1846, it had not yet been published.[12]

If Russell had any inkling of Jefferson's talent at mapmaking, perhaps he would have encouraged him not to leave with Dunleavy's
group. The offspring of a white father and a slave mother, Jefferson
was light-skinned and often passed for white, although there is no
evidence that he ever denied his black heritage. Some scholars and
most T. H. Jefferson descendants contend that it is likely he was the
son of the Monticello slave Sally Hemings and President Thomas
Jefferson, who was also at one time a surveyor and cartographer.[13]

James Reed figured his family and the Donners were definitely
worthy of joining Russell's caravan. Reed also knew the protocol. As
soon as the wagons ground to a halt, he tethered Glaucus, shook off
the trail dust, scrubbed his face, and trimmed his whiskers. He then
sought the captain—Owl Russell—to get approval. Reed dug out
the letter of endorsement signed by the governor of Illinois. Russell,
who took pride in being a quick judge of character, was impressed.
According to a letter Reed wrote the following day to James Keyes,
his brother-in-law in Springfield, Russell "immediately convened the
whole of the men in the center of the incampment and made a speech
or talk to them stating at the same time that he would vouch for me
as a Gentleman that he had been well informed about me before he
left Independ. And on the road Since he left."

The question was put to a vote, and the Reeds and Donners were approved unanimously. As Reed went on in his letter, so were "5 Germans that fell in with us on the road whose Case I represented to the Col. With a request that he put it to a vote which he did and carried, Russle [sic] said that he would vouch for them on my representations, as he had full confidence in what I Said as a Gentle[man]."[14]

The endorsements from people who had met the Reeds and Donners in Independence also helped. Edwin Bryant, a newspaper editor from Louisville, Kentucky, warmly welcomed the Donners and Reeds. "A new census of our party was taken this morning; and it was found to consist of 98 fighting men, 50 women, 46 wagons, and 350 cattle. Two divisions were made for convenience in travelling. We were joined to-day by nine wagons from Illinois belonging to Mr. Reed and Messrs. Donner, highly respectable and intelligent gentlemen with interesting families. They were received into the company by a unanimous vote."[15]

The Donner and Reed teamsters put the cattle out to pasture before they headed out to hunt and fish. The women and girls washed piles of clothing in the creek and spread them to dry on the trees and brush along the stream. "We children, who had been confined to the wagon so many hours each day, stretched our limbs, and scampered off on Mayday frolics," wrote Eliza Donner. "We waded the creek, made mud pies, and gathered posies in the narrow glades between the cottonwood, beech, and alder trees. Colonel Russell was courteous to all; visited the new members, and secured their cheerful indorsement of his carefully prepared plan of travel."[16]

It all seemed too good to be true.

13. THE OTHERS

At first light on May 20, 1846, after a night of merriment to celebrate the acceptance of the Donner and Reed bunch, the Russell Party was aroused by a bugle call at the camp on Soldier Creek. Baylis Williams, the Reeds' albino hired hand, crept into a wagon and covered his face, ready for sleep after tending fires and keeping watch through the night. At least one wagon driver was unable to rally from what was described as "the effects of an over-night's drunken frolic," fueled by "wretched, adulterated whiskey."[1] The comatose man was fitted into the crowded wagon to sleep off his stupor, and another driver was recruited from the ranks.

Before the caravan returned to the trail, James Reed dashed off a letter to his brother-in-law, James Keyes, back in Springfield. Reed included an update on his mother-in-law, Sarah Keyes, who remained bedridden in the Reed family wagon. "I am afraid Your mother will not stand it many week[s] or indeed days, if there is not a quick change," Reed wrote. "Margrat this morning is in good hart. She was visited by several of the Caravan and Russle came with me last night to have an introduction to my family. I have been talking this moment with Your Mother. She says she feels very much like she was going to die one of her eyes pains her so much and She is so blind that she cannot take her coffee or plate if it is not set near her this morning. She cannot eat anything. I am of the opinion a few days will end her mortal carear."[2]

Although Reed wrote a glowing description of the Kansas prairie and its agricultural potential, most of the Donners were not impressed with the rich soil. The exception was Tamzene. She was often seen kneeling on the soft ground busily making notes and collecting wildflowers, forbs, sedges, and grass specimens. But the Donner brothers never wavered. Their only goal was to reach California.

The Donners and others in the party were by no means the only ones who felt that way. People began to move to California in significant numbers in 1846. About the same number of emigrants left from Missouri as the year before, but in 1845, only 260 of a total of 2,760 had gone to California, whereas most emigrants went to Oregon. But the next year, California attracted 1,599, and only 1,200 ventured to Oregon. In 1846, Reed stated in his letter that three large caravans were leaving Missouri for California—274 wagons from St. Joseph and 267 from Independence.[3]

Early in the summer of 1846, the Russell Party—neither the first nor the last caravan to depart Missouri that year—was considered the main body of California emigrants.[4] Eliza Donner later recalled the diversity and hodgepodge of occupations represented. "The government of these emigrant trains was essentially democratic and characteristically American," Eliza wrote. She described Colonel Russell as "the head of a representative body of pioneers, including lawyers, journalists, teachers, students, farmers, and daylaborers, also a minister of the gospel, a carriage maker, a cabinet-maker, a stone-mason, a jeweler, a blacksmith, and women versed in all branches of woman's work."[5]

Several of the "representative body of pioneers" sought new identities, whereas others were going to an unfamiliar land to acquire wealth or regain their health or for adventure. A few, such as James Reed, were starting over from scratch. Tillers of the soil, such as the Donners, saw themselves as claiming their natural inheritance of the land. Unlike the strange and menacing nomads that roamed the prairies, these were people who saw land ownership as critical to their idea of success. Going to California justified their overwhelming desire to possess the earth. It was their manifest destiny and their natural right.

It would be unwise to believe that they shared a common sense of what they were seeking, other than the mutual goal of reaching California. Still, they all realized there was safety in numbers, and everyone on the trail was vulnerable.

These land voyagers considered their journey to be as fraught with peril as an ocean crossing. They would have understood the ancient Islamic historian who, when asked to describe the sea, replied, "The sea is a great creature upon which weak creatures ride—like worms upon a piece of wood."[6] The terrestrial emigrants must have felt "like worms upon a piece of wood" as they stared across the rolling miles before them and their prairie schooners sailed into wind and waving grass.

The colorful leader Owl Russell was not the only person of consequence in the emigrant party. Edwin Bryant, the gregarious Kentucky newspaper editor who had warmly greeted the Donners and Reeds, was a key leader in the wagon train. Bryant had briefly studied medicine, but when he discovered that writing came naturally to him, he quickly turned to journalism. He was the cousin of the celebrated journalist and poet William Cullen Bryant. In 1830, twenty-five-year-old Edwin Bryant moved from Massachusetts to Kentucky, where he edited and owned newspapers in Louisville and Lexington.

However, by the mid-1840s, the mudslinging Edwin Bryant, in poor health and weary of the stress brought on by the daily grind of journalism, was determined to make the journey west and write a book about his experiences. In early April 1846, Bryant and two companions boarded a steamboat in Louisville bound for St. Louis and then up the Missouri River to Independence, where they arrived on May 1.[7] They soon pushed westward, picking up other emigrants along the trail. After a few days, they reached the encampment of Colonel Russell and his party. Bryant surely knew Russell from Kentucky and time spent at Ashland, their mutual friend Henry Clay's plantation near Lexington.

Also included in the party was twenty-seven-year-old Louisiana native Andrew Jackson Grayson, accompanied by his wife, Frances, and infant son, Edward.[8] When the Grayson contingency joined the larger party at the Indian Creek camp, Bryant was impressed with Grayson and his wife. Many years later, Frances Grayson still had fond memories of those times. "I was as full of romantic adventure as my husband," she wrote. "The trip across the plains was one of the most enjoyable episodes of my life."[9]

Among other high-profile emigrants was Lilburn W. Boggs. The Kentucky native was a War of 1812 veteran and former Missouri governor whose second wife, Panthea Boone, was a granddaughter of Daniel Boone.[10] Boggs's first wife, Julia Ann Bent, who had died in 1820, was the daughter of Silas Bent, a Missouri Supreme Court justice, and the sister of William and Charles Bent, well-known traders on the western frontier. They established Bent's Fort, a massive adobe complex that became the hub of mercantile trade on the mountain branch of the Santa Fe Trail.[11]

Lilburn Boggs was an early trader on the Santa Fe Trail. His trading trips to New Mexico solidified his lifelong interest in the West. Even after he entered Missouri politics and served as state senator, lieutenant governor, and governor, Boggs cast his gaze westward.

In 1838, Boggs—while serving as the sixth governor of Missouri— had ordered all Mormon followers purged from the state. This led to his attempted assassination on May 6, 1842, in Independence, where Boggs ran a store.[12] An investigation was launched, and rewards were offered for the apprehension of the assailant. Some people assumed that the attempted murder was a premeditated act of retribution ordered by Joseph Smith, controversial founder of Mormonism. For "the Prophet" and many of his followers, there was plenty of "justifiable provocation" for taking action against Boggs. That remedy called for blood atonement.[13] Publicly, Smith denied any involvement, but almost immediately, his most loyal and lethal bodyguard—Orrin Porter Rockwell—became the chief suspect.

Smith and Rockwell became fugitives and were charged in the shooting. Smith managed to stay on the run and was never brought to trial. Rockwell was arrested in St. Louis in 1843 and spent nine months in jail before he was tried. The charge of attempted murder was dismissed for lack of evidence.[14] It took Boggs nearly a year to recover from his wounds, during which time he was successful in his bid to return to the Missouri senate.

In May 1846, Boggs, with his wife, Panthea, and their son William and wife, Sonora Hicklin, left Independence for California. Traveling with Boggs when he joined the main body of California emigrants were Jessy Quinn Thornton and his wife, Nancy, from Quincy, Illinois, who had met the Donners and Reeds earlier in the month in Independence. Although there are many discrepancies in his account of the journey, Thornton's two-volume work, published in 1848, was the only complete account of the Donner-Reed Party for at least thirty years.

Thornton probably was responsible for giving a glowing endorsement of the Donners and Reeds on May 19, when their group joined the Russell Party. On the morning of May 20, the Donners and Reeds' first full day with the Russell group, everyone except those nursing hangovers was optimistic as the wagons creaked off on the trail toward the Big Blue River. There was not a cloud in the sky. At the nooning, the teams rested, and the families picnicked on the prairie grass. Then in an instant, the mood of the emigrants changed. Eliza Donner recalled that moment.

"Suddenly a gust of wind swept by; the sky turned a greenish gray; black clouds drifted over the face of the sun; ominous sounds came rumbling from distant hills; and before our effects could be collected and returned to cover, a terrific thunderstorm was upon us. We were three hours distance from our evening camp-ground and our drivers had to walk and face that buffeting storm in order to keep control of the nervous cattle."[15]

The rain continued to pelt the travelers when they finally reached the knoll where they would camp for the night. All of them were tired and soaked. Many of them, especially the men, were short-tempered. There could be no fires until wood was gathered from the edge of a swamp a mile from the camp.

"When brought, the green wood smoked so badly that suppers were late and rather cheerless," wrote Eliza Donner. "Still there was spirit enough left in those stalwart hearts to start some mirth-provoking ditty, or indulge in good-natured raillery over the joys and comforts of pioneering. Indians had followed our train all day, and as we had been warned against leaving temptation within reach, the cattle were corralled early and their guards doubled. Happily, the night passed without alarm or losses."[16]

14. PEOPLE OF THE SOUTH WIND

Just before the bugle call at daybreak, after hours of pounding rain, thunder, and lightning, the Russell Party encampment was still asleep. The rain had stopped. Baylis Williams poked at the fires, stirring them to flame. The last shift of night guards sipped a fresh batch of creek-water coffee.

Edwin Bryant had been on watch until the wee hours. By then, the foul tempers brought on by hard travel had waned. The emigrants were shrouded in blankets and tucked inside their tents. Even the dogs had settled down. Almost every family had at least one dog, and most had several. The Reed family had four fine hounds—Barney, Tracker, Tyler, and Trailer—and a lapdog, Cash, a favorite of young Virginia.[1] The relentless rain had made the dogs testy, and they snapped and growled at one another. Once camp was set up and they were fed, the dogs dutifully curled up under the wagons.

"The howls and sharp snarling barks of the wolves; the mournful hootings of the owl; and the rush of the winds through the tree-tops of the neighboring grove, are the only sounds disturbing the deep solitude of the night,"[2] Bryant wrote.

The party had made only eight miles the day before. Bryant and the others rose to see what the new day would bring. "The views from the high elevations of the prairie have, as usual, been strikingly picturesque," observed Bryant. "The country we have passed through for the last one hundred miles, presents even greater attractions to the eye than any that I have ever previously seen. What the climate may be in winter, or how it may effect the health of the settlers in summer and autumn, I have no means of judging."[3]

Bryant would have been wise to conjecture what those cold months would be like in the high country ahead. That week, reports from Fort Laramie, in Wyoming Territory, were just reaching St. Louis. Large quantities of snow had fallen in the western mountain ranges during the winter.[4] But Bryant had no reason to be too worried. Like the others, he was confident that they would bask in the eternal sunshine of California long before the next winter snow fell.

Thick, gummy mud made the going slow. By noon, the party came upon a narrow creek that had no ford, only steep banks on both sides. The caravan ground to a halt. "Our wagons were lowered down by ropes, and by doubling teams, they were all finally drawn out of the bed of the stream, and up the opposite bank," Bryant wrote. "It was four o'clock when this was accomplished. We encamped in a bend of the stream, about a mile from where we crossed it."[5] They ended up progressing only five or six miles that day.

Spirits were up, however, when Alphonso D. Boone, with his seven children and eleven wagons, caught up with the caravan and was warmly greeted by his sister, Panthea Boggs.[6] He was surprised that Lilburn Boggs had lost the election to be captain of the wagon train but was pleased that the two branches of the family were back together.

After the evening meal, the men broke out chewing tobacco or puffed on clay pipes. To mark the arrival of the Boones, a jug of swigging spirits was passed around, and a shooting contest was proposed with targets set up in a meadow at eighty and two hundred yards. It would be good practice for encountering large herds of bison. Besides, it was not every day a man could boast that he had competed in a shooting match with a descendant of the great Daniel Boone. Several sharpshooters took their turns, but in the end, Bryant singled out W. B. Brown, a fellow Kentuckian from Lexington, as the best marksman of the evening.[7]

"The day has been delightful, and a more cheerful spirit seems to prevail in our party than usual," Bryant wrote as everyone settled in for a quiet night. "At dark our cattle were driven into corral to prevent them from straying, and from being stolen by the Indians."

By morning, however, the camp was abuzz with more grumbling

about the slowness of such a large party. As a result, thirteen wagons, half of them from Jackson County, Missouri, decided to strike out on their own. "This is the second division in our party which has taken place since we started, and there is a strong probability that soon there will be others," wrote Bryant. "A restlessness of disposition, and dissatisfaction from trivial causes, lead to these frequent changes among the emigrating parties."[8]

Bryant was not the only one unhappy about the wagon train's slow pace. Several single men became frustrated by fellow travelers encumbered with families, overloaded wagons, and livestock.

One of the most vocal was George W. McKinstry, a thirty-six-year-old native of Hudson, New York. McKinstry had acquired some medical training but chose the life of a merchant in Vicksburg, Mississippi. After hearing stories of California, McKinstry went west.[9] An early recruit for the Russell Party, McKinstry kept a diary of their progress for May and June 1846.[10]

George Law Curry was another young man who chronicled part of the journey. He was already a seasoned traveler after spending part of his childhood in Venezuela.[11] Curry was well read and began a long career in journalism when he apprenticed as a printer. After moving to St. Louis in 1843, Curry became a copublisher of the *St. Louis Weekly Reveille*, published six days a week.[12] When Curry departed for California, he became a correspondent for the paper. Fortunately, a dozen of his letters from the trail survived, most of them addressed to the *Reveille* and signed "Laon," Curry's pen name.[13]

"Life on the plains far surpasses my expectations; there is a freedom and a nobleness about it that tend to bring forth the full manhood," he wrote in one of his dispatches. "A man upon the horizon-bound prairie feels his own strength and estimates his own weakness. He is alive to every thing around him. For him there is a joy in the 'lone elm' grandeur on the mounds, beauty in the grassy and flower-besprinkled couch on which he rests, and a glory forever round him, stretching his spirit to its fullest tension. Bacon and hard biscuit may occasionally interfere with his *fairydom*, but that only occurs twice a day, and the influence is but momentary."[14]

Others in the caravan soon discovered the main reason for Curry's positive attitude. He had taken a shine to one of the "young girls, just blooming into womanhood."[15] Twenty-four-year-old Chloe Donnelly Boone, eldest daughter of Alphonso Boone, caught Curry's eye. The flirtation eventually turned into a full-blown romance.

On May 22, for the first time since departing Independence, the emigrants encountered large numbers of Indians. Fortunately, they were Kaws and not the feared Pawnees, a tribe which the budding author Francis Parkman declared "the genuine savages of the prairie."[16] The Kaw people, or Kanza—the "People of the South Wind"—gave Kansas its name. Like the prairie wind, they were a people in motion, migrating because of tribal disputes, the desires of various chiefs, and most important, in pursuit of the great bison herds that gave them a living. They tried to resist the intruders who wanted the Kaw children to go to the white man's school and speak his language. But by the time the Russell Party encountered Kaws, they were fighting for their survival because of meddling missionaries and the misdeeds of uncaring white men who through economic pressure and intimidation forced Indian leaders into signing treaties to cede land.[17]

The Russell Party had seen Kaw warriors mounted on what Edwin Bryant described as "fat ponies" throughout the day May 22. By late afternoon, the caravan stopped to set up camp on Black Paint Creek, not far from two sizable Kaw villages, comprised of scores of dome-shaped earthen lodges.[18]

Bryant and the others in the wagon train were oblivious to the Kaws' many problems. Bryant described them as "unblushing and practiced beggars" and wrote of young Kaw men trying to trade ponies for whiskey or emigrants' horses. Among the "troublesome visitors" he met was Hard Chief, whose Kaw name Bryant phonetically spelled as Ki-he-gawa-chuck-ee, which loosely translated to "Difficult to Endure Chief."[19] According to Bryant, the Kaw leader was about fifty-five years old and "of commanding figure, and of rather an intellectual and pleasing expression of countenance."

Hard Chief promised Bryant and the other caravan leaders that in exchange for gifts, he would ensure that none of his people would steal from the emigrant herds or camp. Nonetheless, the wagon train posted extra guards throughout the night. There was a slight fracas when sentinels confronted two Kaws in the camp, but they were released when it was determined that they had come to trade a pony for four gallons of whiskey. The next morning, Hard Chief and his wife were seated on the ground near Bryant's tent. They patiently awaited payment for keeping the promise that no thievery would take place. In a rare instance of white men keeping their word with Indians, a large supply of bacon, flour, and other articles was presented to Hard Chief for distribution to his followers.[20]

Before leaving camp, the emigrants once again faced a creek with steep banks and a muddy channel, forcing them to cut down small trees and brush to fill the streambed. When all the wagons and livestock were safely across, the long caravan captained by Russell made good progress. Some young Kaw men, their faces painted with vermilion, rode along as an escort. During a brief rest stop, one of the Kaws spied some bright blue blossoms among the tall grasses. He used a stick to dig up a root about the size and shape of a hen's egg. The Kaw unsheathed his knife and peeled off a coarse brown husk, revealing the white tuber that he proudly presented to Bryant. White pioneers called it a "prairie potato" or "prairie turnip."[21] Plains Indians boiled it, roasted it in embers, or crushed it to a powder to season soup. They also ate the roots raw. That was how Bryant sampled it, declaring that "its flavor is more agreeable than that of the finest Irish potato."

Bryant reveled in the fauna and flora of the prairie. "The wild rose, which is now in full bloom, perfumes the atmosphere along our route with a delicious fragrance," he wrote. "The wild tulip (yellow and variegated), a plume-shaped white flower, and several flowers of the campanella, or bell-shaped classification, have ornamented the prairie to-day."[22]

Tamzene Donner was in heaven. She was amid a profusion of plants she had never seen before, and she found other people in the caravan who were equally impressed and eager to explore the prairies and thickets. "Mr. Edwin Bryant, Mr. and Mrs. Thornton, and my mother were enthusiastic searchers for botanical and geological specimens," Eliza Donner remembered of those late spring days on the trail. "They delved into the ground, turning over stones and scraping out the crevices, and zealously penetrated the woods to gather mosses, roots, and flowering plants. Of the rare floral specimens and perishable tints, my mother made pencil and water-color studies, having in view the book she was preparing for publication."[23]

Andrew Grayson, whose stunning portraiture of birds depicted in natural settings and poses eventually earned him the title "the Audubon of the West," was another frequent and congenial companion on the frequent nature hikes.[24] While Grayson made sketches, the others gathered specimens of buffalo grass, bluestem, indigo, larkspur, creeping hollyhocks, and paintbrush.

On May 23, the caravan met up with four crusty fur trappers from the Rocky Mountains, accompanied by several Delaware Indians. The party was headed east, their saddles loaded with freshly killed game and the pack animals carrying large sacks of furs. The emigrants were envious.[25] The trappers told them to not despair. Just ahead, "some one or two hundred miles," on the Platte River, they were sure to find large herds of bison that would yield much fresh meat.

The Russell outfit and the Kaws who followed them throughout the day established a camp in late afternoon close to a spring of cold, pure water. The next day, May 24, was the Sabbath, and as J. Quinn Thornton noted, "No rest for man or beast." Later that day, Bryant was again taken with fragrant honeysuckle blossoms, sweetbrier, wild tulip, and other plant species along the trail. He later wrote, "Beautiful as the country is, the silence and desolation reigning over it excite irrepressible emotions of sadness and melancholy."[26]

As the travelers pressed on, they came upon two dead oxen left along the trail by one of the forward companies. Most of the day, the caravan had been strung out over several miles. Many of the wagons were slow in arriving at the campsite by a sweetwater spring. A dead elm was divided for firewood. Several people complained of feeling ill and feverish. Bryant recorded his impressions.

"I am beginning to feel alarmed at the tardiness of our movements, and fearful that winter will find us in the snowy mountains of California, or that we shall suffer from the exhaustion of our supply of provisions," he wrote. "I do not fear for myself, but for the women and children of the emigrants. Singular as it may seem, there are many of our present party who have no just conceptions of the extent and labor of the journey before them. They appear to be desirous of shortening each day's march as much as possible, and when once encamped are reluctant to move, except for the benefit of fresh grass for their cattle, and a more convenient and plentiful supply of wood for the purposes of cooking."[27]

Others also were starting to feel uneasy. They knew that no matter what they did, how much they prayed for guidance, and whatever good luck came their way, harder times lay ahead.

15. ALCOVE SPRING

MAY 25–29, 1846

When the long train of wagons returned to the trail on May 25, James Reed on Glaucus and Virginia Reed on Billy rode ahead of the procession, just as they did most mornings.

"In our party were many who rode on horseback, but mama seldom did," Virginia later wrote. "She preferred the wagon, and did not want to leave grandma, although Patty took it upon herself this charge, and could hardly be persuaded to leave grandma's side. Our little home was so comfortable, that mama could sit reading and chatting with the little ones, and almost forget that she was really crossing the plains."[1]

Most women tried their best to avoid trail dust, scorching heat, frequent rainstorms, and the blasphemies of teamsters who encouraged the oxen teams to keep pace. Staying inside the wagon also kept the ladies out of sight in case curious Indians rode by to do some trading or just ogle the odd strangers.

"The staid and elderly matrons spent most of their time in the wagons, knitting or patching designs for quilts," recalled Eliza Donner. "The younger ones and the girls passed theirs in the saddle. They would scatter in groups over the plains to investigate distant objects, then race back, and with song and banter join husband and brother, driving the loose cattle in the rear. The wild, free spirit of the plain often prompted them to invite us little ones to seats beside them, and away we would canter with the breeze playing through our hair and giving a ruddy glow to our cheeks."[2]

The party moved through wide-open prairie country, with only a few trees in sight. By the nooning stop, they had reached Vermillion

Creek, with steep banks on the east but a much gentler slope on the west. The largest stream they had forded since the Kansas, the creek had a rapid current, and the crossing took several hours. Later that afternoon, the travelers camped on high ground. Just as they pitched the tents and were forming a corral with the wagons, a ferocious thunderstorm arose. Sheets of rain and gale-force winds drove everyone to cover. The storm struck with such fury that some of the wagons were nearly turned over. After a half hour, it began to let up.[3]

"The cloud rose from the west, and soon passing over to the east, within a hundred yards of us the most brilliant rainbow I ever beheld was formed, the bases of the arch resting upon two undulations between which we had passed," wrote Edwin Bryant. "No Roman general, in all his gorgeous triumphal processions, ever paraded beneath an arch so splendid and imposing. The clouds soon cleared away, the rain ceased, and the brilliant meteor faded, leaving nature around us freshened and cleansed from the dust and impurities, which for two days past have been excessively annoying."[4]

The next day, the route took them over rolling prairie. Only three miles down the muddy trail, they came to a small stream that was easy to cross despite the gush of rain the night before. The caravan steadily ascended a ridge until they reached the bluffs overlooking the Big Blue River, known by Indians and early travelers as the Great Blue Earth River. Far from being blue, the churning waters were the color of prairie soil. The river was filled with drift, broken branches, and fallen trees of all sizes.[5] Owl Russell huddled with James Reed, George Donner, Lilburn Boggs, and some of his lieutenants to discuss the situation. The river was much too swollen and the current too swift to attempt any crossing. The party would have to give the water a chance to recede. By early afternoon, the wagons and all the animals were settled on a sloping prairie meadow on the east side of the Big Blue.

Despite the delay, most of the Russell Party was ready for a proper rest, and this site near Independence Crossing was ideal. Cool water flowed from a nearby spring. Stands of hackberry, cottonwood, willow, and elm along the river provided an ample supply of wood, and the livestock and horses grazed in a pasture of tall bluestem grass.[6]

By midafternoon on May 26, most of the women and girls were busily scrubbing mounds of clothes and linens in kettles over fires on the banks of a small creek close to the encampment. The bachelors were, as George McKinstry put it, "obliged to do our own washing," adding, "I find I have done my own work badly and am much fatigued."[7] While many of the single men toiled—and perhaps reconsidered their marital status—some looked for a plump deer, but to no avail. Others tried angling in the Big Blue. The current was too strong, and only a lunker catfish about three feet long made it to a waiting skillet.

That evening, under a new moon, Boggs, Reed, George Donner, and several others discussed the established bylaws and regulations governing the caravan which, as Edwin Bryant pointed out, were rarely enforced. "We are a pure democracy," wrote Bryant. "All laws are proposed directly to a general assembly, and are enacted or rejected by a majority."[8] Bryant and the rest of the leaders were optimistic. In his last entry for the day, Bryant wrote, "The day has been delightful. No disagreeable incident has marred the general harmony and good feeling."

That optimism soon vanished. Yet another thunderstorm roared from the night clouds. Some emigrants feared their tents would be swept away. Jessy Thornton, standing watch at the storm's peak, was shaken by the storm's intensity. "The lightning sometimes, as I fancied, ran down my gun barrel, quivered at my feet, and then went out in hissing and darkness. The atmosphere was filled with a sulphureous stench."[9]

Bryant was thankful for the surrounding bluffs and timber that helped to buffet the wind. "The whole arch of the heavens for a time was wrapped in a sheet of flame and the almost deafening crashes of thunder, following each other with scarcely an intermission between, seemed as if they would rend the solid earth, or topple it from its axis. A more sublime and awful meteoric display, I never witnessed or could conceive."[10]

The additional rain meant that it would take even longer before the Big Blue could be crossed. Some emigrants became restless and irritable. A band of disgruntled single men already unhappy with the caravan's sluggishness decided the time had come for some leadership changes.

On May 27, an early morning meeting of the company was held in the camp corral. Ostensibly called to discuss regulations drawn up the previous night, the proceedings turned ugly. Robert Ewing, one of Bryant's traveling companions, disappointed about not being appointed to any post, let loose a barrage of curses aimed mostly at Owl Russell.[11] Ewing then moved to appoint a standing committee to try the caravan leaders, "when charged with tyranny or neglect of duty by any individual of the party." A vote was called, and surprisingly, the motion carried. Stunned and outraged, all the officers, including Russell, immediately resigned. Ewing nominated Boggs, but the former Missouri governor quickly declined.

Now the wagon train had no leaders. Before that fact had a chance to sink in, Bryant stepped forward. He knew most of the party still supported Russell and his cohorts and no one who had voted really understood the Ewing measure. Bryant made a motion of his own—a reconsideration of the vote. "My motion was carried by a large majority; the resolution raising the standing committee was rescinded, and the officers who had re-signed were re-elected by acclamation!"[12]

With the defeat of Ewing and the "Young Men"—as sympathetic journalist George McKinstry called the malcontents—a semblance of order returned to the camp. It was an opportune time for Tamzene Donner, the Thorntons, Bryant, and other nature lovers to explore the prairie, marked by dense undergrowth. While tramping through thickets and clearings in search of bird life, Andrew Grayson came across a bumper crop of juicy prairie peas. He stuffed as many as possible into his pockets and filled his hat with the bounty, knowing that his wife, Frances, had the spices needed to transform the wild peas into delicious pickles. Inspired by the pea harvest, Grayson and others went in search of a honey tree. They proved to be good bee trackers and returned to camp in the afternoon with several pails brimming with delicious wildflower honey.[13]

In the afternoon, Bryant and a few others set out to find the source of the branch running near the campgrounds. Bryant later wrote, "About three-fourths of a mile from our camp we found a large spring of water, as cold and pure as if it has just been melted from ice. It gushed from a ledge of rocks, which composes the bank of the stream, and falling some ten feet, its waters are received into a basin fifteen feet in length, ten in breadth, and three or four in depth. A shelving rock projects over this basin, from which falls a beautiful cascade of water, some ten or twelve feet. The whole is buried in a variety of shrubbery of the rickets verdure, and surrounded by small mound-shaped inequalities of the prairie. Altogether it is one of the most romantic spots I ever saw. So charmed were we with its beauties, that several unconsciously glided away in the enjoyment of its refreshing waters and seductive attractions. We named this the *'Alcove Spring'*; and future travelers will find the name graven on the rocks, and on the trunks of trees surrounding it."[14]

Bryant was credited with naming the spring, but he was not the first person to admire the beauty of the natural grotto. Years before, Frémont had chiseled his name in the rocks. Neither was Bryant the first of the Russell Party to visit the spring. James Reed had been there the day before. His name and the date, May 26, were carved into a rock on the top of the spring. During the time the emigrants camped there, others, including McKinstry, also left inscriptions.[15]

A quiet night passed, with no storms. The campers awoke on May 28 to find that the Big Blue had fallen fifteen inches while they slept. After breakfast, a general call went out for volunteers to gather at nearby Independence Crossing to build a large raft for ferrying the wagons. Men showed up with axes, adzes, and other tools.

The plan, devised by Russell, was to construct a rope ferry consisting of two large dugout canoes united by cross timbers so wagons could be loaded onto the raft. Then, with ropes attached at both ends, the craft could be pulled back and forth across the river by the sheer strength of the men. Two cottonwoods were felled, trimmed, and moved into place. The next step was to hollow out a pair of canoes twenty-five feet long. The men worked on the craft the entire day. They returned to camp exhausted and, soon after supper, turned in for the night.

For the Reed family, it was a long and sleepless night. They kept a deathwatch around the featherbed in the family wagon. The first member of the Donner-Reed Party to die had come to the end of her journey. Near daylight on May 29, Sarah Keyes, the seventy-year-old widowed mother of Margret Reed, breathed her last. Her long struggle with consumption was over.[16] Now she would be laid to rest in a land she never knew.

"The event, although it had been anticipated several days, cast a shade of gloom over our whole encampment," wrote Bryant. "The construction of the ferry-boat and all recreations were suspended, out of respect for the dead, and to make preparations for the funeral."[17]

While James Reed dug a grave beneath an imposing oak, other men felled a cottonwood and built a coffin. John Denton, the Englishman traveling as a teamster for the Donners, found a smooth slab of stone and carved Sarah's name and date of death on it. Reed also cut her name and years into the bark of the oak. Margret and her daughters washed Sarah's body, combed her hair, and dressed her in her best gown. Before the coffin lid was tacked closed, Reed snipped a lock of her hair. He gave it to Patty, the little girl closest to her grandmother, and she treasured it and one of Sarah's pincushions for the rest of her life.[18]

"At 2 o'clock, p.m., a funeral procession was formed, in which nearly every man, woman, and child of the company united, and the corpse of the deceased lady was conveyed to its last resting-place, in this desolate but beautiful wilderness," Bryant wrote. The Reverend Josephus Adamson Cornwall officiated at the brief graveside ceremony. A hymn was sung, and Cornwall delivered what one emigrant called "a sensible sermon."[19] The coffin was lowered into the ground, and the grave was closed and covered with prairie sod and wildflowers.

"It seemed hard to bury her in the wilderness, and travel on, and we were afraid that the Indians would destroy her grave, but her death here, before our troubles began, was providential, and nowhere on the whole road could we have found so beautiful a resting place,"[20] Virginia Reed wrote.

That evening, young Patty Reed cuddled with her mother, the other children, and their pup Cash in the bed where Sarah had died. Patty clutched her wooden doll and the lock of her grandmother's hair. Seventy-one years later, Patty still remembered that night and her simple prayer: "Dear God, watch over and protect dear Grandmother, and don't let the Indians dig her up."[21]

16. THE RHETORIC OF FEAR

Although a pall of death hung over the camp the morning after the burial of Sarah Keyes, some good news dulled the gloom. The river was slowly falling. Work resumed on the construction of the craft, which was christened the Blue River Rover.[1] The makeshift ferryboat was launched to loud hurrahs and cheers, and the ferrying of the wagons commenced.

"She floated down the stream like a cork, and was soon moored at the place of embarkation," Edwin Bryant noted.[2] As expected, every crossing that day was difficult and dangerous. The current was so strong that even near the bank, where the water was only a few feet deep, it took tremendous effort to pull in the Blue River Rover and secure it.

"The banks of this stream being steep, our heavily laden wagons had to be let down with ropes, so that the wheels might run into the hollowed logs," wrote Virginia Reed. "This was no easy task when you take into consideration that in these wagons were women and children, who could cross the rapid river in no other way."[3]

One of the big cottonwood floats was swamped during a crossing, but there was no serious damage or loss except the loss of precious time. Repairs were made and operations resumed. By nightfall, only nine wagons with their contents had made the river crossing successfully.

The next day, May 31, the ferrying process began immediately after breakfast, despite the concern of Jessy Thornton, who pointed out that it was "a desecration of the Sabbath."[4] The water had fallen at least seven more inches, but moving the wagons and swimming the herds of livestock across the stream were just as perilous as the day before. Every man pitched in and did his part.

Heavy masses of dark clouds and a chilling wind rolled in from the northwest. By five o'clock, it commenced raining, and the temperature plunged to the upper forties. The rain did not stop until about ten o'clock that night, just as the last wagon finished the crossing. The men had been working for fifteen hours, many of them standing in water up to their armpits. They were cold, badly cramped, and "shivering violently" as they made their way to the new camp about a mile from the crossing.

Bryant, drawing from the limited medical schooling he had received many years before, described the afflicted men as being "under the influence of a paroxysm of the ague," a painful spasm or fit that often turned into a sudden outburst of violent emotion.[5] Apparently the diagnosis was correct. Two of the teamsters who were usually well behaved got into an argument that quickly turned into a knife fight. Before any serious wounds were inflicted, others jumped in, disarmed both men, and restored order.

That night, after firewood was gathered and the corral was formed by the wagons, some of the men fell asleep without a bite of supper. James Reed and the Donner brothers were pleased that their hired hands stayed clear of any fights. The company was so exhausted that any worry about thieving Indians was put aside, and no guards were posted.

On the first day of June, an unseasonably cold, raw wind greeted the emigrants. It felt more like a chilly November morning. There was much coughing and complaining as they dug through the wagons for heavier shirts and coats. Margret Reed was stricken with one of her worst migraines and wept piteously at having left her mother behind in a prairie grave. Aside from Margret and her girls, the emigrants were pleased to resume their march after the long delay at the Big Blue.

Bryant wrote, "We are now in the territory of the Pawnee, reported to be vicious savages, and skillful and daring thieves. Thus far we have lost nothing of consequence, and met with no disaster from Indian depredation or hostility."[6]

Hostile Indians were not the biggest concern. Incompatibilities within the combined elements of the Russell Party were every bit as dangerous as a Pawnee warrior. Recalcitrant individuals unwilling to bow to authority continually defied the caravan leaders and openly clashed among themselves. Insidious gossip and rumor, as lethal as snake venom, seeped into campfire parleys, turning friends into enemies.

A quarrel that had been brewing for several days erupted between Jessy Thornton and John B. Goode. Both were headed to Oregon—the asthmatic Thornton, along with his sickly wife, Nancy, and Goode traveling alone. Back in Independence, Thornton and Goode had become partners. Thornton financed the wagon, and Goode supplied the oxen. They also hired two teamsters. Problems between them flared not long after the caravan started across the prairie. Goode decided that Thornton was devoting too much of his time to botanical study with his nature-loving cohorts and was not putting in his share of the labor to maintain the wagon and ox team.[7]

On June 1, the disagreement reached a boiling point when Goode threatened removal of the oxen from the wagon, which would have left the Thorntons marooned on the side of the trail. Late that night, as the caravan's appointed council met in an attempt to arbitrate the dispute, tempers flared even more, punches were thrown, and Goode and Thornton had to be separated.

After only a few hours of sleep, the men of the Russell Party were summoned the next morning to consider measures for preventing further disturbances. Ultimately, it was determined that the two individuals at loggerheads over their wagon and oxen and the other eighteen to twenty wagons also bound for Oregon should "in a respectful manner and a friendly spirit" leave the Russell caravan en route to California.[8] The proposition was put to a vote and unanimously passed. The Oregon emigrants immediately withdrew their wagons from the corral and proceeded on their way.

The departure caused much angst for both the future Oregonians and the future Californians. Several of the women broke into tears. After just a few weeks, bonds had been established between mothers from both sides. Likewise, some of the girls were distraught at the thought of being separated from the young men who had been wooing them. As it turned out, anxiousness and tears were for naught. Although from this point of the journey forward the California and Oregon parties remained divided, they were in close proximity much of the way. Usually less than a day's ride apart, they visited back and forth as their own caravans fragmented and regrouped along the trail.

"The Oregon company was never so far in advance that we could not hear from it, and on various occasions, some of its members sent to us for medicines and other necessaries,"[9] wrote Eliza Donner.

Charles Tyler Stanton also described the impact of the Oregon emigrants' departure from the Russell Party. "Friendships and attachments had been formed which were hard to break; for, ever since, our company is nearly deserted, by the young men every day riding out on horseback, pretending to hunt, but instead of pursuing the bounding deer or fleet antelope, they are generally found among the fair Oregon girls!"[10]

A bachelor, Stanton at age thirty-five was much older than the young bucks hired as teamsters. He had read Lansford Hastings's book, *The Emigrants' Guide to Oregon and California*, and convinced himself that he could revitalize his life through travel. Because Stanton sometimes drove one of the Donner wagons, there were claims that he was a Donner employee. It is more likely that he arranged for the Donners to haul his personal belongings in one of their wagons, just as he had done with other travelers earlier on the trail, and occasionally he drove a wagon out of the goodness of his heart. Stanton had caught the big catfish that had provided breakfast for most of the Donners at Alcove Spring. A voracious reader, Stanton desired to improve his mind, and his considerable knowledge of geology and botany endeared him to Tamzene Donner.

For the first few days of June, Tamzene, Stanton, and the other emigrant naturalists stayed close to the wagon train. The unseasonable weather was not conducive to sketching and collecting botanical specimens. It was still cold, and flannels and coats were in order. Many emigrants, especially children, were sick with colds and fever. In addition, as Bryant had pointed out, the Russell Party was now in the territory of the Pawnees, known as tireless warriors, admired and feared for their skill and bravery. The gossips in the caravan spread rumors of Indian sightings that kept everyone on high alert.

Late on June 2, some Indians did approach the wagons—a party of four Shawnees returning home from a hunting expedition along the Platte River. Two of them spoke some English, and that evening, they were invited to camp with the caravan. The Indians sold the emigrants some dried buffalo tongues and jerked meat and slept wrapped in furs and blankets next to the night fires.

June 3 was more bitterly cold than the day before. That morning, the emigrants gave the Shawnees a large bundle of letters addressed to family and friends back east. "We also supplied them with bacon, flour, coffee, and sugar, sufficient for the remainder of their journey," wrote Bryant. "They supped and breakfasted with our mess, and I never saw men swallow food with such apparent enjoyment and in such prodigious quantities."[11]

Despite the friendly encounter with the Shawnee hunters, the Russell Party stayed vigilant. They scanned the ridgelines and occasional groves for any telltale sign of Pawnee scouts on a quest for scalps. To the Pawnees, scalping was an ancient custom that was part of their religious beliefs. The taking of scalps was thought to revitalize the tribe and strengthen their relationship with the sacred powers of the universe.[12]

As a result of the constantly churning rumor mill, there was another threat that the Russell Party emigrants feared as much as an Indian scalping party—Mormons. The Mormons had not forgotten that they had been driven out of Missouri by Lilburn Boggs, now traveling with the Russell Party. After Mormon founder Joseph Smith had been shot and killed by a mob in 1844, Brigham Young was appointed prophet and president of the church. He was committed to a plan conceived by Smith, who had envisioned the Saints establishing a kingdom in the West. Because of continued persecution, the Mormon exodus from Illinois began ahead of schedule. They crossed the ice-covered Mississippi River in February 1846[13] and trudged across Iowa. They were headed for the far West—just like the Russell Party.

17. EBB AND FLOW

The strain and discomfort of trail life took a toll. Disease, injuries, and breakdown forced many emigrants to fall behind. Many joined other wagon trains, but some gave up and went back home. The continual stress and changes of mind about final destinations resulted in a constant ebb and flow in the wagon company. Quarrels were inevitable. Fickle weather, fear of marauding Indians or vengeful Mormons, and concern about the unknown kept nerves frayed and tempers short. Not all the clashes could be settled amicably. When that occurred, it usually led to the splintering off of families or individuals from the main party. Occasionally, it ended in violence.

The evening of June 3, 1846, some of the men were still nursing wounds from the recent brawls at the Big Blue crossing. Without warning, some men who had recently joined the party suddenly went after each other like fighting dogs. When pounding fists and eye gouging had no effect, they drew knives and pistols. "But for the interference of Mr. [William Henry] Kirkendall, who was standing near at the time and rushed between the parties, one or both would probably have been killed,"[1] wrote eyewitness Edwin Bryant.

The violence in camp topped off a chaotic day. While fording a stream that afternoon, one of the wagons had overturned. A pregnant woman—or as Bryant put it, a woman "in a delicate condition"—and her young daughter were thrown from the wagon into a pool of water without serious injury.[2] The long wooden wagon tongue had snapped, and the contents, including clothing, foodstuffs, and bedding, were soaked and covered with mud. Bryant later wrote that the wagon belonged "to a German emigrant named Keyesburgh." A German named Keseberg did in fact own the wagon. It was the first mention in the 1846 trail record of this family that became a significant part of the Donner-Reed Party story.[3]

Johann Ludwig Christian Keseberg, mostly called Lewis, had been born in 1814 in Westphalia, just a year before it became part of Prussia.[4] He wed nineteen-year-old Elisabeth Philippine Zimmerman in 1842. The marriage took place in a Protestant church despite much opposition because the bride was Roman Catholic,[5] and Keseberg's father was a Lutheran minister.

Less than a year later, Philippine gave birth to twin daughters. Juliane Karoline (called Ada) and Mathilde Elise were about a year old in 1844 when the family left Germany. They arrived in New York on Lewis's thirtieth birthday. Two months later, little Mathilde died.[6] The Kesebergs soon settled near Cincinnati. Keseberg worked in a brewery until he decided to move west. Contemporaneous references to Keseberg at the time of the 1846 journey described him as a tall, handsome man with blond hair. Others on the trail noted Keseberg's aptitude for language.

The Kesebergs had left Ohio with two wagons, one of which likely was driven by a Belgian emigrant whose given name remains unknown. His last name was Hardcoop, and he had been a cutler for many years in his native city of Antwerp. At the time of the journey to California, Hardcoop was about sixty years old. Some authors and historians have suggested that one of Keseberg's teamsters was German emigrant Charles Burger, called "Dutch Charley," but other sources from the Russell Party, such as Lilburn Boggs, indicated that Burger worked for the Donners. The most likely candidate for the Kesebergs' teamster remains Hardcoop.[7]

Keseberg had few if any close personal relationships while on the trail. A possible exception was Heinrich Lienhard, a Swiss who was one of the "five German boys" with a caravan just ahead of the Russell Party. He recognized Keseberg's shortcomings but still maintained their friendship. "Keseberg's greatest weakness was his unbridled temper, and one day he confessed that it was the source of considerable embarrassment to him," wrote Lienhard. "After his anger had subsided, he always realized his mistake and was extremely penitent. He gave every indication of being an honorable person."[8]

Other Germans traveling with the Russell Party included the Wolfingers, a young couple about whom very little is known. Some have suggested that Wolfinger's first name was Jacob. It is believed that his wife—Doris or Dorthea—was about twenty years old when the couple joined the Russell Party.[9] According to camp gossip, Wolfinger was wealthy. His pretty wife's appearance seemed to validate that rumor. She was remembered as being a "tall, queenly lady" who wore fine clothing and jewelry, which did not endear the couple to the poorer members of the caravan, especially the other wives.

Joseph Reinhardt and Augustus Spitzer were two other members of the Russell Party's German contingency. Both men were about thirty years old and were said to be partners traveling in their own wagon with the Wolfingers at least part of the way to California.

The German-speaking emigrants tended to travel together and keep to themselves. However, in early June 1846, despite their many differences, all members of the Russell Party had at least one thing in common—they craved fresh meat.

On June 4, as the wagons rolled over what George McKinstry called "the finest road in the world," the hunger for meat was so great that some of the men on horseback, probably led by James Reed on his fine steed and with a brace of hounds, pursued a wolf for miles.[10] They came close, but because of the many ravines, the lobo eluded them. At about noon, the scouts spied large numbers of antelopes grazing about two or three miles in the distance.

"A party started out immediately on the best horses to hunt them," wrote Bryant. "We spread out to the right and left, and the antelopes did not discover us until we had approached within the distance of half a mile. They then raised their heads, and looking towards us an instant, fled almost with the fleetness of the wind. I never saw an animal that could run with the apparent ease, speed, and grace of these.

They seem to fly, or skim over the ground, so bounding and buoyant are their strides, and so bird-like their progress."[11]

The chase was on, but the antelopes easily outdistanced the hunters. They watched the oval-shaped patches of white hair on the animals' rumps grow smaller as the herd dashed over the prairie. "All our efforts to approach them within gunshot was fruitless," wrote Bryant. "The sport, however, was very good for us, but not so agreeable to our horses."

That evening, the hunters made camp on the Little Blue, not far from a large patch of oak, cottonwood, and hickory. Andrew Grayson quietly slipped into the timber and brought down a deer. The plump doe was field-dressed and lugged back to camp, where every bit of roasted venison was consumed. "This is the first game of consequence, that has been killed since we commenced our journey," noted Bryant, "and it was a luxury highly appreciated after subsisting so long upon salted meat."[12]

Refreshed by the venison, the emigrants made good time on the trail for the next few days but were still unable to bag any game larger than a jackrabbit. There were plenty of antelopes around, but they kept their distance. The wagon train also was getting close to buffalo country, and all eyes scanned the broad prairie for signs of the big shaggy beasts known as the monarchs of the plains.

Big game was scarce, but there was no shortage of pesky mosquitoes and gnats that continually harassed humans and beasts. Everyone longed for the sanctuary of tents filled with heavy campfire smoke, although they were liable to spend the night coughing. Horses and cattle got little relief day or night. Clouds of mosquitoes covered the animals. Grazing cattle were so bothered that they pulled up their picket pins and tried to run away. Horses whinnied in pain all night, and in the morning, blood streamed down their flanks. Dogs howled and scratched themselves raw.

Mothers were concerned about the bites inflicted on their families by mosquitoes and ticks. For days at a time, the wagon train would be plagued with sickness, mostly chills, fever, and severe diarrhea.

Emigrants from larger cities who were not used to spending so much time outdoors were particularly vulnerable.

Despite all the travails, compassion was demonstrated. On June 7, as the caravan creaked along, one of the axletrees of a heavily loaded wagon broke. The wagon belonged to Bryant and some of the other single men.[13] Some travelers simply rolled past the marooned wagon without giving it a second look. Finally, a few emigrants stopped to help.

One of them was William H. Eddy, a carriage maker from Belleville, Illinois. Eddy was about twenty-eight years old when he left Illinois in spring 1846 with his wife, Eleanor Priscilla Eddy, about twenty-five, and their young children, James P. and Margaret.[14] They eventually joined up with the Russell Party. Eddy earned a reputation for being skilled with his hands, a good hunter, and a lively and enterprising gentleman. He proved himself to many of the others when he stopped and repaired the wagon belonging to Bryant and the others.

"This would have been a most serious disaster, detaining us probably a whole day, but for the fact that we had brought with us from Independence duplicate axletrees," wrote Bryant. "The tools with which we had provided ourselves in the event of accidents . . . were now found indispensible. . . . The damage was fully repaired, and our wagon as strong if not stronger than before at sunset, when we started for camp."[15]

The Bryant and Eddy wagons, traveling under a bright moon, approached the encampment late that night. Bryant recalled that the tents and wagon covers in the distance "appeared in the moonlight like a cluster of small white cottages composing a country village."[16] Bryant and his companions drove into camp. The teams were unharnessed, and the animals were fed and watered. Tents were pitched. It was time to sleep and dream of the coming days and the Platte River, which was now close.

18. ON THE PLATTE

Mindful of the time they had lost at Alcove Spring, the Russell Party pushed hard during the first week of June. They covered eighteen to twenty miles a day, following the path northward into the future state of Nebraska.

Ahead was one of the journey's major milestones—the Platte River. The broad stream was the convergence point for several pioneer trails and eventually became known as the Great Platte River Road. From the early 1840s until after the Civil War and the coming of the transcontinental railroad, the Platte was considered "the grand corridor of America's westward expansion" and a lifeline to the uplands far to the west.[1] The emigrants knew when they arrived at the Platte that the trail would turn in the direction of their dreams—due west.

"Everyone was anxious to reach the Platte," Charles Stanton of the Russell Party wrote to his brother Sidney that June. "It was in every body's mouth 'when shall we get to the Platte?'"[2]

For several days, the overlanders moved steadily northwest to Thirty-Two Mile Creek, with its gentle banks and easy fords. There had been good water and forage along the Little Blue River valley, but soon the bluestem gave way to shorter grasses, spotty water, and sparse wood for fires.

The ever-observant Edwin Bryant wrote, "The prairie over which we travelled, until we reached the bluffs that overlook the wide valley or bottom of the Platte, is a gradually ascending plane. The soil is sandy; the grass is short, and grows in tufts and small bunches." Given Bryant's love of flora, he added a sad note, "I saw no flowers."[3]

At about three o'clock that afternoon, the wagon train reached the valley of the Platte River. On the bluff above the shining river, James Reed reined in Glaucus and waved his hat in the air. One of the more vocal celebrants was Stanton. "We all hallooed with pleasure and surprise. The valley of the Platte! There is none like it. There is not a single stick of timber to be seen on either side of the river—it is one interminable prairie as far as the eye can extend; yet there is relief found in the numerous islands of the river being generally covered with wood."[4]

Some folks called the river the Nebraska, from *Nebrthaka*, the Otoe Indian name for the region, meaning "flat water." The French trappers called it the Plat, the French word for "flat." Emigrants often said the Platte was "a mile wide and an inch deep."[5] The river began at the confluence of the North Platte River and the South Platte River, streams fed by snowmelt from the Rocky Mountains east of the continental divide. From that point, it flowed more than three hundred miles eastward, where it discharged into the Missouri River.

After descending the bluffs, the Russell Party made camp at the river's edge, opposite a long wooded island formed by the Wood River and a channel of the Platte. It was called Grand Island.

Francis Parkman, the young Brahmin making his tour of the prairies that summer, wrote when he first viewed the Platte River valley, "For league after league, a plain as level as a lake was outspread before us; here and there the Platte, divided into a dozen thread-like sluices, was traversing it, and an occasional clump of wood, rising in the midst like a shadowy island, relieved the monotony of the waste. No living thing was moving throughout the vast landscape, except the lizards that darted over the sand and through the rank grass and prickly pears at our feet. Before us and behind us, the level monotony of the plain was unbroken as far as the eye could reach. Sometimes it glared in the sun, an expanse of hot, bare sand; sometimes it was veiled by long coarse grass."[6]

After spending several days along the river, Bryant wrote, "The general aspect of the scenery is that of aridity and desolation. The face of the country presents here those features and characteristics which proclaim it to be uninhabitable by civilized man."[7]

The key word in Bryant's statement was *civilized*. That excluded people whom he considered uncivilized, such as the Indians who had lived successfully on what was thought to be infertile land for hundreds of years. According to Bryant's way of thinking, if white settlers attempted to live in such an unproductive and inhospitable region, devoid of civilization and cultivation, they would become like wild Indians, dependent on bison for their existence.

That first night on the Platte, the Russell Party emigrants feasted on their first antelope meat, provided by Andrew Grayson. It was the ideal feast to mark their arrival on the Platte. The broad yellow stream was flanked by a dusty trail a quarter mile wide that they would follow for a month to the uplands of the future state of Wyoming.

On the morning of June 9, "copious dew" covered the grass and tents but vanished as the wagons moved westward. The emigrants saw that the river had expanded to at least two miles across. It reminded them of the Missouri or Mississippi except that the Platte was so shallow. In many places a person could wade across the wide stream "without wetting the pantaloons, if well rolled up above the knees."[8]

That evening, one of the hunters came back to camp bearing a human skull he had found in a meadow littered with human bones. It was decided that the skull was from an Indian who likely had been killed during a fight between warring tribes.[9] Several members of the caravan went to the man's tent to see the skull, and some asked to hold it. Others in the caravan urged the man to get rid of the skull. It left them with a sense of the harsh reality of their journey and what they faced on the trail ahead. For them, the skull could bring bad luck.[10]

19. LIFE GOES ON

Each day along the Platte brought new discoveries for the Russell Party. The Donners and other farmers had certain practical skills and wisdom to offer, and others in the party provided knowledge gleaned from academic training and intellectual pursuits. Whenever there was a spirit of cooperation, the results were usually beneficial to all.

When the emigrants found that the primarily treeless "Coast of Nebraska," as the Platte riverbank area was sometimes called, and the surrounding landscape yielded little timber for fires, they turned to an alternative fuel. According to trail guidebooks, what they needed was easy to find—bison manure.

The enormous herds of bison that watered along the Platte left in their wake endless deposits of "buffalo chips" that could be used as fuel when dried out. When wood was scarce, even the more finicky women with the caravan became accustomed to using "Plains oak," the more polite name.[1] As soon as the wagons stopped for the night, women and children bearing pails or gunnysacks hurried to gather buffalo chips for the campfires. It was not unusual to see girls carrying the chips in their aprons. The sun-dried chips burned so rapidly that it often took two or three bushels to cook a meal. Fortunately, there seemed to be an inexhaustible supply.[2]

Although the emigrants saw tracks and other signs of buffalo during the first few days on the Platte, none of the herds had yet been discovered. Hunters turned to other sources for fresh meat. Anything that walked, crawled, or flew was considered fair game.

The river was one of the most important migratory-bird flyway corridors on the continent and attracted many species that ended up on a campfire spit or in a stew pot. Fortunately for the regal sandhill cranes, the Russell Party arrived on the Platte after the spring migration, when hundreds of thousands of the large gray birds sailed north on thermal winds and stopped for a rest in the river's shallow current.³ However, plenty of other birds were considered edible. Besides ducks, the hunters shot long-billed curlews and plovers that were fishing near exposed sandbars and alkali flats where they built nests on the ground, often near conspicuous objects such as buffalo chips. The roasted flesh of the curlew and plover was said to be quite tasty, but the emigrants longed for a haunch of bison.

"We supped last night on curlew, snipe, plover and duck—that's a prairie bill of fare for you!" wrote journalist George Curry, using his pen name, Laon, in a dispatch to editors of the *St. Louis Reveille*. "Don't your mouths water? But they need not, if you let your minds take in the idea of the number of mornings and nights that middling meat, crackers and heavy biscuit comprise our fare. . . . It may be well to say here, that a trip of this kind is the best thing in the world, perhaps, to knock the romance out of a fellow—I mean travelling with emigrating companies. . . . But then we have a glorious time of it in the still night, upon the broad prairie; the solitude gives a profundity to thought, and fancy has no limits."⁴

Curry made no mention of the numerous prairie dogs scampering about or poking their heads from conical entrances to their underground dens. These highly social burrowing rodents got their name from early travelers who thought the little animal's warning call sounded like a dog's bark. They lived in large colonies called towns, networks of tunnels that spanned hundreds of yards. After exploring a large prairie-dog town close to the Platte, some of the emigrants shot several of them. That evening, the camp's supper menu included rodent meat that was said to be tender and flavorful.⁵

Small game enlivened the emigrants' daily diet, but bison was still on everyone's mind. The travelers encountered a party of hunters from Missouri and Kentucky trying to navigate the Platte—no easy task because of its shallowness. Weary and sore, the mountain men tied their two Mackinaw boats loaded with buffalo skins to a cottonwood and spent the night in the Russell Party's camp. The hunters talked of the big herds of buffalo in the area and assured the emigrants that they would find them soon. In the morning, before the hunters moved on to the east with their bounty, they traded some of their buffalo skins for basic foodstuffs such as bacon, flour, and coffee.[6]

On June 12, as the wagon train continued westward, William Boggs, son of Lilburn Boggs, and Andrew Grayson splashed their mounts across the Platte and went north in hopes of finding a herd.[7] Edwin Bryant and his fellow Kentuckian, William Kirkendall, rode off toward some hills where they saw herds of antelopes grazing well out of rifle shot on the distant plain. They spent much of the rest of the day trying to find their way back to the wagon train. They came back with no game but only a specimen of an inedible globular fungi that Bryant had found.[8]

That evening, the overall mood of the company greatly improved when James Reed returned with the carcass of a large elk he had shot that afternoon. He gladly shared his kill with the others, who quickly devoured the tender meat and hunks of fat.[9]

The next morning, Boggs and Grayson returned with choice cuts of a buffalo cow they had killed about fifteen miles from camp.[10] The emigrants already had planned to spend another day in camp making repairs to their wagons, especially the wheels that had loosened and needed to be reset. Now, at long last, they would dine on bison. The morning fires were fed buffalo chips and the dead limbs of some nearby cottonwoods. Soon, plates were filled with generous servings of delicious bison steaks and ribs without a trace of fat. There would be no more suppers of plover and prairie dogs. Over the next few days, the Russell Party came upon herds of bison that stretched across the plains.

"We are now in the midst of buffaloes, and buffalo meat is as 'plenty as blackberries,'" Edwin Bryant wrote to a friend. "I have seen not less than 1,000 of these animals to-day, without going off from the wagon trail. I assisted in shooting one about two hours ago. He fell about 200 yards from our encampment tonight."[11]

Everyone in the company rejoiced with the exception of James Reed. He exposed his competitive nature in the same letter to his brother-in-law in which he had bragged about his prowess as a hunter of elk. "We have had two buffalo killed," wrote Reed. "The men that killed them are considered the best buffalo hunters on the road—perfect '*stars.*' Knowing that Glaucus could beat any horse on the Nebraska [Platte], I came to the conclusion that as far as buffalo killing was concerned, I could beat them."[12]

Reed set out from camp accompanied by a few others, including Hiram Miller, a young teamster for the Donners. Reed's main mission was to prove that he was "the best and most daring horseman in the caravan" and that he "had the best horse in the company." Once bison were spotted, Reed urged on Glaucus and left the others behind as he pursued the herd and quickly closed in on a bull and a large calf. He killed both of them with his brace of powerful pistols. He then watched with great amusement as his companions failed to bring down a bull they were chasing.[13]

"I put spurs to Glaucus and after him I went at full speed," Reed wrote. He made short work of the buffalo and then with little effort killed another calf. "Securing as much of the meat of the calves as we could carry, we took up the line of march for the camp, leaving the balance for the wolves, which are very numerous. An hour or two's ride found us safely among our friends, the acknowledged hero of the day, and the most successful buffalo hunter on the route. Glaucus was closely examined by many today, and pronounced the finest nag in the caravan."[14]

Although the buffalo hunt had been successful, some of the emigrants faced serious problems that had no solutions. Such a situation arose on the morning of June 14 when the Russell Party wagons had gone only about five miles down the trail. Three men from another emigrant company about thirty miles ahead rode up in search of Edwin Bryant, whom they had been told had medical training. The men wanted Bryant to come to their camp at once to tend to a seriously injured boy from Missouri whose family was bound for Oregon. The lad had fallen off a wagon tongue, and his leg had been crushed beneath a wheel. Of all the threats to life and limb on the trail, being run over by wagon wheels was the most frequent cause of injury and death.

The men told Bryant that several other people in the camp were laid up with fevers and various illnesses. Although Bryant had studied medicine briefly in his youth, he was in no way qualified to act as a physician, especially when it came to life-threatening injuries.

"It so turned out that I had acquired the undeserved reputation of being a great 'doctor,' in several of the emigrant companies in advance and in our rear, and the three men who had met us . . . had come for me. I told them, when they applied to me, that I was not a physician, that I had no surgical instruments, and that I doubted if I could be of any service to those who were suffering."[15]

The men were desperate and would not take no for an answer. Finally, Bryant rode with the men to their camp. The ride took several hours and was not easy. When they reached the camp, Bryant was rushed to the Garrison family wagon, where seven-year-old Enoch Garrison was stretched out on some planks. Bryant was stunned when he learned from the boy's mother, Margaret Ellison Garrison, and Enoch's older brother, Henry, that the injury had occurred a week before and that the wounds had been dressed only the night before after the boy had complained that he could "feel worms crawling in his leg."[16] That was when his mother saw that the limb was swarming with maggots, and gangrene had set in.

Besides the boy's kinfolk, Bryant found two former members of the Russell Party at the scene—Jessy Thornton and the Reverend Josephus Cornwall, the minister who had officiated at Sarah Keyes's burial. Their caravan was camped nearby, and they had ridden over that morning so Cornwall could preach at the neighboring encampment. When they arrived, the injured boy's mother beseeched Thornton to amputate the gangrenous leg, but he declined.[17]

Bryant made a cursory examination and determined that from knee to foot, Enoch's leg was in a state of decay. Bryant conferred with Thornton. Both men knew the boy would soon die and could not survive an operation. When they explained the situation to the mother, she became hysterical and pleaded with Bryant to amputate her son's leg. "I told her again, that all efforts to save him would be useless, and only add to the anguish of which he was now dying," Bryant later wrote. "But this could not satisfy a mother's affection. She could not thus yield her offspring to the cold embrace of death, and a tomb in the wilderness."[18]

Frederic Derusha, a French-Canadian cattle driver who was with the wagon train, volunteered to perform the surgery. He claimed he had worked in a hospital and witnessed many operations, including amputations. The desperate mother told him to proceed.[19]

"I could not repress an involuntary shudder when I heard this proposition, the consent of the weeping woman, and saw the preparations made for the butchery of the little boy," wrote Bryant. "The instruments to be used were a common butcher-knife, a carpenter's handsaw, and a shoemaker's awl to take up the arteries."[20]

Just before the surgery, Enoch asked to have one more look at his mangled leg. According to his brother, the boy took his mother's hand and said, "Good by Mother, I am going to heaven."[21] Laudanum, a popular opium-based painkiller used to treat a range of aliments, was given to the boy several times, but with no apparent effect. Derusha made an incision just below the knee and began to saw. Before he cut through the bone, he changed his mind and determined that the amputation should be above the knee.

"A tourniquet was then applied above the upper fracture, and the operation continued," Thornton wrote in his journal. "The boy bore his sufferings with the most wonderful fortitude and heroism. He seemed scarcely to move a muscle. A deathlike paleness would sometimes cover his face, and there can not be a doubt that the pain was most intense but, instead of groaning he used words of encouragement to the almost shrinking operator, or some expression of comfort to his afflicted friends."[22]

At last, one hour forty-five minutes after Derusha had made the initial incision, it was over. The limb was severed, the arteries were secured, and the flap was brought down and bandaged. Within minutes, Enoch's lips quivered, his eyeballs rolled back, and he died.

Bryant's work in the camp was far from over, however. Thornton, Cornwall, and others tried to console the Garrison family while Bryant turned his attention to the dead boy's father, Abraham Garrison, lying prostrate in the tent. The man was in such great pain that for several days, he had been unable to move because of what Bryant diagnosed as inflammatory rheumatism, no doubt brought on by wading through streams and exposure to the rain. Garrison's intense pain, coupled with the news that his son had died, overwhelmed him, and he begged Bryant to help him find some relief.

Bryant dug in his bag and left some medicine, along with stern instructions to not deviate from his dosage directions unless the man had a death wish. "The propensity of those afflicted by disease, on this journey, is frequently, to devour medicines as they would food, under the delusion that large quantities will more speedily and effectually produce a cure," wrote Bryant. "The reverse is the fact, and it is sometimes dangerous to trust a patient with more than a single dose."[23]

Bryant was asked then to examine at least six more people who were complaining of various afflictions. He helped some by doling out sensible advice or some of the medicines he carried with him. Bryant encountered one young man whom he diagnosed with heart disease. "I told him that I could do nothing for him; that the journey might effect his cure, but that no medicine which I possessed would have any other than an injurious effect," recalled Bryant, who later learned that five days after his visit, the young man's heart gave out, and he was buried near the trail.[24]

After making rounds, Bryant accepted an invitation from Thornton to accompany him and Cornwall a mile and a half to their camp for supper. There he was greeted by several of his former traveling companions and Thornton's wife, Nancy, who served a feast of stewed bison and antelope in the open air on a neat white cloth. Later that evening, Bryant and the Thorntons were invited to a wedding ceremony. The fussy Thornton reluctantly agreed, even though he did not like wagon-train marriages. "I can not say I much approve of a woman marrying upon the road," he wrote. "It looks so much like making a sort of a hop, skip, and jump into matrimony, without knowing what her feet will come down upon, or, whether they may be wounded or bruised."[25]

The pretty bride, fifteen-year-old Mary Lucy Lard, was to wed Riley Septimus Moutrey, twenty-two, a teamster hired to drive one of the Lard family's wagons. The nuptials were held in the Lards' tent and were presided over by Cornwall. There were only a few candles, the wedding cake was plain and not frosted with sugar, and there was no music or dancing. "The company separated soon after the ceremony was performed, leaving the happy pair to the enjoyment of their connubial felicities," Bryant wrote.[26]

When Bryant and the Thorntons departed the wedding tent, they looked across the plain and saw in the distance the torches and lanterns of the funeral procession of Enoch Garrison. "It was reported that the Indians was in the habit of opening graves for the purpose of getting shrouding," Enoch's brother Henry Garrison later wrote. "To prevent this, the grave was dug in such a place that the wagons when leaving camp might pass over it. In digging the grave, those who have it in charge was careful to cut and lift the sod in squares so they could be replaced when the grave was filled. Before commencing the grave, bed-quilts were spread on the ground to receive the dirt as it was thrown from the grave. After the grave was filled up, the sods were carefully replaced. The remaining dirt was carried and thrown in the River. When we broke camp next morning, the wagons 74 in number passed over the grave. Fathers wagons was driven to one side and did not pass over the grave."[27]

While Bryant and the others were taking in the mournful scene of the distant funeral procession, a man rode up with news that there was much celebration at his neighboring camp, where a woman had just given birth to a baby boy. Bryant never forgot that moment.

"I could not but reflect upon the singular concurrence of the events of the day. A death and funeral, a wedding and a birth, had occurred in this wilderness, within a diameter of two miles, and within two hours time; and tomorrow, the places where these events had taken place, would be deserted and unmarked, except for the grave of the unfortunate boy deceased! Such are the dispensations of Providence!—such the checkered map of human suffering and human enjoyment!"[28]

20. A LETTER FROM TAMZENE DONNER

NEAR THE JUNCTION OF THE NORTH AND SOUTH PLATTE,[1] *JUNE 16, 1846*

MY OLD FRIEND:

We are now on the Platte, two hundred miles from Fort Laramie. Our journey so far has been pleasant, the roads have been good, and food plentiful. The water for part of the way has been indifferent, but at no time have our cattle suffered for it. Wood is now very scarce, but "buffalo chips" are excellent; they kindle quickly and retain heat surprisingly. We had this morning buffalo steaks broiled upon them that had the same flavor they would have had upon hickory coals.

We feel no fear of Indians, our cattle graze quietly around our encampment unmolested.

Two or three men will go hunting twenty miles from camp; and last night two of our men lay out in the wilderness rather than ride their horses after a hard chase.

Indeed, if I do not experience something far worse than I have yet done, I shall say the trouble is all in getting started. Our wagons have not needed much repair, and I can not yet tell in what respects they could be improved. Certain it is, they can not be too strong. Our preparations for the journey might have been in some respects bettered.

Bread has been the principal article of food in our camp. We laid in 150 pounds of flour and 75 pounds of meat for each individual, and I fear bread will be scarce. Meat is abundant. Rice and beans are good articles on the road; cornmeal, too, is acceptable. Linsey dresses are the most suitable for children. Indeed, if I had one, it would be acceptable. There is so cool a breeze at all times on the plains that the sun does not feel so hot as one would suppose.

We are now four hundred and fifty miles from Independence. Our route at first was rough, and through a timbered country, which appeared to be fertile. After striking the prairie, we found a first-rate road, and the only difficulty we have had, has been in crossing the creeks. In that, however, there has been no danger.

I never could have believed we could have travelled so far with so little difficulty. The prairie between the Blue and the Platte rivers is beautiful beyond description. Never have I seen so varied a country, so suitable for cultivation. Everything was new and pleasing; the Indians frequently come to see us, and the chiefs of a tribe breakfasted at our tent this morning. All are so friendly that I can not help feeling sympathy and friendship for them. But on one sheet what can I say?

Since we have been on the Platte, we have had the river on one side and the ever varying mounds on the other, and have travelled through the bottom lands from one to two miles wide, with little or no timber. The soil is sandy, and last year, on account of the dry season, the emigrants found grass here scarce. Our cattle are in good order, and when proper care has been taken, none have been lost. Our milch cows have been of great service, indeed. They have been of more advantage than our meat. We have plenty of butter and milk.

We are commanded by Captain Russell, an amiable man. George Donner is himself yet. He crows in the morning and shouts out, "Chain up, boys! Chain up!" with as much authority as though he was "something in particular." John Denton is still with us. We find him useful in the camp. Hiram Miller and Noah James are in good health and doing well. We have the best people in our company, and some, too, that are not so good.

Buffaloes show themselves frequently.

We have found the wild tulip, the primrose, the lupine, the eardrop, the larkspur, and creeping hollyhock, and a beautiful flower resembling the blossom of a beech tree, but in bunches as large as a small sugar loaf, and of every variety of shade, to red and green.

I botanize and read some, but cook 'heaps' more. There are four hundred and twenty wagons as far as we have heard, on the road between here and Oregon and California.

Give our love to all inquiring friends. God bless them.

Yours truly,

Mrs. George Donner

THREE

THE PROMISED LAND

21. CHANGE OF COMMAND

Tamzene Donner was not the only member of the caravan who recorded her impressions of the journey on June 16, 1846. George Curry, the young journalist who signed his news dispatches as "Laon," wrote a letter using his true name to friends at the *St. Louis Reveille*. He reported that the Russell Party was only two hundred miles from Fort Laramie and had not yet encountered any Mormons since leaving the United States—good news indeed to the many supporters of former Governor Lilburn Boggs.[1]

"I am in good health, and enjoy the trip as much as the privations will permit," Curry wrote, although the slow pace of the caravan was still not to his liking. Much like James Reed had done in his letter written that same day, Curry bragged about his hunting skills and the speed of his horse. "My pony and myself are greatly attached to each other; he has proved himself a most valuable animal. I tried him in a buffalo hunt yesterday, and he beat all the horses."[2]

Edwin Bryant wrote to a friend of his trip to the sick and dying at the Oregon Party campground, of his bison-hunting successes, and of how life in the outdoors had changed his looks. "If you were to see me now you would scarcely know me. Indeed, when I look in the glass I do not exactly recognize myself. I am as dark, apparently, as the darkest Indian I have ever seen, and bear in many respects a strong resemblance to them. My health has generally been good, although there has been much sickness among the emigrants."[3] Bryant also hinted that he and some of the other single men would soon leave the Russell Party to get away from the slow-moving wagons.

Even Owl Russell, one of many travelers fighting off chills and fever, managed to finish a letter he had started three days before to William F. Switzler, publisher of the *Missouri Statesman*, in Columbia.[4] "We find thousands of buffalo, and kill more than we can destroy [eat], it is really a fine sport," Russell wrote in the postscript.

In the main letter, he vented some of his frustrations as the busy captain of the wagon train. "Well it is a queer life we are living, all our teams are oxen, and our travel of consequence is vexatiously slow not averaging more than 16 or 17 miles a day. My duties as commandant are troublesome beyond anything I could conceive of. I am annoyed with all manner of complaints."[5]

Russell and his party had few concerns about letters reaching the intended recipients. What Bryant called a "sort of post-office communication" proved effective for reaching the outside world and other wagon trains.[6] Eliza Donner wrote in her memoir of this clever way people exchanged news, in addition to giving letters to eastbound travelers. "Another means of keeping in touch with travelling parties in advance was the accounts that were frequently found on the bleaching skulls of animals, or on trunks of trees from which the bark had been stripped, or yet again, on pieces of paper stuck to the clefts of sticks driven into the ground close to the trail. Thus each company left greetings and words of cheer to those who were following. Lost cattle were also advertised by that means, and many strays or convalescents were found and driven forward to their owners."[7]

Fortuitously for the letter writers of June 16, a contingency returning from the Oregon Country came to the camp late in the day. They already had 840 letters from Oregon and from their stop at Fort Laramie, but there was plenty of room for another packet of communiqués.[8] Led by Joel Palmer, the fifteen-man party had no wagons but rode mules and horses.[9] This greatly reduced their time of travel, something that did not go unnoticed by Bryant and some of the other single men who were troubled by the slowness of their caravan.

J. B. Wall, Spencer Buckley, and other young men traveling with Palmer regaled the Russell Party with stories of Pawnee depredations. Such stories stirred the imaginations of the Russell Party emigrants and caused Owl Russell's stomach to churn even more. In the letter he handed over to be delivered to Missouri, he wrote, "I keep up a regular guard, and if I could only keep the militia from falling asleep on their post I should be secure against surprise."[10]

Palmer and his men were ready to depart the next morning. They were anxious to see loved ones, and the single men hoped to snare wives back in civilization. "They designed to do a considerable quantity of courting between this time and next spring, and then return with their wives," a reporter for *The Gazette* in St. Joseph, Missouri, later wrote. "Oregon is no place for bachelors."[11]

Before the Palmer bunch rode out of camp, brothers Nathan and Charles Putnam of the Russell Party scrambled to hand over letters to their parents, filled with news of feasting on buffalo and antelope. They also wrote of their dream of installing a privy "in the hind part of the wagon," no doubt an unrealized dream of many of their modest companions, concerned about privacy when answering nature's call on the open prairie and plains.[12]

The youngsters of the Russell Party managed to put up with the inconveniences of overland travel. For them, the journey was still a grand adventure. "Exercise in the open air under bright skies, and freedom from peril combined to make this part of our journey an ideal pleasure trip," Virginia Reed later wrote. "How I enjoyed riding my pony, galloping over the plain, gathering wild flowers! At night the young folks would gather about the camp fire chatting merrily, and often a song would be heard, or some clever dancer would give us a barn-door jig on the hind gate of a wagon."[13]

On June 17, the Russell Party departed camp at the convergence of the South Platte and North Platte. By two o'clock that afternoon, after traveling seventeen miles, they reached the upper ford of the South Platte, often referred to as the California Crossing. The river was rising, so it was important for all the wagons to get across the broad stream that day. The last wagon made it across before sunset. Virginia Reed's most vivid memory of the crossing concerned the family's hired girl, Eliza Williams, who stayed busy cooking for the Reed family and their teamsters.[14]

"Antelope and buffalo steaks were the main article on our bill-of-fare for weeks, and no tonic was needed to give zest for the food; our appetites were a marvel," Virginia wrote. "Eliza soon discovered that cooking over a camp fire was far different from cooking on a stove or range, but all hands assisted her. I remember that she had the cream ready for the churn as we drove into the South Fork of the Platte, and while we were fording the grand old stream she went on with her work, and made several pounds of butter. We found no trouble in crossing the Platte, the only danger being quicksand. The stream being wide, we had to stop the wagon now and then to give the oxen a few moments' rest."[15]

That evening, two or three buffalo were killed, and early the next morning, a large bull bison was easily shot near the campgrounds while grazing among some of the cattle. Unlike the white newcomers, who often killed more animals than they needed just for sport, the Plains Indians depended on the bison for their very survival. The herds were a major food source and provided everything else the tribes needed for their shelter, clothing, weapons, utensils, and ceremonial objects. Every part of the buffalo was used—hide, hair, flesh, blood, bones, and internal organs.

On the evening of June 18, after all the bison tongues had been devoured and the bones picked clean, word spread through the campground for everyone to gather for a company meeting. Although some of the emigrants appeared surprised, many others knew what was coming when Owl Russell tendered his resignation as captain because of his poor health. Some folks did not believe bilious fever had brought about the change of command, but a faction of travelers unhappy with Russell's leadership skills or lack thereof had deposed him and allowed him to resign to save face.[16]

No matter the cause, the assembled company voted to accept Russell's resignation. Lilburn Boggs, the former Missouri governor who earlier in the journey had been in the running for captain of the caravan, was called forward. Bryant moved to elect Boggs as captain, and the motion was adopted unanimously. Led by Bryant, the company also expressed gratitude to Russell for his service. All the subordinate

officers who had served under Russell, which included George Donner, then resigned out of courtesy to the new leader, and all of them
were accorded a vote of thanks.

Early on June 19, before the day's journey commenced, whispers
circulated through the camp that perhaps eight or ten of the single
men were contemplating striking out on their own. Before the rumor
could be fully verified, the new captain roared out the order to proceed. There were more shouts and the cracking of whips over the
oxen teams. The caravan—now called the Boggs Party—moved on.

22. CHASING MIRAGES

On June 19, 1846, the Boggs Party, with the newly chosen captain leading the way, progressed twenty miles. After climbing steep hills and negotiating the rugged terrain of the high tableland between the North and South Platte rivers, the wagons slowly descended a twisting path into the valley of the North Platte. They stopped at the mouth of Ash Hollow, formerly called Cedar Bluffs, where most caravans paused because of the abundance of wood, lush grass, and sweet spring water that many travelers found to be the best they had drunk since leaving Missouri.[1] Emigrant diaries described Ash Hollow—named for a scattering of ash trees—as one of the most idyllic spots on the trip west, comparable if not better than the oasis at Alcove Spring.

Charles Stanton, the congenial Chicago bachelor with high hopes for a new start in California, wrote of the site in a letter to his brother.[2] "It was a wild dell, and I was told had been a battleground of the Sioux and Pawnees [1835]. For five miles our wagons wound around among hills and steep declivities to a little spring, half a mile from the north fork. . . . At this river we found a company of some twenty wagons encamped. They had had considerable sickness, and this day had buried one of their number. We continued up the north branch some three miles, when we encamped for the night."[3]

After the encampment had been set up, the children gathered chokecherries, wild currants, and gooseberries. Tamzene Donner and the other botanists of the group scrutinized the spring-fed vegetation, including wild roses, ferns, and dwarf cedars. Several emigrants were drawn to a deserted log cabin that some trappers had built as a refuge during the past winter, when they were marooned by snow and ice. Travelers called it the "Ash Hollow Hotel." The walls were covered with messages left by passersby seeking lost cattle or horses. Inside the cabin, the emigrants found a recess in the wall filled with correspondence and requests that the letters be taken back to the States for delivery.[4]

When George McKinstry dug through the pile of letters, he was surprised to find a card addressed to him. It was from Selim Edward Woodworth, a young naval officer who had camped at Ash Hollow eleven days earlier while en route to Oregon bearing dispatches from the secretary of the navy to the Pacific Squadron.[5] The thirty-two-year-old Woodworth was a native of New York and a son of scholar and poet Samuel Woodworth, best known as the author of "The Old Oaken Bucket," a popular poem written in 1817. The younger Woodworth was well acquainted with McKinstry and his family.[6]

When he read the note, McKinstry must have been amused that the adventurous Woodworth finally had his chance to cross the continent. Woodworth was making excellent time. He had left Westport on May 14, vowing to reach Oregon in one hundred days or less. He was already far ahead of the Boggs Party. That did not go unnoticed by McKinstry, much annoyed by his caravan's pace.

That evening, McKinstry met with Edwin Bryant, George Law Curry, William Kirkendall, Benjamin Lippincott, Robert Ewing, and several other men to finalize plans for breaking away from the main caravan. "A party of eight or ten persons, including myself, had determined on our arrival at Fort Laramie, to change our mode of travel, provided we could make suitable arrangements," Bryant wrote in his journal. "If mules could be obtained for packing, our design was to abandon our oxen and wagons, and all baggage not absolutely necessary to the journey. This would enable us to proceed with much greater expedition towards the point of our destination."[7]

The next morning, Bryant and the others left for Fort Laramie, about 150 miles away. Later in the day, they overtook a train of wagons under the command of Captain Gallant D. Dickerson. This was the company that had gone out on its own on May 22, the day the

Donners and Reeds joined the Russell Party. "We accepted Captain D's invitation to encamp with him for the night," wrote Bryant. Free of the wagon train, the riders had made thirty miles that day and would travel eighty miles in the next two days.

Meanwhile, the Boggs Party also proceeded up the arid valley, angling over to the North Fork of the Platte and staying close to the south bank. After the travelers had spent weeks on the grassy plains, the changes in terrain and landscape were dramatic. By that time and for much of the journey to come, the emigrants often experienced the optical phenomenon of mirages. At times, the mirages appeared to be pools of water, animal herds, trees, and even cityscapes dancing and shimmering far ahead of the wagons or on the great expanses of land flanking the broad trail. Mirages on the prairie fooled everyone, including Indian hunting parties, mountain men, and soldiers.

Edwin Bryant and Jessy Thornton made notes about some of the more memorable flickering images. "The mirage has displayed itself several times to-day with fine effect, representing groves of waving timber and lakes of limpid water," Bryant jotted in his journal one hot June evening.[8]

The travelers also came upon rock formations unlike anything they had ever seen. Sometimes in the glaring sun or the shadows of late afternoon, the formations seemed to take on the shapes of palaces, castles, and other buildings. The first such formations they saw were two massive outcroppings of sandstone, clay, and volcanic ash. About four miles south of the trail, the larger of the two formations rose four hundred feet above the river valley. It was known as McFarlan's Castle until the late 1830s, when most travelers began to call it Courthouse Rock because it was said to resemble the new courthouse under construction in St. Louis.[9] Bryant and the other men who had left the main wagon train visited the site. On June 22, the Boggs Party reached the campsite near the two monoliths. Several emigrants visited the big rocks and scratched their names and the date or made drawings on the towering walls.

Ahead of them loomed one of the most noted landmarks on the trail—the five-hundred-foot-tall Chimney Rock.[10] The night before,

Bryant's group had camped near there. Because there were so few of them, every man had to stand guard duty. Bryant's turn came early in the evening. It was memorable. "The dark masses of clouds which had been rising from the west for many hours, continued to become more and more threatening. I never witnessed more brilliant displays of electricity, or heard more deafening crashes of thunder," he later wrote. "While standing in our camp with a pistol in my hand, sparks of electricity rolled along the barrel and dropped to the ground. I was several times sensibly but not violently affected by electrical shocks."[11]

For two days, as the wagons moved closer, the emigrants became entranced by Chimney Rock. Once they arrived, they etched their names on the base or as high as they dared go up the column. They chipped off pieces of the formation, and some folks fired guns at the spire for target practice or to get souvenirs.[12]

By June 24, the Boggs Party had reached Scotts Bluff, a gigantic rock formation named for an old fur trapper, Hiram Scott. They made camp at Frémont Springs, and several of the party found the names of John C. Frémont and his guide Kit Carson engraved on a rock in 1842.[13]

The next morning, the travelers rose as one, and the wagons rolled early. Fort Laramie was only two days ahead. There was no time to chase mirages.

23. SAGE ADVICE

The wagon train led by Lilburn Boggs continued to follow the North Platte River. By June 26, it unknowingly entered what became the state of Wyoming forty-four years later.[1] The overlanders knew that in only one more day, they would reach Fort Laramie, considered the point of no return for emigrants on their way to Oregon and California.

Situated on the lower Laramie River near its confluence with the North Platte, the fort was not yet a military garrison but an outpost of the American Fur Company. It was a gathering place for Plains Indians, trappers, traders, and travelers. Fort Laramie supplied a vast area of the central Rocky Mountains to the west and the sprawling bison range to the east, where the developing buffalo-robe trade was replacing the beaver-fur trade.[2]

For two days, ever since Laramie Peak had loomed on the horizon, giving the emigrants their first glimpse of the Rocky Mountains, they had become increasingly excited. That afternoon, however, when the caravan was just eight miles southeast of Fort Laramie, Boggs ordered the wagon party to stop at Fort Bernard, a smaller trading post on the North Platte. Established the year before, it had become competitive because westbound overlanders came to it before reaching Fort Laramie. That summer, as emigrants found they could make better deals at Fort Bernard, an intense rivalry developed between the two posts. When the Boggs Party reached Fort Bernard, the trading post was doing a brisk business with the wagon trains by underselling Fort Laramie by 30 to 40 percent.[3]

Francis Parkman, fighting dysentery with small doses of opium and freshly shaved after six weeks on the trail, was camped in the vicinity the same time as the Boggs Party. Parkman enjoyed hunting with the Sioux and visiting their encampment near Fort Laramie. Parkman called the Fort Laramie traders "a set of mean swindlers" and the "natural enemies" of the emigrants.[4] "They [the emigrants] were plundered and cheated without mercy," Parkman wrote to his mother.[5]

When word spread along the trail that the gatherings of Sioux, with large herds of horses, camped around Fort Laramie had greatly diminished the meadows, the grassy bottomland along the river at Fort Bernard provided an attractive alternative.

Boggs had another reason for halting the wagons at Fort Bernard. It was the site chosen for a rendezvous with the men who had left the main party earlier. Edwin Bryant, George McKinstry, George Curry, and the others had arrived days before and become familiar with both forts, especially the available mule stock. They awaited the arrival of their former traveling mates, who were bringing the men's wagons and oxen to exchange for pack mules and trail supplies.

"I returned to Fort Bernard yesterday, and have received much attention from the gentlemen of the establishment," wrote George Curry in a dispatch to the *St. Louis Weekly Reveille*.[6] "Already it has become, though situated so near its more powerful rival, a position of no small importance. Its proprietors and inmates are agreeable and courteous to the extreme, and among them a stranger feels himself at home. It is my intention, if it can possibly be carried into effect, to leave the wagons at this point, and with fifteen others, all young men, perform the remainder of the journey with pack animals. To procure pack animals was the reason for my pushing ahead to this place."

Edwin Bryant wrote in his journal, "From Laramie, I proceeded back to the small trading post, known as 'Fort Bernard,' where I ascertained that arrangements could be made with the traders from Mexico for mules, by exchanging them for our oxen and wagons. I was joined here by other members of the party which accompanied me from the wagons, and here we determined to encamp until the wagons came up."[7]

The next day, June 26, when the Boggs Party reached Fort Bernard, Bryant and others from his group gave them a rousing welcome and reclaimed their wagons and oxen. That evening, all the emigrants, trappers, and traders were entertained at a supper. "The banquet was not very sumptuous, either in viands or the manner in which it was served up; but it was enjoyed,"[8] wrote Bryant. He failed to mention the traders' ample supply of aguardiente (fiery water), a potent concoction that came to be known as Taos Lightning.[9]

Despite a late night of hard drinking, many of the travelers who were camped at Fort Bernard rose early on June 27. Bryant completed his trade of a wagon and three yoke of oxen for seven sturdy mules with packsaddles. He and his companions, most of them battling headaches from imbibing "Ol Touse," spent the rest of the morning going through baggage, selecting only essential belongings. In the afternoon, a friendly shooting match was arranged, featuring some Sioux warriors using bows and arrows, rifles, and pistols.[10]

That morning, while George Donner's wife, Tamzene, and Margret Reed "botanized among the cottonwoods," Donner scribbled a letter to a friend in Illinois. "We arrived here on yesterday without meeting any serious accident. Our company are in good health. Our road has been through a sandy country, but we have as yet had plenty of grass for our cattle and water. . . . Two hundred and six lodges of Sioux are expected at the Fort today on the way to join the warriors on the march against the Crows. The Indians all speak friendly to us. Two braves breakfasted with us. Their ornaments were tastefully arranged, consisting of beads, feathers, and a fine shell they got from California, bark variously colored and arranged, and the hair from scalps they have taken in battle."[11]

George Donner's young daughter Eliza also recalled the great congregation of Sioux warriors "smeared with war-paint, and armed with hunting knives, tomahawks, bows and arrows," and their large herds of horses. "Many of the squaws and papooses were gorgeous in white doe skin suits, gaudily trimmed with beads, and bows of bright ribbons," Eliza wrote in her memoir. "They formed a striking contrast to us, travel-stained wayfarers in linsey dresses and sun-bonnets.

Many of the white men connected with the fort had taken Indian wives and many little children played around their doors."[12]

At noon on June 27, the Oregon wagon train that included Jessy and Nancy Thornton and others from the former Russell Party stopped for the day and camped near Fort Bernard.[13] The Thorntons were warmly greeted by their former traveling companions, who were washing clothes and hanging them to dry on trees along the riverbank.

At about the same time, Parkman joined a friend who was riding to Fort Bernard to make a horse trade.[14] From previous encounters on the trail, Parkman knew many of the emigrants camped near the fort, and he went in search of familiar faces.

He later wrote that he "entered an apartment of logs and mud, the largest in the fort; it was full of men of various races and complexions, all more or less drunk."[15] Then Parkman spied some "fine-looking Kentucky men" whom he had met in St. Louis and others from the former Russell Party. He learned that the overlanders, especially those who were forsaking wagons for mules, were trying to lighten their load by ridding themselves of their "very copious stock of Missouri whisky." They were selling it to traders and Indians and drinking the rest.

Parkman described "maudlin squaws stretched on piles of buffalo robes . . . squalid Mexicans, armed with bows and arrows . . . Indians sedately drunk," and Canadian and American trappers sporting pistols and bowie knives.[16] Parkman then turned his attention to a tall man wearing a "dingy broadcloth coat" who stood in the middle of the crowd "haranguing the company in the style of a stump orator" while waving one hand wildly in the air and clutching an empty jug with the other. It was Owl Russell in all his glory.

"Instantly the colonel, seizing me, in the absence of buttons, by the leather fringes of my frock, began to define his position," Parkman wrote. "His men, he said, had mutinied and deposed him; but still he exercised over them the influence of a superior mind; in all but the name he was yet their chief. As the colonel spoke, I looked round on the wild assemblage, and could not help thinking that he was but ill fitted to conduct such men across the deserts to California."[17]

Disgusted by what he had witnessed at Fort Bernard, Parkman and his friend rode back to Fort Laramie by midday June 27. Between the two posts, they must have passed another small party of men, women, and children on packhorses on their way to Fort Bernard from the west. Their leader was a fifty-four-year-old seasoned mountain man and trail guide of some renown— James Clyman, former messmate of James Reed and Abraham Lincoln in the Black Hawk War.[18]

At the time, no one realized that Clyman would give the emigrants the best advice offered during the entire journey. Clyman, while talking with a cluster of curious men full of questions, spied James Reed.[19] Neither Reed nor Clyman had heard the news that Abraham Lincoln had been nominated as the Whig candidate for U.S. Congress.[20]

Born in Virginia on land once owned by George Washington, Clyman led a challenging life filled with adventure and danger. This veteran of the War of 1812 had already thoroughly trekked the Rocky Mountains when he took part in the brief Black Hawk fracas. Clyman eventually returned to the West, where he forged trails, trapped and traded, fought hostile Indians, faced grizzly bears, and managed to survive.[21] Clyman was literate—rare for a mountain man—and enjoyed reading Shakespeare, the King James Bible, and Byron's poetry. He recorded his thoughts and movements in a daily log.

His current expedition had begun in April, about the time the Reed and Donner families departed Springfield, Illinois. Clyman had just finished a bear hunt when he decided to join with other travelers and go to Illinois and Wisconsin for a visit. One of the men in the group was Lansford W. Hastings, author of *The Emigrants' Guide to Oregon and California*, one of the most popular sources of information for men such as Reed and the Donner brothers.[22] All of them read every word more than once before they left Illinois. At many evening encampments, Jacob Donner's well-thumbed copy was passed around and discussed.

Clyman considered Hastings to be largely a schemer and dreamer who had not even crossed the Sierras but was telling other folks how to do it. Hastings, mindful of this as well as his opportunity to sell land in California to grateful newcomers, thought it wise to travel the route he was touting to others. At the same time, he would encourage all the wagon trains he met along the way to forget about Oregon and wind their way to California.

Clyman especially questioned the feasibility of a proposed cutoff through the Wasatch Mountains, passing to the south of the Salt Lake and then across the salt flats to rejoin the California Trail at the Humboldt River. Hastings was sure this shortcut would save travelers valuable time. Clyman did not agree.

Ultimately, Hastings and Clyman parted ways. Hastings decided to go no farther but to greet the approaching caravans and keep them on the right path. Clyman and others from the party continued eastward. As they encountered emigrants, he always told them the hard truth. Just days before reaching Fort Laramie, he wrote in his journal, "To day we met all most one continual stream of Emigrants wending their long and Tedious march to Oregon & California and I found it allmost impossible to pass these honest looking open harted people without giving them some slight discription of what they might Expect in their newly adopted and anxious sought for new home but necessity only could compel us onward." [23]

When Clyman and his small band stopped at Fort Bernard and stumbled across Reed, Clyman found yet more "honest looking open harted people." Besides Clyman and Reed, the Donner brothers, Boggs, Bryant, and possibly Thornton, Russell, and others talked late into the night. They listened intently to Clyman's recommendations about how to proceed on their westward journey. A few of them, such as Bryant, took Clyman for just another frontier character and put no stock in his advice. [24] Others took heed, and some decided to change their destination from California to Oregon. James Reed was not one of them.

Reed did not doubt Clyman's wisdom, but he was sure that the best way to reach California was by using the shortcut Hastings had mentioned in his guidebook: "The most direct route, for the California emigrants, would be to leave the Oregon route, about two hundred miles east from Fort Hall; thence bearing west southwest, to the Salt Lake; and thence continuing down to the bay of San Francisco, by the route just described."[25]

Those few lines had caught Reed's eye early on, and he was convinced that the cutoff was the way to go. Clyman persisted. "I told him [Reed] to take the regular wagon track [via Fort Hall] and never leave it—it is barely possible to get through if you follow it [before early snowfall] and it may be impossible if you don't."[26]

Reed quickly responded. "There is a nigher route, and it is of no use to take so much of a roundabout course."[27]

Clyman tried again and again to make Reed see the recklessness of diverting from the proven trail. He told him of "the great desert and the roughness of the Sierras, and that a straight route might turn out to be impracticable."

Finally, only Clyman and Reed were left. The others had gone to their wagons. The fire was reduced to glowing coals, and there was nothing more to say.

24. A SENSE OF URGENCY

JUNE 28–JULY 12, 1846

Nothing was quite the same for the emigrants after that long night with James Clyman at Fort Bernard. For the rest of their days on the trail, the thin veneer of civility that had made the party a cohesive unit was chipped away a piece at a time. They all realized there was no turning back. They had to push forward, but seeds of doubt had been sown that would yield strife and dissension later.

On the morning of June 28 when the Boggs Party moved on, many of its members knew they were behind schedule. A sense of urgency swept over the wagon train. There was no need for panic, but there was no time to squander.

Some of the emigrants, including Lilburn Boggs, had been swayed by Clyman's routing advice, especially his warning about avoiding the shortcut suggested in Lansford Hastings' guidebook. They knew that when the time came, they would opt for the proven route. For the time being, however, all they wanted was to make up some time. Although Boggs remained, at least in name, the captain of the caravan in early July, many emigrants started to call themselves the "California train" or the "Californians."

The newly reconstituted Boggs wagon train returned to the trail, as did Edwin Bryant and eight other men on their mules.[1] "Not one of us had ever seen a mule packed before this morning," Bryant wrote in his journal. "Some New Mexicans who came in with the trading-party gave us our first lesson, and it was a very valuable one, although experience and necessity, the best of tutors, instructed us afterwards, so that many became adepts in the art of handling and packing mules. . . . The mules, stupid as we regarded them, knew more about this business than we did; and several times I thought I could detect them in giving a wise wink and silly leer, as much as to say, that we were perfect novices, and if they could speak, they would give us the benefit of their advice and instruction. A Mexican pack mule is one of the most sagacious and intelligent quadrupeds that I have ever met with."[2]

Francis Parkman and some Sioux who were camped at Fort Laramie watched the pack mules and emigrant wagons pass by. The caravan went only a few miles up the Laramie fork before camping. Parkman spent July and early August hunting with the Sioux beyond the Laramie Mountains. Before he headed east in August, a mysterious fire burned Fort Bernard to the ground. Although never proved, it was widely believed that some men from rival Fort Laramie had started the fire.[3]

It was still uncertain whether or when the Sioux warriors would go in pursuit of foes from other tribes. Some of the Sioux chiefs urged Boggs and the emigrants to move on because the warriors had grown restless and were primed for conflict.

"We, in turn, were filled with apprehension, and immediately hurried onward in the ruts made by the fleeing wagons of the previous day," wrote Eliza Donner in her account. "Before we got out of the country of the Sioux, we were overtaken by about three hundred mounted warriors. They came in stately procession, two abreast; rode on in advance of our train; halted, and opened ranks; and as our wagons passed between their lines, the warriors took from between their teeth, green twigs, and tossed them toward us in pledge of friendship, then turned, and as quietly and solemnly as they had come to us, rode toward the hills. A great sigh of relief expressed the company's satisfaction at being left alone; still no one could feel sure that we should escape a night attack."[4]

Eliza, the youngest of George and Tamzene Donner's children and only three years old at the time, still had colorful memories sixty-five years later when she recounted the incident with the Sioux. Other youngsters from the wagon train had their own remembrances. One of them was Virginia Reed, whose birthday was June 28. She turned thirteen years old that day and marked the momentous occasion by riding her pony, Billy, around the camp, accepting birthday greetings from well-wishers packing their wagons.

As she rode, Virginia and her handsome pony caught the eye of some of the Sioux warriors camped around Fort Laramie. "The Sioux are fine looking Indians and I was not in the least afraid of them," Virginia recalled. "They fell in love with my pony and set about bargaining to buy him." They also had an interest in trading for the pert young lady riding him.

"They brought buffalo robes and beautifully tanned buckskin, pretty beaded moccasins, and ropes made of grass, and placing these articles in a heap alongside several of their ponies, they made my father understand by signs that they would give them all for Billy and his rider," wrote Virginia. "Papa smiled and shook his head; then the number of ponies was increased and, as a last tempting inducement, they brought an old coat, that had been worn by some poor soldier, thinking my father could not withstand the brass buttons."[5]

Reed artfully managed to convince the Sioux that he could not possibly trade his own daughter and her cherished pony for anything. The crippling migraine that had been building in a worried Margret Reed's head soon vanished.

Charles Stanton's headache was just beginning. The kindly bachelor, who had joined the caravan after fleeing his "dull and monotonous life" in Chicago, decided to stay in camp and complete one of his lengthy letters to his brother. When he finished writing, Stanton saw that the wagons had "long since disappeared behind the hills." He was alone and set out on foot to catch up with the party.[6] "I was soon surrounded by ten or twelve Sioux," Stanton wrote. "I believe there are few men, no matter how brave, that would not have a queer sort of feeling come over them, by being thus suddenly surrounded by these children of the plains."[7]

Stanton could not understand anything the warriors said as each of them shook his hand. But then some of the Indians made an ominous gesture by drawing their knives across their throats. "This struck me as not being a very pleasant amusement, especially if they were to amuse themselves in this manner on me." The quick-thinking Stanton presented them with pieces of tobacco, which the Sioux happily accepted and rode off.

"I was now left on my solitary walk—but I was soon surrounded by another party, and then another, and still again another until I caught up with the wagons. Here I felt in perfect safety. The Indians seldom attack a large body, but only straggling parties of one, two or three. These they seldom kill unless they resist, but strip them and send them back naked to the camp."[8] Stanton arrived with all his clothes on and his scalp in place and was missing only his supply of tobacco.

Some overlanders such as Stanton had become accustomed to seeing large numbers of Indians. They reflected the views that Tamzene Donner plainly stated in a letter: "We feel no fear of Indians."[9] Most emigrants, however, remained wary. They believed it was only a matter of time before open conflict erupted between the various tribes and the white intruders.

"The extraordinary rapidity with which the bisons have disappeared within a few years, has often been the subject of remark by travelers as well as by traders," wrote Jessy Thornton. "The Indian tribes in the country around Fort Laramie, and especially the Sioux and Cheyenne, become each year more and more hostile to, and jealous of the whites; and nothing but a dread of bringing upon themselves the military force of the United States, of whose power and strength they seem to have some confused idea, restrains them from making an open war upon the emigrants, as they pass through their country, on their way to Oregon."[10]

In addition to concern about confrontation with Indians, there was growing antipathy between factions of the wagon train stemming from ethnic, cultural, and religious differences. Lewis Keseberg and other recent immigrants from Germany, Ireland, and Belgium, especially those from the "lower classes," were often subjected to discrimination and prejudice.

Disputes and jealousies were an inevitable characteristic of all overland travel at the time. It was also true that parties that had splintered from the main body often stayed in contact, at least until the perceived danger of Indian attack had passed.

On July 1, the wagon train headed to Oregon that included the Thorntons and the Bryant-Russell pack-mule party camped close to the Boggs company. The next day, Bryant rode over to visit. He was on a mission. One of his group, persuaded by stories he had heard at Fort Bernard, had decided to change his destination from California to Oregon. That left Bryant with a spare mule.[11] Bryant convinced teamster Hiram Miller, one of the original members from Springfield, Illinois, to join his band of mule riders.

July 2 was the last day Miller wrote in the diary he had started on May 12 in Independence. He relinquished the journal to Reed, whose first entry appeared July 3: "We made this day 18 miles and camped on Beaver Creek here is a natural Bridge 1 1/2 miles above camp."[12] At camps near Beaver Creek, the parties found plentiful grass, water, and firewood.

Trail tradition held that wagon trains had to reach Independence Rock by the Fourth of July if they wanted to arrive safely in California and Oregon before winter. Although the emigrants were about a week away from the great loaf-shaped granite rock, it was decided to celebrate the nation's seventieth birthday at Beaver Creek.

"At nine o'clock, a.m., our united parties convened in a grove near the emigrant encampment," wrote Bryant. "A salute of small-arms was discharged. A procession was then formed, which marched around the corral, and returning to the grove, the Declaration of Independence was read, and an address was delivered by Col. Russell. A collation was then served up by the ladies of the encampment, at the conclusion of which, toasts suitable to the patriotic occasion were given and drunk with much enthusiasm, a discharge of musketry accompanying each sentiment."[13]

James Reed provided most of the beverages for the many toasts. True to his promise to friends in Springfield, Reed broke out a special bottle of brandy. He faced the east at the prearranged time and raised his glass, while his friends in Illinois faced westward and drank a toast to his success from a companion bottle.[14]

Patriotic songs were sung, including a few solos from Bryant, all to the accompaniment of fiddle, flute, and drum. After a feast of roasted bison, bread, and beans, Bryant summed up the festivities in his journal by declaring "the 'glorious fourth' was celebrated here in this remote desert with more spirit and zest, than it usually is in the crowded cities of the States."[15]

By early afternoon, Bryant and the other mule riders, including newest recruit Hiram Miller, took their leave. Thornton and the other Oregon emigrants had departed early in the morning. They were farther down the trail at a new campsite, picking black currants "which, upon being cooked, however, were not so agreeable to the taste as they promised to be."[16]

Although time was of the essence, those bound for California decided to stay put for recuperation. The teamsters and other men made repairs to the wagons and harnesses, the women washed clothes and bedding, and the children played in grassy meadows along the creek. When the emigrants finally departed, Reed scribbled in the journal, "We left camp much rested and our oxen moved off in fine style."[17] They had not gone very far before the caravan encountered a great number of Sioux.

"On the sixth of July we were again on the march," wrote Virginia Reed. "The Sioux were several days in passing our caravan, not on account of the length of our train, but because there were so many Sioux. Owing to the fact that our wagons were strung so far apart, they could have massacred our whole party without much loss to themselves."[18]

Some members of the company were alarmed. A few emigrants brandished rifles to show that they were prepared to defend themselves, but the Sioux showed no sign of hostility. They were simply inquisitive about the strange people traveling across their land.

"Their curiosity was annoying, however, and our wagon with its conspicuous stove-pipe and looking-glass attracted their attention," Virginia Reed later recalled. "They were continually swarming about trying to get a look at themselves in the mirror, and their desire to possess my pony was so strong that at last I had to ride in the wagon and let one of the drivers take charge of Billy. This I did not like, and in order to see how far back the line of warriors extended, I picked up a large fieldglass which hung on a rack, and as I pulled it out with a click, the warriors jumped back, wheeled their ponies and scattered. This pleased me greatly, and I told my mother I could fight the whole Sioux nation with a spy-glass, and, as revenge for forcing me to ride in the wagon, whenever they came near trying to get a peep at their war-paint and feathers, I would raise the glass and laugh to see them dart away in terror."[19]

The emigrants tried to hasten the pace. They crossed the North Platte River. Hunters killed eight bison in two days, more than enough to feed everyone.

"The buffalo and other game are becoming plentiful," wrote Charles Stanton. "Every day one or more is killed, and we are again luxuriating on fresh meat. I think there is no beef in the world equal to a fine buffalo cow—such a flavor, so rich, so juicy, it makes the mouth water to think of it."[20]

As the wagon train made its way to the Sweetwater River, Alphonso Boone, brother-in-law of Lilburn Boggs, rode up with news that he and his company, headed to Oregon, had just killed eight bison, mostly fat cows and calves. Boone invited those who wanted more buffalo meat to take all they liked.[21] "We waited some two hours for those who went out, when they came in loaded with nice bits of buffalo, leaving the remainder for the wolves," wrote Stanton.

The next day, the emigrants heard bursts of gunfire and soon were joined by young William Boggs, son of the former governor, who had just killed two buffalo. A short time later, Reed charged into camp in pursuit of a buffalo bull he had wounded and quickly dispatched it in front of a cheering crowd.[22]

At nightfall on July 11, the emigrants made it to the location they had hoped to reach a week before. That evening, Reed took out Miller's journal and wrote, "Sat [July] 11 made this day 20 miles to Independence Rock Camped below the Rock good water ½ way."[23]

The Bryant-Russell pack train had reached Independence Rock three days earlier. Unlike the Bryant mule riders, those headed to

California remained in camp two nights at Independence Rock. On Sunday, July 12, Tamzene Donner caught up with her journal entries and examined botanical specimens. Several of the emigrants hiked over to the huge turtle-shaped rock to leave their names and the date on the granite surface.

Virginia Reed used her free time to write to her cousin, Mary C. Keyes, in Illinois. Virginia related some of the major incidents involving the party, such as the death of their grandmother, Sarah Keyes, at Alcove Spring, encounters with a variety of Indian tribes, and the recent Fourth of July commemoration. "We are all doing well and in hye sperits so I must close your letter, you are for ever my affectionate couzen," Virginia wrote in closing.[24]

On that quiet Sabbath, several heads of households got together to look over maps and guidebooks and discuss plans for the rest of the journey. It did not take long to see that not many minds had been changed in the past week. Major differences of opinion about the routing had only widened the chasm. Before suppers were cooked, the decisions made would ensure that these emigrants would be known forever in the annals of American history.

25. PARTING OF THE WAYS

A bugle blared on the morning of July 13, 1846, and preparations were made to depart the camp near the base of Independence Rock on the Sweetwater River. James Reed left his teamsters to chain up the oxen while he investigated the massive monolith, known as the "Great Register of the Desert." Tens of thousands of names, dates, and initials had been painted on with axle grease made from pine tar and hog fat or had been carved into the surface. Reed saw the names of trappers, traders, and countless emigrants, including some from his own company.

Reed must have been pleased that the wagons had finally reached this place on the Sweetwater, which would lead to South Pass on the continental divide. Although he wished the wagons were farther down the trail, he felt confident that any lost time could be made up by using the shortcut recommended in Lansford Hastings's book.

At the same time, Reed also might have been concerned. Just the day before, the number of emigrants in the company had been greatly reduced when differences of opinion caused another division within the ranks. Because of reports from others they had met on the trail and especially the warnings of James Clyman, several families struck out on their own for Oregon. This party included some of the more influential emigrants, such as Lilburn Boggs, who at least in name was still captain of the wagon train. Charles Stanton provided some explanation in a letter to his brother.

"Today, a division of our company took place. Governor Boggs, Colonel Boon, and several other families 'sliding' out, leaving us but a small company of eighteen wagons.[1]

"Just as the new Oregon company was leaving, there was an important arrival—a single traveller, with his horse and pack mule, who came alone all the way from Oregon. . . . [He] gave the preference decidedly in favor of California. Of course this pleased all of us whom had not changed our minds, and made some of the others feel a little chagrined that they had so suddenly changed their course. But Gov. Boggs is actuated by different motives—he is afraid of the Mormons. He has heard that they are [on] the route, and thinks they will go to California. Should they do so, that will be no place for him. You may be aware that he was shot by [Porter] Rockwell, and came very near losing his life; consequently, he has something to fear."

It is doubtful that a fear of Mormon retaliation was Boggs's primary concern or his reason for "sliding out." He was more troubled by the Hastings routing that others in the wagon train wanted to take, in spite of warnings.

Ironically, the Oregon traveler mentioned in Stanton's letter brought news directly from Hastings himself. Wales B. Bonney, the emissary from Hastings, showed up at camp just before the Boggs Party left. He was returning home to Ohio and brought hundreds of emigrant letters that he was taking back east.[2] Bonney gladly added the letters of Virginia Reed, Stanton, and others, promising safe delivery.

Bonney also bore an open letter from Hastings addressed: "At the Headwaters of the Sweetwater: To all California Emigrants Now On the Road." Bonney already had shared the contents of the letter with many other emigrants, such as the Bryant-Russell mule train that was well to the west of South Pass by that time.[3] Hastings wrote of the ongoing war between the United States and Mexico, urging the various companies to "concentrate their numbers and strength" in case of Mexican attacks.[4] He advised them to take the new route from Fort Bridger around the south end of Salt Lake to shorten the distance by at least two hundred miles. Hastings added that he planned to meet the emigrant parties at Fort Bridger. From there, he promised to guide them across deserts and mountains over his new route in the future states of Utah and Nevada and into California.

Boggs and others ignored Hastings' advice and stuck to the proven route. Reed, the Donner brothers, and others who put their faith in Hastings were even more encouraged by his open letter, especially his offer to act as a guide. Without taking time to elect an official captain of their company, the Donner and Reed families and their companions left Independence Rock. They nooned eight miles southwest at Devil's Gate, where the Sweetwater had cut a chasm through a wall of granite so narrow and steep that wagons had to detour around it.[5]

The party did not halt again until sundown, when they caught up with the Boggs wagons, which had left the day before. The two factions became somewhat contentious about which of the caravans should take the lead. The next day, July 14, the Californians got a jump on the nearby Boggs camp. After a grueling drive of twenty miles, staying about one mile ahead of the Boggs Party, they again halted to set up camp on the Sweetwater.

The Donners, Reeds, Stanton, and the rest could not help but note the chilly winds and freezing nighttime temperatures. Then they had their first view of "the snow clad mountains," as the distant sawteeth of the Wind River Range to the northwest came into view. The Winds, as mountain men affectionately called the rugged mountains, contained scores of peaks more than thirteen thousand feet high, dotted with lakes and glaciers. "It was now midsummer," Stanton wrote. "We had been travelling for the past ten days under a boiling sun, and it was strange thus suddenly to see this winter appearance on the distant hills."[6]

The company pushed on. Everyone cheered when they passed the Boggs Party at one of the Sweetwater crossings shortly before stopping for the day. The emigrants got a late start on July 17 because of a "difference of opinion among our company . . . as to whether we should lay by or go on," according to Stanton. Those who wished to "lay by" were the younger men and some of the families who had run out of fresh meat. They wanted to spend the day hunting before leaving bison country. They also pointed out that the cattle badly needed a day's rest.[7] The others, led by Reed and the Donners, said if they spent another day in camp, the other companies would get ahead of them, and their livestock would eat all the available grass. "The go-ahead party finally ruled," noted Stanton, "and we 'rolled out.'"

The next day, July 18, the caravan reached a monumental landmark, South Pass, a saddle twenty-eight miles wide on the continental divide.[8] From that backbone of the continent, streams flowed east to the Mississippi River or west to the Pacific Ocean. The gentle ascent to South Pass—between the Wind River Range to the north and the Antelope Hills to the south—was so gradual that many emigrants did not even know when they reached the summit. Nonetheless, they were elated. "Thus the great day-dream of my youth and of my riper years is accomplished," gushed Stanton in a letter written the next day from South Pass. "I have seen the Rocky mountains—have crossed the Rubicon, and am now on the waters that flow to the pacific!"[9]

After nooning at South Pass, the caravan descended the trail and soon came to Pacific Spring, the first good water west of the Great Divide. After a brief rest, they followed the trail to the southwest along Pacific Creek until it merged with Dry Sandy Creek. True to the name, there were only a few puddles of water in what Stanton called a "dry gully" and not a blade of grass for the animals.[10] It was nearly sundown, but the company continued until James Reed, who with George Donner had been scouting for a campsite, returned to the wagons at full gallop. There was no suitable site ahead, so the party returned to the gully. It was dark before suppers were cooking, and Donner still had not returned. Jacob Donner and several others, fearing George was lost, shot guns and lighted small fires on the nearby hills. At midnight, Donner rode into camp, hungry, weary, and parched.[11]

The emigrants quickly packed up camp the morning of July 19. It was a Sabbath, but everyone was eager to reach fresh water, ten miles ahead on the Little Sandy River. En route, there were serious problems. Some of the oxen appeared to have been poisoned. Someone pointed out that the oxen had lapped up the few puddles of standing water at Dry Sandy Creek the night before. The wagon train halted while teamsters tended to the beasts, but nothing could be done. The water had been tainted with alkali. Three oxen died that morning—each of the Donner brothers lost one, and Reed's ox "old Bulley" died.[12]

When the emigrants reached the Big Sandy, they found that several other wagon trains going to Oregon and California were already camped there. There were fragments of the original Owl Russell Party and the sixteen wagons of the new Boggs Party that a few days before—just east of South Pass—had merged with the small Oregon company that included the Thorntons.

Unlike previous nights spent under summer stars, the emigrants refrained from revelry and celebration. It was a serious moment, a somber time for all of them. In the morning, there would be yet one more divide. It would be a last good-bye. Some wagons would turn to the right on the proven trail to Fort Hall that would lead to Oregon or continue on the standard route to California, and the rest would turn left and take the road to Fort Bridger and just beyond to Hastings's cutoff. They had all come to the proverbial fork in the road that came to be called "the parting of the ways."[13]

James Reed, who for so long had pondered the question of which way to go, was now fully confident that the smart move was to follow his instincts and take "a nigher route." George and Jacob Donner fully agreed with Reed, and so did many others. The party would be assembled at daybreak and head out for Fort Bridger, where they hoped Lansford Hastings was still waiting to guide them. All of them were excited, but before they tried to get some sleep, it was decided to elect a captain for the company. Ever since Boggs had left, Reed and George Donner had led the emigrants, but there had to be an official election of a leader of the new company before it departed.

Some emigrants might have wanted Reed for the post, but most of them considered him too headstrong and arrogant. It is not known whether Reed campaigned for the job or whether any of the other heads of household put their own names forward. Reed did not mention the election in his daily journal. Instead, writing in the third person as always, he only noted the oxen that had died from drinking poisoned water.[14]

The man of the hour was the affable George Donner, who was

considered hardworking and reliable. When the votes were counted, he would be the one to lead them on the final leg of their journey, using the route that Hastings had devised. Everyone went to bed eager for the travel adventure to continue. At least one person, however, although confident about Donner, was not so sure about Hastings.

"The Californians were generally much elated, and in fine spirits, with the prospect of a better and nearer road to the country of their destination," Thornton wrote of his former comrades. "Mrs. George Donner was, however, an exception. She was gloomy, sad, and dispirited, in view of the fact, that her husband and others could think for a moment of leaving the old road, and confide in the statement of a man of whom they knew nothing, but who was probably some selfish adventurer."[15]

Tamzene Donner was a bright and capable woman. Perhaps she thought she could change her husband's mind and get him to take the other route. Maybe her brother-in-law Jacob could also be swayed and even the foolhardy Reed. She hoped there was plenty of time to convince them while the caravan traveled to Fort Bridger, where an old trail branched off to Fort Hall and the proven route to California.

26. THE DONNER PARTY

On July 20, 1846, the Donner Party was born. For the first time since the Donners and Reeds and their friends and employees had left Springfield, Illinois, more than four months before, the company of emigrants bore the name that would live in history.

At the Little Sandy camp, as the various parties prepared to go their separate ways, Tamzene Donner and the Thorntons had a tearful good-bye. Tamzene was losing yet another of her botanizing companions. Not all the emigrants were headed to Oregon. Some of the California pilgrims, who did not want to risk the Hastings Cutoff, took the standard route to Fort Hall.

Lilburn Boggs and his family bid farewell to the Donner Party at the Little Sandy and left for Fort Hall with the Boone family, the Thorntons, and some former members of Edwin Bryant's mule caravan. Boggs had left Missouri bound for California but changed his mind after meeting James Clyman and hearing the horror stories about the Hastings route. Only days after leaving for Oregon on July 20, Boggs would change his mind once again at Fort Hall, the fur-trading post on the Snake River where the Oregon and California trails split in southwesterly and northwesterly directions.[1] After he shook hands with his brother-in-law, Alphonso Boone, who was going on to Oregon, Boggs took the turn to California, as originally planned.

The thirteen members of the Murphy, Foster, and Pike families were one of the largest groups that chose to continue with the Donner Party. This alliance consisted of Levinah Jackson Murphy, a thirty-six-year-old widow traveling with her seven children. The two oldest were married with children of their own.[2] Levinah Murphy and the younger children made the journey in two wagons, and the two married couples each had a wagon. They had joined what was then the Russell Party in late May while waiting for the Big Blue River to subside. Levinah and her deceased husband, Jeremiah Murphy, had joined the Mormons in 1836 while living in Tennessee, and members of her family were also said to be Saints.[3] Oddly, there was no record of any conflict between the greater Murphy group and former Governor Boggs during the journey.

Patrick and Margaret Breen and their brood were ready to depart before George Donner could bellow out "Wagons ho!" Destined to have an important role in the remainder of the journey, the Breens had played cat and mouse with the main California emigrants much of the way since leaving Independence.[4]

Born in 1795 in Ireland, Breen immigrated to Canada in 1828 and two years later married Margaret Bulger. The couple left Canada with two infant sons in about 1834 and farmed at Springfield, Illinois, where they first met George and Jacob Donner and James Reed.[5] In 1835, the Breens moved to Iowa, where more children were born to them.[6]

Patrick Breen, a lifelong Catholic, wanted to better the lives of his family in a land that promised great opportunity. He sold his farm, and he and his family began their journey to California on April 5, 1846. Breen was fifty-one, and Margaret, also known as Peggy, was forty. The family traveled in three wagons drawn by a total of seven yokes of oxen. They also took cows, horses, and their beloved dog, Towser.[7]

Another Irishman, Patrick Dolan, about thirty-five years old, joined the Breens. One of the Breen children later described Dolan as "red-faced, light-hired, handsome, well-built, honest, very religious."[8] Dolan was a bachelor farmer and the Breens' neighbor and friend. He sold his farm in exchange for a wagon and team.

Once the Breens and Dolan got to Independence and headed down the trail, they often encountered the Owl Russell caravan. Early on, the Breens decided, at least for a time, to cross the plains alone so they would not have to vie for water and grass at the nightly camp-sites. When they occasionally visited another party's camp, Patrick Breen broke out his fiddle, much to the delight of the young folks who loved to dance.[9] The Breen Party spent the Fourth of July at Fort Laramie, some days behind the Boggs Party. When they caught up with them, Breen and Dolan decided they were ready to join the Donner wagon train.

After all the farewells and the last-minute check of wagons, the new Donner Party was ready to go. Tamzene Donner was still concerned that the company was following a route suggested by a "selfish adventurer," as she called Lansford Hastings.[10] With the late start, the train went only six miles before making camp on the Little Sandy.

The next day, they were forced to stay in camp. The poison water from Dry Sandy Creek was still taking a toll on the oxen and cattle. Reed's journal entry that night told the story: "Tues [July] 21 we encamped on little Sandy all day Geo. Donner lost one steer in the encampmt J. F. Reed lost old George & one Bald faced steer, by poisoned at dry sandy on Saturday night last."[11]

On July 22, the emigrants arrived at Big Sandy Creek, where one of Patrick Dolan's steers fell dead because the Breens and Dolan also had made the mistake of halting at Dry Sandy. At least there was plenty of grass at the next camp, established on July 23. The next day, they pressed on.[12] The wagons reached the Green River crossing.

In late July, everyone began to make better time. On July 26–27, the company went thirty-six miles, putting them just below where they wanted to be—Bridger's Fort. They camped in a lush meadow near a stream of cold, clear water without a hint of alkali. There was a collective sigh of relief. Tomorrow, they would go to the trading post to resupply and meet the illustrious Jim Bridger and his partner, Louis Vasquez. And if their luck had turned, there would be another man to shake hands with—Lansford Warren Hastings.

27. BETRAYED

James Reed and George Donner rode lickety-split from their camp to nearby Fort Bridger. Haggling over the price of supplies and acquiring more oxen at the trading post could wait. First they had to find Lansford Hastings, whose guidebook had brought them to this place.

There was one problem—Lansford Hastings was not at Fort Bridger that morning as he had told the emigrants he would be. He had been there, but he was gone. The news came as a terrible blow to Reed and Donner, but before they could fully comprehend the situation, their hosts, Jim Bridger and Louis Vasquez, explained that Hastings had indeed been at the fort for the sole purpose of assisting emigrant parties headed to California. Then earlier in the month, large numbers of emigrants had showed up at Fort Bridger, all of them impatient and eager to take advantage of Hastings's offer. He decided to lead them.

On July 20, the same day the Donner Party had started its trek from the Big Sandy camp, the Bryant-Russell pack train, including three new members from another emigrant party, had left Fort Bridger with Hastings's partner, mountain man James Hudspeth, as their guide.[1] The former members of the original Russell wagon train—cold, wet, and shivering from a rainstorm—had arrived at Fort Bridger on their sturdy mules four days before. Prior to reaching the fort, their pace had slowed because of weather and sickness.[2] At Fort Bridger, they pitched their tents near the camp of Hastings and Hudspeth and pumped them for information.

Bryant and the others had also listened to stories told by Bridger and Vasquez. Pierre Luis Vasquez had been well educated in St.

Louis. By the time he reached his twenties, he was fully engaged in the fur trade.[3] Vazquez partnered with Bridger, and in 1843, they built Fort Bridger on Black's Fork of the Green River.

By then, Bridger had arguably earned the title "King of the Mountain Men." In 1822, when he was seventeen, he had responded to an advertisement seeking enterprising men to "ascend the Missouri" and collect furs. Although Bridger could not write his own name, he had learned several languages and had an endless supply of tall tales.[4] Fort Bridger was an ideal venue for a yarn spinner of Bridger's caliber.

It was also a popular stop for mountain men who wanted to do some trading. One who happened to be at Fort Bridger in July 1846 was Joseph R. Walker, an exceptionally knowledgeable trailblazer who led countless emigrant parties to California. He had a reputation for looking a man in the eye and telling the truth, even if it was cold and hard. That appealed to Edwin Bryant when he and Walker talked at the trading post.

"Captain W. [Walker] communicated to me some facts in reference to recent occurrences in California, of considerable interest," Bryant wrote in his daily journal. "He spoke discouragingly of the new route via the south end of the Salt Lake."[5] Before he and Walker talked, Bryant was already reconsidering his decision to take the Hastings Cutoff. "My impressions are unfavorable to the route, especially for wagon trains and families; but a number of the emigrant parties now encamped here have determined to adopt it, with Messrs. Hastings and Hudspeth as their guides; and are now waiting for some of the rear parties to come up and join them."[6]

On July 17, several emigrant parties had arrived at Fort Bridger and others had departed, taking the old trail to Fort Hall. By midafternoon, rain clouds had risen from behind the mountains to the south. When the rain stopped, the clouds broke, revealing snow across the summits. In fifteen minutes, the temperature fell from eighty-two degrees to forty-four.[7]

The next morning, perhaps because of the shift in the weather, Bryant and most of his party ultimately decided to take the Hastings route with Hudspeth as their guide as far as the salt plain just west of the Salt Lake. "Although such was my determination, I wrote several letters to my friends among the emigrant parties in the rear, advising them not to take this route, but to keep to the old trail, via Fort Hall," Bryant wrote. "Our situation was different from theirs. We were mounted on mules, had no families, and could afford to hazard experiments, and make explorations. They could not."[8] Bryant gave the packet of letters to Bridger and Vasquez for safekeeping. They promised to distribute them to the incoming emigrants on arrival.

While waiting for the wagon caravan to form, some emigrants dashed off letters. Hastings rode around the camps on horseback assuring emigrants that his route was "perfectly practicable for wagons" and would save precious time. This was good news to travelers such as Bryant, who saw that the surrounding mountains at Fort Bridger were "covered as deeply with snow as if it were the middle of winter."[9]

The emigrants gave letters to Walker to take back east.[10] A few days later, he came upon the Donner Party making its way to Fort Bridger. He told them the same thing he had told Bryant and the others—do not follow Hastings. Walker probably could tell that his warning would be ignored.[11]

On July 20, the Bryant-Russell pack train took its leave from Fort Bridger. "We resumed our march, taking, in accordance with our previous determination, the new route already referred to," Bryant wrote in his journal. "Our party consisted of nine persons. Mr. Hudspeth and three young men from the emigrant parties, will accompany us as far as the Salt Plain."[12]

That same day, the first wagon train left Fort Bridger led by Lansford Hastings himself. Known as the Harlan-Young Party, it was comprised of forty emigrants from four family groups.[13] Many of the members of the caravan had traveled with the former Russell Party earlier on the trail and were well acquainted with the recently formed Donner Party.

During the next few days at Fort Bridger, more small parties and stragglers got their wagons repaired and replaced oxen that were worn out or lame. On July 26, a third organized group, the Hoppe Party, led by Jacob D. Hoppe, left Fort Bridger to follow Hastings's tracks. In the train was Heinrich Lienhard, one of the "German boys."[14] Another member of the company was the cartographer Thomas H. Jefferson.[15] According to Lienhard, on the afternoon of July 26, Hastings left the Harlan-Young Party at a camp on the Bear River and "turned back again with us and remained overnight." The next day, Hastings led the Hoppe Party to the other camp on the banks of the Bear River.[16]

Also on July 26, there were more comings and goings at Fort Bridger. Andrew Jackson Grayson, the observer of natural history who would win accolades for his paintings of birds, wisely listened to Joe Walker. Grayson and his family took the trail to Fort Hall and from there hooked up with the known route to California.[17]

At the trading post, Bridger and Vasquez sold supplies and live-stock and turned a good profit peddling endless pints of what Bryant called "miserable whiskey" at an outrageous price. But their busi-ness was driven by traffic.[18] When the timesaving Greenwood Cut-off (named for mountain guide Caleb Greenwood) had opened in 1844 to the east at the "parting of the ways" near Big Sandy, much of the traffic to Fort Bridger stopped. That is why Bridger and Vasquez were pleased with the Hastings route, which brought the customers they needed so badly. They despised losing any trade because of the alternative route to Fort Hall.

That is why on the morning of July 28—when Reed and Donner went to the trading post to confer with the absent Hastings—Bridger and Vasquez strongly encouraged them to follow the Hastings route after allowing the emigrants and animals to rest and revitalize. It sounded good to the two tired men, even if they were concerned about losing more time. They were given assurances that there was plenty of time to catch up with the others. Hastings had left them instructions and directions, and it would be easy to follow the tracks of the wagons he was leading.

What Bridger and Vasquez chose not to share with Reed and

Donner were the letters that Bryant had left behind, warning his friends to avoid the cutoff and instead take the trail to Fort Hall. Bridger and Vazquez knew what Bryant had written, and they would not take any chances of losing business. Reed and Donner returned to camp with reassurances that all was well.

Tamzene Donner, the most vocal critic of Hastings and his short-cut and saddened because most of her fellow nature enthusiasts had left the party, had her mind on another project. She was caring for Luke Halloran, a twenty-five-year-old native of Ireland. He had consumption and had left his business in St. Joseph, Missouri, to regain his health in California.[19]

"He was a stranger to our family, afflicted with consumption, too ill to make the journey on horseback, and the family with whom he had travelled thus far could no longer accommodate him," Eliza Donner later wrote. "His forlorn condition appealed to my parents and they granted his request" to travel with the Donners.[20] Without a moment's hesitation, Tamzene had the young man placed in a wagon. Halloran's trunk full of personal possessions and his saddle and tack were squeezed into a wagon, and his horse was brought along in hopes that Halloran would recover enough to ride.

Caring for Halloran was another example of George and Tamzene Donner's capacity for embracing those in need. They had given the lone bachelor Charles Stanton a place as a driver. While in the Fort Laramie area, Donner had found a spot for a young man known only as Antonio, probably from Santa Fe, New Mexico Territory. Described as both a Spaniard and a Mexican, he helped to drive wagons and herded the family's loose cattle.[21]

Donner used his time at Fort Bridger to get his horses shod, purchase new oxen, and lay in provisions. He recruited a new driver to replace Hiram Miller, who had quit earlier in the month to join the Bryant-Russell mule team. Donner found just who he was looking for in Jean-Baptiste Trudeau, a sixteen-year-old who was hanging around the fort.[22] The lad remained with the Donner Party for the duration of their journey.

At Fort Bridger, another family joined the Donner company

—William McCutchen, his wife, Amanda, and their toddler daughter, Harriet.[23] They were from Jackson County, Missouri, where the six-foot-six-inch-tall McCutchen farmed and became known as "Big Bill." The McCutchens were likely traveling with Samuel Young when they ran into problems with their wagon or oxen and were detained at Fort Bridger. Even though they had only a horse and a mule, they were elated to join the last emigrant team of the season taking the Hastings path.

On July 31, after three days at Fort Bridger, the Donner Party was ready to leave and catch up with the forward companies and Hastings. That day, Reed wrote to the Keyes family in Springfield. He shared news of the loss of oxen to poison water and his enjoyment in hunting grouse, antelope, and mountain sheep with his three teamsters. Mostly, he sang the praises of Bridger and Vasquez, calling them "two very excellent and accommodating gentlemen" who "can be relied on for doing business honorably and fairly. . . . The independent trappers, who swarm here during the passing of emigrants, are as great a set of sharks as ever disgraced humanity, with few exceptions. Let the emigrants avoid trading with them. Vasques & Bridger are the only fair traders in these parts."[24]

Reed's opinion of Vasquez and Bridger would have been quite different if he had known they had intentionally failed to distribute Bryant's letters of warning about the shortcut. Consequently, Reed had only good things to report about the path the wagon train was soon going to follow.

> The new road, or Hastings Cut-off, leaves the Fort Hall road here, and is said to be a saving of 350 to 400 miles in going to California, and a better route. There is, however, thought to be, one stretch of 40 miles without water; but Hastings and his party are out ahead examining for water, or for a route to avoid this stretch. . . . On the new route we will not have dust, as there are 60 waggons ahead of us. The rest of the Californians went the long route—feeling afraid of Hasting's Cut-off. Mr. Bridger informs me that the route we design to

take, is a fine level road, with plenty of water and grass, with the exception before stated. It is estimated that 700 miles will take us to Capt. Suter's Fort, which we hope to make in seven weeks from this day.[25]

At the campground, nineteen wagons were in good repair. The stock and horses were rested. The signal was given. Whips cracked like pistol shots, and seventy-six wheels rolled as one. The Donner Party—at that point numbering seventy-four men, women, and children—moved into the unknown.

28. THE HASTINGS CUTOFF

AUGUST 1–22, 1846

The first days "on the Hastings" went reasonably well. As Eliza Donner said, "The trail from the fort was all that could be desired."[1] James Reed noted that the company had traveled only twenty-seven miles in two days but had been fortunate to find springs "as cold as ice" and "several valleys well watered with plenty of grass."[2]

By the third day, there were problems. The emigrants got a late start when an ox went missing. After they finally got moving, they traversed ridges and rises on what Reed said was at best a "tolerable rough road."[3] After setting up camp on the Bear River, a pair of spirited thirteen-year-olds—Virginia Reed and Edward Breen—took their ponies out for a jaunt. The youngsters were galloping along when Edward's pony stepped into a badger or prairie-dog burrow and took a hard fall. Seeing that Edward was knocked unconscious, Virginia raced back to camp for help.[4] When Patrick Breen and others arrived, they found that the boy had come to his senses but was in much pain from a compound fracture between the left knee and ankle.

Eddie was carried back to camp, where Margaret Breen saw that her son had a serious break. Ragged ends of the tibia protruded from his bloody leg. With no doctor in camp, a rider was sent back to Fort Bridger. He eventually returned with "a rough looking man with long whiskers" riding a mule. The gnarly mountain man—who no doubt had doctored many people with bone breaks as well as victims of bear attacks and Indian skirmishes—took one look and reached into his bag for a short meat saw and a long-bladed knife.[5]

Eddie had heard about Edwin Bryant witnessing the amputation of young Enoch Garrison's leg and his horrible death at an emigrant camp on the Platte. Eddie cried and begged his parents to let him keep his leg. The Breens could not bear to see their son in such anguish and called off the old-timer before he could cut. Breen gave him some money for his trouble and sent him back to the fort. With assistance from her husband and perhaps from Reed, Margaret got the broken bones back in place. They carefully cleaned and dressed the leg and made splints from wooden strips. Eddie would be confined to riding in a wagon, feeling every bump and enduring constant pain.[6] The Breens, knowing that young bones mended quickly, told him he would be on his feet again soon after they arrived in California.

Eddie Breen's leg healed in about eight weeks, just as his parents had predicted, but not in California. He started to walk again in late September, when the company finally made it to the Humboldt River in present-day Nevada and rejoined the original California Trail.[7]

After the excitement over the broken leg, the Bear River camp settled down. Earlier that day, Charles Stanton had approached the old man who had come to tend to Eddie Breen and gave him a letter to take back to Fort Bridger.

"I may not have another opportunity of sending you letters till I reach California," Stanton wrote to his brother, "but I have brought you to the top of the mountains; hereafter, I will give to you the descent to the Pacific. We take a new route to California, never travelled before this season; consequently our route is over a new and interesting region. We are now in the Bear river valley, in the midst of the Bear river [Uinta] mountains, the summits of which are covered with snow. As I am now writing, we are cheered by a warm summer's sun, while but a few miles off, the snow covered mountains are glittering in the sun."[8]

The next day, following the fresh tracks carved by the many wagons of the Harlan-Young Party, the caravan wound its way into present-day Utah. They rested for a night at the top of Echo Canyon in the Wasatch Mountains. This range formed the eastern wall of the Great Basin, a huge expanse bordered by the Sierra Nevada range on the west, the Columbia Plateau on the north, and the Mojave Desert on the south.⁹ The names of many trappers, mountain men, and overland travelers—some dating to the 1820s—had been inscribed on the walls of Cache Cave, a well-known rendezvous spot high above the canyon trail.

On August 6, the Donner company approached the mouth of Weber Canyon, where they found a piece of paper secured to some sagebrush. It was a message from Hastings. The news was not good. Virginia Reed wrote, "We were seven days reaching Weber Cañon, and Hastings, who was guiding a party in advance of our train, left a note by the wayside warning us that the road through Weber Cañon was impassable and advising us to select a road over the mountains, the outline of which he attempted to give on paper."¹⁰

It seemed that Hastings had left the wagon train he was leading to check on one of the smaller groups coming up from the rear. In his absence, James Hudspeth, who was guiding the Bryant-Russell mule team, decided to visit the Harlan-Young emigrants. Hudspeth advised them to take the Weber Canyon route.¹¹ They would be the first wagon train to make the attempt. From the outset, it was regrettable. The Harlan-Young party had lost a wagon and oxen that were hurled over a precipice seventy-five feet high.¹² The remaining wagons had to be almost lifted through the canyon.¹³

When members of the Donner Party read Hastings's note explaining that it had been a terrible mistake to take a wagon train up the steep and narrow Weber Canyon, they were thunderstruck. The note implored them to not go forward. Hastings told them to send a messenger ahead to him, and he would provide the Donner Party with an alternative route so they could avoid Weber Canyon and reach the Great Salt Lake in a timely manner.

The company had no choice but to comply with Hastings's request. They set up camp and quickly appointed James Reed, Charles Stanton, and William Pike to ride in advance to Hastings and, as Virginia Reed would write, "induce him to return and guide our party."¹⁴

Reed did not want to risk injuring his valuable mare Glaucus, so he saddled one of the spare horses. Early on August 7, the three men rode as fast as they could over the rugged terrain. They had not gone far when it became evident why traversing Weber Canyon—with a river bottom littered with huge boulders and choked with brush and trees—would have been a dangerous and time-consuming endeavor. "Our conclusions were that many of the wagons would be destroyed in attempting to get through," wrote James Reed, who marveled that only one wagon had previously been lost in the canyon.[15]

By the evening of August 8, Reed and the others had caught up with Hastings. He and the Harlan-Young Party had crossed the Wasatch and were camped just south of the Great Salt Lake at Adobe Rock in the Tooele Valley.[16] The rueful Hastings received a chilly greeting from Reed and his companions but offered assurances that he had a backup plan they would find acceptable. Both Stanton and Pike were as spent as their poor horses were. It was agreed that they would stay at this camp and recover and then hurry back to the caravan. Early the next morning, Hastings and Reed, riding a fresh horse he had swapped for his worn-out mount, started back to the Donner Party camp.

They had not yet returned to the Wasatch when Hastings announced that he was having second thoughts. He told Reed that he was obliged to continue guiding the Harlan-Young Party. This meant that he would not be able to return to the Donner camp to guide that company. Instead, he would show Reed a potential route to follow.

"Mr. Hastings, finding the distance greater than anticipated by him, stated that he would be compelled to return the next morning to his company," Reed later wrote. "We camped this evening in a canyon." In the morning, Hastings took Reed to Big Mountain, on the great divide east of the Salt Lake. Reed recalled that they ascended to "the summit of the mountain where we could overlook a portion of the country that lay between us and the head of the canyon, where the Donner party were camped. After he gave me the direction, Mr. Hastings and I separated."[17]

It was the last time anyone in the Donner Party saw Hastings, whom many of them had considered their guiding star.

Reed rode eastward and took what he thought might be an Indian trail. Thinking that it could be a suitable path for the company, he used his hatchet to blaze trail markers on trees in case the company decided to use the route.

On the evening of August 10, Reed rode into the camp on the Weber River. His children flocked around him, and Margret breathed a sigh of relief. The rest of the company was surprised that once again, Hastings had let them down, but they anxiously listened as Reed laid out the options. He explained that they could try to take the difficult and risky Weber Canyon route or go to another path that Reed had found on his ride. Reed told the emigrants that the reason the Harlan-Young Party was able to make it through the treacherous canyon at all was because they had far more able-bodied members than the Donner Party. He asked them to consider the new route he had just blazed, but with the understanding that it would not be easy, just less dangerous.[18]

After some discussion, the verdict was in—the company would take the route suggested by Reed. His journal entry, written in the third person, told the story: "Tues [August] 11 left Camp and took the new rout with Reed as Pilot he having examined the mountains and vallies from the south end of the Lake this day made 5 [miles]."[19]

Five miles did not seem like much, but the company learned quickly enough that for the next two weeks, any progress at all would be hard to come by. Some days, the wagons sat still while the men hacked their way through aspen groves and ravines covered with dense brush. Large trees had to be felled and dragged off and boulders rolled aside. At times, the loads of debris were so great that it required double- and triple-yoked oxen teams to get the loads up the steep rises. Women and children stayed in the wagons. They prepared meals for the ravenous work parties and helped Tamzene Donner and Peggy Breen care for Luke Halloran and little Eddie Breen. The long, hard days took a toll on the emigrants and the animals.

"Only those who have passed through this country on horseback can appreciate the situation," wrote Virginia Reed. "The canon wound around among the hills. Heavy underbrush had to be cut away and used for making the road bed."[20]

Shortly after Reed had returned and the struggle to penetrate the Wasatch commenced, more wagons of overlanders appeared from out of nowhere. It was the family of Franklin Ward Graves, a fifty-seven-year-old farmer from Marshall County, Illinois. Graves, a native of Vermont, was more of a hunter than a farmer. He was accompanied by his wife, Elizabeth, their daughter and son-in-law, and eight younger children. With the Graves family was a teamster, John Snyder.[21] The Graves family had traveled just behind the Donner Party most of the spring and summer. They had pulled into Fort Bridger just a few days after the Donners had left and had hurried to join them for the rest of the trip. They were warmly received and put right to work.

With the addition of the Graves family, the company reached its full number—eighty-seven men, women, and children traveling in twenty-two wagons. Now the Donner Party was complete.

While the emigrants continued to fight their way through the Wasatch, a search party scoured the countryside looking for Stanton and Pike, who had not yet returned from the Harlan-Young camp. Soon after the Graves family joined the caravan, the two lost men were found, just on the verge of killing their horses for sustenance.[22] There was a brief celebration when Stanton and Pike returned. They provided some useful trail information, wolfed down a hot meal, and picked up shovels and axes to work on the road.

For several days, the men and older boys labored as hard as galley slaves, only to find that the eight-mile stretch of wagon road they had just completed ended abruptly in a box canyon. Some members of the party became so depressed and angry that they considered striking out on their own and leaving the others behind. George Donner and Reed restored order and got the company turned around and on the right path. Supplies were dwindling, as was morale. The party kept moving by sheer will and the knowledge that they were close to escaping the Wasatch.

Finally the company entered what came to be called Emigration Canyon, the last geographic obstacle they faced before entering the Salt Lake Valley. This was a tight passage with eighteen deep creek crossings. It would require harnessing at least six or eight yokes of oxen to drag each of the twenty-two wagons up the steep slope that still bears the name Donner Hill.[23] As they made the slow descent, some of the emigrants claimed they smelled salt from the lake.

On August 22, Reed recorded in his journal, "this day we passed through the Mountains and encampd in the Utah vally." [24]

Altogether, the delay of four days at the Weber River camp plus the painful thirty-six-mile crawl through the Wasatch to the Salt Lake Valley—a distance that was supposed to take a few days—had cost the Donner Party at least eighteen days.

Sadly, the worst was yet to come.

29. THE FEARFUL LONG DRIVE

The last days of August were bittersweet for the Donner Party. They had managed to hack out a road up East Canyon through the tangled wilderness of the formidable Wasatch Range without any loss of life or limb. Miraculously, all the oxen, horses, and other livestock and the faithful hounds had survived. The emigrants had endured every challenge they faced on the first stretch of the Hastings Cutoff, but the experience had taken a toll on humans and animals. They were exhausted, utterly drained physically and mentally. Worst of all, they were demoralized.

Travel across the Wasatch had been tediously slow. The many unanticipated delays had cost valuable time, and summer was almost gone. Farmers such as the Donners and Patrick Breen and others who knew seasonal patterns from spending much of their time outdoors could not help but notice the changing path of the sun and the shifting shadows. At evening campgrounds, they no longer discussed the Hastings guidebook but smoked their pipes and thumbed through a reliable almanac.

After descending into the Great Salt Lake Valley, the company crossed a stream that Mormon settlers later named the Jordan River. "Worn with travel and greatly discouraged we reached the shore of the Great Salt Lake," Virginia Reed wrote.[1]

Several of the emigrants had crossed the Atlantic Ocean in coming to America. Others who were from the eastern United States had also seen the ocean. But for a fair number, particularly children, the Great Salt Lake was by far the largest body of water they had ever beheld. Situated between the Wasatch Range on the east and the Great Salt Desert on the west, it was the largest salt lake in the Western Hemisphere, with much higher salinity than any ocean.[2] In describing the Great Salt Lake, James Reed noted that the salty water was "strong enough to brine beef."[3]

While the company tried to recover from the ordeal of the Wasatch, they moved to other campsites in the area in search of spring water, which they found brackish but at least potable. By August 24, they had picked up the tracks of the wagons and livestock of the Harlan-Young Party piloted by Lansford Hastings and followed the trail around the south end of the lake. The wagon train was starting to build up momentum again, knowing that just to the west awaited the Great Salt Lake Desert—the most desolate place on the California Trail.

The angel of death visited the camp the next day. On August 25 at about four o'clock in the afternoon, Luke Halloran, the young merchant from St. Joseph, Missouri, who had consumption, quietly died.[4] "The tedious delays and high altitudes wrought distressing changes in Mr. Halloran's condition, and my father and mother watched over him with increasing solicitude," Eliza Donner wrote.[5]

It was said that he took his final breath with his head cradled in Tamzene Donner's lap. She had cared for him as if he were one of her own children. The exact place where he was buried is unknown. At least two known emigrant camps south of the lake were said to be the site. What is known is that the "stranger" he was buried next to was John Hargrave, a member of the Harlan-Young Party. While helping to get his company's wagons across the Wasatch, Hargrave had caught a cold that developed into typhoid pneumonia. He had died on August 11 and was laid to rest the following day, making him the first known overland emigrant buried in Utah soil.[6]

Although Halloran's death from tuberculosis was inevitable, it was hastened by the rigors of crossing the Wasatch. Both he and Hargrave were victims of the Hastings Cutoff. Some of the men who made Halloran's coffin and dug his grave cursed Hastings, and a few of them, under their breath, damned Reed for advocating the cutoff route.

Just days before Halloran died, he had talked with Reed, who later wrote that Halloran "being in a dying condition . . . made himself known to me as a Master Mason."[7] Thus the graveside service was a formal Masonic funeral. Reed, who also was a Master Mason, officiated. After Halloran was buried in the salty soil, his trunk was opened. It contained clothing, some keepsakes, a Masonic emblem, and about $1,500, all in coins. All of it was bequeathed to George Donner, as well as Halloran's saddle, tack, and horse.[8]

This death was the first for the Donner Party since the passing of the elderly Sarah Keyes almost three months before at Alcove Spring, but the number of people in the company remained at eighty-seven. During those same days in the Great Salt Lake Valley, there was another addition to the company roster. Philippine Keseberg, the young German woman headed to California with her husband, Lewis, and their three-year-old daughter, delivered a healthy baby boy. Named Lewis Keseberg Jr., the baby looked none the worse for wear even though his pregnant mother had been thrown from an overturned wagon into the water in early summer.[9]

Keseberg, known to have physically abused his wife and thought by some to have defiled an Indian burial site, was not the most popular person in the wagon train. Still, most of the emigrants came around to pay a call on the newborn and his mother. These were folks who valued the old family proverb that from death comes life. They had already witnessed it on the trail before and had witnessed it again. Some of them took it as a sign, direct from the Old Testament God they worshipped who—just as the Prophet Isaiah promised—would help them "make a way in the wilderness, *and* rivers in the desert."[10]

After the internment of Halloran, the caravan journeyed to Twenty Wells, a pleasant resting place named for twenty pothole sweetwater springs. The travelers did not linger. Days of leisure and long rests were no longer a consideration. The wagon train remained on the move in a race with the coming winter. From Twenty Wells, the party rounded the Stansbury Mountains and camped at Burnt Spring in the north end of what Hastings called Spring Valley. It soon became better known as Skull Valley because of ancient bison skulls and old Indian bones found in the area.[11]

On the evening of August 28, the company came upon what Reed described as "delightful fresh water wells" at an oasis fittingly named Hope Springs. While imbibing, the emigrants found more waiting for them than thirst-quenching water.[12]

Eliza Donner, three years old at the time, never forgot what she witnessed. Many years later she wrote, "Close by the largest well stood a rueful spectacle—a bewildering guide board, flecked with bits of white paper, showing that the notice or message which had recently been pasted and tacked thereon had since been stripped off in irregular bits. In surprise and consternation, the emigrants gazed at its blank face, then toward the dreary waste beyond. Presently, my mother knelt before it and began searching for fragments of paper, which she believed crows had wantonly pecked off and dropped to the ground."

Others were soon on their knees, scratching among the grasses and sifting through the loose soil with their fingers. What they found, they brought to Tamzene Donner. After the search ended, she laid the guide board across her lap and thoughtfully fitted the ragged edges of paper together, matching the scraps to marks on the board. The writing was that of Hastings, and Tamzene's patchwork brought out the following words: "2 days—2 nights—hard driving—cross—desert—reach water."[13]

Once the scribbled note had been pieced together and deciphered, the emigrants tried to make sense of the message. Then it began to sink in. Just like the message that Hastings had left for them at the mouth of Weber Canyon, his latest epistle evoked an array of emotions ranging from unbridled anger and shock to disbelief and fear. Hastings had told them that the upcoming desert crossing was flat and easy. He had said it was only thirty-five or forty miles and could be crossed in a day and a night with a scattering of brief rests. But now this warning from Hastings indicated that the journey would be much longer and more difficult and the travel time at least doubled.

George Donner held a quick conference with the family heads, but they had no choice but to go on. They honed their knives, cut bunches of grass, and bundled it up for livestock feed. Every cask, jar, pail, or any receptacle that could hold even a little water was filled to the brim. "This would be a heavy strain on our cattle, and to fit them for the ordeal they were granted thirty-six hours indulgence near the bubbling waters, amid good pasturage,"[14] Eliza Donner wrote of that day.

On August 30—a Sunday—many prayers had been said by the time the wagon train moved on. The company paused to top off their water supply at Redlum Spring but found the water brackish. Ahead, they scrambled up Hastings Pass through the Cedar Mountains, the range forming the western boundary of Skull Valley, and then they crossed the Grayback Hills. They were now in the Great Salt Lake Desert. They were on the brink of making the crossing that cartographer Thomas H. Jefferson called "The fearful long drive 83 miles no grass no water."[15] Jefferson's description was spot-on—eighty-three miles of barren salt flats to cross and not thirty-five or forty miles, as suggested by Hastings.

That same day, the quick-moving Bryant-Russell Party, with its mules, had already crossed the Sierras in Alta California and were less than a day's journey from Captain John Sutter's fort. The party spent that evening at John Calhoun Johnson's Six Mile Ranch, a popular encampment for emigrant companies. The mule riders were treated to a "pile of small cheeses and numerous pans of milk with thick cream upon them."[16]

Also on that day, Hastings and his advance wagons—having already made the desert crossing—were far to the west, quickly making their way through the Ruby Valley in present Nevada. They would soon reach the Humboldt River and get back on the original California Trail.[17]

The Donner Party was not concerned about all the companies ahead of them. They had their own worries. They knew they were alone, the last wagon train on the California Trail. "We started to cross the desert traveling day and night only stopping to feed and water our teams as long as water and grass lasted," James Reed later explained.

Virginia Reed also provided her impression of the start of the desert trek. "It was a dreary, desolate, alkali waste; not a living thing could be seen; it seemed as though the hand of death had been laid upon the country. We started in the evening, traveled all that night, and the following day and night—two nights and one day of suffering from thirst and heat by day and piercing cold by night."[18]

By September 1, the emigrants had separated. The Eddy and Graves families had healthier and hence faster oxen teams. They surged ahead of the pack on the hard surface of salt and made a beeline to the northwest for Pilot Peak, the highest mountain in the Pilot Range and the landmark everyone aimed for when traversing the desert. The nine heavy wagons of the Donner brothers and the Reed family fell behind from the start. They soon ended up far to the rear of the caravan, which stretched out over a mile.

The travelers, with few exceptions, walked alongside the wagons to lighten the load for the oxen, stumbling along and straining at their yokes.[19] The emigrants walked by day beneath the relentless sun and at night under a canopy of blazing stars and wrapped themselves in blankets to ward off the night chill. Both day and night, the desert was quiet. The only sounds they heard were their own muffled steps and those of the plodding livestock.

Farther into the desert, the hard and dusty salt flats gave way to a sink with a shallow lake below the thin crust. When the wagons and herds tramped into this stretch, the alkali turned into a mush that slowed down the wagons and herds even more. One observer said that for the emigrants, it was much "like walking through deep oatmeal mixed with glue."[20] People and animals became mired, and wagon wheels had to be cleaned off repeatedly.

The company, moving in distinct family groups, also found that they were isolated in a land of illusions. They had been seeing mirages on the trail since Nebraska, but now on these scorching days as heat waves rose from the salty soil, they were taunted by images of floating islands, grassy meadows, and vanishing water holes. Some of the Donner family thought one of the mirages was Hastings and a caravan moving through tall grasses toward a shimmering lake.[21]

"Alas, as we advanced, the scene vanished," Eliza Donner wrote. "A cruel mirage, in its mysterious way, had outlined a lake and cast our shadows near its shore. Disappointment intensified our burning thirst, and my good mother gave her own and other suffering children wee lumps of sugar, moistened with a drop of peppermint, and later put a flattened bullet in each child's mouth to engage its attention and help keep the salivary glands in action."[22]

William Eddy, whose family was ahead of most of the others in the company, was completely fooled by an optical illusion. He later shared his experience with Jessy Thornton. "Mr. Eddy informed me that he was surprised to see twenty men all walking in the same direction in which he was traveling," Thornton related in 1848. "They all stopped at the same time, and the motions of their bodies corresponded. At length he was astounded with the discovery that they were men whose features and dress were like his own, and that they were imitating his own motions. When he stood still, they stood still, and when he advanced, they did also. In short, they were living and moving images of himself, and of his actions. Subsequently he saw the caravan repeated in the same extraordinary and startling manner."[23]

Well to the rear of the spread-out company, if Reed encountered any mirages, he never mentioned it. Instead, he was devoting all attention to his struggling family, hired hands, and horses and livestock. All were showing definite signs of stress, particularly the oxen. It was September 2, the company's third day on the desert, and the supply of food and water was almost gone. The oxen would soon begin to fail and perish, and if that happened, everyone else would soon follow.

Reed took immediate action. He decided to ride out alone and find water. After saddling Glaucus, he told his main teamster, Milt Elliott, to wait until the oxen became so exhausted that they could go no farther before removing them from the wagons and driving them up the road until they reached water.[24] He also instructed his workers, Walter Herron and Baylis Williams, to remain behind with the wagons and look after his family. Reed then rode off toward Pilot Peak.

Other families in the company were also forced to take drastic measures when their oxen could not go on or fell dead in their tracks.

The Donner brothers left their families in their wagons, unyoked the oxen, and herded them down the trail. The Eddys, who had been so far ahead of the others, also were forced to leave their wagon before reaching Pilot Peak. Carrying their two small children, the couple drove their cattle ahead of them in the moonlight.

By nightfall, Reed, riding Glaucus, had covered more than twenty miles and reached Pilot Peak, where he eventually found the freshwater spring. He left his racehorse behind to rest and started back on a borrowed mount with water for his stranded family. Along the way, Reed met up with the teamsters herding all the cattle and horses. He told them to be careful when approaching Pilot Peak. If the cattle caught the scent of water, they could stampede and become lost, which was exactly what happened not long after Reed went on his way.[25]

When he got to his three wagons, Reed dispersed water to Margret, the children, and the hired hands. Walter Herron immediately left on the borrowed horse to return to Pilot Peak and wait for the family to catch up. The rest waited for the teamsters to return with fresh oxen, but by day's end, there was no sign of anyone, and the water Reed had brought was almost gone.

Virginia Reed described the dire situation.

> Towards night the situation became desperate and we had only a few drops of water left; another night there meant death. We must set out on foot and try to reach some of the wagons. Can I ever forget that night in the desert, when we walked mile after mile in the darkness, every step seeming to be the very last we could take! Suddenly all fatigue was banished by fear; through the night came a swift rushing sound of one of the young steers crazed by thirst and apparently bent upon our destruction. My father, holding his youngest child in his arms and keeping us all close behind him, drew his pistol, but finally the maddened beast turned and dashed off into the darkness. Dragging ourselves along about ten miles, we reached the wagon of Jacob Donner. The family

were all asleep, so we children lay down on the ground. A bitter wind swept over the desert, chilling us through and through. We crept closer together, and, when we complained of the cold, papa placed all five of our dogs [Tyler, Barney, Trailor, Tracker, and the family favorite, Cash] around us, and only for the warmth of these faithful creatures we should doubtless have perished.

At daylight papa was off to learn the fate of his cattle, and was told that all were lost, except one cow and an ox. The stock, scenting the water, had rushed in ahead of the men, and had probably been stolen by Indians, and driven into the mountains, where all traces of them were lost. A week was spent here in a fruitless search. Almost every man in the company turned out, hunting in all directions, but our eighteen head of cattle were never found. We had lost our best yoke of oxen before reaching Bridger's Fort from drinking poisoned water found standing in pools, and had bought at the fort two yoke of youngsters, but now all were gone. . . .[26]

Young Virginia was right. It did take almost a week for all the members of the wagon train to reach Pilot Peak and partake of the refreshing water from a spring that would one day be renamed for the Donners. All the emigrants survived the hellish days and nights in the desert, including the newborn Keseberg baby, but many oxen, cattle, and horses were dead or missing. Reed lost eighteen animals, and other members of the company could not account for twenty more. Several wagons filled with the makings for new lives in California remained abandoned on the salt flats. Days were spent trying to find lost livestock, cull through belongings from the wagons left in the desert, and transfer what little food and supplies remaining in the wagons were still trailworthy.

Many animals were still alive but were so weakened that they were abandoned and left to fend for themselves until death came. Most of the emigrants knew it was best to put the animal down with a shot to the head. Some of the teamsters and families had become so close

Lansford Warren Hastings
(1819–1870), author of *The
Emigrants' Guide to Oregon
and California*, promoted the
infamous Hastings Cutoff as a
shortcut across present-day Utah.
*(Used by permission, Utah
State Historical Society)*

Hastings's *Guide* cover.
*(Yale Collection of Western
Americana, Beinecke Rare
Book and Manuscript
Library, Yale University)*

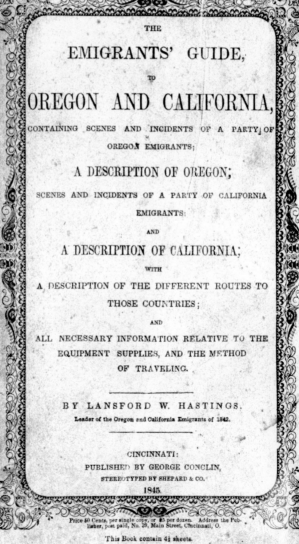

THE

EMIGRANTS' GUIDE,

TO

OREGON AND CALIFORNIA,

CONTAINING SCENES AND INCIDENTS OF A PARTY OF

OREGON EMIGRANTS;

A DESCRIPTION OF OREGON;

SCENES AND INCIDENTS OF A PARTY OF CALIFORNIA

EMIGRANTS;

AND

A DESCRIPTION OF CALIFORNIA;

WITH

A DESCRIPTION OF THE DIFFERENT ROUTES TO
THOSE COUNTRIES;

AND

ALL NECESSARY INFORMATION RELATIVE TO THE
EQUIPMENT SUPPLIES, AND THE METHOD
OF TRAVELING.

BY LANSFORD W. HASTINGS,

Leader of the Oregon and California Emigrants of 1842.

CINCINNATI:
PUBLISHED BY GEORGE CONCLIN,
STEREOTYPED BY SHEPARD & CO.
1845.

Price 50 Cents, per single copy, or $5 per dozen. Address the Pub-
lisher, post paid, No. 39, Main Street, Cincinnati, O.

This Book contain 4½ sheets.

Daguerreotype taken by Nicolas H. Shepard shortly after Abraham Lincoln was elected to Congress in 1846, the earliest known image of the future president. *(Attributed to Nicholas H. Shepherd. Source: Gibson William Harris, "My Recollections of Abraham Lincoln," Woman's Home Companion, November 1903, Library of Congress, Prints and Photographs Division)*

James and Margret Reed.
(Used by permission, Utah State Historical Society)

Eliza Donner.
(From The Expedition of the Donner
Party and Its Tragic Fate *by Eliza
P. Donner Houghton, 1911)*

Frances Donner Wilder.
(From The Expedition of the Donner
Party and Its Tragic Fate *by Eliza
P. Donner Houghton, 1911)*

Immediately after their rescue by
the Third Relief, Georgia Donner
(left) and Eliza Donner were put in
the care of Mary Brunner *(center)*
and her husband, Christian, a Swiss
couple at Sutter's Fort.
(From The Expedition of the
Donner Party and Its Tragic Fate *by
Eliza P. Donner Houghton, 1911)*

Leanna Donner.
(From The Expedition of the Donner
Party and Its Tragic Fate *by Eliza
P. Donner Houghton, 1911)*

William Eddy.
*(Clyde Arbuckle
Photograph Collection,
San Jose [California]
Public Library)*

Eleanor Eddy.
*(Clyde Arbuckle
Photograph Collection,
San Jose [California]
Public Library)*

Mary Graves.
(Courtesy of ushistoryimages.com)

Lewis Keseberg.
(Courtesy of ushistoryimages.com)

Charles Stanton.
(Courtesy of ushistoryimages.com)

THE BREEN FAMIY.

1. PATRICK, Sr.   2. MARGARET.   3. JONN.   4. EDWARD P.   5. PATRICK, Jr.
6. SIMON P.   7. JAMES F.   8. PETER.   9. BELLA M.   10. WILLIAM M.

The Breen family.

(Courtesy of ushistoryimages.com)

Interior of covered wagon.
(Courtesy Robert G. McCubbin Collection)

Alcove Springs in present-day Kansas.
(Rebecca Perry Irons)

Sand Hills of the Platte Valley, by William Henry Jackson.
(Scotts Bluff National Monument, National Park Service)

Lightning Storm, by William Henry Jackson.
(Scotts Bluff National Monument, National Park Service)

River crossing.
(© North Wind Picture Archives)

Wagon ruts on the trail west.
(Scotts Bluff National Monument, National Park Service)

Wagon train at rest by Independence Rock.

(L. Tom Perry Special Collections, Harold B. Lee Library, Brigham Young University, Provo, Utah)

Freighter's Grub Pile, by William Henry Jackson.

(Scotts Bluff National Monument, National Park Service)

Fort Laramie.
(Alfred Jacob Miller/The Walters Art Museum)

Sutter's Fort.
(Courtesy of UC Berkeley, Bancroft Library)

Donner Lake.

(iStock.com/yulhun)

Patrick Breen's diary, page 28.
(Courtesy of UC Berkeley, Bancroft Library)

Patty Reed's doll.
(AP Photo / The Sacramento Bee,
Anne Chadwick Williams)

Daniel Rhoads.
*(Annie R. Mitchell History Room, Tulare
County Library, Visalia, California)*

William McCutchen.

(Courtesy of ushistoryimages.com)

to the animals that they could not kill them but simply walked away and did not look back.

This was most likely the time when Virginia Reed parted with her beloved pony, Billy. In her writings, she did not disclose exactly when it happened, but only wrote that "a day came when I had no pony to ride, the poor little fellow gave out. He could not endure the hardships of ceaseless travel. When I was forced to part with him I cried until I was ill, and sat in the back of the wagon watching him become smaller and smaller as we drove on, until I could see him no more."[27]

James Reed, with others in the company, returned to the marooned wagons to retrieve essentials, including valuables and documents. Much of the furniture, clothing, and items considered nonessential were left behind, cached in the desert sands with the owners' intent to return someday and retrieve them, or were given away to others. Sadly for the youngsters, they were expected to part with most of their personal things such as books and toys. Patty Reed, just eight years old, could not bear leaving her most prized possessions buried in the salt desert sand. Without anyone else knowing it, she carefully hid in the hem of her apron her wooden doll named Dolly that was small enough to fit in the palm of her hand and was a gift from her grandmother, Sarah Keyes. She also kept a lock of her grandmother's hair, Sarah's pincushion, and a few other keepsakes.[28]

George Donner left a wagon behind, and so did Keseberg. Only one of the three Reed wagons was salvageable and was brought back to the camp at Pilot Peak. Reed placed what goods and belongings the family kept in the larger family wagon, where his mother-in-law had ridden in a featherbed until her death.[29] The bed and cookstove remained in the desert. Others in the company loaned Reed a yoke of cattle. He still had an ox and a cow to make up a second yoke.

On September 10, it was determined that all strays had been rounded up, and the emigrants and livestock were somewhat rested.[30] At last, the journey to California resumed. The toll of the desert crossing was the loss of three dozen animals, four wagons, many of the emigrants' belongings and, most important, eleven precious days.

That morning, the wagons moved out, and nature sent the emigrants another sign. They had traveled only six miles, following the trail around the base of Pilot Peak, when a severe snowstorm swept down upon them. They eventually passed through it, but it made an impression. Years later, Patrick Breen's son John recalled the "considerable fall of snow" and the "apprehension of delay from this cause." Most of all, he remembered that it "made the mothers tremble."[31]

30. RACE AGAINST TIME

Back on the trail, in what would become the state of Nevada, the mothers described by John Breen were not trembling from the unseasonably cold wind and snow. They were shaken to the core from fear, worry, and anger. The women of what had become an increasingly acrimonious company of emigrants knew that they and their children were in a precarious situation. A glance at an almanac calendar confirmed what most of them had suspected for some time. Time was running out and hope was in short supply, as was something they could not live without—sustenance.

Everyone in the party—from suckling infant to gray-headed grandfather—was hungry. Pickings were thin. The many delays and setbacks throughout the passage on the Hastings Cutoff had badly depleted all the food stores, and for several days, no game had been seen on the salt desert.

At camp on the evening of September 10, an inventory was taken of the entire party's remaining provisions. James Reed was asked to tally the findings.[1] It was apparent that among all the emigrants, there was not nearly enough food to get the company through to California. Someone was going to have to get help.

"After receiving the estimate of each family, on paper, I then suggested that if two gentlemen of the company would volunteer to go in advance to Captain Sutter, in California, I would write a letter to him for the whole amount of provisions that we wanted, and also stating that I would personally become responsible to him for the amount," Reed recounted years later. "I suggested that from the generous nature of Captain Sutter he would send them. Mr. [William]

McCutchen came forward and proposed that if I would take care of his family he would go. This the company agreed to. Mr. [Charles] Stanton, a single man, volunteered, if they would furnish him a horse. Mr. McCutchen, having a horse and a mule, generously gave the mule."[2]

It was no surprise that none of the men traveling with large families volunteered to ride to Sutter's Fort. Likely, the young teamsters and hired hands were reluctant to step forward and leave the jobs they had been hired to do. McCutchen, who had no wagon but only his horse and mule, saw it as an opportunity to get his wife and little girl into a more comfortable traveling situation. Stanton had no family in the caravan and chose to go out of a sense of duty. Taking blankets and meager rations, they started for California.

With Amanda McCutchen and baby Harriet safely ensconced with the Reed family, the Donner Party pressed forward. They had to follow Hastings's route for several days on a detour around the Ruby Mountains to the Humboldt River and once again pick up the true California Trail.

On September 13, they stopped at a basin of water that Reed christened "Mad Woman Camp." As he put it, "all the women in Camp ware mad with anger."[3] No further explanation was needed. There was plenty to be mad about. Maybe there was something in the water at this particular site that made folks angry. More than five weeks before the Donners' arrival, the Bryant-Russell mule team had stopped at the same place. During the evening around the fire, a disagreement over a "very trivial matter" had fueled an altercation between two members of the party who leveled rifles at each other.[4] Fortunately, the cool-headed Bryant jumped between the two and talked them out of continuing the duel.[5]

No rifles were leveled at Reed, but the angry stares directed at him—the one who had convinced the party to follow Hastings's route—looked just as lethal as lead shot. Hastings had lost all credibility with the company, but there was plenty of blame to spare for Reed.

On September 16, while camped on the east side of the rugged

Ruby Mountains, two of George Donner's horses went missing. A little gray pony and one of George's favorite saddle horses, a cream-colored mare named Margaret, presumably had been stolen by Shoshone Indians during the night.[6]

Like the others in the caravan, Donner realized that soon they would reach the Humboldt River and get back on course. He hoped that by then or soon after, McCutchen and Stanton would be back from California with victuals that would enable the company to cross the Sierras. After the wagons made the turn around the south end of the Ruby Mountains, the days still dragged on, even though the travelers tried with all the energy they could muster to make as many miles as possible.

They stopped at several springs, including a few that were warm and even hot. Clean clothes and baths helped their morale, as did the antelope, sage hens, and Rocky Mountain sheep brought in by the hunters.[7] Roasted meat, even prairie-dog haunches, boosted spirits and helped to squelch the gnawing feeling in the emigrants' bellies. By September 24, the company was camped near the entrance to the canyon of the South Fork of the Humboldt River. The next day, after what Reed described as "a perfect Snake trail," they camped in the winding, narrow gorge.[8]

On Saturday, September 25, the whole company heaved a collective sigh of relief. After what must have seemed like a lifetime, the wagon train had reached the South Fork of the Humboldt River. After sixty-eight days of heartbreak and pain, the Donner Party had completed the Hastings Cutoff and rejoined the established California Trail.[9]

The first order of business was to investigate the river they would follow until it emptied into the Humboldt Sink. The sink was a body of water during the snow melt-off in spring, but by late summer, it was a wide, sandy low spot where what little water remained in the river was absorbed into the sand. The Donner Party had heard many stories about the Humboldt, mostly concerning lack of shade, turbid water, twisting loops called oxbows, and the many stagnant sloughs that could mire unsuspecting oxen and mules.[10]

The Humboldt had gone by many names and would not officially become the Humboldt before 1848, when the name appeared on a map published by John C. Frémont.[11] No matter what it was called, most travelers found the river disgusting. Unlike the native Shoshone and Paiutes who used the river and surrounding marshes for sustenance, emigrants maligned the Humboldt every chance they got. They filled their diaries with diatribes such as: "[The] Humboldt is not good for man nor beast . . . and there is not timber enough in three hundred miles of its desolate valley to make a snuff-box, or sufficient vegetation along its banks to shade a rabbit, while its waters contain the alkali to make soap for a nation."[12]

When the Donner Party emigrants surveyed the river, they found it low, with very little grass along the banks. After a brief council, it was decided to split the company into two groups. The Donner brothers would take the lead because their oxen appeared to be in better condition than most of the other livestock. The slower-moving wagons, which included the Reed and Eddy families, would follow.

Some of the migrants later claimed the division was because of the scarcity of forage. In truth, the company had been in the process of splitting up as far back as the crossing of the salt desert. They had been out on the trail so long that petty disagreements escalated and nerves were frayed. Families now tended to keep to themselves and traveled apart, joining others only at the nightly campsite.

Another concern was the growing number of Indians the travelers had encountered since entering the homeland of the Shoshone people and the Paiutes farther west along the Humboldt. To tribal people, the strangers in their wagons were a curiosity. At first, the Indians were willing to give the emigrants advice or answer their questions. The Shoshones—even though they had little to share—gave food to needy whites in dire straits. But as more caravans came, there was less grazing grass, the waters became polluted, and the game became scarce.

When it became evident that white men took what they needed from the land and the rivers, the Indians decided to retaliate by robbing the intruders. The emigrants considered all Indians to be the same, and the Indian stereotype was formed. All Indians, especially in the Great Basin and especially in California, became known as "Diggers," a pejorative term that came into use when the emigrants saw Indians foraging for roots and bulbs, an important part of their diet.[13]

The Donner Party had seen large gatherings of Indians, including one sizable group of people near the Humboldt who were completely naked. One diarist reported that they "hovered around in the vicinity, but did not come into camp."[14]

Some days later, farther down the Humboldt, the last group of the company—made up of the Reed, Graves, Murphy, Eddy, and Breen families—was greeted by a friendly Paiute who spoke some English picked up from previous emigrant parties. They dubbed him "Thursday" in homage to Robinson Crusoe's companion, Friday. Soon, another Paiute who spoke some English joined them. The two Indians traveled with the party and camped with them that evening at a place called Gravelly Ford, where the gravel riverbed made a good wagon crossing. During the night when a campfire ignited some dry brush, all hands turned out to fight the blaze, including the two Paiutes. Afterward, the party, including the Indians, ate a supper with whatever could be thrown together, and the campers went back to sleep. When everyone arose in the morning, the Indians were gone, and so were a yoke of oxen and a shirt belonging to Franklin Graves.[15]

The emigrants had no time to look for the oxen. They crossed to the south side of the river at Gravelly Ford and continued down the trail. Two nights later, on October 1, one of Graves's horses—"a fine mare"—was stolen. Again, there was nothing to do but keep going.[16]

James Reed's diary entries became more terse and incomplete. "Frid [Oct.] 2 Still down the River Made to day 12 miles. Sat [Oct.] 3 left Camp early mad[e] a this day 10 miles."[17]

By then, the geese were headed south. Their honking could be heard all through the long, chilly nights. There was still no sign of McCutchen and Stanton with provisions. There seemed to be game along the river and in the sagebrush, but Eddy and the other hunters had no luck.

The Breens and others of the party who were true believers constantly uttered prayers as they traveled. They thought it could not have gotten any worse.

Reed's diary entry for October 4 read: "Son [Sunday] [Oct] 4 Still."[18]

Just the single word—"Still"—and no more. It was the last dated entry in the diary.

The next day, it got worse.

31. BLOOD RAGE

It was over in a few minutes. Like many eyewitnesses, those of the Donner Party who beheld the shocking acts of October 5, 1846, had very different stories to tell.[1] It happened so suddenly—angry words turned to curses followed by a rain of blows, the flash of a knife, and then blood. About that, they all were in full agreement. There was a lot of blood.

That Monday started quietly enough for the Reed, Graves, Keseberg, and Breen families, the group that followed the lead band of emigrants headed by George Donner. There were perfunctory housekeeping chores and a slim breakfast, rationed out by women who tried to stretch what little food remained. The night before, camp had been set up where the trail left the south bank of the Humboldt. Reed had just started writing his diary entry for the day when he was interrupted, and he managed to write only the word "Still." He probably thought he could finish the entry later, when they stopped for the night. But that was not to be.[2]

When the party got moving, they followed the trail over bluffs on the south side of the river. After their nooning stop, they approached the steep and sandy slope up what mapmaker T. H. Jefferson had called Pauta Pass. Before making the ascent, the caravan came to a halt. Because of the grade, they were forced to double-team the oxen and pull the wagons up the hill one at a time.

The wagons queued up at the bottom of the steep grade. Two of the Graves family wagons, with double teams of oxen straining beneath the yokes, were pulled to the top. Next in line was the family's third wagon, driven by teamster John Snyder, who decided that he and his oxen were capable of making the climb without any help. He did not want to lose time waiting for another Graves team to be brought down the hill and hitched to the wagon. Snyder cracked his whip, and the oxen slowly moved forward, but it was obvious that the steep grade was too much. Behind Snyder, driving the large family wagon shared by the Reeds and Eddys, teamster Milt Elliot had already joined another yoke of oxen from William Pike with his team and was ready to go.[3]

Tempers were already ragged and nerves were raw from the pressure of knowing that time was running out to get over the Sierra Nevada range before the first heavy snowfall. Becoming impatient, Elliot finally pulled his wagon around Snyder's to go up the hill. The headstrong Snyder was put off by this maneuver, and he and Elliot exchanged angry words and curses when Elliot's lead yoke of oxen became entangled with Snyder's team. Everything came to a standstill. The furious Snyder lost all control and began to beat the oxen on their heads with the heavy wooden whip handle, or stock.[4] As Snyder flogged the pitiful beasts, James Reed rode up on Glaucus.

"Snyder was beating his cattle over the head with the butt end of his whip, when my father returning on horse-back from a hunting trip, arrived and appreciating the great importance of saving the remainder of the oxen, remonstrated with Snyder, telling him that they were our main dependence, and at the same time offering the assistance of our team," Virginia Reed explained.

> Snyder having taken offense at something Elliot had said declared that his team could pull up alone and kept on using abusive language. Father tried to quiet the enraged man. Hard words followed. Then my father said: "We can settle this, John, when we get up the hill." "No," replied Snyder with an oath, "we will settle it now," and springing upon the tongue of a wagon, he struck my father a violent blow over the head with his heavy whip stock. One blow followed another. Father was stunned for a moment and blinded by the blood streaming from the gashes in his head. Another

blow was descending when my mother ran in between the
men. Father saw the uplifted whip, but only had to time to
cry: "John, John," when down came the stroke upon mother.
Quick as a thought my father's hunting knife was out and
Snyder fell, fatally wounded.[5]

Reed had stabbed Snyder just below the collarbone and punctured
his left lung. Despite the knife wound, Snyder brought Reed to his
knees with two more vicious blows to his head before Snyder collapsed into the arms of Billy Graves, who laid him on the ground.
When John Breen rushed forward to help the young man he had
taken a liking to, it was said that Snyder whispered just before he succumbed, "Uncle Patrick, I am dead."[6]

Reed—staggering, in shock, and with blood running into his
eyes—flung the knife into the river. Margret and the girls rushed
to his side to staunch the bleeding, but Reed broke away and went to
Snyder. Some emigrants who were present claimed they heard Snyder
murmur, "I am to blame" just before he died.[7] Reed was overwhelmed
with grief and likely some guilt, even though he had brandished the
knife in self-defense and to protect his wife.

Travel was over for the day. Camp was pitched near the top of the
hill, and the Graves family took their teamster's body to wash and
prepare for burial. Reed volunteered boards from his wagon to use
for a coffin, but Franklin Graves summarily rejected the offer.

Reed, seeing that Margret was stricken with a migraine and badly
bruised from the blow she had received, asked Virginia to help him
only after she finished tending to her mother in the family tent. Once
Margret was settled, Virginia turned to her father in the wagon. She
fetched a basin of water and sponge, gently washed away the caked
blood, and dressed each wound.

"When my work was at last finished, I burst out crying," Virginia
wrote. "Papa clasped me in his arms, saying: 'I should not have asked
so much of you,' and talked to me about my feelings, so that we could
go to the tent where mama was lying down. We then learned that
trouble was brewing in the camp where Snyder's body lay."[8]

That evening at the council, there was consensus that the death of Snyder could not be ignored. The emigrants who had witnessed the mayhem on the sandy slope were mostly in agreement about the sequence of events, up to a certain point. But those same eyewitnesses came up with different scenarios. If the person was not fond of Reed, of which there were quite a few, then he was cast as the aggressor who challenged Snyder and then attacked him with a knife.

The issue of what to do about Reed stirred great debate and a range of possible solutions. One was to take everyone's written statements to be used against Reed in court when the emigrants reached California. That did not suit those whose mind-set was an eye for an eye. One of those was Lewis Keseberg, who loathed Reed from past conflicts on the trail stemming from Keseberg's abuse of his wife. Keseberg raised a wagon tongue in the air and demanded that Reed be hanged from it at once. The Graves family and some others would have gone along with the measure, but Milt Elliott and William Eddy, armed and ready, made it clear that they would not allow a kangaroo court to decide the fate of a man who had acted in self-defense.[9]

Late in the evening, the stalemate ended when all agreed that Reed's punishment would be banishment from the party. At first it was decreed that he was to go out on foot, but based on his friends' pleas, a compromise was reached. He still would go alone, but he was permitted to take his horse. He could leave with the clothes on his back and nothing more. By not being allowed to take a weapon or any provisions, he would have no way to procure food or defend himself.[10] His chance of survival was extremely low. Most of the emigrants considered Reed's banishment a death sentence.

At first, so did Reed, and he refused to accept the punishment. He also said that he could not desert his wife and children. His few allies told him that he must leave, and they vowed to look after his family. They also pointed out that Stanton and McCutchen had not returned with food. Maybe they never would return. But if Reed successfully reached the other side of the Sierras, he could bring back more provisions. Reed was still hesitant.

"Then came a sacrifice on the part of my mother," wrote Virginia. "Knowing only too well what her life would be without him, yet fearful that if he remained he would meet with violence at the hands of his enemies, she implored him to go, but to no avail until she urged him to remember the destitution of the company, saying that if he remained and escaped violence at their hands, he might nevertheless see his children starving and be helpless to aid them, while if he went on he could return and meet them with food. It was a tearful struggle; at last he consented, but not before he had secured a promise for the company to care for his wife and little ones."[11]

In the morning, the entire party—including Reed, with his head wrapped in bandages—gathered for the burial of Snyder. There were tears and some prayers, but no coffin. The body was laid in a grave shrouded in a sheet and sandwiched between two boards.[12] While some of the men and boys shoveled in sand, Reed turned to his family. He embraced a sobbing Margret and his children and promised them he would return. Then he mounted his dependable Glaucus and rode away.

Despite Reed's stubborn allegiance to Hastings and the disastrous cutoff, his departure was a real loss and had a shattering impact on the party. They had banished one of the most capable, diligent, and resourceful men in the wagon train. It was often said that if the steady, stable, and reasoned George Donner would have been there instead of miles ahead with his own group, the verdict against Reed would have been different.

Reed's devoted family believed in his value and worth. They were not about to allow such a man to be deprived of every advantage necessary to stay alive on a wilderness trail, even if it took an act of bold defiance. That evening, Virginia Reed and the loyal Milt Elliott slipped out of camp.

"I followed him [Reed] through the darkness," Virginia recalled, "taking Elliott with me, and carried him his rifle, pistols, ammunition and some food. I had determined to stay with him, and begged him to let me stay, but he would listen to no argument, saying that it was impossible. Finally, unclasping my arms from around him, he placed me in charge of Elliott, who started back to camp with me—and papa was left alone. I had cried until I had hardly strength to walk, but when we reached camp and I saw the distress of my mother, with the little ones clinging around her and no arm to lean upon, it seemed suddenly to make a woman of me. I realized that I must be strong and help mama bear her sorrows."[13]

With no wagons and family to care for, Reed rode hard and long. After two days, he caught up with the Donners. Reed gave them a sanitized story about why he had left the other group and led them to believe he was going after supplies that had still not been delivered by Stanton and McCutchen.

After breakfast the next morning, Reed's former teamster, Walter Herron, who had been traveling with the Donners, volunteered to accompany Reed to California and help with supplies. Reed welcomed his help. Although Herron had no horse, Reed suggested that they share riding time.[14] He wanted to move at a slower but steady pace so as not to wear out Glaucus. One of them could walk while the other rode, and they would still make good time.

They set out, taking rations for only a few days and a letter from George Donner to John Sutter asking for enough oxen teams and provisions to enable the company to reach California. In the letter, Donner gave his personal pledge that Sutter would be paid in full once the company arrived.

After a few days, the little food Reed and Herron had was gone. "I supplied our wants by shooting wild geese and other game when we could find any," Reed later wrote. Then there was "no game to be seen; hunger began to be felt, and for days we traveled without hope or help."[15]

Meanwhile, the larger party of emigrants back at the Humboldt River struggled to rally their broken spirits and continue the journey. They were completely splintered and lacked the leadership and will to reunite and work together as a cohesive unit. Only family mattered. All sense of community was gone.

"We traveled on, but all life seemed to have left the party, and the hours dragged slowly along," was how Virginia Reed described that challenging October passage. "Every day we would search for some sign of papa, who would leave a letter by the way-side in the top of a bush or in a split stick, and when he succeeded in killing geese or birds would scatter feathers about so that we might know that he was not suffering for food. When possible, our fire would be kindled on the spot where his had been. But a time came when we found no letter, and no trace of him. Had he starved by the way-side, or been murdered by Indians?"[16]

Indians were very much on the minds of all the emigrants. On October 7, while William Eddy and William Pike were out in the brush on horseback hunting for some badly needed game, they were attacked by a band of Paiutes. The arrows missed their marks, and the men returned safely, although empty-handed. Back at camp, Eddy and Pike learned that one of the emigrants was missing.[17]

The man about sixty years old known only by his surname, Hardcoop, a driver for the Keseberg family, was nowhere to be found. When Keseberg was questioned about Hardcoop's whereabouts, he claimed he had no idea but acknowledged that something was wrong. A rider backtracked the trail and found Hardcoop about five miles in the rear. He was returned to the camp, and he told the others that Keseberg had forced him out of the family wagon.[18] Keseberg, who had started the long journey with two wagons, had abandoned one of them in the salt desert of Utah. He told the others that Hardcoop was worn out and could not walk like everyone else, but there was not enough room for him in the remaining wagon. Keseberg pointed out that his family was walking, including his wife, carrying their infant son.

The next morning, it was decided to cache the last Reed wagon, the big one that had carried Sarah Keyes. Some of the Eddy family's clothing and tools also were cached to lighten the load. A smaller wagon was procured from Franklin Graves for the remaining belongings of the Reeds and Eddys. The emigrants continued to trudge along the Humboldt.[19]

About an hour after they had started, Hardcoop caught up with Eddy and let him know that Keseberg had once again put him out of the family wagon. Hardcoop said it was impossible for him to travel on foot, and he begged Eddy to let him ride in his wagon. His pleas were touching, but because the wagons were moving through deep loose sand, Eddy explained that he could not stop then but would as soon as he could.[20] Hardcoop said that he would try his best to keep up until that time.

As it turned out, the emigrants could not stop again until early evening. When they made camp, Hardcoop was not there. Some of the boys who had been driving livestock far behind the wagons said they had last seen him earlier that day. He was completely worn out, sitting shoeless under a clump of sagebrush. His feet had turned black and were so swollen the skin had split open.

A signal fire was set on a hillside in hopes that Hardcoop would see it and find his way into camp. The guards and Baylis Williams kept the fire going until morning, but there was no sign of Hardcoop. Margret Reed, Milt Elliott, and Eddy pleaded with Keseberg to go back and look for the old man, but he rebuffed them. Patrick Breen also refused to help or even lend them a horse, as did William Graves. They said it was not worth the risk of a man or horse to rescue an old man who was unfit to travel and had probably already been killed by Indians. When Pike, Eddy, and Elliott proposed to go on foot to search for Hardcoop and bring him back, the other emigrants told them they would not wait but would go on without them.[21] There was no time. That was the constant refrain—no time, no time, no time.

The book had not only closed on Hardcoop, it had slammed shut. The few who cared and gave a damn hoped his death was swift. The rest of them tried to forget about the nice old gent from Belgium whose first name they never knew . . . the man who was not worth their time.

The next day, in what could have been taken for an act of Old Testament retribution for their role in the abandonment of Hardcoop, the group hit a long stretch of exceptionally deep, loose sand that took more than twelve hours to cross. Finally, at four o'clock in the morning on October 10, they came upon the camp of the other part of the Donner Party.

There was an ominous feeling about the place. A month earlier, another party of emigrants, including several known to the Donner Party, had buried a fallen comrade. He had lingered for three days after having been wounded farther upstream on the Humboldt in a retaliatory attack on a sizable band of Paiutes who had stolen some of the emigrants' cattle.

Andrew Grayson, whose family had once traveled with the original Russell Party, also took part in that fight with the Paiutes but was unscathed. Another former member of the Russell Party, Benjamin S. Lippincott, took an arrow tipped with rattlesnake venom in his right leg but survived.[22]

The lone fatality was William Pierre Sallee, who was buried in a shallow grave in the middle of the trail. The emigrants ran their wagons over the grave to conceal it. Indians found it anyway and dug up the remains to get the dead man's clothing. They also took his scalp and mutilated his body. Wolves picked over Sallee's rotting remains and sun-bleached bones. They were still on display for the Donner Party, along with a board stuck in the sand on the side of the trail, bearing a warning about hostile Indians and a few words that told of the fight and Sallee's death.[23] The image of the dead man's scattered bones and the sign's stark warning stayed with the Donner Party that day as they consolidated even more and abandoned another wagon.

At camp that evening, those who were not with the second group heard the details, both true and false, about the death of Snyder and the abandonment of Hardcoop. An outpouring of accusations and finger pointing resulted, causing more bitterness in the ranks.[24] The squabbling created an opportunity for some Paiutes to quietly make off with all of the Graves family's horses. That put a damper on what already was a miserable forty-sixth birthday for Elizabeth Graves.[25] It also gave the emigrants who had wanted to go back for Hardcoop a chance to gloat because the horses Graves had refused to let them borrow were now gone.

The next day at the company's camp in a marshy area known as Big Meadows, Paiutes made another raid. They stole or killed with poisoned arrows eighteen head of cattle belonging to the Donner brothers and Wolfinger and snatched a milch cow from Graves. The Donners had no more oxen and would have to yoke cows to their wagons.

That night, the emigrants camped on boggy ground with little edible forage and difficult access to what turned out to be bad water. When Patrick Breen's mare became mired in a sinkhole, he turned to William Eddy for help. Eddy reminded Breen of his unwillingness to lend a horse to rescue Hardcoop and refused to give any assistance. Breen struggled alone but to no avail, and the horse smothered in the thick mud.[26]

At midnight on the cusp of October 12–13, the company reached the Humboldt Sink. In the final push that night, one of Eddy's oxen collapsed and was left beside the trail. The emigrants were barely out of sight when some lurking Paiutes appeared, brandishing knives, and quickly dispatched and butchered the animal.

Camp was made, and several guards stayed with the remaining livestock through the night. In the morning, all was quiet, and the weary sentries came into camp for breakfast. Before they could take a bite, the vigilant Paiutes pounced again and riddled twenty-one head of cattle with arrows. Most of the animals did not die outright but were wounded so badly that they had to be butchered for what little meat was left on their bones. There was no time to properly dry and preserve the meat, so it had to be eaten on the spot. Between the Indian depredations and the grueling journey itself, the company had very little livestock left. The Eddys and Wolfingers had one ox each. Both families had to leave their wagons behind.[27]

William Eddy buried the family's last few possessions, not sure if he would ever be able to retrieve them. The family would now have to travel only on foot. Eleanor would carry their infant, Margaret, and William would tote their son, James, and the only food left—a bit of tea and about three pounds of loaf sugar.[28]

Fortunately, the young German couple—Jacob Wolfinger and his wife—were traveling without the responsibility of children. Wolfinger had been a prosperous merchant and was thought to be carrying a large sum of money in gold coin and other valuables. That might have accounted for his decision to not leave until he had buried the wagon for safekeeping with his possessions inside.[29]

The rest of the company would not wait. Their hunger was unbearable. It had been more than a month since Stanton and McCutchen had gone for help. There were serious doubts that they ever would return. The emigrants faced a forty-mile march across an unforgiving alkali desert. They could not waste any more time. Wolfinger was on his own. No one even wished him luck.

At the last minute, Joseph Reinhardt and Augustus Spitzer—both of whom worked for Wolfinger—volunteered to stay behind and help bury the wagon. They would get the work done and catch up with the company while Wolfinger's wife continued with those who were leaving. The couple embraced, and the ragtag company departed. From the bluffs above, they could hear the Paiutes' laughter. Doris Wolfinger, who had started the westward journey wearing fine gowns and jewelry, walked into the desert empty-handed with a group of women and children. She would never see her husband again.[30]

The company's wagons, pulled by mixed teams of scrawny oxen and cows, reached a fork and took the right branch, called the Truckee Route. It was named for the friendly Paiute chief known for guiding emigrants along the edge of the desert and through the Sierra Nevadas. The route had no grass, water, or shade, only saltbush, greasewood, and a carpet of crusty salt and silt. The emigrants traveled at night to escape the punishing sun. Along the path, they saw discarded furniture and many dead horses, mules, and oxen, all of them with staring eyes and their tongues hanging from their mouths. If there was no moon, the emigrants set fire to abandoned wagons to show the way.[31]

About halfway across the desert on the Truckee Route, they reached Boiling Springs, where James Clyman's beloved spaniel had leaped into one of the pools and instantly been burned to death. The emigrants, who had heard about the incident earlier, scrambled to tie their dogs to wagons and keep livestock away from the water that would have scalded their muzzles and tongues.

At the hot springs, William Eddy took a bit of coffee that one of the Donner women had given him and mixed it with some boiling water. Eddy did not drink a drop but gave it to Eleanor and their two children. The bitter brew revived them, but their thirst was so great that Eddy feared they would die. Knowing that the Breen family had at least ten gallons of good water, Eddy asked for just a small amount for his children. Breen supposedly denied having any water at all, but when pressed by Eddy, admitted that he did have some but had to keep it for his own family. Eddy looked Breen in the eye and told him he was going to take some water or die trying. Eddy pushed past Breen, took some water, and returned to his family with it.[32]

A ridge of extremely deep sand made the final ten miles of the desert crossing some of the most challenging of the journey. Six more oxen dropped dead. The party pushed on, all of them aware that just ahead, on the banks of the Truckee, waited lush grazing grass, shade trees, and clean, cool water. Suddenly the desert seemed to disappear. After hundreds of miles of travel, they thought they saw trees. It was not a mirage. It was real. They saw glistening water and heard it rushing over smooth stones. They had reached the green banks of the Truckee River. The banks were soon lined with people and animals drinking in water until they were bloated.

But they were still hungry. Some of them had squirreled away a little food, but most had nothing or almost nothing. William and Margaret Eddy had not tasted any food at all for two days and two nights. All that their two children had was lumps of sugar to suck on. Eddy went to Elizabeth Graves for a piece of meat for his hungry children. She flatly refused. He went to Peggy Breen with the same request, and like her husband, she told him they had nothing to spare.

Breen heard the squawking of geese and saw some on the wing over the river. His gun had been broken on the trail, so Eddy borrowed Keseberg's weapon. He returned to camp with nine plump geese. A story that circulated for many years was that despite their rude behavior, Mrs. Graves and Mrs. Breen were given two geese each, and Keseberg got one as payment for the loan of his gun. Whether this tale was true or not, the Eddy family ate quite well that night.[33]

As the company headed up Truckee Canyon, Reinhardt and Spitzer rode in with a story to tell. They explained to the distraught Doris Wolfinger and others that some Paiutes had attacked them and killed Wolfinger. They said they were fortunate to have escaped. Some of the others in the party later said they found the story of Wolfinger's death at the hands of Indians plausible, but something did not seem quite right about the two survivors. They offered few details, and their behavior was guarded.[34] Philippine Keseberg, who of course also spoke German, comforted the shocked and grieving widow, as did other women from the party. Wolfinger was the third member of the Donner Party to die that October.

The company resumed moving in two groups up the south side of the winding Truckee. Thirst was quenched with ice-cold river water, but the emigrants needed nourishment. There was still no sign of Stanton and McCutchen. The canyon continued to be narrow, forcing as many as twenty-seven crossings. Then on October 20, the lead wagons of the Donner Party reached a broad valley known as Truckee Meadows.[35]

The Donner Party was now about forty miles from California and the Sierra Nevadas. The name, which translated as "snow-covered mountain range," was most fitting. Even in late October, under a gunmetal gray sky, the Sierra Nevadas stood high and silent, already covered with snow.

32. PERSEVERANCE

Stragglers from the fragmented Donner Party continued to drag into Truckee Meadows. They were the last emigrants of the season still on the trail, a full month behind the Bryant-Russell mule train. Even the children were aware that time—or rather, the lack of it—was a serious issue. Nevertheless, the emigrants were sharply divided about when to proceed.

"On Truckee River, the weather was already very cold, and the heavy clouds hanging over the mountains were strong indications of an approaching winter," John Breen later recalled. "This of course alarmed several people, while others paid no attention."[1]

Some emigrants—in fear of snowstorms blocking their passage through the mountains—wanted to push on as soon as possible. Others were relieved to find such an inviting, lush meadow. They wished to rest and give the few animals that remained time to recuperate. In what was by then a rare show of compromise, it was decided that in the company's best interest, they would stay in camp for at least a few days. People and livestock needed rest before tackling the Sierra Nevadas, the most difficult obstacle in their entire journey. Whether the emigrants showed good judgment by staying in camp was soon to be learned.

Meanwhile, on the other side of the mountains, James Reed and Walter Herron still struggled to reach Sutter's Fort. Both men were in desperate need of food. One week, they had only wild onions to eat. They had to keep on the move, and that made hunting game difficult. Herron became so ravenous that he wanted to kill Glaucus for food. The mare was worn out and could no longer bear the weight of a saddle. Reed calmed Herron by telling him that if they did not find relief soon, he would kill his beloved horse himself.[2]

"Soon after this he [Herron] became delirious," Reed explained later. They moved on, and Reed spied a single bean lying on the trail. He picked it up and gave it to Herron. They got down on their hands and knees and searched for more. "We found in all five beans," wrote Reed. "Herron's share was three of them."[3] It was not exactly a feast, but it inspired them to not give up.

"Next morning, after traveling a few miles, we saw some wagons," Reed recalled. "We soon reached and ransacked the wagons, hoping to find something to eat, but we found nothing. Taking the tar bucket [used for greasing wagon wheels] that was hanging under one of the wagons, I scraped the tar off and found a streak of rancid tallow at the bottom. . . . I handed the tar bucket to him having some of the tallow about the size of a walnut on it. This he swallowed without giving it a smell. I then took a piece myself but it was very repulsive."[4]

Herron, who apparently had a stronger constitution, wolfed down another portion and would have eaten still more, but Reed told him to stop. After walking a short distance, Reed experienced a wave of nausea and fleeting blindness, not uncommon with poison victims. He purged what little was in his shrunken stomach and stretched out in the grass.

After a rest, Reed rallied. When confronted with what appeared to be an insurmountable problem, he kept in mind his personal motto—persevere. All his life, it was that intense determination that helped Reed get through many difficulties. Often, it worked against him with others, who saw his perseverance as nothing more than stubbornness. On that October afternoon, Reed was not motivated solely by a fervent and heartfelt desire to rescue his wife and children. He also was very much driven by the same ambition that motivated so many others to make the risky and challenging pilgrimage to an unknown land.

After Reed recovered at least partially, he and Herron, leading a wobbly Glaucus, descended a steep slope into Bear Valley, where they came across more wagons at a campsite. The emigrants who greeted them had more than putrid grease for their hungry guests. Sitting by a fire and wrapped in blankets, Reed and Herron ate hunks of bread and slurped down sugared tea. Glaucus was fed and watered.

When a figure emerged from the shadows, they saw it was Charles Stanton on his way back to the Donner Party. At first glance, he did not recognize the hollow-eyed Reed and Herron, both so thin and drawn. But when they spoke, he knew who they were, and the three of them hugged and sat together. They talked for a long time, exchanging news of the emigrant party and the war with Mexico.

Stanton explained that in early October, after a hard and furious ride, he and William McCutchen had reached John Sutter's New Helvetia on the banks of the Sacramento River. Sutter lived up to his reputation of being a generous host for needy overlanders. His fort was considered a logical terminus of the California Trail, and he had welcomed and employed newly arrived emigrants ever since the first significant parties arrived in California in 1841.[5]

"At times my buildings were filled with immigrants. . . . Often it was necessary for me to go with my men and cattle to drag them in to safety out of the snow," Sutter later recalled.[6]

Sutter might have appeared to be the consummate host, but he was also a shrewd businessman with a growing enterprise to finance and manage. Profit was of great importance to the pragmatic Sutter. All those who partook of his generosity ultimately had to account for services and goods rendered. He was not opposed to giving credit, but with the clear understanding that the debt would be relieved as soon as possible. Once he had reviewed the letter Stanton gave him, signed by James Reed and promising payment in full, Sutter gladly supplied seven mules and what he thought would be enough provisions to last the Donner Party for the rest of the journey.[7]

Sutter also offered the services of two Miwok Indians, known only as Salvador, about nineteen years old, and Luis, about twenty-eight.[8] The Miwok people, indigenous to northern California, had endured the cruelty of the Spanish, who brought diseases along with the sword and cross in an attempt to force their culture and religion on Indian tribes they encountered. The same was true when Mexico claimed the land and kidnapped tribal people to work on large ranches along the coast. The Miwoks soon found that when white settlers came to their homeland, they were no different than the others. In some ways, they were worse. One of those who consistently preyed on the Miwoks was John Sutter.

When Sutter presented Luis and Salvador to Stanton and McCutchen, he called them "my good vaqueros," or cowboys, because they were skilled horsemen. In truth, both men were little more than slaves. Sutter had first become involved with the slave trade in 1838 when he bought an Indian boy once owned by Kit Carson.⁹ A native labor force was indispensable to Sutter's frontier enterprise, which operated much like a southern plantation. Sutter supplemented his income by selling Indians to rancheros and used slaves as payment for overdue debts. He kept Indian girls for his own pleasure and was known to have made a gift of a young girl to one of his friends.¹⁰

"The Capt. [Sutter] keeps 600 to 800 Indians in a complete state of Slavery and as I had the mortification of seeing them dine I may give a short description," James Clyman wrote after a visit to Sutter's Fort in 1846. "10 or 15 Troughs 3 or 4 feet long were brought out of the cook room and seated in the Broiling sun. All the Labouers grate and small ran to the troughs like so many pigs and fed themselves with their hands as long as the troughs contained even a moisture."¹¹

If Stanton and McCutchen witnessed the barbaric feeding procedure, they failed to mention it. Once they arrived at Sutter's Fort, "Big Bill" McCutchen, the robust outdoorsman, had become so ill he was not able to return with Stanton but had to stay behind to recover. Stanton was anxious to get back to the rest of the company. By October 18, he was back on the trail on a fresh horse with the mule train and the two Indian helpers.¹²

Sutter had no worries about "his Indians" going astray and not returning to the fort. Luis and Salvador knew only too well that Sutter would have them hunted down and punished. The diminutive Stanton was delighted to have two Miwok companions, especially since McCutchen had dropped out. Before the mule team left the emigrant camp in Bear Valley, Stanton gave Reed and Walter

Herron dried meat and flour to tide them over until they could reach Sutter's Fort.

Back at Truckee Meadows, the members of the Donner Party had given up on seeing Stanton and McCutchen again. Many emigrants were using their time to repair the few wagons that were left and to doctor livestock that had been wounded by Paiute arrows. It was not long before misfortune struck again.

Brothers-in-law William Pike and William Foster, two of the thirteen members of the extended Murphy-Pike-Foster family group, decided that instead of waiting for others to return with provisions, they would go themselves. The two men had been close friends for several years. They had been shipmates on the Mississippi steamship *La Salle* when it departed from Warsaw, Illinois, in the winter of 1842 and became icebound while headed for St. Louis.[13] Among the passengers was Levinah Murphy, a widow with seven children, including her eldest daughters, Sarah and Harriet. While the ship was marooned by ice, romance blossomed, and shortly after Christmas, Sarah married Foster and Harriet married Pike in a joint ceremony. Now with children of their own, the two couples were sharing a great adventure that would take them to the "wonderful land west of the Rocky Mountains," where Mother Murphy wanted to live with all her children and grandchildren.[14]

In preparing to ride off for the Sierra crossing, Pike and Foster packed a few things in saddlebags and curried their horses. They checked their weapons, including a small multibarreled handgun called a pepperbox because it resembled a household pepper grinder. Accounts differ about what happened next, but while Foster was holding the pistol—and perhaps loading it—the gun accidentally discharged and sent a bullet into Pike's back.[15]

The wound at such close range was mortal, but not instantly so. Pike writhed in pain and gasped for breath while his wife, Harriet, and other family members tried to comfort him. One of the Murphy children, Meriam (known as Mary), witnessed Pike's death and later wrote that "he died in about one half hour and in that time he suffered more than tongue can tell."[16] Harriet, only eighteen years old, was left a widow with two daughters, an infant and a toddler. The distraught Foster, a Roman Catholic convert, wept and prayed as he dug a grave in rocky soil. Once more, the pall of death hung over the emigrant camp.

By the time Pike was in his grave, several elements of the company were preparing to quit the meadowlands and head to the Sierras. They no longer operated as a functioning wagon train but for purposes of traveling fell into three distinct bands. The Breen family took the lead, with their friend Patrick Dolan out front. They had lost fewer cattle and generally fared better than the others. They also were the most vocal about pushing on to make the steep crossing before the snow became too deep. Accompanying the Breens and Dolan were the Eddys and Kesebergs.

The second group was comprised of the Murphys, Margret Reed and her children, and the extended Graves bunch, still the largest family unit despite the loss of Pike. Bringing up the rear and going at a slower pace were the Donner brothers with their families and teamsters and the Wolfinger widow.[17]

As had been the case for some time, the Donner Party did not travel as a single unified company. Even within the groups, each individual's only allegiance was to self or family. Survival was all that mattered. But what the emigrants had to bear in mind was that when their survival was threatened, struggles were bound to erupt between people and within families. Survival did not depend on being fearless. It was about the ability to make decisions, even if the decision was sometimes wrong. Calculated risks were worth taking. There was a thin line between survival and disaster. The Donner Party found it difficult to keep its balance on that line. In so doing, they often failed to persevere.

While they traveled upriver beneath heavy snow clouds, it was already cold, and the temperature fell lower. The cold numbed their minds and bodies. The cold was more lethal than poisoned arrows. It was a dangerous threat because it subdued the will to survive.

It was late October when the Breen faction moved farther into higher ground. Pat Dolan, riding just ahead of the others, saw what appeared to be another party coming toward him. He strained his eyes and let out a whoop and a holler. It was no mirage but the intrepid Charles Stanton and the Miwok escorts, Luis and Salvador. They had seven mules loaded with flour, jerked beef, sugar, beans, tea, coffee, and other foodstuffs.

The emigrants broke into cheers and the men waved their hats in the air as the mule train halted. The "excellent Stanton," as John Breen called him, and the Miwoks broke open the packs and doled out food to folks who had not had a decent meal for weeks.[18]

"Capt. John A. Sutter had given him [Stanton] the mules and provisions, for the mere promise of compensation, an act for which he deserves the love of every soul of that suffering company," young Breen later wrote. "He will always be remembered by me, with gratitude and reverence, for that generous act. And Mr. Stanton, who sacrificed his life to assist his companions—for he had no family or relations in the company—should be held in honored remembrance by every one who can appreciate a noble act. The clouds on the mountains looked very threatening, but he naturally looked at the bright side of things, and assured us there was no danger."[19]

Once the Breen group was resupplied, Stanton and his team continued to ride east to the next party of emigrants. There was another jubilant celebration. The Graves and Murphy families crowded around the three men, hailing them as heroes while they reached out for sacks of flour and packages of dried meat.

"Hungry as we were, Stanton brought us something better than food—news that my father was alive," wrote Virginia Reed. "Stanton had met him not far from Sutter's Fort; he had been three days without food and his horse was not able to carry him. Stanton had given him a horse and some provisions and he had gone on."[20]

The news that her husband was alive brought tears to Margret's eyes. She kindled a fire and baked a batch of biscuits, and Virginia gave one to each of her siblings. Later, after Stanton had made the rounds with the mule train and the provisions had all been distributed, he and the Indians returned to the Reeds. Thanks to Stanton, the family would no longer have to walk.

"We now packed what little we had left on one mule and started with Stanton," wrote Virginia. "My mother rode on a mule, carrying Tommy in her lap; Patty and Jim rode behind the two Indians, and I behind Mr. Stanton, and in this way we journeyed on through the rain, looking up with fear towards the mountains, where snow was already falling although it was only the last week in October. Winter had set in a month earlier than usual. All trails and roads were covered; and our only guide was the summit which it seemed we would never reach. Despair drove many frantic."[21]

The lead group, led by Dolan and the Breens, left the Truckee River after endless crossings and worked their way northwest up a narrow canyon. They crossed over a low range dotted with ponderosa pines and through what came to be called Dog Valley because of large packs of feral dogs that roamed the area. At camp just north of Crystal Peak—a huge block of solid quartz—William Eddy stood guard duty, toting a borrowed weapon because the lock of his rifle was still broken.

"They encamped on the top of a hill," Jessy Thornton later wrote, based on interviews with Eddy. "Here nineteen oxen [not likely all oxen but mostly cows] were shot by an Indian, who put an arrow in each ox. The cattle did not die. Mr. Eddy caught him in the act, and fired upon him as he fled. The ball struck him between the shoulders, and came out at the breast. At the crack of the rifle he sprung up about three feet, and with a terrible yell fell down a bank into a bunch of willows."[22]

At about this same time, the five wagons of the combined Donner families, along with Doris Wolfinger's wagon being driven by a teamster, were well behind the rest of the company but slowly closing the gap. George and Jacob Donner figured that if they could get in a good day or two of travel on the Truckee, they might catch up with the others.

All was going well until an axle on one of George Donner's wagons snapped on a steep rise. The wagon overturned with his daughters Eliza and Georgia inside. Four-year-old Georgia was located and pulled free, but there was no immediate sign of three-year-old Eliza.

Everyone frantically searched through the massive heap of quilts and clothing in the wagon box. Finally, Jacob Donner freed Eliza. She quickly came to and was still being fussed over by Tamzene when George and Jacob Donner felled a tree and went to work hewing a new axle. They were in a hurry to get the wagons rolling once again.[23]

"Uncle [Jacob Donner] was giving the finishing touches to the axle, when the chisel he was using slipped from his grasp, and its keen edge struck and made a serious wound across the back of Father's right hand which was steadying the timber,"[24] Eliza later wrote. Once Jacob stopped the flow of blood from George's wound, Tamzene carefully washed and dressed it with strips of clean cloth. Jacob was able to put the new axle in place, and with George's hand bandaged, the Donners moved on. To ease his brother's guilt, George joked that the gash was just a scratch, and they had more important things to worry about. He was partly correct. As Eliza would later put it, "The consequences of that accident, however, were far more wide-reaching than could have been anticipated."

Far ahead of the Donners, the rest of the company faced different consequences that resulted from poor decisions, inadequate preparation, quirks of fate, squandered opportunities, and failure to learn from mistakes. There was also plenty of bad advice. The old adage that good advice comes from a bad experience might have been true for some emigrants, but not for the Donner Party. They failed to heed good advice in favor of bad advice. As a result, they had already suffered through countless bad experiences.

Now, finally in California and so close to fulfilling their dreams, they would have to endure the worst.

FOUR

OUT OF TIME

33. SNOWBOUND

Death no longer startled the Donner Party, but it continued to stalk them in California. Now death tracked them from the Gulf of Alaska, ringed by mountains, forests, and tidewater glaciers that spilled onto the coastal plains.[1] As clouds grew and low pressure strengthened, the jet stream was forced south along the coastline. Clouds loaded with moisture rolled over sea and shore. The storm punched to the east, cascading over the coastal ranges. It climbed the High Sierras as moist air inside the clouds rose and cooled. The temperature was below freezing, changing the moisture to icy droplets that hardened into crystals. The crystals soon turned into snowflakes in a furious tempest that produced the heaviest snowfalls.

One such storm would have made the crossing over the Sierras challenging but possible. That was not the case in the autumn of 1846. Starting on October 16, much earlier in the season than usual, a large snowstorm struck the Sierras. Another big storm soon followed. Between mid-October and early April 1847, ten major snowstorms descended on the Sierras.[2] Each storm brought huge snowfalls.

It was almost November when the first two parties, almost two-thirds of the company, approached Truckee Lake (later renamed Donner Lake). Carved by glaciers and called the "Gem of the Sierras," the lake was slightly less than three miles long and about three-quarters of a mile wide. Fed by snowmelt and numerous creeks and springs, the lake was at the foot of the east flank of the Sierras, an almost vertical massive wall of smoothly rounded granite boulders.

To enter the promised land, the emigrants had to ascend more than seven thousand feet to Frémont Pass. Sutter's Fort was less than ninety miles away. The remnants of an early snowfall remained, but the emigrants, most of them lowlanders, were confident that it would not last. They had experienced plenty of snowstorms, even blizzards, where they came from in the Midwest. They knew that after a few days, the snow and ice always melted, and the sky cleared until the next storm. But weather systems in Illinois, Missouri, or Kentucky were not the same as in the High Sierras, where fierce storms could come in rapid succession and with a vengeance.

As the forward parties neared Truckee Lake, another early winter storm roared to life. It would continue for two weeks, with only a few pauses. "On the 30th of October, 1846, we camped in a pretty little valley about five miles from Donner Lake; that night it snowed about eight inches deep,"[3] William Graves, whose family was part of the second group of emigrants, recalled.

The next day, the lead party reached the lake, skirted the north shore, and headed toward the granite wall of the Sierra Nevadas. The grass was covered with snow and difficult to get to, so the men and boys cut pine boughs to feed the hungry cattle, worn out from moving through the snow. They also came across an abandoned "shanty"—as Patrick Breen called the small cabin—that looked promising as a refuge in case they had to turn back.[4]

"In the morning it was very cold, with about an inch of snow on the ground," recalled John Breen, the family's oldest son. "This made us hurry our cattle still more, if possible, than before. We traveled on, and, at last, the clouds cleared, leaving the towering peaks in full view, covered as far as the eye could reach with snow. This sight made us almost despair of ever entering the long sought valley of the Sacramento; but we pushed on as fast as our failing cattle could haul our almost empty wagons. At last we reached the front of the main ridge, near Truckee Lake. It was sundown."[5]

Young Breen and his father were pleased that by early evening, the wind had died down and the sky had cleared. October was turning to November. When the moon rose full, a large circle was around it. A lunar halo foretold an approaching storm.[6]

"Daylight came only to confirm our worst fears," John Breen wrote.

> The snow was falling fast on that terrible summit over which we yet had to cross. Not withstanding, we set out early to make an effort to cross. We traveled one or two miles—the snow increasing in depth all the way. At last it was up to the axle on the wagons. We now concluded to leave them, pack some blankets on the oxen, and push forward; but by the time we got the oxen packed, it was impossible to advance; first, because of the depth of the snow, and next, because we could not find the road; so we hitched to the wagons and returned to the valley again, where we found it raining in torrents. We took possession of a cabin and built a fire in it, but the pine boughs were a poor shelter from the rain, so we turned our cattle at large, and laid down under our wagon-covers to pass the night. It cleared off in the night, and this gave us hope; we were so little acquainted with the country as to believe that the rain in the valley was rain on the mountain also, and that it would beat down the snow so that we might possibly go over. In this we were fatally mistaken.[7]

The cabin where the Breens took shelter was the "shanty" they had found earlier. It had been built in the winter of 1844 by eighteen-year-old Moses Schallenberger and two other men of the Stevens-Townsend-Murphy Party, the first emigrants to take wagons over the Sierra Nevadas, opening the Truckee Route of the California Trail. The cabin leaked so much that the nine members of the Breen family spent the night in the wagon, bunched with their dogs under blankets and heaps of dirty clothing. They listened to the steady rainfall and heard the second group of emigrants arrive. The Breens were still determined to reach the pass, but a monsoon struck the next day. Everyone stayed in camp and watched the downpour. Some of them realized that rain at the lake meant it was snowing at the pass.

It seemed that the day would never end. By first light, the Breens and those traveling with them had yoked up their oxen. The snow at the lake was three feet deep, and the oxen, already weakened from a diet of pine branches, had problems just maneuvering around the lake, where the snow was deepening.

"We set out next morning to make a last struggle, but did not advance more than two miles before the road became so completely blocked that we were forced to retrace our steps in despair," John Breen later wrote. "When we reached the valley, we commenced repairing the house; we killed our cattle and covered it with their hides."[8]

As the Breens cached the butchered meat in the growing snow-drifts and repaired the cabin roof with hides, Charles Stanton with the two Miwoks, Luis and Salvador, and the rest of the middle group prepared to make their own attempt to scale the mountains. They were confident that with John Sutter's mules in the lead, a trail could be broken.

Besides Stanton and the Indians, others in the group included the Reed, Graves, and Eddy families. Lewis Keseberg also decided to go despite being lame. While hunting earlier in the journey, he had stepped on a willow stub that pierced his buckskin moccasin and penetrated the ball of his foot.[9] Keseberg and his wife washed and dressed the wound, but his foot became so swollen and inflamed that he was unable to walk for several days. He got some relief after another emigrant lanced the foot and Keseberg extracted a piece of the willow stub.[10] Determined to continue on the journey, Keseberg asked some of the men to boost him up on his horse. Once he was comfortable, they tied his foot into a sling attached to the saddle.

Before the emigrants could leave, it was determined that the wagons were too burdensome and had to be left behind. Instead, the remaining oxen and cattle would be used as pack animals to follow Stanton's mules. This decision caused much confusion in the ranks about which items should be left behind. Franklin Graves's main concern was what to do with his hoard of silver coins. Some of the women were determined to bring bolts of calico, and some men argued that a

crate of tobacco absolutely had to be packed.[11] The clearheaded emigrants knew that lugging such things was ludicrous. All they needed
was enough food to support them for six days, by which time they
would have reached Johnson's Ranch on the Bear River.

Regrettably, the more realistic emigrants did not prevail. That
became evident when a few emigrants who could not decide what was
essential chose to bring their wagons. Others were not overly anxious
to tackle the Sierras. They thought waiting out winter at the lake
might be a better option.

The rest of the party soon found that turning oxen into pack animals bearing unfamiliar loads on their backs was not easy. The oxen
bucked and bellowed and wallowed in the snow. They rubbed against
pine trees in an attempt to get rid of the packs. Finally, with ample
encouragement and prodding from the teamsters, the poor beasts
accepted their fate and complied.

It was midday by the time the party approached the pass. The
snow was waist deep and difficult to walk through, especially if one
was carrying a child or a sack of provisions. It was impossible to find
even a trace of the trail. One of the Indians, with Patty Reed clinging to him, rode a mule that kept its head down and barreled into
the snowdrifts, breaking a path for the others to follow. Emigrants
with wagons soon had to abandon them, unyoke the oxen, and trudge
through the snow with the others. There was a lull in the snowfall. The snow already on the ground, however, got deeper until the
exhausted pilgrims could go no farther.[12]

Stanton and one of the Miwoks went on by themselves to scout
ahead. They pushed through snow chest deep and reached the summit. Before them was the promise of life. Behind them was the threat
of death. Stanton had left the company once before to fetch provisions and had returned. Now he had another opportunity to leave.
If the possibility of not returning crossed his mind, he must have
considered the shivering people who waited for him. He also had
those borrowed mules that belonged to Sutter and the loyal Luis and
Salvador.

"Stanton had stoutly insisted upon taking the mules over the mountains," Charles F. McGlashan wrote in 1880. "Perhaps he did not wish to return to Capt. Sutter without the property which he had borrowed. Many in the train dissented from this proposition, and endeavored to induce the Indians, Lewis and Salvador, to leave Stanton, and guide them over the summits. The Indians realized the imminent danger of each hour's delay, and would probably have yielded to the solicitations of these disaffected parties, had not Stanton made them believe that Capt. Sutter would hang them if they returned to the Fort without the mules."[13]

Whatever the motivation, Stanton and the Miwoks made their way back through the drifting snow to the place where the rest of their party waited. As they neared the site, they saw what appeared to be a great column of roaring flames. In their absence, the others had decided they could go no farther in either direction and would spend the night. Someone had set fire to a tall pitchy pine covered in oozing resin. The emigrants were digging out places to sleep.[14] Stanton beseeched them to stop. He told them the summit was only about three miles ahead, and they could still get across before more snow fell.

No one heeded Stanton's plea, with the exception of Keseberg, who hobbled about on his one sound leg trying to persuade the others to resume their journey. "I begged them for God's sake to get over the ridge before halting," Keseberg later told McGlashan. "The weather looked very threatening, and I exhorted them to go on until the summit was reached."[15]

It was no use. The idea of a "forced march," as Virginia Reed referred to Stanton's plan, held no appeal for anyone.[16] The entire tree was consumed in flames, and the huddled emigrants basked in its warmth. Stanton and Keseberg saw that nothing they could say would get the party to budge. Stanton lit his pipe and probably second-guessed his decision to stay with the party. One of the Miwoks wrapped himself in a blanket and, like a sentinel, stood all night leaning against a tree. The makeshift camp was quiet except for the pop and crackle of pockets of resin in the burning wood.

Then the snow returned. Its arrival was like a scene from Celtic lore when the dead rose from their graves. Years later, Keseberg provided a description: "In the night I felt something impeding my breath. A heavy weight seemed to be resting upon me. Springing up to a sitting posture, I found myself covered with freshly-fallen snow. The camp, the cattle, my companions, had all disappeared. All I could see was snow everywhere. I shouted at the top of my voice. Suddenly, here and there, all about me, heads popped up through the snow. The scene was not unlike what one might imagine at the resurrection, when people rise up out of the earth. The terror amounted to panic. The mules were lost, the cattle strayed away, and our further progress rendered impossible."[17]

The few emigrants who managed to get some sleep awoke to find that another foot of snow had fallen overnight. Drifts ten feet tall surrounded them. The big pine was a charred, smoldering stump. They shook the snow off their clothing and blankets and managed to light a new fire. It was painfully clear that they could not continue to the summit. The pass was blocked.

If Lansford Hastings had somehow magically appeared before those wretched souls, he would have been hanged or buried alive in a snowbank. Many of them faulted Hastings for inspiring James Reed to take the now infamous shortcut route that was spelled out in just a single sentence in the guidebook. Once highly touted, the book was of no further use to the emigrants except as fire tinder or for use after bowel movements. Yet six pages after Hastings wrote of the alternative route, he offered another tip that probably would have worked if the Donner Party had managed its time better. It was short and to the point: "Unless you pass over the mountains early in the fall, you are very liable to be detained, by impassable mountains of snow, until the next spring, or, perhaps, forever."[18]

Those were words to live or die by. Those were words for the whole lot of them to chew over as they retreated to Truckee Lake, which in itself was far from easy. Even going downhill was a struggle. It was late afternoon before they reached the lake. The Breens were firmly ensconced inside the cabin. The rest of the emigrants made do. They would begin to build their own shelters in the morning.

There was still no sign of the Donner family entourage. Their progress had been hampered by the wagon accident and the injury to George Donner's hand when he and Jacob replaced the broken axle. The last persons from the lake camp to see the Donners were two messengers who had ridden back to warn them that the pass above the lake was blocked with snow.

The Donners were far behind the rest of the company. Although George made light of his injury and tried to help with the work, he could not use his right hand and was in constant pain. The deep gash was more serious than first thought. Tamzene cleaned the wound every day and wrapped the puffy hand in the cleanest cloth she could find, but it was not healing. It remained inflamed and tender to even Tamzene's gentle touch. Donner "was like a one armed man when we reached camp," Jean-Baptiste Trudeau, the young teamster hired by the Donners at Fort Bridger, recalled years later.[19]

Tamzene realized George's wound needed proper medical attention as soon as possible. She wanted the party to keep moving. Even if the pass was blocked, Tamzene—like all the others—told herself the snow would stop and they could go ahead. Besides, there was strength in numbers, and it would be in her family's best interest to be with the rest of the company. George and Jacob disagreed with Tamzene. They decided that before continuing, they would cache everything but the bare essentials and then take the wagons apart and build carts that could be pushed and pulled on the trail. After further discussion and more time lost, that idea was scrapped.

"Their next scheme was to pack the oxen, ours were gentle and packed all right but Uncle Jake's did not like their new burden and jumped and kicked until they had scattered everything," Frances Donner wrote many years later.[20]

Ultimately, they repacked the wagons and moved on, not stopping until they reached the junction of Alder Creek and Prosser Creek, about six or seven miles northeast of Truckee Lake.[21] Wary of the storm clouds hovering over the mountains ahead, George thought they had found a suitable winter campsite near water in a valley that at the time was free of snow. The wagons were unloaded, the oxen unhooked, and work commenced on building a cabin. George tried to help despite his injured hand, and Jacob was already feeble. Much of the work was carried out by the hired hands and the women and children who were able-bodied or big enough to lend a hand. Some felled trees and cut them into logs. Others trimmed off the branches, and the teamsters wrapped chains around the logs so the oxen could drag them into place.

The cabin walls were only four logs high when work suddenly stopped. Snow began to fall. The emigrants could see it coming, like a great curtain of white ashes bearing down on them. It was the same storm that forced the other two groups to dig in at the lake. By the time the snow reached the Donners at Alder Creek, the storm had worked itself into a swirling frenzy. Trudeau remembered the ferocity of that storm for the rest of his life. "The snow came on with blinding fury and being unable to build cabins we put up brush sheds" in "that camp of snow and suffering," he recalled.[22]

Leanna Donner, one of George's daughters from his second marriage and only twelve years old during the winter of 1846–1847, shared similar memories of the snowstorm in a letter in 1878. "We had no time to build a cabin," she wrote. "The snow came on so suddenly that we barely had time to pitch our tent, and put up a brush shed, as it were, one side of which was open. The brush shed was covered with pine boughs, and then covered with rubber [rain] coats, quilts, etc. My uncle, Jacob Donner, and family, also had a tent, and camped near us."[23]

George Donner's camp—a tent and brush shed—was on the north side of the creek next to a large pine. A shallow hole was dug near the tree trunk to serve as a hearth for cooking. The tent was sleeping quarters. Crude beds were fashioned from poles and pine boughs. It was a tight but cozy squeeze for George and Tamzene, the five Donner daughters, and the recently widowed Dorthea Wolfinger. In addition, although many accounts of the Donner Party purported that the teamsters lived apart from the family in a wigwam-style hut, no evidence of it was ever found. Most members of the Donner family stated that the single men, Baptiste Trudeau and Joseph Rein-hardt, lived in their shelter.[24]

Jacob Donner's camp was about three hundred yards up the creek in a clearing with no trees nearby. Members of George Donner's family later remembered that as the snow continued to fall, Uncle Jake's camp could not be seen because of the high snowdrifts. When anyone from the other camp wanted to visit, they had to look for smoke rising from behind the snow to show the way.

George Donner's children sensed that they were in dire straits just by watching their father. His hand throbbed with pain, but he did not complain. He spoke very little but spent much of the time staring into the fire with dull and lifeless eyes. George and Jacob Donner must have been depressed. They had figured that by now, they would be acquiring land for their first spring crop in California. Likewise, Tamzene, who long before had stopped collecting botanical specimens, had to be wondering if her dream of opening a school for young ladies would ever come true. Outside, the howling wind stopped, and the snow fell silently and deep.

"For eight consecutive days, the fatal snow fell with but few short interruptions," wrote Eliza Donner.

> Eight days, in which there was nothing to break the monotony of torturing, inactive endurance, except the necessity of gathering wood, keeping the fires, and cutting anew the steps which led upward, as the snow increased in depth. Hope nigh-well died with us. Axes were dull, green wood was hard to cut, and harder to carry, whether through loose, dry snow, or over crusts made slippery by sleet and frost. Cattle tracks were covered over. Some of the poor creatures had perished under bushes where they sought shelter. A few had become bewildered and strayed; others were found under trees in snow pits, which they themselves had made by walking round and round the trunks to keep from being snowed under. These starvelings were shot to end their sufferings, and also with the hope that their hides and fleshless bones might save

the life of a snow-beleaguered party. Every part of the animals was saved for food. The locations of the carcasses were marked so that they could be brought back piece by piece into camp; and even the green hides were spread against the huts to serve in case of need.[25]

At the Truckee Lake camp, the emigrants had no time to worry about those at the Donners' camp. They had more than enough to deal with, especially the priorities of food and shelter. Keseberg's injured foot prevented him from building a proper cabin for his wife and two children. Instead, he and fellow Germans Augustus Spitzer and Charles Burger slapped together a lean-to shed from cut poles and pine branches. They constructed it on the west end of the old Schallenberger cabin, which had been appropriated by the Breens.[26] Besides the nine members of the Breen family, the cabin also provided shelter for their friend Patrick Dolan and the drover known only as Antonio.

The other emigrants built sturdy cabins. About two hundred yards south of the Breen cabin, William Eddy, with assistance from William Foster and some of the Murphys, erected a cabin of unpeeled pine logs against the flat side of a huge boulder. The boulder was used as a natural hearth that allowed smoke to rise through a gap between the flat roof and the boulder. When completed, the cabin was home for sixteen people—the Eddy, Murphy, Foster, and Pike families.[27]

Franklin Graves selected a site for a cabin that would house his family, the Reeds, and several others about a half mile downstream from the other cabins. "Father built his cabin where it was most sheltered from wind and storm and wood near by regardless of company interest, I supposed," was how Graves's daughter Mary explained it in 1879. Patty Reed had her own theory. She later wrote that Graves built the cabin away from the other emigrants "because he wished to for he, & all of his family, had minds & wills of their own."[28]

It was a large double cabin—two rooms, each with its own fireplace, separated by a log wall. The Graves family and Amanda McCutchen, whose husband was at Sutter's Fort, and her infant daughter lived in one chamber, and Margret Reed and her five children and their employees took the other side. They were joined by Stanton and the two Miwok guides. Like the other cabins, there were no windows, and each side had its own door. That reduced the tension between the Graves family and the Reeds that resulted from James Reed having killed the Graves family's teamster, John Snyder.

Although some emigrants still had a glimmer of hope that they would escape the Sierras sooner rather than later, the realists among the company knew that the stage was set for a long winter siege. Of the eighty-seven members of the Donner Party plus the addition of the Miwoks, Luis and Salvador, eighty-one people were trapped in separate camps in the Sierra Nevadas. Fifty-nine were at the lake camp, and twenty-two were dug in at the Alder Creek camp about six miles away. More than half were under eighteen, and many of those were young children or infants.[29]

All of them—for better or worse—were sheltered, but the provisions that Stanton and the Miwoks had brought from Sutter's Fort were almost gone. The emigrants had started to kill their cattle, but once all the livestock was gone, there would be no way to get the wagons over the summit. Even more serious was the fact that some emigrants still had cattle and oxen and others did not. Would anyone share what little food they had with others? How far would people go to feed their hungry children? When would the snow stop? Was any more help coming? Where was James Reed?

34. DESPERATE TIMES, DESPERATE MEASURES

In the Sierra wilderness, the shared dream of the members of the Donner Party became a nightmare. Marooned by a deep ocean of snow that almost never stopped falling, they were constantly cold, hungry, and afraid. Their prospects were not good. Neither was morale. Yet all was not lost. They had not been forgotten. On the other side of the Sierras was the dogged James Reed, who rode a horse named for a Greek sea god and whose personal motto was "Persevere." Reed was committed to rescuing his wife and children and in so doing save the overlanders who had seen fit to banish him from their company.

On October 28, 1846, the emaciated and haggard Reed and Walter Herron reached Sutter's Fort. John Sutter greeted them, as did several former comrades from the Russell Party who had opted to not take the Hastings Cutoff, including Edwin Bryant, William "Owl" Russell, George McKinstry, Benjamin Lippincott, Andrew Grayson, and others. That same day, Lilburn Boggs and his family arrived at Sutter's Fort and joined in the reunion.[1] In the evening, after enjoying a meal he had dreamed about for weeks, Reed caught up on news of the ongoing war between Mexico and the United States.

Reed must have been intrigued to learn about the Bear Flag Republic and a short-lived rebellion that had broken out in Alta California in June when rumors circulated that the Mexican authorities were about to exile all foreign settlers who were not citizens. This news would have been of particular interest to Reed because the leader of the Bear Flag Revolt was William Brown Ide, the former Springfield farmer and schoolteacher whose emigrant company that had gone to California in 1845 included Robert Caden Keyes, Reed's brother-in-law.[2]

Keyes's presence in California was one reason why his elderly mother, Sarah Keyes, had traveled with the Reed family in 1846. She wished to see her son, but she had died before reaching California. The family later received word that Keyes disliked California and had gone to Oregon. Now Reed found out that Keyes had changed his mind and returned to California.[3]

Reed was told that another acquaintance from Springfield, William Levi Todd, nephew of Mary Todd Lincoln and a member of the Ides caravan, had taken an active role in the revolt.[4] Todd had designed the distinctive California Bear Republic flag, made from unbleached cotton, which depicted a lone red star, a grizzly bear, and the words CALIFORNIA REPUBLIC.[5] Although the revolt had lasted only twenty-two days, Todd and the "Bear Flaggers" then joined the forces of John C. Frémont in the effort to wrest California away from Mexico. Frémont was in command of the California Battalion, a combined force of members from his surveying crew and volunteers from the Bear Flag Republic.

But that night at Sutter's Fort, Reed and his friends received fresh war news sent from Frémont at his headquarters in Monterey, California. According to Frémont, a large number of enemy troops had driven off a force of Americans, and the garrisons at Los Angeles and Santa Barbara had escaped or retreated.[6] Unknown to anyone in California until that evening, Frémont had been commissioned a lieutenant colonel the previous May by President James K. Polk. Frémont was now sending out a call for volunteers to join a new regiment of riflemen to engage the enemy.[7]

Bryant wrote in his memoir, "On receipt of this intelligence, I immediately drew up a paper which was signed by myself, Messrs. Reed, Jacob, Lippincott, and Grayson, offering our services as volunteers, and our exertions to raise a force of emigrants and Indians which would be a sufficient reinforcement to Colonel Fremont. This paper was addressed to Mr. Kern [U.S. Navy Lieutenant Edward M. Kern], the commandant of Fort Sacramento [Sutter's Fort], and required his sanction. The next morning (29th) he [Kern] accepted our proposal, and the labor raising the volunteers and procuring the necessary clothing and supplies for them and the Indians was apportioned."[8]

Reed signed the document that committed him to serve with the volunteer force, but with the caveat that first he be allowed to take provisions back to the Donner Party. "The companies were to be officered by the petitioners," Reed later explained. "Being requested to take command of one of the companies, I declined, stating that it would be necessary for the Captain to stay with the company; also, that I had to return to the mountains for the emigrants; but that I would take a Lieutenantcy. This was agreed to, and I was on my return to the emigrants to enlist all the men I could between there and Bear Valley."[9]

William McCutchen stepped forward. Worried about his wife and infant daughter and fully recovered from the illness that had stopped him from returning with Charles Stanton, he was eager to accompany Reed.

Sutter was just as eager to equip Reed, especially when cash collateral was offered until the animals were safely returned and a promise was made to pay off the balance.[10] It appeared that Reed, who had traveled to California because of bankruptcy, had kept a secret stash. Perhaps Abraham Lincoln, who by then was serving in Congress, had helped Reed find a way to keep a cash reserve. Sutter immediately allotted Reed and McCutchen thirty horses, a mule, a hindquarter of beef, and an ample supply of flour and beans. Sutter also assigned two more of his Miwok Indian vaqueros to help drive the pack train through the snow.[11]

In early November, Reed, McCutchen, and the two Miwoks departed Sutter's Fort leading the long string of horses. They rode through rain for four consecutive days before reaching the head of the Bear River, where they found eighteen inches of snow. Reed hoped that by the time they reached the valley, they would come across the Donner Party, but the emigrants were nowhere to be seen. On the evening of November 5, heavy rain turned to sleet and continued all night. "We drove on until a late hour before halting," Reed wrote. "We secured the flour and horses, the rain preventing us from kindling a fire."[12]

The next morning, the snow was more than two feet deep at the foot of Emigrant Gap when they came upon the camp of Jotham Curtis and his wife.[13] Overlanders from Missouri, they had broken away from their wagon train because of a disagreement. Because of the threatening weather, they chose to take their chances in a winter camp. It seemed to Reed that the couple had used their last chance. Their oxen had run off, and their food supply was gone.

"They hailed us as angels sent for their delivery, stating that they would have perished had it not been for our arrival," Reed wrote.

> Mrs. Curtis stated that they had killed their dog, and at the time of our arrival had the last piece in the Dutch oven baking. We told them not to be alarmed about anything to eat, for we had plenty, both of flour and beef; that they were welcome to all they needed. Our appetites were rather keen, not having eaten anything from the morning of the day previous. Mr. Curtis remarked that in the oven was a piece of the dog, and we could have it. Raising the lid of the oven, we found the dog well baked, and having a fine savory smell. I cut out a rib, smelling and tasting, found it to be good, and handed the rib over to Mr. McCutchen, who, after smelling it some time, tasted it and pronounced it very good dog. We partook of Curtis' dog. Mrs. Curtis immediately commenced baking bread, and in a short time had supper for all.[14]

Before leaving the Curtis campsite in the morning, Reed promised to retrieve the couple on his return trip to Sutter's Fort. He also left enough flour and beef to tide them over. The Reed party slogged through deep snow all day before making camp on the mountain. During the night, they heard what sounded like horses moving down the trail and discovered that the two Miwoks had sneaked away, taking some of the horses with them. McCutchen quickly saddled his horse and rode back to the Curtis camp, where he learned that the Indians had stopped there to rest by the fire before continuing to the valley.

McCutchen returned to Reed, and they went on. Before long, they could not find a trace of a trail because of the snow. The long string of horses, carrying heavy packs, struggled to move forward. "We pushed them on until they would rear upon their hind feet to breast the snow, and when they would alight they would sink in it until nothing was seen of them but the nose and a portion of the head," Reed later recalled. "Here we found that it was utterly impossible to proceed further with the horses. Leaving them, we proceeded further on foot, thinking we could get in to the people, but found that impossible, the snow being soft and deep."[15]

They were only about ten or twelve miles from the summit but could go no farther. Even if they had been able to reach the summit and descend to the emigrant camps, it would have done no good since they had left the packs of food behind. Reluctantly, they returned to their horses, dug them out of the snow, and backtracked to the Curtis camp. There they hung the dried meat in trees and cached the flour and other provisions in a wagon while Curtis and his wife packed a horse for the trip to Sutter's Fort. In the valley, there was little snow, and there was plenty of underbrush for the hungry horses to browse on.

"As soon as we arrived at Capt. Sutter's, I made statement of all the circumstances attending our attempt to get into the mountains," Reed wrote in 1871. "He was not surprised by our defeat. I also gave the Captain the number of head of cattle the company had when I left them. He made an estimate, and stated that if the emigrants would kill the cattle, and place the meat in the snow for preservation, there was no fear of starvation until relief could reach them. He further stated that there were no able-bodied men in the vicinity, all having gone down the country with and after Frémont, to fight the Mexicans. He advised me to proceed to Yerba Bueno, now San Francisco, and make my case known to the naval officer in command."[16]

Reed, disappointed that his first two attempts to reach his family had failed, pondered his next move. Meanwhile, his wife, Margret, stranded with the rest of the company on the other side of the Sierras, tried to come up with a way to keep her children alive. If she had had just a little of her husband's secreted money, her worries would have been over.

The Breen and Graves families still had about six oxen each. The Murphys had a few, and the Eddys had just one. Margret Reed had none. She was in dire straits, just like all the single men who had to trust in the good will of their employers to survive. Despite her migraines, Margret—who knew no one would be willing to just give her food—found the strength to approach Franklin Graves to see about buying an ox.[17] Graves was still upset with the Reeds because of the killing of his teamster, but he could not let a woman and children starve to death. He sold Margret two of his lean oxen on credit with the stipulation that the money had to be paid back double if the party ever made it across the mountains. The Breens sold Margret another pair of oxen and must have been somewhat pleased that William Eddy was forced to come up with $25 to purchase a dead ox from Franklin Graves. Levinah Murphy's son-in-law Jay Fosdick talked Breen into selling two oxen in exchange for a gold watch.[18]

The families began the process of slaughtering the oxen. They spared the mules for the time being because they would have to be accounted for at Sutter's Fort. The farmers, such as Breen and Pat Dolan, were used to killing and butchering, but even they had a difficult time. Most of these beasts had served the company faithfully for many months and shared in all the hardships along the way. Now they were seen solely as food.

After the ox was shot in the head or struck on the head with a sledge, its throat was quickly cut, and as much blood as possible was captured in vessels.[19] The deep snow likely resulted in the animals being butchered on the ground instead of being hung by the hind feet from a stout tree limb. Large cuts of meat were stacked in the snow and froze quickly, and the blood was consumed while it was still warm or was used for cooking. The emigrants harvested the ox's brain and organs and cut out the tongue. The tail was sliced into sections for soup. Bones were cracked open to get at the marrow. Hide was good for shelter covers. Like the Indians on the open plains who used every part of the bison for their needs, the emigrants finally learned to do the same with their oxen.

To further supplement his food supply, almost every day, Eddy borrowed a rifle from William Foster and went hunting. All the deer had retreated to lower elevations for the season, and there was sparse game in the snowdrifts. He succeeded in bagging a prairie wolf (coyote) that made a good supper for Eddy's entire cabin. On another day, he shot an owl, but the stringy meat did not go far after Eddy gave half to Foster as the fee for borrowing his gun.[20]

By November 12, the snow had stopped, and the skies were clear. This change inspired some of the emigrants to make another attempt to climb the mountain and go through the pass to find help for those left behind. The party was made up of thirteen men, led by Graves and Charles Stanton, and two women, sisters Mary Graves and Sarah Foster.[21] They left the camp with the best of intentions, all bundled up and each with just a piece of meat for rations. They somehow managed to work their way through high snowdrifts and up ravines, but the soft snow was at least ten feet deep. They had to call a halt to the trek well short of the divide. They made it back to the lake camp at about midnight, not in time to get even a whiff of the two ducks Eddy had killed that afternoon.

The following day, Eddy—claiming to feel faint from hunger—went out again, hoping to return with something larger than fowl. He found some large tracks in the snow that he surmised could have been made only by a bear, probably a grizzly.[22] It was not long until Eddy found the bear busily digging through the snow to get at some roots. Eddy took careful aim and fired. The bear immediately reared up on its hind legs and charged Eddy, who was standing behind a tree. By the time the wounded bear reached him, Eddy had reloaded, and after a brief chase around the tree, he shot the bear and brought it down. Eddy used a tree branch to club the bear to death and went for help.

He returned with Graves. They chained the bear to an ox and dragged the carcass back to the camp. Eddy gave Foster half the meat for the use of the gun and gave a portion to Graves for the loan of the ox. He also gave a share to the Reed family.[23] Meat from the bear, estimated to have weighed eight hundred pounds, and oxen meat sustained the emigrants for a while as they shored up their shelters and wondered how they could hold out until the spring thaw.

On November 20, Patrick Breen began to keep a diary. It was the only daily chronicle of events at the Donner Party camps that survived that terrible winter of 1846–1847. This remarkable document was written on eight small sheets of paper folded to make a thirty-two-page book, of which three remained blank except for the word "Journal" written by Breen on the last page. The writing style was succinct, straightforward, and often understated, like the monotone brogue of the author.[24]

In the first entry, one of the longest in the diary, Breen summarized the emigrants' situation from the time of arrival at what became their winter home.

> Friday Nov. 20th 1846. Came to this place on the 31st of last month that it snowed we went on to the pass the snow so deep we were unable to find the road, when within 3 miles of the summit then turned back to this shanty on the lake, Stanton came one day after we arrived here we again took our teams & waggons & made another unsuccessful attempt to cross in company with Stanton we returned to the shanty it continueing to snow all the time we were here we now have killed most part of our cattle having to stay here until next spring & live on poor beef without bread or salt it snowed during the space of eight days with little intermission, after our arrival here, the remainder of time up to this day was clear & pleasant freezing at night the snow nearly gone from the valleys.[25]

While Breen was writing his first diary entry, other emigrants, encouraged by the melting snow around the camps, prepared to make another effort to cross the mountains on foot.

"My father was a native of Vermont, near the Green Mountains, and had some idea of the snow Mountain," William Graves wrote in 1877 of Franklin Graves. "He would not risk the snow going off, but kept trying to get over. About two weeks after we stopped here [Truckee Lake], the weather was clear and pretty, the snow nearly all gone in the valley, so father proposed trying to cross on foot; about 20 started with him."[26]

In fact, that party numbered twenty-two—six women and sixteen men—including Stanton and the two Miwoks, concerned with what John Sutter thought about their prolonged absence. On the morning of November 21, the party set off with only a few supplies in packs and loaded on seven mules. Breen recorded their departure in his diary:

"Sat. 21st Fine morning wind N:W 22 of our company are about starting across the mountains this morning including Stanton & his Indians, some clouds flying thawed to day wnd. E."[27]

Most of the men and all of the women in the party came from the lake camp. Lewis Keseberg, still nursing his wounded foot, stayed put. So did Breen, suffering from "the gravels"—painful kidney stones. The only one from the Donner camp at Alder Creek who hiked up to join the party was young Jean-Baptiste Trudeau. The first day out, they made good time. Much of the snow had melted, and that which remained was covered with a thick crust. They made it through the pass, where Eddy measured the snow and found it was twenty-five feet deep.[28] That evening, they camped in a valley on the west side of the Sierras. It was bone-chilling cold, and kindling a fire was not easy in the wind with six feet of snow at seven thousand feet above sea level. As it turned out, that was as far as the party would go.

A squabble erupted between Stanton and some of the others over the mules. Although the crusted snow made it easier for humans to walk, the mules were too heavy and broke through the thick crust. They were totally exhausted and slowed down the party. When it was suggested that the mules be left behind so the emigrants could make a quicker descent to the valley, Stanton strongly disagreed. He argued that the mules were the property of John Sutter, and neither Stanton nor the Miwoks, Luis and Salvador, would consider leaving the mules to die.

Without the three men most familiar with the trail to guide them, the rest of the party knew they could go no farther. Eddy tried his best to change Stanton's mind, but it was no use. The next day, the dejected members of the expedition—and all seven of the mules— plodded into an icy wind back over the pass and made it to the dark and silent camp at about midnight. At the same time, in the Gulf of Alaska, another storm was coming to life.

Breen wrote, "Tuesday 24th Fine in the morning towards evng cloudy & windy wind W looks like snow freezeing hard. Wendsday 25th Wind about W N W cloudy looks like the eve of a snow storm our mountaineers intend trying to cross the mountain tomorrow if fair froze hard last night."

The next day—the last Thursday in November—was celebrated in some states as Thanksgiving Day. That very month in the United States, a campaign was started to make the last Thursday of November a national holiday.[29] There were no observances and certainly no feasts in the Sierras. After a gale of snow made its entrance, the "mountaineers," as Breen called Graves, Eddy, and the others intent on escaping their snowy prison, sensibly determined that another attempt was too risky.

That morning at the Alder Creek camp, some of the emigrants remained confident that relief would come or someone would get over the mountains and find help. With that in mind and despite the fact that his wounded arm had not healed, George Donner managed to scribble a note. It read:

Donners Camp Nov 28 1846
This is to certify that I authorize Milford Elliott and make
him my agent to purchase and buy whatever property he may
deem necessary for my distress in the mountains for which
my arrival in California I will pay the Cash or goods or both

2 Gallons salt

$3 worth Sugar

150 # Flour

3 Bus Beans

50 # Cake Tallow

5 pack mules and two horses—purchase or hire[30]

During the first month of that terrible winter entrapment, other emigrants, such as Jacob Donner and William Foster, wrote similar authorization notes. None of them was fulfilled. Nothing was certain except that more snow would fall. For days, Breen's diary told the story—"Continues to snow," "Snowing fast," "deep soft wet snow," "still snowing," "Killed my last oxen today," "hard to get wood," and, as December was about to commence, the ominous: "Snowing fast wind W about 4 or 5 feet deep, no drifts, looks as likely to continue as when it commenced no living thing without wings can get about."[31]

The first days of December brought more snow. When it cleared briefly, the emigrants emerged from their shelters to find that the remaining horses and cattle were dead and buried under snow. Sutter's mules were also gone—the mules that Stanton had refused to abandon. They likely were buried in the snow or had been stolen by Washoe Indians who wintered in the area and got around on snowshoes. It made no difference how the animals had disappeared. They were gone, and so was a valuable source of food. The men and boys had no luck probing the snow with long poles in hopes of at least finding the dead animals to butcher.

The deep snow also made it difficult for anyone to gather firewood. All the wood that could be uncovered was wet, and dead wood was impossible to find. The tops of pines poking out from the snowbanks were cut off for firewood, but the green wood created so much smoke in the cabin fireplaces that it drove the occupants out into the elements. Some of the more desperate emigrants began to chip away at the logs of their cabins for tinder. In time, the wagons, built of oak, were taken apart and burned for kindling.

At the lake camp, there was still a little meat, but not much else. Augustus Spitzer was so sick and weak from hunger that he no longer could sit up. The Breens took pity on him and moved him from the crowded Keseberg lean-to into their cabin, where he would find more comfort. Margret Reed's time was spent doling out small rations of meat to her children and helping the family servant, Eliza Williams, nurse her half brother, the albino Baylis Williams, as he steadily succumbed to malnutrition.

Meanwhile, the stronger emigrants looked for ways to stay alive. Throughout the first two weeks of December, Franklin Graves and Charles Stanton put their knowledge of making snowshoes to good use. None of the others in the company had ever used snowshoes, but Graves and Stanton convinced the flatlanders that if they knew how to walk, they could snowshoe,[32] distributing their weight over a larger area so their feet would not sink. They dug through the snow to salvage discarded wooden oxbows to make into frames for snowshoes. Women and girls were enlisted to cut long strips of rawhide from cattle skins for bindings. The goal was to make at least fifteen pairs of snowshoes, wait for a clear day, and then slog through the deep snow and glide across the powder to freedom. Graves made the rounds of the camp, recruiting candidates for the snowshoe party.

In preparation for the next expedition, Stanton wrote a note to Tamzene Donner at Alder Creek asking her to send him a pound of their "best tobacco" and the loan of a pocket compass to use on the trek.[33] Tamzene complied, but tobacco and compasses were the last things on her mind. Her husband's arm was badly infected, and from all appearances, his health would only decline. Her brother-in-law, Jacob Donner, was on his deathbed, and three of the party's young men—Sam Shoemaker, Joseph Reinhardt, and James Smith—were close to that point.[34]

"Three of our men became dispirited, said that they were too weak and hungry to gather wood, and did not care how soon death should put an end to their miseries," Eliza Donner wrote in her memoir.

"The out-of-door duties would have fallen wholly upon my Aunt Betsy's two sons and on John Baptiste and on my crippled father, had the women lost their fortitude. They, however, hid their fears from their children, even from each other, and helped to gather fuel, hunt cattle, and keep camp."[35]

But as the long, frigid December days passed at the Alder Creek camp, there were no more cattle to be hunted. Wood was scarce. The only things to eat were roasted mice and a gelatinous broth of the glue that formed in cooking pots when cattle hides and a moldy bison robe were boiled. It was repulsive, but it helped to quell the gnawing feeling in a shrunken belly. Cradled in George Donner's good arm and with all the children snuggled close, Tamzene could escape in sleep to her parlor in Illinois, filled with friends, books, laughter, and flowers—lots and lots of flowers.

35. THE FORLORN HOPE

DECEMBER 1846

The time for dying began less than two weeks before Christmas. At the lake camp, the first to go was Baylis Williams, the Reed family's albino hired man who, because of his sensitive eyes, had slept in the wagons by day and tended fires and took care of chores at night. He had been sickly throughout the long journey, and by the time the company became trapped in two camps, he was laid low with fever, diarrhea, and what appeared to be pneumonia.[1]

Williams stayed curled up beneath a blanket in the Reeds' half of the cabin, shared with the Graves family. His half sister, Eliza, and Margret Reed tended to him, but there was little food, and he had no interest in eating. Near the end, Williams displayed symptoms consistent with malnutrition, including delirium. On December 15, Williams—said to have been crazy with fever—cried out and died.[2] He was twenty-five.

"Baylis Williams, who had been in delicate health before we left Springfield, was the first to die; he passed away before starvation had really set in," was how Virginia Reed later described it.[3]

William Graves, a seventeen-year-old boy who was quickly growing up, and the Englishman John Denton were given the task of cleaning and clothing the corpse. They wrapped Williams in a sheet and with little ceremony buried him in the snow not far from the cabin.

As the emigrants at Truckee Lake laid Baylis Williams to rest, four lives ended at the Alder Creek camp at almost the same time. The first to die was Jacob Donner, a kindly man who had been overshadowed for much of his life by his older brother George. Jacob was just fifty-six.[4] Described as "a slight man, of delicate constitution," it was said that Jacob acted older than his years.[5] That was why some of the younger Donners always thought Uncle Jake was the eldest of the brothers when in fact he was four years George's junior. Many years later, Jacob's niece Eliza Donner still was confused when she wrote about her uncle's death.

"Uncle Jacob, the first to die, was older than my father, and had been in miserable health for years before we left Illinois," she wrote. "He had gained surprisingly on the journey, yet quickly felt the influence of impending fate, foreshadowed by the first storm at camp. His courage failed. Complete prostration followed."[6]

Neither his wife, Betsy, nor his children could get Jacob to rally. Even George had no luck. "The trials of the journey reduced his strength and exhausted his energy," Eliza told C. F. McGlashan, the first author to chronicle the Donner Party story.[7] "When we reached the place of encampment in the mountains he was discouraged and gave up in despair. Not even the needs of his family could rouse him to action. He was utterly dejected and made no effort, but tranquilly awaited death."

His family gathered around him near the end. Some of them later remembered that Jacob died while sitting at a table in his shelter, with his head in his hands, as if in deep meditation. George, racked with pain, rallied from his sickbed to be at the side of the brother he had been with all his life. From North Carolina to Kentucky, Indiana, Illinois, and finally across the plains and mountains to a snowy camp by a wild mountain river, they had never been far apart.

"My father and mother watched him during the last night, and the following afternoon helped to lay his body in a cave dug in the mountain side, beneath the snow,"[8] wrote Eliza.

George Donner, who had buried two wives before finding his beloved Tamzene, tried to use his one good arm to help carve the icy tomb. Before the snow fully encased Jacob's body, three of the young single men in camp died in rapid succession—Sam Shoemaker, James Smith, and Joseph Reinhardt.

"That snow had scarcely resettled when Samuel Shoemaker's life

232 OUT OF TIME

ebbed away in happy delirium," wrote Eliza Donner. Like many of the other hired hands in the company, little was known of Shoemaker. He was about twenty-five years old and was thought to have come to Illinois from Ohio. In September, on the scalding Utah sands, Shoemaker had pitched in and helped William Eddy repair one of the Reed family's wagons. At the end of his life, "He imagined himself a boy again in his father's house and thought his mother had built a fire and set him before the food of which he was fondest,"[9] Eliza noted. He spoke of those visions and then died smiling and at peace.

James Smith, a Reed teamster who was about twenty-five, also died quietly. Eliza Donner recalled that his death was like "a tired child falling asleep." He was wearing a new pair of brogans, heavy work shoes he had purchased less than a month before from Jacob Donner.[10]

Joseph Reinhardt was far from being at peace when he died. For days before his death, he babbled on—sometimes in German and sometimes in English—about his thirty years on earth. Members of the George Donner family remembered Reinhardt's passing, especially his final words when he spoke of the death of Wolfinger at the Humboldt Sink.

"Joseph Rhinehart was taken sick in our tent, when death was approaching and he knew there was no escape, then he made a confession in the presence of Mrs. Wolfinger that he shot her husband; what the object was I do not know," Leanna Donner stated in a letter she dictated thirty years later.[11] Her sister, Eliza, had a similar recollection, when she wrote that "when Joseph Rhinehart's end drew near, his mind wandered, and his whitening lips confessed a part in Mr. Wolfinger's death; and my father, listening, knew not how to comfort that troubled soul. He could not judge whether the self-condemning words were the promptings of a guilty conscience, or the ravings of an unbalanced mind."[12]

The dying declaration as the result of a "guilty conscience" was soon accepted as the truth. Dorthea Wolfinger was present when Reinhardt made his confession, and at last, she knew what had happened to her husband. He had not been killed by Indians, as Reinhardt and Augustus Spitzer had claimed. Instead of helping him cache his goods, they had shot him for his gold. George Donner assured the young widow that once the emigrants were rescued, there would be an inquiry to ensure that Spitzer was held accountable for his role in the slaying.

With an injury that would not heal and that prevented him from doing any work, George Donner was hard-pressed to muster any optimism. He was the last adult male Donner left, and he had trouble just staying on his feet. Tamzene and his widowed sister-in-law, Betsy, went over and above the call of duty when it came to keeping up the camp.

Fortunately, Milt Elliott and Noah James, two of the teamsters from the camp at Truckee Lake, had arrived at the Donners' camp on the Alder several days before Jacob Donner and the three others died.[13] They helped to bury the four men, gathered firewood, and showed Jean-Baptiste how to probe the deep snow for the carcasses of cattle. Elliott brought with him the letter Charles Stanton had written to Tamzene, asking for tobacco and the loan of a compass. They also told the emigrants about the proposed snowshoe expedition and invited anyone who felt strong enough to come back to the lake camp. There were no takers.

Elliott and James planned to return to the lake camp as quickly as possible, but a blizzard began the day they arrived, followed by another wave of big snowstorms. Finally, when it seemed there was a break, Elliott, anxious to join the snowshoers before they departed, took his leave from the Donner camp. James, who had been one of George Donner's drivers, remained behind to help Jean-Baptiste search for food.

"It was weary work, for the snow was higher than the level of the guide marks, and at times they searched day after day and found no trace of hoof or horn," Eliza Donner recalled in her memoir. "The little field mice that had crept into camp were caught and then used to ease the pangs of hunger. Also pieces of beef hide were cut into strips, singed, scraped, boiled to the consistency of glue, and swallowed with an effort; for no degree of hunger could make the saltless, sticky substance palatable. Marrowless bones which had already been boiled and scraped, were now burned and eaten, even the bark and twigs of pine were chewed in the vain effort to soothe the gnawings which made one cry for bread and meat."[14]

The children of the Donner Party never forgot what it was like trying to survive in their prisons made of snow. They had no interest ever again in snowball fights, building snowmen, or riding in a horse-drawn sleigh beneath a winter moon. For them, freshly fallen snow was no longer beautiful. It was menacing and loathsome. The children retained many of their memories—both good and bad—from their experiences on the wagon trail and in the Sierra camps. Surprisingly, many of the children did not repress the times of trauma.[15] What they recalled was not always accurate and often was influenced by the memories of others. Yet often even a seemingly simple moment was never lost but was tucked away and shared many years later.

Such was the case with little Eliza Donner, almost four years old during that brutal winter, who spent much of her time in the small shelter snuggled between her sisters Frances and Georgia. Eliza later wrote that they "gave me of their warmth . . . from them I learned many things which I could neither have understood nor remembered had they not made them plain."[16]

Eliza held onto one of those innocent memories and shared it more than sixty-five years later:

> Just one happy play is impressed upon my mind. It must have been after the first snow, for the snow bank in front of the cabin door was not high enough to keep out a little sunbeam that stole down the steps and made a bright spot upon our floor. I saw it, and sat down under it, held it on my lap, passed my hand up and down in its brightness, and found that I could break its ray in two. In fact, we had quite a frolic. I fancied that it moved when I did, for it warmed the top of my head, kissed first one cheek and then the other, and seemed to run up and down my arm. Finally I gathered up a piece of it in my apron and ran to my mother. Great was my surprise when I carefully opened the folds and found that I had nothing

to show, and the sunbeam I had left seemed shorter. After mother explained its nature, I watched it creep back slowly up the steps and disappear.[17]

Sunbeams were in short supply in the Sierras throughout much of December. Milt Elliott found that out as he made his way through deep snow, trying to get back to the lake camp before the snowshoe party left without him. He did not make it in time. The snow had finally stopped, at least for a few days, and the brave souls recruited by Franklin Graves and Charles Stanton were eager to start their snowshoe trek while the sky was clear. As much as they wanted the compass they had requested from Tamzene Donner, they thought they could rely on dead reckoning to get them over the hump into the Sacramento Valley. Thinking that Elliot and James might have been lost in the recent blizzard, the snowshoers left without waiting for them to return.

On December 16, Patrick Breen wrote, "Fair & pleasant froeze hard last night so the company started on snow shoes to cross the mountains wind S.E. looks pleasant."[18]

The party that left the Lake Truckee camp that morning was made up of seventeen emigrants—ten men, five women, and two children. At fifty-seven, Franklin Graves was the oldest. The youngest were brothers Lemuel Murphy, thirteen, and William Murphy, ten. Most of the snowshoers were in their twenties and thirties. As evidence of how desperate these emigrants were to find help for themselves and their families, four of the men were fathers and three of the women were mothers who entrusted their babies and small children to other women in the camp.[19]

The party included Graves, his two oldest daughters, Mary Ann and Sarah, and Sarah's husband, Jay Fosdick. Amanda McCutchen, whose husband, William, had left the company in September and was still at Sutter's Fort, handed over her baby daughter, Harriet, to the care of Elizabeth Graves, who remained behind with her seven youngest children. Besides the two young Murphy brothers, others from that extended family were the boys' big sisters Harriet, the widow of William Pike, and Sarah, with her husband William Foster, who had accidentally shot and killed Pike. Harriet's baby son and the Fosters' two toddlers were left with their grandmother, Levinah Murphy. William Eddy had a difficult time bidding farewell to his wife, Eleanor, and their young son and daughter.[20] Like the others who were leaving children and loved ones, Eddy knew that what he was doing was for the best. Besides seeking help for those left behind, just having fewer people in the camp meant there were fewer to feed.

The half dozen single men included in the party were Patrick Dolan, the Irish farmer who had left Iowa with the Breens; Charles Burger, a German teamster often referred to as "Dutch Charley"; Antonio, who had hired on with the wagon train at Fort Laramie; and one of the snowshoe-party organizers, Charles Stanton, with the long-suffering Miwok Indian guides, Luis and Salvador.[21]

On that cold, crisp morning, there was one last inspection before bidding farewell to those who remained behind. All seventeen snow-shoers were of course dressed as warmly as possible in layers of linen shirts, woolen coats, pants, cloaks, and socks. The women pulled on flannel pantaloons beneath loose trousers made from their heaviest dresses. Everyone had scarves or wraps around their necks. Each also had a makeshift backpack and a blanket.[22]

They took an ax, rifle, flint, a few pistols, three horns of gunpowder, and as much tobacco as could be spared to help with stress and subdue hunger pangs. The men would alternate carrying the ax, rifle, and powder horns. The rations for each person consisted of some tea or coffee, a bit of loaf sugar, and about eight pounds of stringy dried meat that was described as "poor beef." It was thought to be just enough food for the six days the emigrants calculated it would take to cross the mountains and reach Johnson's Ranch in the foothills.[23]

There were only fourteen pairs of snowshoes to go around since Milt Elliot had used a pair to get to the Alder Creek campsite. The two Murphy brothers and Burger, without snowshoes, brought up the rear so they could walk in the footsteps left by the others. That turned out to be easier said than done.

After tearful good-byes, the party made its way through deep snow around the north side of Truckee Lake. They did not go very far before it was apparent that for every step an adult took on snowshoes, the boys had to take two steps. The short and stocky Burger found the going tough. His thick legs pushed deep into the snow and buried him to his hips. It was not long before Burger was gasping for breath and, like the two boys, falling far behind. The party halted several times to allow the three without snowshoes to catch up. When they had made it about halfway around the lake, they had to stop again. This time, William Foster agreed to lead ten-year-old William Murphy and Burger back to the lake camp and then try to return to the party when they camped. Lemuel Murphy wanted to keep going and promised to keep up.[24]

The party made little progress the first day. They camped that evening just beyond the head of the lake, close enough to the lake camp to see smoke rising from the cabins. At that rate, they knew the chances of their meager rations holding out were slim to none. Foster easily caught up with them that evening after taking William Murphy back to camp and was surprised that they had not gone farther. He joined the others at the fire, where Graves managed to improvise a smaller pair of snowshoes for young Lemuel from some packsaddles found along the way.[25]

The next morning, the party—now at fifteen members—continued, hopeful that they would improve on the four miles they had made the first day. They did just that. They went six miles over a snowpack twelve to sixty feet deep and made camp west of the summit.

"We had a very slavish day's travel, climbing the divide," Mary Ann Graves recalled. "Nothing of interest occurred until reaching the summit. The scenery was too grand for me to pass without notice, the changes being so great; walking now on loose snow, and stepping on a hard, slick rock a number of hundred yards in length. Being a little in the rear of the party, I had a chance to observe the company ahead, trudging along with packs on their backs. It reminded me of some Norwegian fur company among the icebergs. . . . Well do I remember a remark one of the company made here, that we were about as near heaven as we could get."[26]

Close to heaven, perhaps, but still so far from where they needed to be, the emigrants once again strapped on their snowshoes at first light. Most of them had frostbitten hands and feet. The rising sun felt good on their faces, but as the day passed, the sun became as dangerous as the bitter cold wind, the snow, and the altitude that left the emigrants, so weakened by hunger, panting for air. The sun's rays reflected off the snow and ice and burned the corneas of some of the emigrants' eyes. After a few days' exposure, Stanton, the dependable gent from Chicago, was snow-blind. So was Franklin Graves, but his daughters and son-in-law helped him to stay on track, and he quickly recovered. Stanton was in far worse shape. At first, his eyes turned red and watery, followed by an uncontrollable twitching before swelling shut. The pain was almost unbearable. The two Miwoks led the way, while Stanton fell behind and was the last one to drag into camp.

By then, the emigrants were in snow at least eleven feet deep, and brief snowstorms continued. Since leaving Truckee Lake, they had seen no game, and their rations were almost gone. Sometimes as they shuffled along, they saw things that were not there—not mirages but hallucinations. They were not sure whether they were lost, and they wished Milt Elliot had made it back in time to bring the compass.

They did what they always did whenever they faced a dilemma. They questioned themselves. Should they have waited? Should they have never left camp in the first place? So many questions, so much doubt, so little hope. Thirty-three years later, when Charles McGlashan wrote his book about the Donner Party, he coined the name that the snowshoe party would always be known by—the Forlorn Hope. McGlashan took the term from the Dutch *verloren hoop*, literally "lost troop," a small detachment of soldiers sent on a dangerous mission with little hope of success.[27] It proved to be an apt name for the snowshoers.

On December 21—the shortest day of the year and the first day of winter—William Eddy was digging through his backpack when he discovered a package that his wife had concealed there before the party left camp. He unwrapped a half pound of bear meat from the grizzly he had killed earlier in the month. A note Eddy found with the package said the meat might save his life. It was signed, "Your own dear Eleanor."[28] In the past, Eddy had shared the game he shot with others in return for borrowing a weapon or, as was the case with the bear, the loan of an ox to drag the carcass to camp. This time, there was no sharing. Eddy kept the meat for himself and tried to make it last as long as possible.

That morning, just before the party moved on, Mary Graves noticed Stanton sitting on a log near the smoldering fire. He was smoking his pipe and staring into the flames. She asked if he was coming with them. Stanton, by then not only blind but somewhat delirious, turned toward her voice.

"Yes, I am coming soon," he replied.[29] Those were the last words the emigrants ever heard Stanton utter. When they left, Stanton, with his pipe smoke spiraling upward, seemed to be at peace with himself and the icy world that surrounded him. The diminutive but courageous bachelor, who had performed acts of kindness and made heroic attempts to save his starving companions, was never seen alive again.

"He was always noble and generous, even to a fault—always ready and willing to share his last cent with his less fortunate brothers and sisters," Philip Stanton, one of Charles's brothers, wrote almost two years later. "This characteristic he bore from his earliest childhood. He was ever ready to sacrifice his own interest and means to the welfare of others, and hence it is not so surprising that he should be found willing to yield up his life in endeavoring to relieve his perishing companions."[30]

Stanton, who had cared for his widowed mother until her death in 1838, left his own benediction in the final stanza of a poem he had written in tribute to her:

> *When death shall close my sad career,*
> *And I before my God appear—*
> *There to receive His last decree—*
> *My only prayer there will be*
> *Forever to remain with thee,*
> *My mother.*[31]

36. CAMP OF DEATH

DECEMBER 1846

After more than a week of traversing the Sierras, the members of the snowshoe party were not sure where they were or even if they were going in the right direction. In short, they were lost. They also were in denial. It had been days since they had last seen Charles Stanton, but they still looked for him to catch up as they struggled through the snow. At night, they nibbled like hungry mice on the last bits of dried beef and prayed for the return of the man they had come to rely on for guidance. At the top of a prominent hill, they built a large signal fire and waited all day for Stanton to appear, but all that came were cold rain and more snow.[1] Finally, they had to face the reality that Stanton was not coming and never would.

The party was now fourteen in number, and each of them recognized that snow meant death. Snow was their enemy. So was the cold. It numbed mind and body and subdued the will to live because it caused people to forget the ultimate goal—survival. Once a person gives up, it becomes surprisingly easy to die. Some of the emigrants figured that out early in the journey. Survival calls for commitment. Survival was about living. To survive, one must live.

Some of those with the snowshoe party and others back at the camps were concerned only about saving themselves. They were prepared to do anything to stay alive, no matter the cost to others. Although there were exceptions, the emigrants were apt to fight not only for their own survival but also for the survival of loved ones. They rallied time and again to outsmart death and spare the lives of their families.[2]

With each passing day, staying alive became increasingly difficult.

Whether huddled in a shelter at one of the campsites or wrapped in a blanket with the snowshoe party, the emigrants felt that time itself had frozen solid. Days and nights blended into light and darkness. The people were lost in an icy limbo.

Patrick Breen, at the lake camp, had become the timekeeper. Only he knew for sure what day it was, and he mentioned ordinary and extraordinary events of each day in his diary. Like a patient monk transcribing scripture, Breen faithfully wrote of the comings and goings of emigrants, such as "Dutch Charley" Burger's failed attempt to hike to the Donners' camp. He also noted the return of Milt Elliot with the compass that the snowshoers so desperately needed and of Elliott's news that Jacob Donner and three others had perished at Alder Creek.

The emigrants were stunned to learn of the deaths of the four men. They were not as surprised when Elliott told them about Joseph Reinhardt's deathbed confession to murdering Wolfinger at the Humboldt Sink.[3] There was no rush to punish Reinhardt's accomplice, Augustus Spitzer. Too weak to rise, he lingered in the Breen cabin.

Yet beyond the actions of his fellow emigrants, Breen never neglected to record the status of one of the Donner Party's greatest concerns—the weather. "Tuesd. 22nd Snowed all last night Continued to snow all day with some few intermissions had a severe fit of the gravel [kidney stones] yesterday I am well to day, Praise be to the God of Heaven."[4]

The next day, Breen began to read the Thirty Days Prayer to the Blessed Virgin Mary, a devotional in the Irish-language prayer book that faithful Catholics such as he read at times of hardship and trouble.[5] If there was ever a time to seek celestial help, that time had come.

Unlike Breen, the members of the snowshoe party on the west flank of the Sierras were about "prayed out." They had prayed for many days, wandering like zombies through the snow. They prayed at night huddled around a fire. They prayed for Stanton's return, prayed for the snow and rain to stop, prayed that the Miwoks, Luis and Salvador, would find the way, and prayed that some game would cross their path so they could eat. None of those prayers had been answered.

The snowshoers found themselves in a desperate state. Surrounded by deep snow, they were chilled to the bone and ravenous. Bodies and minds began to deteriorate. They shivered constantly, which generated body heat but also caused fatigue that lowered their body temperature.

Any exposed skin was vulnerable to frostbite. At first, the skin took on a dull whitish pallor and was numbed. If the frostbite went deeper, the soft tissues tended to harden and became almost immovable. To treat frostbite, the emigrants vigorously rubbed their fingers and hands with snow, the accepted remedy of the day. In fact, that was the worst thing they could have done. It was like rubbing gravel on open wounds and could cause permanent damage.[6] Drinking plenty of water increased the blood's volume, which helped to prevent frostbite.

Water was even more important than food. (Humans can survive only a few days without water but can live for eight weeks or more without food.) At least the vast deposits of snow provided a water supply. By checking the color of their urine on the snow, they could determine if they were becoming dehydrated. When the piss was the color of butter, they knew they were fine, but if it looked like dark beer, it was time to drink water.[7] They slugged down cups of melted snow, unaware that eating snow instead of drinking it lowered the body's core temperature and caused further dehydration.

By Christmas Eve, the fourteen members of the snowshoe party limped along aimlessly through fast-falling, heavy curtains of snow. At one rest stop, all the men except William Eddy and the two Indians announced that they could go no farther. They wanted everyone to turn around and return to the camp at Truckee Lake. Every woman in the party vehemently opposed the plan. Given the distance they had traveled and the lack of rations to fuel them, the odds were fully against ever making it back.[8]

"Some of those who had children and families wished to go back, but the two Indians said they would go on to the Captain Sutter's,"

Mary Graves wrote in an 1847 letter. "I told them I would go too, for to go back and hear the cries of hunger from my little brothers and sisters was more than I could stand. I would go as far as I could, let the consequences be what they might."[9]

By then, most of the snowshoers had gone without any food for at least three days. Eddy had his secret stash of bear meat, but it was almost gone. It had been more than two months since any of them had eaten a complete, nourishing meal. Many of them showed the classic signs of starvation. They grew weaker and frequently felt dizzy as their fat reserves and muscles were depleted. The simplest tasks became difficult. Diminished circulation caused feet, ankles, and hands to swell. With continued weight loss, the emigrants experienced painful constipation followed by uncontrollable diarrhea. Their immune systems broke down, which made them susceptible to various infections.[10]

Soon, they experienced disturbances in heart rhythm, severe muscle pain, listlessness, apathy, insomnia, and hallucinations. When they slept, the emigrants dreamed of food and eating large feasts. They were miserable in body and mind, knowing it would be a painful death marked by extreme discomfort and the loss of all bodily functions. Not so well known was that many people who starved or froze to death succumbed to a resulting infectious disease and went into cardiac arrest at the end.[11]

All of them knew the end was near. Their confused minds raced in search of a survival plan. It was uncertain how many of the emigrants came up with the final solution. It must have crossed the minds of more than one. Finally, someone—likely Patrick Dolan—put the unthinkable into words. For the party to survive, extreme action had to be taken at once. Someone had to die so the flesh could be used to sustain all the others. Even if they had thought of it, hearing those words must have been shocking. That would be the ultimate taboo—cannibalism.[12]

Members of the snowshoe party fell silent. Who would be the sacrificial lamb? Who would act as executioner? What would be the manner of death? Could they bring themselves to eat from a human body?

Dolan, already in the later stages of starvation and what came to be known as hypothermia, suggested that the emigrants draw lots to see who would be sacrificed for the others.[13] Eddy quickly agreed, but some of the others expressed concern, and William Foster was totally opposed to the plan. Eddy then proposed that two of the men in the party draw lots, face off in a duel, and shoot it out. That idea was also rejected. Finally, Eddy and the others concluded that because they were all in poor condition and some were near death, the best solution would be to keep going and let nature take its course. It would not be long before death would overtake one of them. This plan must have been more acceptable to Eddy, the strongest because of the hidden bear meat he had consumed.[14]

Weary and confused, they set out again. It was slow going. The emigrants were so weak and exhausted that they found it difficult to keep their balance. With much effort, they took a step at a time, floundered in the snow and, panting like spent hounds, sucked in mouthfuls of thin mountain air. There was little or no talking because there was nothing more to say. The sole purpose of the trek was to completely wear out one of the weaker ones and cause death. Staggering through the falling snow, with their wrapped heads down in the howling wind, they must have hoped, maybe even prayed, that the weakest among them would fall and die.

The party did not go very far before stopping for the night. All of them were too tired and cold to go farther. The most able-bodied set out to make a fire. They cut some green logs for a platform in the snow and then collected as much wood as possible. With much difficulty, they kindled a fire. The mostly unseasoned wood was soaked, producing more smoke than flames, but it provided some comfort for those who were far gone, especially Franklin Graves and the Hispanic hired man, Antonio.[15] Graves was the oldest member of the party, and Antonio, about twenty-three, was one of the youngest.

That evening, the emigrants nestled by the fire. The exhausted Antonio was so close that when he turned in his sleep and flung out his arm, his hand fell into the flames. Eddy saw what had happened and was surprised when Antonio did not react but continued to sleep, oblivious to what must have been excruciating pain. When Eddy jumped up and pulled Antonio's hand from the fire, he saw that the young man was unconscious and his breathing was labored. Then Antonio again flung out his arm, and his hand shriveled in the fire and burned to a crisp.

Eddy saw that there was nothing that could be done for the young man. Antonio's raspy breathing became a death rattle, and then it stopped. The first of the snowshoers was dead.[16]

Less than an hour after Antonio's passing, another storm—a furious combination of hail, snow, and wind—swept down on the thirteen remaining emigrants. This prompted them to pile more wood on the fire until it became a roaring inferno. The wood supply was quickly exhausted, but not before the intense fire burned the foundation logs and melted the snow beneath the logs.

"The camp and the fire had been built over a stream of water, and the fire had melted through the overlying snow until it had fallen into the stream," wrote C. F. McGlashan. "Those who peered over the brink of the dark opening about which they were gathered could hear, far down in the gloom, during the lull of the storm, the sound of running water. . . . When the fire disappeared, it became apparent that the entire forlorn hope would perish before morning if exposed to the cold and storm."[17]

Again, fingers thick with numbness fumbled to ignite the driest tinder. Once the fire was lit, it was not easy to keep it going because of the lack of dry wood. That situation worsened when the head of the hatchet flew off the handle and was lost in a deep snowbank.[18] That left the emigrants no choice but to wade into the snow and tear off any dead branches and green boughs they could find for fuel. Without a log platform for a foundation, the fire melted the snow and continued to settle. Try as they might to keep the fire going, it soon was extinguished—as was another life.

At about eleven o'clock that night, Franklin Graves, who had been in steady decline for several days, died. His two daughters, Sarah and Mary Ann, were at his side. Just before Graves passed, Eddy told him what was already obvious—death was near. Graves replied that he did not care. The Vermonter who could make snowshoes and—like the Donner brothers—had farmed the rich Illinois soil was ready for the sweet release of death. He told his daughters he was prepared to die and asked them to tell their mother and the other children how much he loved them. Graves also urged them to do all they could to stay alive, including eating human flesh and even using his body for nourishment if it came to that.[19]

Graves's corpse was laid in the snow next to the frozen body of young Antonio. On that Christmas Eve, the fierce wind and the wailing of the young women who had just watched their father die became a funeral hymn that echoed in some hearts and minds forever.

The twelve survivors returned to the task of staying alive. To that end, the emigrants resorted to a cold-weather survival technique favored by mountain men and trappers. Perhaps the snowshoers had heard about it from James Clyman or one of the other frontiersmen they had encountered on the trail. They created a makeshift tent by sitting close together in a circle on some blankets and then draping more blankets over their heads. The emigrants took turns holding the blankets aloft and occasionally shook off the accumulated snow so their shelter would not collapse on top of them.[20]

Beneath the blanket tent, the emigrants found protection from the wind. Their trapped body heat gave them some comfort during the long night. "The delirium of death had attacked one or two, and the pitiful wails and cries of these death-stricken maniacs were heart-rendering," McGlashan wrote. "The dead, the dying, the situation, were enough to drive one crazy."[21] The sun rose on Christmas morning, but the storm did not stop, and neither did the dying.

The shrieking Patrick Dolan awakened the emigrants who had managed to get some sleep. The Irish farmer was delirious and deranged with hypothermia and starvation. He raved and thrashed beneath the blankets. Eddy and others tried to calm him down, but he became so anguished that he tore off his boots and clothing. The other emigrants were frightened, unaware of the compulsion of people in the final stages of hypothermia to strip off their clothing as they lose all rationality and are overwhelmed by the sensation of extreme heat against their skin.[22]

Disrobed, Dolan tried to crawl out of the tent but was stopped and wrestled back under the blankets. He persisted and managed to break free. Some emigrants brought him back. He immediately escaped again, and again the others dragged him through the snow to the shelter. Eddy held him, and eventually Dolan calmed down and grew quiet. In late afternoon, he fell into a deep sleep and never awoke. His lifeless body was placed alongside the two other corpses.[23]

In the morning, the snowshoers emerged from the makeshift tent. Except to relieve themselves or help move a dead body, they had been confined to the shelter for almost thirty-six hours. The snow was still falling, and the glare of the sun blinded them. Eddy tried to start a fire using gunpowder for tinder but ended up blowing up his powder horn. His hands and face were burned, and two of the women sustained minor burns. Later, when the storm moved on, the emigrants again tried to make a fire. For tinder, one of the women cut a patch of dry cotton batting from the lining of her cloak, and it was ignited by a spark from the flintlock rifle. They set fire to a large dead pine. Everyone gathered around as flames quickly spread through the tree branches.

The blaze would soon become a cooking fire. The time had come to face the inevitable. The starving emigrants could wait no longer. It was time to eat the dead to stay alive.

All of them agreed that none of the emigrants would have to eat from their own kinfolks' bodies. Likely, William Foster and Jay Fosdick volunteered to do the butchering. William Eddy, smarting from the powder burns, might have joined in this gruesome task even though he and the Miwoks, Luis and Salvador, initially declined to partake of any human flesh.[24]

The body of Patrick Dolan, who had no familial ties to anyone else in the party, was the first to be cannibalized. Honed knives cut strips of flesh from his arms and legs. The frozen meat was skewered on sharpened sticks and roasted over the fire. The aroma stimulated appetites, but it was said that when the emigrants ate the first human flesh, they avoided eye contact and wept.[25]

There was no attempt to render Dolan's entire frozen body. That would have required a great amount of time and effort and would have been difficult with only knives. For the time being, they took only enough flesh to satiate their hunger and restore their vitality. As long as the bodies remained frozen, the flesh could be used as needed. Cutting the meat into small pieces helped make eating it more palatable. The strips could be cooked over a fire and some could be dried in the sun to preserve the meat. Then it looked more like jerky and was not recognizably human.[26]

Members of the Donner Party were not the first or the last to resort to starvation cannibalism. The human consumption of human flesh is as old as mankind. During food shortages, Neanderthals survived by killing other Neanderthals. Cannibalism is mentioned in the Bible and in Greek mythology. The universal social taboos of incest and cannibalism were motifs in William Shakespeare's works. The brutal winter of 1609–1610 at the Jamestown colony in Virginia came to be known as the "Starving Time" when hundreds of British colonists perished, reducing the survivors to cannibalism.[27] Of all the taboos, including incest and bestiality, any kind of cannibalism was the absolute epitome of savage behavior.[28]

To get beyond any horror at the idea of consuming human flesh, the stigma of cannibalism had to be quickly assuaged. The emigrants trapped in the Sierras rationalized that what they were doing was a far cry from ritualistic or ceremonial cannibalism. To the emigrants, the bodies of the dead represented sustenance and nothing more. They were not ghouls. It was either eat the dead or die.

The two Murphy sisters—Sarah Foster and Harriet Pike—tried to coax their younger brother, Lemuel Murphy, into eating some of Dolan's flesh. The boy had been steadily declining and behaving irrationally, much as Dolan did in his last days. Only thirteen, Lemuel was "dearly loved by his sisters and full of courage," but when they put some of the roasted meat to his lips, he could not eat.[29] Just the day before, he had been desperate for food like everyone else. When a mouse scurried from its winter hole across the snow, several emigrants tried to catch it, but it was Lemuel who grabbed it. He stuffed the squirming rodent into his mouth and ate it alive.[30]

Lemuel was no longer the same boy who, back at the lake camp, had tried to give his share of food to others. As he became more delirious, he thrashed about and tried to bite the arms of those who subdued him, the whole time screaming, "Give me my bone!"[31] But as night fell, the delirium was gone. Lemuel's pulse weakened, and his breathing became shallow. His emaciated body had exhausted its energy supply, and he stopped shivering.

During the night, he grew still and softly moaned. His sister Sarah held Lemuel's head in her lap and stroked his hair. She wept and whispered her love. The fire made shadows on the snow, and in the clear night sky, the moon rose and set. At that moment, Lemuel died. For the rest of her life, whenever Sarah Murphy Foster gazed at the moon, her mind would take her back to that winter's night in the snow-covered Sierras in the place they called the Camp of Death.[32]

37. THE STARVING TIME

The surviving snowshoers—five men and five women—spent the final days of 1846 regaining their strength in the Camp of Death. One after one, the bodies of Patrick Dolan, Antonio, William Graves, and Lemuel Murphy were systematically dismembered with knives, and the fleshy and fatty parts were sliced into various cuts. Smaller pieces of flesh were roasted for immediate consumption. Livers, hearts, lungs, and brains were extracted and eaten. Much of the meat was dried over the fire and packed away.

Those doing the butchering made every effort to ensure that no one ate the flesh of a relative. Everyone shared the flesh of the single men, Dolan and Antonio. The Graves daughters avoided going near their father's corpse, just as Murphy's sisters and brother-in-law stayed away from his body. Despite the precautions, heartbreaking incidents occurred. The worst was the evening Sarah Murphy Foster sat by the fire, deeply grieving the death of young Lemuel. She looked up and noticed some of the emigrants on the other side of the fire roasting meat spitted on sticks. Suddenly, Sarah realized she was watching someone eat the broiled heart of her cherished younger brother.[1] Immediately, William Foster rushed to his hysterical wife and spirited her away.

Many years later, the survivors spoke little about the cannibalism, and several of them vehemently denied that it had ever happened. But there was no denying that on December 30, 1846, the snowshoers, bearing packages of dried flesh, departed the Camp of Death.[2] Not one of them turned to look at the remains of their four companions whose deaths had saved their lives.

Back on the move after a long layover and reenergized by the meat, the emigrants also were in pain. Their frostbitten feet were so swollen that the skin cracked and burst. They wrapped strips of blankets and rags around their bloody feet, but the pain was agonizing. By the end of the day, they had walked only four miles. That night, William Eddy felt so weak and faint from lack of any food that he could barely stand. The others implored him to eat some of their rations of dried flesh, and he reluctantly agreed. He could not hold out any longer.[3]

The next day, the last one of the year, the snowshoers managed to make six miles after traversing a steep ridge and crossing ravines on tenuous snow bridges. By the time they camped on the edge of a deep canyon, a trail of blood from their feet marked the snow behind them. That night, still cursing the loss of their hatchet, the emigrants set fire to a pine tree. Basking in the glow, they silently ate the last of the dried human flesh. Eyes darted from face to face, but no one spoke. There was nothing to say. All that mattered was when they would have their next meal and who would provide it.

Back at Truckee Lake, some of the emigrants had given up on the snowshoe party. They had been gone more than two weeks, which seemed like plenty of time to find help. Some folks concluded that the party had perished.

Although there had been no open talk of cannibalism, the possibility of having to use it as a means of survival was being considered at the lake camp. "The prospect is appalling but hope is in God," Patrick Breen noted in his diary.[4]

Since the departure of the snowshoe party in mid-December, life had only become worse at the Truckee and Alder Creek camps. The nutritional value of the boiled-hide muck most people gagged down was questionable. The marrow was picked clean from the slaughtered animal bones that were boiled repeatedly until they were so soft they could be chewed. Only a few families at the lake had scraps of meat. There was none for the Donner families, dug in at Alder Creek, only field mice that at least provided some nourishment.

"Snowy Christmas brought us no 'glad tidings,' and New Year's

Day no happiness," was how Eliza Donner remembered the holidays that year. "Yet, each bright day that followed a storm was one of thanksgiving, on which we all crept up the flight of snow steps and huddled about on the surface in the blessed sunshine, but with our eyes closed against its painful and blinding glare."[5]

At Truckee Lake, after a night of rain, another snowstorm began at about noon on Christmas Day. Patrick Breen's kidney stones laid him low, but he managed to lead his family in Christmas prayers before sending sons John and Edward out in the storm to replenish the woodpile.[6] Most of the emigrants in camp slurped the now familiar broth of boiled hides and bones. Levinah Murphy, however, surprised everyone in her cabin by adding an oxtail to her cook pot.

After everyone had eaten supper, Levinah put all the babies in her charge to bed. Later, young William Murphy, who had tried to go with the snowshoe party but had to return to camp, was reading Levinah's favorite psalm to her when she suddenly became ill. That was the start of her decline, but she continued to care for the children. She also prayed every day for her family members with the snowshoe party, unaware that her beloved son, Lemuel, had died and his body had been used for food.[7]

The most memorable Christmas dinner took place in the Reed family's half of the Graves cabin. Virginia Reed described the meal.

"The misery endured during those four months at Donner Lake in our little dark cabins under the snow would fill pages and make the coldest heart ache," Virginia wrote. "Christmas was near, but to the starving its memory gave no comfort. It came and passed without observance, but my mother had determined weeks before that her children should have a treat this one day. She had laid away a few dried apples, some beans, a bit of tripe, and a small piece of bacon. When this hoarded store was brought out, the delight of the little ones knew no bounds. The cooking was watched carefully, and when we sat down to our Christmas dinner mother said, 'Children, eat slowly, for this one day you can have all you wish.' So bitter was the misery relieved by that one bright day that I have never sat down to a Christmas dinner without my thoughts going back to Donner Lake."[8]

Two additional feet of snow fell on Christmas night, and by December 27, the snow at the lake was at least nine feet deep. Wood was becoming more difficult to find. The trees that were felled sank into the deep snow and had to be dug out. This totally exhausted the emigrants who were still capable of working and drained what little energy they had left. Several of them were declining rapidly. Most people stayed in their shelters and kept to themselves.

Charley Burger died in Lewis Keseberg's lean-to on the night of December 28. He had not been well since he dropped out of the snowshoe party after just one day. Back in camp, Burger's health had quickly deteriorated, and the "chunky little Dutchman," as Lilburn Boggs called him, died at the age of thirty. After depositing the body in the snow, Keseberg and Augustus Spitzer, not far from death himself, divided up Burger's personal possessions. Spitzer took a coat and rain slicker, and Keseberg pocketed $1.50 in cash, along with a gold pin, two silver watches, three boxes of percussion caps for guns, and a straight razor.[9]

Burger was the first emigrant to die at the lake camp since Baylis Williams, the Reeds' hired man. Patrick Breen briefly noted Burger's death in his journal, along with his usual weather report and prayers. Just a day later, another storm was gathering over the Pacific.

Virginia Reed wrote, "The storms would often last ten days at a time, and we would have to cut chips from the logs inside which formed our cabins, in order to start a fire. We could scarcely walk, and the men had hardly strength to procure wood. We would drag ourselves through the snow from one cabin to another, and some mornings snow would have to be shoveled out of the fireplace before a fire could be made. Poor little children were crying with hunger, and mothers were crying because they had so little to give their children. We seldom thought of bread, we had been without it so long. Four months of such suffering would fill the bravest hearts with despair."[10]

On New Year's Day 1847, Margret Reed was forced to do something that those who knew her would never have thought she was capable of doing. The last real food her children had eaten was the surprise Christmas dinner, and it could barely be called a meal. Margret had done her best to find food. She even traded her husband's watch and a Masonic medal for some meat. She could not give up now. She considered her husband's credo—persevere.

Margret pulled on her coat and slipped a knife into a pocket. She told the children she was going to take little Cash for a walk. He was the last of the family's five dogs still living and the children's most beloved pet. Cash dutifully followed Margret out the cabin door. She let him run in the snow and then picked him up and stroked his head. Her hand found the knife, and she quickly cut the dog's throat. He died in the snow. Margret wept as she cut up his body.[11]

The children cried for hours. Margret told them why she had had to sacrifice the dog, but it was hard for them to understand. Virginia, who adored Cash almost as much as her beloved Billy, the pony she had had to leave to die in the desert, took up for her mother. She gently explained to the younger children why Cash had to die so that all of them could stay alive. The Reeds lived on Cash for several days. They ate all his flesh, entrails, head, paws, and tail. Spare pieces of the dog made a pot of soup. As Virginia later wrote, they ate "everything about him."[12] Margret knew full well that once Cash was gone, her family had nothing more to eat except hides and a small stash of dried meat. Their chances of survival were slim at best.

Once again, Margret took stock of the situation. She was a thirty-two-year-old woman who had been in poor health ever since she survived the cholera epidemic that took the lives of her first husband and her sister. Staggering migraines and chronic illnesses kept her bedridden much of the time, including the day she wed James Reed. Just before leaving Springfield, Illinois, with her family on the California Trail, Margret had buried an infant son next to the grave of her father. While on the westward trail, she had watched her mother die and had witnessed Reed kill a man in a fight. She had no idea where her banished husband was or if he was even alive.

Margret tapped into the reservoir of strength that had helped her through all the hard times. She became the proof that no love is stronger than maternal love, and there is nothing fiercer than a mother protecting her children. She would shield them from death and disaster by sheer force of will. She also devised an exit strategy. Unwilling to sink into lethargy like some of the others in camp, Margret decided to form her own party and find a way over the Sierras. Some of the others were critical of the plan, but Margret's mind was made up. The risk was worth taking.

"Time dragged slowly along till we were no longer on short allowance [of food] but were simply starving," Virginia would later recall. "My mother determined to make an effort to cross the mountains. She could not see her children die without trying to get them food."

Margret knew that her three youngest children could not keep up. She went from cabin to cabin asking other emigrants to look after her children until rescue parties arrived at the lake. She found obliging families who, in a rare show of cooperation, were willing to help. Eight-year-old Patty went to stay with the Kesebergs, five-year-old James went to the Graves family, and three-year-old Thomas was left with the Breens. Margret would take with her thirteen-year-old Virginia, her faithful teamster, Milt Elliott, and the hired girl, Eliza Williams.

On January 4, the party left the camp with only a small ration of dried meat. The three youngest children cried and begged Margret to take them with her. Virginia later recounted how difficult it was for her mother to say good-bye. "It was hard to leave them but she felt it must be done. She told them she would bring them bread, so they were willing to stay, and with no guide but a compass we started—my mother, Eliza, Milt Elliott and myself. Milt wore snow shoes and we followed in his tracks."[13]

Margret's attempt to cross the Sierras to find help was unsuccessful. The trek lasted only five days, and much of that time was spent returning to the lake camp. Eliza managed to make it through the first day before the freezing temperatures and snow convinced her to turn around. The others went on, but when Elliott's compass began to behave oddly, they soon were lost. They also were frostbitten and ready to admit that going any farther would be foolhardy.

"Often I would have to crawl up the mountains, being too tired to walk," Virginia wrote.

> The nights were made hideous by the screams of wild beasts heard in the distance. Again, we would be lulled to sleep by the moan of the pine trees, which seemed to sympathize with our loneliness. One morning we awoke to find ourselves in a well of snow. During the night, while in the deep sleep of exhaustion, the heat of the fire had melted the snow and our little camp had gradually sunk many feet below the surface until we were literally buried in a well of snow. The danger was that any attempt to get out might bring an avalanche upon us, but finally steps were carefully made and we reached the surface. My foot was badly frozen, so we were compelled to return, and just in time, for that night a storm came on, the most fearful of the winter, and we should have perished had we not been in the cabins.[14]

By the time the weary threesome reached Truckee Lake, they were done in after four bone-chilling nights in the snow. The first order of business was to find a new home. Most of the oxen hides making up the roof on the Reeds' side of the cabin had been pulled down to be used for food. Elliott took Eliza with him and headed to the Donner camp on Alder Creek, Virginia moved in with the Breens, and Margret found a place with the Kesebergs.

That arrangement did not last long. Soon the Breens invited Margret and all the Reed children to move in with their family. The merger totaled fifteen people in the Breen cabin. It was a very snug fit, but it made for a very warm cabin. The timing was good. Just as everyone was settled, another great storm hovered over the Sierras for several days, dumping so much snow that all the cabins were completely buried.

It looked as though 1847 was going to be every bit as punishing as 1846 had been for the emigrants of the Donner Party.

. . .

THE NEW YEAR had not improved the circumstances of the surviving members of the snowshoe party, stumbling through the canyon country. By the first days of January, they were out of food. All the packaged human meat they had carved from the four corpses at the Camp of Death had been eaten. At least the snow was crusted hard, allowing them to take off the crude snowshoes.

For sustenance, they toasted the rotting rawhide strings and some shoes and boots that were falling apart. The emigrants managed to choke them down. Even though there was no nutritional value, just the act of chewing and filling their stomachs eased the pangs and brought some comfort.[15]

To replace their footwear, the emigrants wrapped more strips of blankets around their feet. The blood soaked through the cloth, leaving a swath of red in the snow. Frostbite took a toll. The Miwok guide Luis was in such poor condition that one of his blackened toes fell off at the first joint.[16] Jay Fosdick showed signs that he was in decline. He moved slowly and was unsteady on his feet. When he began to lag behind, his dutiful wife, Sarah, fell back with him, causing the rest of the party to stop and wait for them to catch up. Eddy and Foster recognized that before long, Fosdick could go no farther, and they would again have fresh meat.

Foster was impatient and hungry and was beginning to show signs of delirium. Instead of waiting for Fosdick to die, Foster proposed killing the two Miwoks and using their bodies for food. Like the majority of Anglo pioneers hoping to gain a foothold in California, Foster apparently had no compulsion about taking the life of an Indian. Indians were seen as almost subhuman.[17]

After enduring so much with Luis and Salvador as his companions, Eddy was firmly opposed to Foster's proposal. Some of the others were in agreement with Foster and indicated that they would support his plan. Realizing his Indian friends were in eminent danger, Eddy warned Luis. That evening, the two Miwoks slipped away and disappeared into the darkness.

The next morning, Eddy, toting his flintlock rifle, announced that he would go ahead and try to bag a deer. At last the party was out of the snow on bare ground, and there were signs of game. Mary Ann Graves went along with Eddy.[18] They followed the bloody footprints of Luis and Salvador while scanning the brush for game. The rest of the party followed—William and Sarah Foster, Amanda McCutchen, and Harriet Pike in one group, followed by Jay and Sarah Fosdick well to the rear and falling farther behind.

The hunters quickly picked up deer tracks. When they spotted the browsing deer, Eddy took aim and fired, with some difficulty because of his weakened arms. The deer was wounded and on the run, with Eddy and Mary Ann in close pursuit. The chase ended when the deer could no longer run and fell to the ground. Eddy and Mary Ann ran to the dying animal. Eddy took hold of the antlers and slit the deer's throat. Then both Eddy and Mary Ann drank the warm spurting blood. They immediately felt strength returning to their withered bodies. Later they built a fire, cut the deer open, and ate its heart and part of the liver.

Eddy fired the rifle several more times to alert the others to their location, but by that time, the rest of the party had stopped to make camp. Foster and the women with him spent another night without any food. So did the Fosdicks. They were well behind, wrapped in a single blanket and without a fire. Sarah later said that when Fosdick— who could no longer walk—heard the gunshots, he exclaimed, "There! Eddy has killed a deer. Now if I can only get to him, I shall live!"[19]

It was not to be. During the night, Fosdick slowly lost consciousness and died in his wife's arms. They had not yet reached their first wedding anniversary. Sarah stayed with her husband's body, praying that she would freeze to death. She survived, however, and in the morning was making her way to rejoin the party when she encountered William and Sarah Foster. Certain that both of the Fosdicks had perished, they were backtracking to butcher their bodies so the party would again have fresh meat. Instead, they took Sarah Fosdick back to their camp where Eddy and Mary Ann Graves had arrived and were sharing venison with the others.

After they ate and rested, Sarah Fosdick, accompanied by the Fosters, returned to her husband's body to say farewell and retrieve a few keepsakes. The Fosters had other plans. Despite protests from the young widow, they proceeded to butcher the corpse. They removed the edible organs, cut off Fosdick's limbs, and packed all of it back to camp to be roasted along with the deer meat.[20]

During the next several days, the emigrants climbed steep canyon walls and forded streams, pausing only at springs to wash and tend their wounded feet. The dried flesh—deer and human—was eventually gone.

Of the seven surviving members, the women were in the best physical shape and showed no signs of failing any time soon. That might have been the primary reason for Foster and Eddy, the lone males, to discuss killing one of the women for food. Foster's behavior had become quite erratic. He seemed depressed and mentally unbalanced. Some accounts, largely based on the word of Eddy, said it was Foster who came up with the idea to kill and eat Amanda McCutchen. When Eddy pointed out that she was a wife and mother, Foster then suggested killing Mary Ann Graves or Sarah Fosdick. Eddy claimed he not only put a stop to such talk but also faced off with Foster and threatened him with a knife.

Other accounts make Eddy out to be the villain, based on the premise that Eddy's true motive for taking Mary Ann Graves on the hunting trip was to get her alone and then kill her and eat her flesh. No matter who came up with a murder scheme, none of the five females was murdered.[21] Two other innocents were not so lucky.

Just after the fracas between Foster and Eddy was settled at what Jessy Thornton called the Camp of Strife, the emigrants spied two sets of fresh bloody footprints in the mud.[22] They must have been the footprints of Luis and Salvador. Rushing forward as fast as their aching bodies could move, the emigrants had gone only about two miles when they came upon the two Miwoks. After going without food for so many days, the Indians could go no farther and were lying prone on the ground. Foster, with his mouth watering and his eyes filled with madness, took up the flintlock and, ignoring Eddy's plea for mercy, made it clear that this time, he would not be denied. Eddy and the women moved on a little way so they would not see what was about to happen.

Foster later explained that he walked over to Luis and told him that he had to die before shooting him point-blank in the head. Foster reloaded and shot Salvador. Eddy and the women heard both gunshots. They went back, and some of the women helped Foster slice off the flesh and dry it.[23]

None of them held Foster accountable for murdering the two men. They reasoned that he was deranged and not acting out of sheer malice. They also believed that the Indians were close to death anyway, so what Foster did was really a mercy killing. What went unsaid was that Luis and Salvador were "just Indians." Indians had no rights. Killing an Indian was like killing a varmint. To many white folks, Indians needed to be treated like a contagious disease and eradicated. At that time, Foster never would have been charged or tried for the slayings. The deaths of the Miwoks were the only time during the entire Donner Party ordeal that anyone was killed for food.[24]

After Luis and Salvador were butchered, the emigrants ate generous helpings of their flesh, but Eddy ate only dry grass. For the rest of the journey, neither Eddy nor the three women who were not related to Foster would sleep anywhere near him when they camped. They kept watch in case his desire to kill returned.[25]

That sleeping arrangement did not last very long. Just two days after the murders, the emigrants came upon an Indian trail. Wisely, they followed it, and in the afternoon, they reached an Indian village. The inhabitants were Miwoks, the tribe of Luis and Salvador.[26]

When the ragged and gaunt party first came into view, the Indians took them for ghosts and ran away. Then they heard pleas for help, and they responded. Once the emigrants were all in the village, the Miwoks cared for them. Acorns were one of the mainstays of the Miwok diet during the winter months, and the Indians gave their guests acorn bread and a thin soup made from the nuts. The Miwoks knew that starving people often died from overeating, so they kept the portions small even when the emigrants begged for more. The tannin in the acorns made them bitter to the taste.[27] Eddy could not eat them, so he stuck to his grass diet for the time being.

In the next several days, the emigrants were guided from village to village. At each stop, they continued to be cared for and fed. On January 17, after a week of recovery, Eddy had developed a taste for pine nuts and was the strongest of the party. With the help of two sturdy Indians, he hobbled along and finally was carried to Johnson's Ranch, fifteen miles away. The six other survivors remained behind.

After a difficult hike, the Indians and Eddy arrived at the cabin of a recent emigrant, Matthew Dill Ritchie. He and his family had made it to California just in time to spend the hard winter of 1846–1847 at Johnson's Ranch. When his young daughter, Harriet, opened the door and saw Eddy being held upright by two Indians, she was so stunned by his appearance that she burst into tears.[28] Ritchie brought Eddy inside, fed him, and put him to bed. Meanwhile, Harriet ran to neighboring cabins, spreading the word that lost pilgrims had been found and needed help. Everyone knew they must be some of the Donner Party that had been the source of rumors for weeks.

In no time, men and boys from the cabins scattered around Johnson's Ranch formed a party. The rescuers gathered blankets, food, medicine, and clothing and took off for the Indian camp. They arrived at about midnight, and by the following morning, they had returned to the ranch with each of the emigrants holding on to a rider on horseback.

The journey of thirty-three days was over for what was once a party of fifteen men and women. Eight of them—all males—were dead in the Sierra snow. Two men and five women survived to tell the tale. And what a tale they told! It spread like quicksilver across the land.

38. IN DIRE STRAITS

When the survivors of the snowshoe party were rescued and the out-side world learned the fate of the snowbound Donner Party, most of the emigrants were still trapped in their miserable camps. But on the west side of the Sierras, there was a whirlwind of activity focused on this group of people whose dreams had turned into nightmares.

As that was happening, the godforsaken emigrants were dealing with the tedium and utter horror of daily life at Truckee Lake and Alder Creek. They had become dislocated in time and knew nothing of what was happening elsewhere. Many of them no longer knew who they were or where they were. Not only did they not recognize the land, they did not recognize themselves.

Probably more than any of the emigrants, the mothers at the Truckee Lake cabins constantly experienced that sense of disconnection and loss of identity. Some retained their compassion for those outside their family, but others totally detached themselves from everyone except their own children. Like wounded animals, these women became she-wolves from the necessity of safeguarding their families' survival.[1]

There were exceptions. At the Breen cabin, overflowing with the Breens and the Reed family, Margaret Breen ran a tight ship. She was especially frugal when it came to dispensing the precious dried oxen meat she kept in a hidden larder. Fixated on keeping her seven children nourished, she could ill afford doling out any meat to others. Several emigrants who tried to coax her into giving them a little bit of the meat found that out. Still, she also had a softer side. She thought well of the Reed children, and her favorite was spunky Virginia.

When Peggy noticed that Virginia could not tolerate eating hides, she slipped the grateful girl small pieces of meat.[2] Patrick Breen also was a comfort to Virginia, who missed her father and came to appreciate Breen's presence as a protector and spiritual guide.

"I often went to the Catholic church before leaving home, but it was at Donner Lake that I made the vow to be a Catholic," Virginia later wrote. "The Breens were the only Catholic family in the Donner Party and prayers were said aloud regularly in that cabin night and morning. Our only light was from little pine sticks split up like kindling wood and kept constantly in the hearth. I was very fond of kneeling by the side of Mr. Breen and holding those little torches so that he might see to read."[3]

There was other reading material in the lake camp besides Breen's well-used Bible. Many of the emigrants had cached their books in the desert to lighten the load, but some had held on to a few favorite titles. Virginia Reed read and reread a thick tome that chronicled the life of Daniel Boone. Reading about Boone's colorful life and the trials and tribulations he faced probably took Virginia's mind off her own misfortunes.

Whenever she could, little Patty Reed was comforted by playing with the tiny wooden doll she could not bear to part with when the emigrants dumped most of their personal possessions. She kept Dolly hidden in the folds of her clothing. Patty and the other children also were expected to devote some of their time to studying Samuel Kirkham's *English Grammar in Familiar Lectures*, considered the best primer of the day.[4]

In the evening, the Reed children enjoyed having their mother or big sister Virginia read to them. They especially liked *The Flock of Sheep; or Familiar Explanations of Simple Facts*, a slim chapbook of sixteen pages illustrated with small wood engravings. It told a simplistic story of a mother teaching her little daughter, Ann Green, about the origins of food, shelter, and clothing.[5]

Patrick Breen, still urinating blood and fighting off nausea and pain from kidney stones, found comfort in reading the Scriptures and offering up prayers that went unanswered. He revealed some optimism in the entries that peppered his diary for January and February, such as ". . . very pleasant today sun shineing brilliantly renovates our spirits prais be to God, Amen," and when another storm approached, ". . . expecting some account from Siuters [Sutter's Fort] soon."[6]

In reality, there was not nearly enough food for everyone in the camps. The weather was horrendous, and the fickle sun that Breen praised usually peeked through the clouds only by high noon. As far as rescuers, there was no way of knowing whether James Reed and "Big Bill" McCutchen or the snowshoe party were still alive or had even come close to Sutter's Fort.

At the Murphys' cabin, Levinah Murphy—the family matriarch at only thirty-seven—was failing fast.[7] She had been in a rapid decline ever since falling ill after a Christmas supper of boiled bones. She tried her best to care for the little ones, including three grandchildren left in her care when her daughters went with the other snowshoers to find help. Levinah lost her sight from snow blindness and was becoming emotionally unstable from stress and strain. She experienced wide mood swings and would break into laughter and then suddenly burst into tears. It was all she could do to make a thin gruel from snowmelt and some coarsely ground wheat flour, which she spoon-fed to the nursing baby, Catherine Pike.[8]

Levinah became more distraught when her son John Landrum, who had turned seventeen while in camp, also started to fail from lack of nourishment. At one time a big strapping youngster, he could no longer eat hides and became delirious and difficult to control, much like his brother Lemuel just before he died with the snowshoe party.[9]

At the Alder Creek camp, the Donners and others kept vigil during the daylight hours, hoping a relief party would come into view. Sometimes young Jean-Baptiste Trudeau shinnied up a pine to scan the snowfields for any sign of movement. There was no food in the camp except some unsavory beef hides and field mice. Trudeau and Noah James continued to search for buried cattle. "They made excavations, then forced their hand-poles deep, deeper into the snow, but in vain their efforts—the nail and hook at the points brought up no sign of blood, hair, or hide," Eliza Donner wrote in her memoir.[10] George Donner, totally incapacitated, was still hanging on because of Tamzene's constant care of his badly infected hand.

Occasionally, various emigrants—usually the younger single men—went back and forth between the two camps to finagle some scraps of food under the guise of checking on everyone's well-being. They were seldom if ever successful. One January morning, Trudeau and John Denton came from the Alder Creek camp with Eliza Williams, the Reeds' servant girl, in tow.[11] It was the second time in a week that Eliza, who could not digest boiled hides, had begged Margret Reed for meat. There was no meat to give. The Donner Party was in dire straits. Margret tried to explain the situation, but Eliza insisted that she could not eat hides. As Breen noted in his journal, Margret then "sent her [Eliza] back [to Alder Creek] to live or die on them."[12]

Snow slowly began to fall just after sunrise on January 22. It increased in strength and ferocity all day and into the night. By the next day, it had become a full-blown blizzard. Breen declared it "the most severe storm we experienced this winter."[13] Over the next few days, the snow stopped occasionally and everyone's hopes rose before the storm returned, as fierce as ever.

On January 27, during a break in the storm, a ghostly Philippine Keseberg came to the Breens' cabin with sad news. Three days before, as the blowing snow raged outside the Murphy cabin where the Kesebergs had moved, Philippine's baby boy had died. Born on the trail and named Lewis for his father, the infant was less than six months old. Keseberg, shattered by the loss of his son, was still bothered by his infected foot and could not help his wife tuck the tiny corpse into a snowbank.

Philippine told the others of the poor conditions in the Murphy cabin. Levinah Murphy seemed to be going insane and needed any help she could get to take care of the babies left in her care. Three of the Murphy boys—Landrum, Bill, and Simon—were in a bad way, but Landrum was the worst.[14] Philippine predicted that he could not endure much longer.

Just a few days later in a cold cabin under a full moon, Landrum was lying on the cabin floor next to his two sick brothers and not far from Keseberg, still inconsolable after his son's death. Before Landrum passed, his mother pulled herself together enough to go to the Breens and beg for food to revive her boy. No one was in a giving mood at the lake camp. That same day, Elizabeth Graves called in the Reeds' loan of some meat many weeks before and seized some of the family's hides for collateral. But even Peggy Breen could not turn away a grieving mother. She graciously gave Levinah a small piece of meat.[15]

"I remember the little piece of meat; my mother gave half of it to my dying brother, and he ate it, fell off to sleep, with hollow death-gurgling snore, and when I went to him, and he was dead—starved to death in my presence," William Murphy said later.[16]

The first month of 1847 was over, but no relief was in sight. Three arduous months had passed since the emigrants had been trapped in the snow. As February started, the emigrants would again bear witness to a rapid succession of deaths.

On February 2, another snowy day with strong winds from the southwest, Harriet McCutchen, the one-year-old only child of William and Amanda McCutchen, died without her parents. Her father had left the wagon train long before, and her mother was with the snowshoe party. Lovina Graves had promised to take care of Harriet along with her grandchildren. When Lovina began her rapid physical and mental decline, things went terribly wrong for all the children.

As if malnutrition and bitter cold were not enough, Harriet's body hosted an infestation of lice on her scalp and all over her tiny body. As the parasites crawled over the child, feeding on her blood, their painful bites caused such intense itching that her agonizing cries could be heard throughout the camp. Many years later, Patty Reed could still hear "the terrible screams of that poor little one."[17] Near the end, Levinah tied the baby's arms to her sides to stop her from continually scratching her bloody arms and legs. The screaming got louder and then suddenly stopped. Harriet's death was merciful. The emigrants dug a grave inside the Graves cabin and laid her to rest.

Two days later, on February 4, another toddler perished. Margaret Eddy was withered like a peach struck by frost. Her mother, Eleanor, like the other young nursing mothers, was so sick and starving that she had no more milk for the girl. It was said that Eleanor was almost beyond grieving. She lingered a few days and died on February 7. John Breen later buried the mother and baby together in the snow.[18]

The next day, Augustus Spitzer, one of the accused killers of Wolfinger on the trail, died after weeks of suffering. Spitzer had become an outcast who probably would have been hanged if there been enough healthy men to do the job. Instead, he was simply ignored and left to die on his own. Some emigrants recalled that just before he died in the dark morning hours of February 8, he pleaded with Peggy Breen to give him a morsel of meat to put in his mouth so that he could die at ease. She ignored him and went back to sleep.[19]

On February 9, Breen reported that "Milt [Elliott] at Murphys not able to get out of bed."[20] The teamster had collapsed on the floor and could not get up. He was one of the most beloved members of the Donner Party and a young man whom the Reeds considered part of their family. Elliott's health had gradually declined but had gone unnoticed. His main wish was to not die alone surrounded by strangers. He tried to move into the Breen cabin to be close to the Reeds, but Breen was concerned about Elliott's condition and did not want his children to witness death. Margret Reed, whom Elliott had called "Ma," helped him make his way to the Murphy cabin, where he died. He was twenty-eight years old.

"When Milt Elliott died—our faithful friend, who seemed so like a brother—my mother and I dragged him up out of the cabin and covered him with snow," Virginia Reed later wrote. "Commencing at his feet, I patted the pure white snow down softly until I reached his face. Poor Milt! It was hard to cover that face from sight forever, for with his death our best friend was gone."[21]

Life, such as it was, went on at the lake camp. Death could not be ignored. It slept in the dampness of the prison cells the emigrants called cabins. It rose up with the steam of boiling bones and beef hides. It was in the eyes of the next person to die. Like the cunning thief, death found a home in darkness and turned dreams into nightmares.

"One night we had all gone to bed—I was with my mother and the little ones, all huddled together to keep from freezing—but I could not sleep," Virginia Reed remembered. "It was a fearful night and I felt that the hour was not far distant when we would go to sleep—never to wake again in the world. All at once I found myself on my knees with my hands clasped, looking up through the darkness, making a vow that if God would send us relief and let me see my father again I would be a Catholic. That prayer was answered."[22]

39. MAN ON A MISSION

JANUARY–FEBRUARY 1847

James Reed—the subject of his daughter Virginia's desperate prayers —was neither dead nor lost. He had been a busy man since early November 1846 when he and William McCutchen tried to reach the trapped emigrants but had to return to Sutter's Fort because of the impassable snow. After that disappointment, Reed persevered in utter defiance of the unrelenting wrath of nature and the bothersome war in Alta California.

Reed's most important objective was to recover his family and the rest of the Donner Party. At the same time, he wanted to make his mark in California. As he scrambled to find a way to carry out the rescue mission, Reed also managed to pave the way for his family's transition to their new home in the West.

Reed must have been painfully aware that he had failed to connect with fellow emigrants. Whether he would have admitted any culpability was another matter. Arguably, he could have been the Donner Party's most effective leader, but what was perceived as his arrogant attitude and overbearing personality worked against him. So did his insistence that the company take the Hastings Cutoff. Even though the other emigrants went along with Reed of their own free will, that decision made him no friends. Certainly, the death of a teamster at Reed's hand was the crowning blow that resulted in his expulsion from the company.

Yet if the members of the Donner Party were foot soldiers in the vanguard for Manifest Destiny, then Reed was a classic standard-bearer for the cause. He never proselytized to "subdue the continent" or "teach old nations a new civilization," as William Gilpin, a fervent proponent of Manifest Destiny, put it.[1] Reed exemplified another profile—the mid-nineteenth-century American capitalist whose failed business caused him to pack up his family and head to California for a fresh start. James Reed believed in his own manifest destiny. That strong belief, combined with stubbornness and perhaps some Irish luck, kept Reed going during those long and difficult months of separation from Margret and the children. The first time he went to Sutter's Fort in late October 1846, Reed immediately began to plan a rescue mission. He also looked for property in the Promised Land.

On October 29, just one day after arriving, Reed, Edwin Bryant, and the Reverend James Dunleavy had drafted a petition to seek land rights on an island in the Sacramento River.[2] The men knew one another from the trail. Bryant was one of the leaders of the packmule train. Dunleavy, whose party had been asked to leave the Russell Company early on because his 140 head of cattle were slowing down the wagon train, was a Methodist preacher and missionary.[3] The document they signed was sent to Washington Bartlett, the alcalde, or chief magistrate, in Yerba Buena, soon to become an important city of commerce named San Francisco.[4] Bryant had come across Long Island, so named because it was "twenty to thirty miles in length," while exploring the territory around Sutter's Fort. Later, he recorded his favorable impressions of the river and the potential of the land they intended to use for farming and grazing.[5]

Based solely on Bryant's word, Reed invested in land he had never seen. That became a trend. When Reed and McCutchen returned to Sutter's Fort after their first rescue attempt was aborted, Reed continued to buy property. He desperately wanted to retrieve his family, but if an opportunity arose, he was ready to make deals and conduct business.

Reed was not dissuaded even when John Sutter explained that further rescue attempts would have to be postponed until the winter storms had ceased. Few men in the Sacramento Valley were available for relief parties. Most able-bodied males had gone off to fight in the war. Reed could not sit still and wait for winter to end. Taking Sutter's advice, Reed departed from New Helvetia (Sutter's Fort) to seek help from Commander Joseph B. Hull, senior military authority and highest-ranking naval officer in Yerba Buena.[6] Reed rode south bearing a letter of introduction to Hull as well as official papers allowing him "and three companions to pass to the 'Pueblo de San José' without molestation," signed by Lieutenant Edward Meyer Kern, military commander for the District of the Sacramento.[7] In no time, Reed encountered a problem. "When I arrived at San José, I found the San Francisco side of the bay was occupied by the Mexicans."[8]

Forced to lay over in San José, Reed put his time to good use by finding out what the area could offer an ambitious forty-six-year-old in search of a new home for his family. Founded in the Santa Clara Valley by the Spanish in 1777 as El Pueblo de San José de Guadalupe, the settlement of irregular streets lined with adobe houses was the oldest in Alta California. Reed found it all strange and exotic—the main plaza where bears and bulls fought to the death for the crowd's entertainment and gambling dens where handsome dark-eyed women played monte and other games of chance alongside men.[9] Most appealing were the town's proximity to the sea, ample freshwater sources, and vast expanses of arable land.

Reed quickly made friends and sought out others he had known in Illinois or had met on the emigrant trail, using his network of contacts and a proven instinct for seizing the right opportunities. He also wisely used some of his secret stash of money that might have been as large as $10,000, a tidy sum for a man who had declared bankruptcy.[10]

One of the most important contacts Reed made in San José was John Burton, a Massachusetts native who had deserted a New England merchant ship and taken up residence in the pueblo of San José in 1830. He married a Mexican woman, assumed the title of captain, and made his living as a merchant and rancher. Among the Anglo population, Burton was known as "a pioneer of the pioneers," but the native Californios dubbed him Capitan Viejo, the "Old Captain."[11] In October 1846, Burton was appointed the first American alcalde of San José. Although he had little formal education, he was blessed with "considerable common sense" and was "reputed to have been very honest and to have the esteem and confidence of the native population."[12]

Before long, Reed was a frequent visitor at the Juzgado, the hall of justice that housed the courts, the calaboose (jail), and the alcalde's office. In that old adobe building built in 1798, Burton listened to citizens' grievances, meted out justice, settled disputes, and carried out other duties of the office.[13] Chief of those other duties was approving the many requests to purchase property.

Reed's timing was ideal. Great change would soon impact commerce, government, the legal system, and every aspect of daily life. The war with Mexico, at least in Alta California, was grinding to an end. Burton would not remain the chief magistrate much longer.

Although Reed was thwarted from assembling a rescue party right then, he astutely used his time to grab as much land as he could by filing claims with the accommodating Capitan Viejo. It was a smart maneuver. It was doubtful whether Burton even examined the documents before giving his blessing. On a few occasions, Reed turned in petitions to purchase land in the names of family members and friends and forged their signatures.

In the midst of his land acquisition, Reed was forced to face up to an important obligation he had committed to weeks before at Sutter's Fort. In the company of Edwin Bryant, William "Owl" Russell, George McKinstry, Lilburn Boggs, and several other emigrants, Reed had signed a document promising to serve with the American forces in the war against Mexico. The only caveat was that he first be given a chance to rescue the Donner Party emigrants.[14] That mission had not succeeded, and now the time had come to step up and accept his commission as a lieutenant.

Reed was hesitant. He remained hopeful that if he could get to Yerba Buena, he would find enough men for a rescue party. Captain Joseph María Weber, the stern German-born commander of the U.S. volunteers at San José, would have none of it. "You must fight," Weber told Reed. "If you don't it will be murder. You have been in the Black Hawk War, and you understand fighting.[15] Besides unless you help us you'll never reach Yerba Buena alive. Every gringo's life is in danger."[16]

Reed realized that Weber was right. By fulfilling his duty and participating in the war, Reed could expedite the assembling of a relief team. Helping the other Americans also could benefit him in the future. A reluctant but stoic Reed accepted the lieutenancy of thirty-three mounted riflemen, later described as a "motley band" mostly comprised of "sailors, whalers, and landsmen," some of whom Reed already knew.[17] By most accounts, Reed's brief tenure as an officer went reasonably well. He cut a fine figure leading his band of volunteers on routine patrols through the countryside and reconnoitering the stands of tall timber.

The lone personnel problem Reed dealt with was Jotham Curtis, the overlander from Missouri whom Reed and McCutchen had come upon during their first failed rescue attempt. Reed said Curtis and his wife had "hailed us like angels" when he and McCutchen rescued the snowbound couple at the foot of Emigrant Gap in the Sierras. Reed and McCutchen had shared the couple's supper of roasted dog and later led them to sanctuary at Sutter's Fort. En route, McCutchen and Curtis had a row about the couple's slow pace of travel.

Later, Reed suffered the defiant Curtis's abusive tongue during his military service. Neither patient nor long-suffering, Reed quickly had his fill of sass. The contrary Curtis, once referred to as "a peculiar character," was immediately discharged from further military service for insubordination and failure to obey orders.[18]

That winter, Reed and his ragtag dragoons stayed on the move. While out scouting, they lived off the land, much to the displeasure of many Californios who were angry about the massive land grab by squatters and gringo newcomers.

The Californios had long been dissatisfied with their relationship to the Mexican government and had even contemplated a revolution. Still, they had little reason to be supportive of the American emigrants who schemed to colonize the land. The Americans' main objective was to turn California into an independent territory like Texas and soon after, make it one of the largest states in the Union. The war with Mexico divided the American people who monitored the conflict from afar. The majority of citizens supported the conflict, but some important political and public circles called it "Mr. Polk's

War." One of the most vocal in his opposition was James Reed's friend and lawyer Abraham Lincoln, the Whig Congressman from Illinois, who saw the war as immoral and a threat to the nation's values.[19]

In California, the Reverend Walter Colton, a highly respected U.S. Navy chaplain and the first American alcalde of Monterey, condemned the tactics of his countrymen in early 1847.[20]

"There is one feature in our military operations here [in Alta California] which is far asunder from that system of order which appertains to a well-disciplined army. Every one who can raise among the emigrants thirty or forty men becomes a captain, and starts off to fight pretty much on his own hook. Nor is he very scrupulous as to the mode in which he obtains his horses, saddles, and other equipments."[21]

As a lowly acting lieutenant, Reed likely did not act independently or "on his own hook," as Colton put it, when it came to the plundering and pillaging of Californios. Reed stayed busy carrying out orders and keeping up morale, especially when the weather turned sour. The monotonous days and nights of hard riding with hardly any sleep took a toll. Then at last, Reed and his troops were ordered into combat. It was a far cry from a real battle, but even a skirmish would do.

The incident was triggered by the actions of Reed's commanding officer, Captain Weber—a German expatriate and former Mexican national. Acting with no legal authority, Weber ordered his junior officers to confiscate as much livestock as they needed to feed the militia that was recruited from the local American population. Instead of being repaid at a fair market value for any property or animals, the rancheros were left high and dry or were given worthless scrip.[22] The gangs of volunteers—fueled by aguardiente, a potent brandy made of mission grapes, apples, or pears—repeatedly raided the horse and cattle herds of every rancho between Yerba Buena and San José on the San Francisco peninsula.[23]

When a delegation representing the besieged rancheros asked Naval Commander John B. Montgomery to remove Weber from his post, their petition was denied. Montgomery said Weber had not violated any rules or regulations and chided the delegation for questioning the integrity of one of his officers.[24]

Weber and his volunteers were not the only ones who commandeered horses and livestock. Lieutenant Washington Bartlett, the naval officer who acted as the American alcalde in Yerba Buena, scoured the ranchos for fresh provisions and stock. Eventually, the requisitioning became nothing more than pillaging. The rancho patrons, including the highly respected Don Francisco Sanchez, a former alcalde of Yerba Buena whose family had come to California in 1776, lost all patience.[25]

When Lieutenant Bartlett and five armed sailors from the U.S. sloop *Warren* came ashore to procure more cattle and horses, they rode to Sanchez's San Mateo rancho. A large force of Californios led by Sanchez seized the Americans and took them hostage. This act of defiance was not against the United States but was in protest of the transgressions of the volunteer militia led by officers such as Bartlett and especially Weber, who was considered "to be the principal culprit of the misdeeds."[26]

On January 2, 1847, an expeditionary command led in part by Captain Weber stumbled upon Sanchez and his sizable force of Californios just west of the mission Santa Clara de Asis. Intent on rescuing Bartlett and his sailors, the Americans, including Reed's motley volunteers, backed up by a detachment of U.S. Marines, engaged the Californios in a scuffle called the Battle of Santa Clara. Sometimes referred to as "The Battle of Mustard Stalks" because much of the site was covered by a large mustard field, the skirmish lasted only a few hours before a truce was called.[27]

The most reliable casualty numbers claimed that four Californios had been killed and four wounded, whereas the Americans reported two wounded and one horse killed.[28] Eventually, a treaty was signed and prisoners were swapped, including Bartlett and his men.

Acting Lieutenant James Reed wrote to John Sutter on January 12, "I am heartily glad that I had such an opportunity to fight for my country. . . . Every man in the fight acted well his part. The reason that there were so few killed was because we could not get close to them. Their horses were fine, while ours were broke down."[29]

The Mexican-American War in Alta California was effectively

over after the fray at Santa Clara. In his official report dated March 15, 1847, General Stephen W. Kearny summed it up. "The Californians are now quiet, and I shall endeavor to keep them so by mild and gentle treatment. Had they received such treatment from the time our flag was hoisted here, in July last, I believe there would have been but little or no resistance on their part. They have been most cruelly and shamefully abused by our own people—by the volunteers (American emigrants) raised in this part of the country and on the Sacramento. Had they [the Californios] not resisted they would have been unworthy of the name of men."[30]

Reed not only emerged unscathed from the clash at Santa Clara, his streak of good luck continued. Although his short-lived military hitch stymied efforts to put together a rescue party, the war ultimately proved to be beneficial for him and his family. Soon after Reed returned to San José, Naval Lieutenant Robert F. Pinkney (sometimes spelled Pinckney) appointed him the officer in charge of the Mission San José. Years before, it had been one of the twenty-one Spanish missions in Alta California established by Catholic priests of the Franciscan order to convert and "civilize" the native Indian tribes.[31]

But when Mexico gained independence from Spain, everything changed. The government of Mexico—unable to financially support the upkeep—secularized the missions and eventually divided up and sold the vast landholdings.[32] Reed quickly issued a public mandate that "any person taking tiles or timber or in any way disturbing the houses belonging to the Mission of San José will be punished according to the law."[33]

Pinkney had given Reed control not only of the mission buildings but also of the surrounding land, which included productive orchards and vineyards, some of which had been planted before the mission was established in 1797. In December, Reed had already filed for land claims near the mission for his family. He enlisted William Daniels and John Stark to help plant crops. On January 21, Reed and his helpers appeared before Magistrate John Burton, who gladly declared that Reed had satisfied the homestead provisions for improving the land claim he had filed.[34] Later, Reed and Padre José María Suarez del Real of the San José Mission came to an agreement that allowed Reed to lease the premises and cultivate the valuable orchards and vineyards "on the shares," meaning both parties would share in the profits or losses of the undertaking.

Now the only thing keeping Reed from proceeding with his plans to rescue his family was his release from service as an officer. On January 26, Reed's commanding officer, Captain Weber, signed the discharge document.

Reed immediately saddled up and rode to Yerba Buena (San Francisco), where he hoped to raise funds and enlist men for a relief party. It was already February. Reed was unaware that word was spreading about the wagon train's disaster in the Sierra Nevadas. As early as January 16, the day before William Eddy staggered into Johnson's Ranch just ahead of the rest of the Forlorn Hope snowshoers, a brief news item had appeared in the *California Star*, a newspaper only a week old. Under the headline "Emigrants in the Mountains," the report did not name the caravan or any of the emigrants but stated that a party of about sixty from the United States was prevented from crossing the mountain range by an early, heavy snowfall. It also mentioned that John Sutter had provided mules and provisions but an early rescue attempt failed. The story ended with a plea: "We hope that our citizens will do something for the relief of those unfortunate people."[35]

As he rode, carrying a petition signed by friends and citizens of San José asking the authorities in Yerba Buena to aid the stranded emigrants, Reed had no knowledge that a rescue party had already been formed. He knew nothing of how dire the situation had become at the snowbound camps where people were dying. He did not know of the snowshoe party's survivors eating the flesh of the dead to stay alive. The only thing that James Reed knew for sure was that he had to get help.

40. TO THE RESCUE

James Reed rode into San Francisco on February 1, 1847, two days after Yerba Buena's new name had become official.[1] It felt like spring, but more winter weather was yet to come, especially for the Donner Party, awaiting another snowstorm in makeshift camps on the other side of the Sierras.[2]

Shrouded in sea fog, the San Francisco that greeted Reed was a far cry from the metropolis it was to become. In 1847, it was a village of fewer than five hundred people, not counting Indians, even though they vastly outnumbered all other racial groups in California.[3]

Once he had his bearings, Reed struck out in search of funding for a rescue party. He carried a petition signed by prominent citizens of San José, beseeching Commodore Robert F. Stockton, the U.S. military governor of California Territory, to outfit a snowshoe expedition to retrieve the trapped emigrants.[4] When Reed went to the commodore's headquarters, however, he found that Stockton was elsewhere.

Instead of waiting for Stockton, Reed sought out Captain Joseph B. Hull, the officer whom Reed had originally wanted to contact before the call to military duty in the Mexican War interrupted his plans. "I presented my petition to Commodore [Captain] Hull, also making a statement of the condition of the people in the mountains as far as I knew; the number of them, and what would be needed in provisions and help to get them out," Reed recalled in 1871. "He made an estimate of the expense that would attend the expedition, and said that he would do anything within reason to further the object, but was afraid that the department at Washington would not sustain him, if he made the general out-fit. His sympathy was that of a man and a gentleman."[5]

Reed wanted more than sympathy, however. He wanted immediate action, and he spent the rest of the day drumming up support. He sought out acquaintances from the California Trail as well as veterans who had served in the recent military expeditions. One of Reed's most enthusiastic supporters was the Reverend James G. Dunleavy, the Methodist minister who had left the Owl Russell wagon train in May 1846 just as Reed and the Donners brothers joined it.[6] In October, Reed and Dunleavy—a brother Mason—had first reunited at Sutter's Fort. Dunleavy was willing to use his influence and oratorical skill to further Reed's mission.

Reed found another staunch advocate in Washington Bartlett. After briefly being held hostage by the Californios, the young lieutenant was still alcalde of San Francisco. After conferring with Captain Hull, Bartlett called for a public meeting so Reed could make an appeal for manpower and financial aid. The gathering was set for the evening of February 3 at the City Hotel—the first real hotel in town.[7] News of the event spread quickly.

Despite a steady rain, the popular hotel saloon was crowded, with "nearly every male citizen" of the town in attendance,[8] including Sam Brannan, publisher of the town's first newspaper, the *California Star*.[9] Reed saw a few familiar faces, such as Andrew Grayson, who had been part of the Donner-Reed caravan until it reached the Little Sandy, where Grayson wisely opted to not take the Hastings Cutoff.[10]

At 7:00 P.M., there was standing room only. Bartlett welcomed everyone, read the San José petition aloud, and introduced Reed. Reed began to tell the story of his family and the families of George and Jacob Donner and all the others they had met on the long wagon trail to California. Reed felt deeply buried emotions that had never been released. His voice cracked, and he could no longer speak. He burst into tears and sank into his chair, sobbing hard and loud. No one could have called Reed arrogant that rainy night.[11]

Instantly, Dunleavy leaped to his feet and picked up where Reed had left off, based on his own trail experiences and pieces of news and gossip.

"Those who heard that thrilling address of Mr. Dunleary [sic] will never forget the effect upon his attentive audience, while he related the trials of their journey and the probable fate of the starving company, unless relief was soon carried them—perhaps already too late," wrote J. Quinn Thornton, who visited with some Donner Party survivors during an 1847 stop in San Francisco.[12]

Dunleavy's final words were barely out of his mouth when the saloon erupted in cheers and huzzahs. A mass of men, many of them weeping and some clutching fistfuls of silver dollars, rushed forward to give money to a stunned Reed. Lieutenant Bartlett and some attentive Marines restored order. Committees were appointed, including one to receive contributions, and lines formed for the donors.[13] At least $800 was collected that night to purchase provisions, horses, and mules for a rescue team. In the following days, the amount rose to more than $1,500.[14]

Just as it looked as though the expedition was ready to depart, everything ground to a temporary halt when John Sutter's launch *Sacramento* sailed into the harbor.[15] Aboard was a courier with an urgent letter for Alcalde Bartlett. Dated January 29, 1847, it was written by John Sinclair, alcalde of the Northern District.[16]

Bartlett read the letter and was stunned. It spelled out the story of how five women and two men from the fifteen members of the snowshoe party had stayed alive by eating the flesh of six of the eight men who had perished along the way. Sinclair's account was based on a letter dictated by William Eddy, recovering with the others at Johnson's Ranch.

Sinclair also reported that a party of able-bodied men was being raised to recover the remaining members of the Donner Party, and he urged Bartlett to do the same. According to Sinclair, a thrifty Scotsman, every man would be paid three dollars per day "from the time they start until they return" unless the emigrants themselves could cover the costs. "We likewise hold ourselves responsible for the provisions, at the same time we feel confident that our government will be willing to pay all expenses incurred in such a case as this, and we know that there is not one of our fellow citizens but is willing to aid and assist us in saving the lives of those helpless women and children."[17]

Sinclair's shocking news caused serious concern for the committee leadership in San Francisco. The condition of the Donner Party was far worse than had been thought, and any rescue attempts would require more support. Knowing that another relief party was being formed at Johnson's Ranch, the group decided that more preparation time was needed before leaving San Francisco. It seemed prudent to devote a few days to recruit additional men and collect more food and supplies. In addition, the second party would establish a base camp along the way for replenishing supplies. Everyone agreed that this change in strategy was for the best, even the anxious Reed.

Rescue would not be easy. More than one team would be needed to retrieve anyone still alive, but there was still a chance.

41. THE FIRST RELIEF

WHILE JAMES REED and the U.S. Navy brass in San Francisco raised money and collected a boatload of food and supplies, a few men and boys at Sutter's Fort and Johnson's Ranch prepared to do battle with the stormy Sierras. Their aim was to reach the mountain camps as quickly as possible and bring back alive whoever was left of the Donner Party. Thus, their letter to John Sinclair, alcalde of the Northern District, came about in this way.

Soon after the seven survivors of the snowshoe party were accounted for and tucked into feather beds at Johnson's place, the men who had retrieved them—in the words of one of the rescuers—"commenced to devise some plan to releeve" the emigrants who were still snowbound in the mountains.[1] Because of the serious shortage of manpower among the scattering of emigrant families wintering at Johnson's Ranch, it took two weeks to find enough recruits, and there were no surplus provisions. The nearest settlement of any size was Sutter's Fort, forty miles to the south. Like the rest of the Sacramento Valley, many of the men there had not yet returned from the waning war.

To gain Sinclair's sympathy so that he would rally more men, it was determined that William Eddy—one of the survivors of the snowshoe party—would be the one to make the impassioned plea. Still weak but much improved after some sleep and a few meals, Eddy, from his bed, dictated a letter to be taken to Sinclair. The missive was given to a Miwok runner who crossed the floodwaters of the Bear River on a makeshift raft and reached Sinclair's ranch that same evening.[2] The alcalde was away on business for a few days, so his wife, Mary, accepted the letter. The Indian messenger did not leave empty-handed. Mary gave him a bundle of undergarments to tote back for the women of the snowshoe party.

The next morning, she took Eddy's letter to Captain Edward M. Kern at Sutter's Fort. With both Sinclair and Sutter away, Kern was left with the task of enlisting volunteers for a rescue team. He called for a meeting at the fort's armory, but only a few men showed up, mostly emigrants just off the trail and some sailors who likely had taken "French leave"—popular military jargon for deserting their ships—to work for Sutter.[3]

By all accounts, Kern was an unlikely recruiter. An epileptic suffering from numerous health problems, he was not a trained military officer but an accomplished illustrator and cartographer who longed to be outdoors drawing and collecting botanical specimens. He would have been far better suited discussing fauna and flora with Tamzene Donner than trying to convince strangers to risk their lives on a dangerous rescue mission.

Kern began his pitch by briefly describing the importance of the task ahead. The few men at the meeting sat silent and poker-faced. That quickly changed when Kern announced that he could offer volunteers as much as three dollars per day, a princely sum for that time. It was the same pay that Kern received as a cartographer. By comparison, monthly pay for most soldiers fighting in the Mexican War ranged from eight dollars for a private to seventy-five dollars for a full colonel.[4] When pressed for details, however, Kern sadly admitted that he lacked authority to set the pay for volunteers. All he could do was recommend an amount. That changed everything. Without a guarantee for compensation, only three men stayed in the armory.[5]

The oldest of the recruits was Aquilla Glover, a forty-year-old Kentuckian. Glover had left Missouri for California in the spring of 1846 with his wife and son in a wagon train headed by the Reverend James G. T. Dunleavy—the minister who had parted ways with Owl Russell's caravan and was helping James Reed to muster his own rescue party in San Francisco.[6]

Riley Septimus (Sept) Moutrey also stepped forward and signed on with Kern. Moutrey was another 1846 emigrant who had crossed paths with the Donner Party. He had been married along the Platte to fifteen-year-old Mary Lucy Lard, daughter of the man he worked for as a teamster.[7]

The third enlistee was a man of mystery named Joseph Sels, remembered as being "good-humored" and thought to be a runaway sailor called "Jack the Sailor."[8] He signed the rescue party's roster using the name Joe Foster.

Kern's recruitment efforts stalled until Sinclair returned to Rancho del Paso. After reading Eddy's letter soliciting help, Sinclair incorporated details of the plight of the Donner Party in the communiqué he sent to Lieutenant Bartlett in San Francisco. Next, Sinclair and Sutter jointly announced that they personally would pay each member of the party three dollars a day if the U.S. government failed to make good on Kern's promise. They also promised to provide horses, pack animals, and provisions. Straightaway, four more volunteers came forward.[9]

Daniel Rhoads, a strapping twenty-five-year-old overland emigrant, was one of them. After five months on the California Trail, he and his wife, Amanda, had arrived in the Sacramento Valley in October 1846. They made the journey with fifty-one members of their family in a ten-wagon caravan led by his father, Thomas Foster Rhoads, a Mormon elder. It was said to be the largest single-family wagon train to ever make the long trek to California.[10]

Rhoads wrote, "They gave the alarm that the people [the Donner Party] would all die without assistance. It was 2 weeks before any person would consent to go. Finally we concluded we would go or die trying for not to make any attempt to save them would be a disgrace to us and California as long as time lasted."[11]

Sinclair, knowing his letter to Bartlett in San Francisco would prompt more help for the stranded emigrants, set out on foot for Johnson's Ranch ahead of the volunteers to help oversee preparations for the rescue party. As soon as he arrived, Sinclair made sure recruitment efforts there went well and that as many horses as possible were rounded up for the mission.[12]

On January 31, the rescue team from Sutter's Fort was ready.

Seven mounted men trailing a string of packhorses rode through the fort gates, crossed the American River, and headed north. Aquilla Glover was at the head of the slow-moving pack train. The recent rains had resulted in thick mud that slowed travel. It took two days for the volunteers to reach Johnson's Ranch. When they got there, no time was wasted. All of them immediately joined in with the others already hard at work butchering the half dozen fat beeves that William Johnson had donated to the cause.[13]

"We killed some beef cattle and dried the meat over fires," Rhoads later wrote. "We pounded some wheat in Indian stone mortars and ground some in coffee-mills (no grist mills nor flour nor meal of any kind in those days). We cut the hides of the animals we killed into strips for future construction of snow-shoes. Although we worked night & day without intermission except for short intervals for sleep these preparations occupied us three days."[14]

What came to be called the First Relief Party was ready to go. It was a diverse bunch, numbering fourteen. Some of them would be in support roles and not on the team that went all the way to the camps. None of the rescuers was an experienced mountaineer, but several had plenty of moxie and—as the old scouts put it—were stout enough to hunt bear with a switch.

Originally, Captain Kern was to lead the party, but he and several of the men recognized that he was not the best choice. Instead, Kern would remain at the base camp to oversee logistics and make sure a supply line was kept open.[15]

Aquilla Glover and Reason Penelope Tucker were chosen to lead the First Relief. Both men were levelheaded and had the respect of everyone in the party. One of Tucker's neighbors, John Rhoads, joined the team. Rhoads was not about to allow his younger brother, Daniel, to go without him. Tucker picked his fifteen-year-old son George W. Tucker to go along and assigned him to guard a stockpile of provisions and to tend spare horses at a base camp in the foothills. Another young man, William Coon, was chosen to help young Tucker. The few mentions of Coon in print claim that he was feebleminded.[16]

The elder Tucker and Glover were already acquainted with most of the members of the First Relief, such as forty-year-old Matthew Ritchie. It was the Ritchie residence at Johnson's Ranch where the exhausted Eddy had appeared, looking so ghastly that young Harriett Ritchie became hysterical when she opened the door. Ritchie's nineteen-year-old son, William Dill Ritchie, was hired to haul supplies to the rescuers as they descended from the Sierras.

Some members of the rescue team were not overland emigrants. Edward "Ned" Coffeemeyer, like Joseph Sels, was a sailor on French leave, likely from a whaler.[17] A German named Adolph "Greasy Jim" Brueheim also hired on.[18] Joseph Verrot, a French-Canadian who had left John Frémont's second expedition at Sutter's Fort in 1844 after crossing the Sierras, rode with the rescue party. A skilled woodsman, or *voyageur*, Verrot had helped to bring back the six survivors of the snowshoe party.[19]

Although he quickly proved inconsequential as far as contributing to the efforts of the First Relief, Jotham Curtis was listed on the roster. He had been trapped in the snow with his wife just ahead of the Donner Party and rescued by James Reed and William McCutchen. Only a few days before he appeared at Johnson's Ranch, Curtis had been discharged from military service for insubordination and failing to obey the direct orders of his superior officer, James Reed.

William Eddy, still emaciated and feverish, was the last man to join the party. Although Sinclair and others tried to discourage him from going on the mission, Eddy was determined to return to the camp where he had last seen his wife and two children. He was going even if he had to be tied in the saddle.

On February 4, the First Relief Party was ready to depart Johnson's Ranch for the Sierras when some of the horses being saddled broke away.[20] According to the party's diary, by the time the horses were rounded up, "there was every appearance of a storm coming on the day being nearly spent the party considered it best to remain until morning rather than risk the destruction of their provisions by the rain which in a short time after fell in torrents accompanied by one of the heaviest hurricanes ever experienced on the Sacramento."[21]

It was still raining on February 5 and would do so for a few more days, but the rescue party would not wait any longer. The string of pack animals was in place. The volunteers ate a hot breakfast and mounted their horses. Eddy was so weak he had to be helped into the saddle. He was still hopeful about the rescue, not knowing that just the night before, his daughter, Margaret, had died in the camp at Truckee Lake. His wife, Eleanor, would die two days later and be buried with her baby in a snowbank.

Before the rescue party left the ranch, John Sinclair offered a few words of encouragement, "requesting them to never turn their backs on the Mountains until they had brought away as many of their suffering fellow-beings as possible."[22]

The long procession moved out. They were still in sight of Johnson's Ranch when travel became challenging. The path they followed was a quagmire made worse by persistent rain. More than once, animals bearing heavy loads of food and supplies bogged down in the belly-deep mud. This required the removal of all the goods so a team of mules could pull them free. By the end of the first day, the party had traveled ten miles but in the next two days managed only a total of fifteen miles.[23]

When the sun peeked through the clouds, the party devoted one entire day to drying out their soaked clothing and provisions. They made scaffolds from tree branches and hung their stores of meat, blankets, and clothing on rope lines to dry in the sunshine. They stoked fires throughout the day and night. In the morning, they set out, stopping only when they came upon a good stand of grass for the horses and mules.

"The next day, we got to Steep Hollow Creek, one of the branches of the Bear River," George Tucker recalled in 1879. "The stream was not more than a hundred feet wide, but it was about twenty feet deep, and the current was very swift. We felled a large pine tree across it, but the current swayed down so that the water ran over it about a foot deep. We tied ropes together and stretched them across to make a kind of hand railing, and succeeded in carrying over all our things."[24]

It did not go so well when they tried to get the animals to swim across the stream. The first two horses had to be forced into the water, but the current was too much. They were carried downstream, and one almost drowned. "We then tied ropes together, part of the men went over, and tying a rope to each horse, those on one side would force him into the water, and the others would draw him across," explained Tucker. "We lost a half day at this place. That night we climbed a high mountain, and came to snow. Camped that night without any feed for our horses."[25]

The next day, the party reached Mule Springs, on a high ridge north of Bear River. In some places, the snow was four feet deep, making it impossible to go any farther on horseback. It was decided to continue the trek on foot. Mule Springs would serve as a base camp. Some of the men unloaded the pack animals while others cut poles and cedar boughs and built a shelter to store the provisions.

In the morning, Verrot and Eddy took the pack animals back to Johnson's Ranch. Desperate to reach his family, Eddy objected but finally had to admit that he was too weak to continue the journey on foot. The teenaged boys George Tucker and Billy Coon made themselves as comfortable as possible.[26] They were assigned to guard the supplies and tend to the horses until the other people returned.

On February 11, the ten remaining members of the relief party left Mule Springs. Each of them brought a hatchet, a tin cup, and a blanket. Each also carried fifty to seventy-five pounds of dried beef and flour, with the exception of Curtis, who claimed he could tote only half a load. They hiked "Indian file" in the hard-crusted snow, each stepping in the footprints of the man in front of him.[27] When the leader who was breaking the trail wore out, he went to the rear of the line, and the next man took his place.

"Of course we had no guide and most of our journey was through a dense pine forest but the lofty peak which overlooks the lake was in sight at intervals and this and the judgment of our two leaders were our sole means of direction," Daniel Rhoads recalled twenty-six years later. "When we first started from the fort Capt Sutter assured us that we should be followed by other parties as soon as the necessary preparations could be made. For the guidance of those who might follow us and as a signal to any of the emigrants who might be straggling about in the mountains as well as for our own direction on our return trip, we set fire to every dead pine tree on and near our trail. At the end of every three days journey (15 or 20 miles) we made up a small bundle of dried meat and hung it to the bough of a tree to lighten the burden we carried and for subsistence on our return."[28]

The snow became deeper as the relief team climbed higher. Frustration grew with each agonizing step. At one point, they stopped so each member of the party could make snowshoes using pine boughs and rawhide. Reports were mixed about the value of the snowshoes. According to most accounts, the snow became so soft and wet from the sun that it stuck to the snowshoes in heavy clumps and made them useless.[29]

The men continued in single file, plunging ahead in the deep snow one step at a time. On February 13, the relief party at last reached Bear Valley. The snow was at least ten feet deep, but the crust was so hard, they did not sink in. Curtis led them to the far end of the valley to the remains of his wagon, where Reed and McCutchen had stashed some food the past November when they rescued Curtis and his wife.[30] Some of the men dug through the snow but found that the cache of provisions had been ripped apart. Just bits and pieces of food remained. Bears were blamed for the destruction, but the more likely culprits were wolverines, opportunistic scavengers that do not hibernate, will eat anything that was once alive, and once ranged throughout the Sierra Nevadas.[31]

That evening, a cold rain turned to snow. In the morning, the sun emerged, but morale was low. Once again, they stayed in camp stoking fires of wet timber to dry their soaked clothing and blankets. Another day had been lost.

Even worse, three members of the party announced that they had had enough. Matt Ritchie, "Greasy Jim" Brueheim, and Curtis said they would go no farther.[32] Ritchie, one of the older men, admitted that he did not realize that the trek would be so physically demanding. Brueheim pointed out that he had signed on to go only as far as

Bear Valley. Once Curtis found that there was nothing salvageable from his wagon, he had no interest in continuing a mission of mercy for people he did not know.

The sudden decision rattled the other members of the party. Some were so discouraged that it seemed that even more men might quit, and the entire mission would end in failure. Then Tucker, one of the party leaders, vowed that he would guarantee payment of five dollars a day—back to the first day of the mission—to every man who completed the rescue.[33] The offer, although more than generous, was not enough to change the minds of the three who were leaving, but all six of the other members of the party assured Tucker they would stay.

Aware that plenty of food was waiting for them back at the Mule Springs base camp, the men who were leaving cached most of their provisions for when the party returned with survivors. The three defectors, free of the heavy packs, headed off on the trail through Bear Valley leading to Mule Springs. Before Ritchie left, he gave his diary to Tucker. The seven remaining members of the First Relief pushed on into the snow.

The storms continued and the snow got deeper, but the team pressed on. They continued to torch dead pines for trail markers, left more caches of food for themselves and others to use, and gradually climbed the west slope of the Sierras. When Aquilla Glover and Daniel Rhoads became ill from altitude sickness, the others helped by carrying their backpacks.[34] Despite Rhoads's protests, they also tended to his infected hand, which he had injured during his journey on the California Trail.

Just as the party thought the worst was over, another snowstorm walloped them. Nevertheless, they advanced fifteen miles closer to the summit. They camped above the Yuba River bottoms, but after a good sleep, they rose to face more snow. After just a few miles, the conditions became so poor, they stopped and once again made snowshoes from pine boughs. The higher they climbed, the more the altitude sickened Glover and the younger Rhoads brother. The party made little progress, but the next day brought clear skies. Dan

Rhoads later explained that they continued to use the snowshoes "to travel continuously except at brief intervals on hill-sides & bare spots where we took them off."[35]

On February 17, the relief party was almost at the summit. That evening, Tucker wrote in the diary, "Travelled 8 miles and camped at the head of Juba [Yuba] on the Pass we suppose the snow to be 30 feet deep."[36]

The next morning, the seven men beheld a grand vista that stretched forever to the east. They could see no signs of life, only an ice-covered lake and unending snow. Just after high noon, they began the descent. It took the entire afternoon. By the time they reached Truckee Lake, the last of the sun was about to disappear. They crossed the frozen lake and made their way toward the trees and the place where Eddy said they would find the cabins and—it was hoped—people still alive. But they did not see any trace of the cabins, only piles and piles of snow. They heard nothing, not even the song of a night bird.

"We looked all around but no living thing but ourselves was in sight and we thought that all must have perished," Dan Rhoads recalled. "We raised a loud halloo and then we saw a woman emerge from a hole in the snow. As we approached her several others made their appearances in like manner coming out of the snow. They were gaunt with famine and I never can forget the horrible ghastly sight they presented. The first woman spoke in a hollow voice very much agitated & said 'are you men from California or do you come from heaven.'"[37]

42. THE SECOND RELIEF

AT THE SAME TIME members of the First Relief came upon the withered specters emerging from their icy limbo at Truckee Lake, James Reed was chafing at the bit. Reed's family and the rest of the Donner Party had been trapped for four months.

Reed had just finished scouring the ranchos and settlements of the Sonoma and Napa valleys in search of volunteers, horses, and supplies. He did not travel alone. After the successful public meeting in San Francisco to organize and fund rescue teams, the old trail guide Caleb Greenwood had showed up to help Reed raise volunteers. Eighty-three years old and clad in buckskin, Greenwood had learned about the Donner Party's plight from William McCutchen, who was in Sonoma pursuing his own recruitment effort. At the close of a letter urging Reed to join him, McCutchen wrote, "If you come [and] we are gone you can over take us at Sutter's we will go that way you had better come in hast [sic] as there is no time to delay your compliance will mutch oblige yours & mine."[1]

Reed knew very well the need for haste. He also knew Greenwood's savvy and many years of wilderness experience would be of great value. So did the influential Californio political and military leader Mariano Vallejo. He donated horses and mules from his rancho and generously contributed hundreds of dollars to the rescue cause, including a hefty stipend for Greenwood's services.[2] Naval Commander Joseph Hull became another funding source for Greenwood. The agreement made with Greenwood was clearly spelled out in the official orders that Hull sent to Reed.

Reed and Greenwood spent almost two weeks enlisting personnel and gathering horses. At Fort Sonoma, they acquired ten army horses and five men. Reed bought more horses and engaged three men at the rancho of George Yount.[3] Reed was pleased to find that McCutchen was still at Yount's and had not left for Sutter's Fort. McCutchen was healthy again, and he was raring to return to the Sierras.

On February 13, Reed and the nascent rescue party pressed on, unaware that a story criticizing the actions of the Donner Party had appeared that morning in Sam Brannan's newspaper, the *California Star*, beneath the headline "Distressing News."[4] It was written by George McKinstry, one of the bachelor emigrants who, to make better time, had left the wagon train that eventually became known as the Donner Party. McKinstry arrived at Sutter's Fort in October. When his poor health kept him from serving in the Mexican-American War, he accepted an appointment as sheriff of the Sacramento District.[5]

In the newspaper story, McKinstry related what he knew based on his own experiences and what he later learned when Reed first stumbled in to Sutter's Fort. According to McKinstry, the decision to build a new road in Utah to avoid the Weber River canyon was the most detrimental error in judgment made by the Donner Party.

"Mr. Reed and others who left the company, and came in for assistance, informed me that they were sixteen days in making the road, as the men would not work a quarter of the time," McKinstry wrote. "They were then some 4 or 5 days travel behind the first waggons; which were traveling slow, on account of being obliged to make an entire new rout for several hundred miles through heavy sage and mountains, and delayed four days by the guides hunting out passes in the mountains; and these waggons arrived at the settlement about the first of October. Had they gone around the old road, the north end of the great Salt Lake, they would have been in the first of September."[6]

McKinstry also described the snowshoe party's "horrid journey over the mountains" and how some of them had "made meat of the dead bodies of their companions" to stay alive.[7]

The newspaper editor's note to introduce the story bluntly summed up McKinstry's attitude about the Donner Party and their predicament. It read: "The writer who is well qualified to judge, is of the opinion that the whole party might have reached the California Valley before the first snow fall, if the men had exerted themselves as they should have done. Nothing but a contrary and contentious disposition on the part of some of the men belonging to the party prevented them from getting in as soon as any of the first companies."

The newspaper story spawned rumors about the Donner Party that spread faster than cholera. And with each telling, the story changed. Whether or not Reed ever read McKinstry's critique, he made no mention of it in his trail diary or subsequent writings.

On the day the story appeared, all of Reed's attention was focused on the men of the new rescue party. For the most part, Reed was pleased with the enlistees. Greenwood snared some fellow mountaineers who were younger and heartier versions of himself. The rest of the volunteers looked fit enough and capable of riding with the herd of horses at a quick pace through the hills and into the Sacramento Valley. They seldom stopped except for water and to camp. Reed briefly paused to buy five more horses at William Gordon's ranch on Cache Creek, where the water at the crossing ran so deep that it came up to the horses' backs.[8]

Reed thought he had all the men and horses he needed, but instead of already scrambling up the Sierra Nevadas, the rescue team was still trying to reach Johnson's Ranch. They soon learned that they would have to try harder.

When they reached the designated rendezvous site at the confluence of the Sacramento and Feather rivers north of Sutter's Fort, no one was there to meet them. The launch from San Francisco loaded with lifesaving cargo was nowhere in sight. Reed sent a man to follow the river and look for the boat. When the scout returned, he told Reed that the craft was moored at Sutter's Fort, supposedly taking refuge from strong head winds.[9]

The overdue sloop was under the command of Passed Midshipman Selim Woodworth, the young solo traveler who had left a note in a deserted cabin on the trail in Nebraska for family friend George McKinstry, then still a member of the Owl Russell caravan. In early

February, Commander Hull put the junior officer in charge of the relief operations. At the same time, Reed was chosen to direct the rescue party known as the Second Relief.[10]

On the morning of February 18, while the First Relief started the final leg of the trek to the lake camp, Reed knew that the amount of the supplies and provisions on Woodworth's launch—all either donated or paid for with contributions—was staggering. The inventory included barrels of flour and pork, four hundred pounds of sugar, tins of ground coffee, and one hundred pounds of cocoa contributed by Hull, along with a large cash gift. The funds collected also paid for frying pans, axes and hatchets, blankets, woolen stockings, shoes for adults and children, mittens, bolts of calico and flannel, pantaloons, buck and elk skins, comforters, and seventeen pounds of tobacco.[11]

"I was here placed in a quandary—no boat to take us across the river, and no provisions for our party to take to the mountains," Reed later wrote of the predicament.[12]

Because of the wise advice of Greenwood and his mountain men, Reed came up with a bold new plan. They would not wait for Woodworth and his stalled schooner. Instead, the hides from elk that Greenwood and the woodsmen shot the night before would be used to fashion bullboats by making bowl-shaped frames with bent willow branches and covering them in animal skins with the furry side out.[13] Often used by Indians and trappers, the tublike craft were slow and difficult to steer. It was going to take a good deal of time to swim the horses across the river and then transport men and supplies in the small boats.[14]

Just as Greenwood and some of the others began to construct the bullboats, they spied a schooner sailing toward them. It was the *Indian Queen*, a sloop of ten tons commanded by Perry McCoon, coming to the rescue.[15] The twenty-five-year-old McCoon worked for John Sutter in various capacities, established a ranch on the Cosumnes River, and acquired the schooner for ferrying people up and down the Sacramento River.[16]

As soon as the *Indian Queen* tied up, a ramp was put in place for loading horses and mules. Reed did not want to waste another minute. He and "Big Bill" McCutchen coaxed their horses aboard before the rest of the party, and the schooner headed for the opposite bank with Reed shouting orders to his men. He urged them to follow and ride as fast as possible to Johnson's Ranch.[17] By the time McCoon turned the boat to shuttle the rest of the party across, the wind had picked up. McCoon had to wait for the wind to ease before returning to the other side. By then, Reed and McCutchen were long out of sight, riding hell-bent-for-leather through the brush.[18]

When they reined in their panting horses at the ranch headquarters on the Bear River, William Johnson greeted them and put Reed and McCutchen to work. "Making known our situation, he drove his cattle up to the house saying, 'there are the cattle, take as many as you need,'" Reed later recalled. "We shot down five head, staid up all night and with the help of Mr. Johnson and his Indians, by the time the men arrived the next morning, we had the meat fire dried, and ready to be placed in bags, Mr. Johnson had a party of Indians making flour by hand mills, they making during the night nearly 200 lbs."[19]

In the morning, the rest of the party reached the rancho and helped to bag the dried beef and pack up supplies. Unlike the courageous but inexperienced blend of runaway sailors and farmers of the First Relief, the heart of Reed's company was comprised of veteran frontiersmen, all of them trackers with many survival skills. "Old Greenwood," rawboned and wily, brought along his son, Britton Greenwood. Brit, in his late teens, had spent his young life in the wilderness with his father.

John Turner, as big and burly as McCutchen and recently discharged as a guide for John Frémont, was a welcome addition to the relief party. He was considered one of the best trappers west of the Rockies and was notorious for uttering profanities that could make the saltiest of sailors blush.[20]

Little was known about Matthew Dofar and Joseph Gendreau, French-Canadian woodsmen.[21] Three other young men chosen for the party—Charles Cady, shoemaker Nicholas Clark, and Charles Stone—had little wilderness experience, but they were vigorous. Reed liked their spunk and referred to them as "the boys."[22]

Reed's longtime friend Hiram Miller, the blacksmith who had left Springfield, Illinois, to work as a teamster for the Donners, was also in the relief party. Miller had started to keep a daily diary on May 12, 1846, when the caravan left Independence, Missouri. He had left the company on July 2 to join the other single men who continued the trek on pack mules.[23] The diary had become Reed's responsibility. When Miller heard about the Donner Party's predicament and the rescue efforts, he went to Johnson's Ranch. He wanted to help the people he knew and some, such as the Reed children, whom he cherished.

Several more hands were added, mainly to tend the horses and shuttle supplies to Mule Springs. Most of them would drop out or remain at the base camp. Reed had faith that the ten core members would hold fast and carry out the mission, but his confidence in Woodworth was another matter.

There still was no sign of Selim Woodworth and the store of supplies. Reed would not wait any longer. The hundreds of pounds of dried meat and flour he and the men had prepared would have to do. Just after sunrise on February 22, everyone was ready to ride. Reed shook Johnson's hand and told him that when Woodworth finally made it to the ranch, he should be told to move on as quickly as possible to deliver the lifesaving provisions.[24]

The Second Relief moved ahead along the Bear River. The group started for the Sierras, following the same path taken by the men of the First Relief, who had left frozen Truckee Lake that same morning with twenty-three members of the Donner Party considered strong enough to travel. Most were children. Not all of them would survive.

WHEN THE SEVEN MEN of the First Relief arrived at the mountain camp on the evening of February 19, the more delusional emigrants, overcome by famine and delirium, mistook them for guardian angels. The rescuers were shocked by what they found—creatures that seemed human but were stripped of all humanity. Withered bodies shrouded in ragged clothing crawled from the cabins, looking like the dead rising. The weaker ones could scarcely get to their feet and walk in the snow.

Others stood still and stared with blank eyes, their lips barely moving as they whispered to themselves. The vermin-infested cabins reeked of soiled bedding, wood smoke, and rotting rawhide roofs, mixed with the disgusting odor of the gummy boiled hides and bones caked in cooking pots. The infirm people huddling under quilts in the darkness seemed oblivious to the stench.

After a while, the emigrants realized the ruddy-cheeked men were neither angels from heaven nor a band of Indians. They flocked around their seven saviors, hugging and thanking them, shouting their praises, and crying tears of pure joy. Reason Tucker wrote in his diary, "The sight of us appeared to put life into their emaciated frames." He later recalled that his men were so moved by the people's reaction that they "cried to see them cry and rejoiced to see them rejoice."[25]

Some of the more vocal were members of the Reed family after they found out that James Reed was alive. Virginia Reed instantly remembered the vow she had made, that if God would send relief to the camps and let her see her father again, she would become a Catholic. Her prayer had been answered.[26]

"On the evening of February 19th, 1847, they reached our cabin, where all were starving," she wrote years later. "They shouted to attract attention. Mr. Breen, clambered up the icy steps from our cabin, and soon we heard the blessed words, 'Relief, thank God, relief!' There was joy at Donner Lake [at that time called Truckee Lake] that night, for we did not know the fate of the Forlorn Hope and we were told that relief parties would come and go until all were across the mountains. But the joy [and] sorrow was strangely blended. There were tears in other eyes than those of children; strong men sat down and wept. For the dead were lying about on the snow, some even unburied, since the living had not had strength to bury their dead."[27]

To avoid making a horrible situation worse, when emigrants asked about the welfare of family and friends with the snowshoe party, they were assured that everyone was safe. It was better to lie. Soon enough, the survivors would learn the fate of the snowshoers who had died and been cannibalized.

The relief party made the rounds of the camp, visiting all the cabins and carefully doling out small portions of dried beef and biscuits. Fortunately, some of them knew the danger of giving a starving person too much food.

"They had been without food except for a few work oxen since the first fall of snow," Dan Rhoads later recalled. "We gave them food very sparingly and retired for the night having some one on guard until morning to keep close watch on our provision to prevent the starving emigrants from eating them which they would have done until they died of repletion."[28]

By the time the First Relief arrived, nine members of the Donner Party had died at the lake camp.[29] When the first deaths occurred, the survivors had buried the bodies deep in the snowbanks. But the emigrants later became so weak that they could only manage to slide a body out of the cabin on an inclined plane and wrap it in a quilt.

"So far the survivors had not been compelled to partake of human flesh," noted Dan Rhoads. He also made another interesting observation—most of the dead were adult males. "I remember seeing but 3 living men. Louis Keeseberg was lying on his back unable to rise. Patrick Breen and one other were the only ones left. Very few women or children had died up to that time."[30]

On the morning of February 20, there was a tenth death in the camp—little Catherine Pike, less than a year old. No bigger than a china doll, she died in the arms of her grandmother, Levinah Murphy, who had become the sole caretaker of Catherine and her three-year-old sister, Naomi, when their mother, Harriet Pike, had left with the snowshoe party. When Harriet left the lake camp with her sister at the insistence of their mother, she was so malnourished that her body could no longer produce milk to feed her nursing baby.[31] Levinah tried her best to care for Catherine by feeding her thin gruel made of flour and snow water. It was miraculous that the baby stayed alive for so long. At last her suffering was over.

By then, death had become so expected that the baby's passing was hardly noticed by ravenous survivors. They were concerned only about their family or themselves.

Besides preventing the starving people from overeating, the rescuers were concerned that their supply was running low after caching so much food along the trail. Breen, the camp's observant diarist, made note that the relief party arrived "with som provisions but left the greater part on the way."[32]

After breakfast, Reason Tucker, John Rhoads, and Sept Moutrey packed up some food and set out to check on the Donners and others at Alder Creek. "We found them in a starving condition," Tucker wrote in his diary. "Most of the men had died and one of them [Jake Donner] leaving a wife and 8 children. The two families had but one beef head amongst them. . . . There was two cows buried in the snow but it was doubtful if they would be able to find them."[33]

Fortunately, there had been no losses since Jacob Donner and three other men had died in late December. But when the rescuers saw George Donner, it was apparent to them that he was failing. Mortification had set in. There was a stench of rotten flesh, and when the men kneeled by Donner's side, his breath was sickly sweet.[34] In spite of Tamzene's valiant efforts, the massive infection in her husband's hand had spread, leaving his arm so gangrenous that he could not move.

John Rhoads never forgot the few minutes he spent trying to boost Donner's spirits. Many years later on his own deathbed, Rhoads confessed that his "conscience had always pricked him" because he told the dying Donner "that he would come back to get him, all the time knowing that he could not keep that promise."

Tamzene appeared to be in fair health, especially compared with the other adults. The relief team decided she had the stamina to make the return trip. But Tamzene flatly refused. She told them her stepchildren were strong, and they should go. She would not leave her husband and their three young daughters. Efforts to convince her otherwise failed, so the rescuers chose her stepdaughters, Elitha and Leanna.

Betsy Donner, Jacob's widow, also chose to remain with her youngest children. Solomon Hook, Betsy's oldest son and Jacob's stepson, also stayed at the camp. Eliza Donner later explained that her stepcousin had become "snow-blind and demented, and at times restless and difficult to control."[35] Solomon's younger brother, William Hook, and stepbrother George Donner Jr. joined their cousins who were going out with the rescue party. Besides the four youngsters, two others were selected from the Alder Creek camp—Dorthea Wolfinger, the young widow of the man murdered on the trail by his companions, and teenage teamster Noah James. Much to his dismay, young Jean-Baptiste Trudeau was left behind to cut firewood and look after the women and children.

As a goodwill gesture and to inspire Trudeau, the rescuers chopped off the top of a tall pine for the woodpile. Each person remaining at the camp was given a cup of flour, two small biscuits, and some thinly sliced jerked beef.[36] That was all that could be spared until the next relief party arrived.

Tucker told Tamzene and Betsy to stay strong. He assured them that more help was on the way. Tamzene said that had better be the case, for once the little bit of food they had was gone, there would be only one recourse to keep the families alive.[37] Tucker knew what Tamzene meant and saw that she was dead serious.

Just before the party struck out for the lake camp, Tamzene took aside her stepdaughters, Leanna and Elitha, and told them to never speak about what they had seen and experienced in the Sierras. After much hugging and many tearful good-byes, the rescuers and their six charges left. Even after they were long out of sight, their loved ones at the camp still watched and cried.

"Mother stood on the snow where she could see all go forth," Eliza Donner later wrote. "They moved in single file—the leaders on snowshoes, the weak stepping in the tracks made by the strong. Leanna, the last in line, was scarcely able to keep up. It was not until after mother came back with Frances and Georgia that I was made to understand that this was the long-hoped-for relief party. . . . Oh, it was painfully quiet some days in those great mountains, and lonesome upon the snow. The pines had a whispering homesick murmur, and we children had lost all inclination to play."[38]

Back at the Truckee Lake camp, the four other rescuers spent the day deciding which emigrants to take. Much like the selection process at Alder Creek, priority was given to families with no food, single adults and older boys, and small children or infants who could be carried. Parents would remain to care for the younger children, as would anyone seriously ill or physically impaired.[39] Ultimately, seventeen of the thirty-four emigrants at the lake were deemed acceptable to return with the First Relief.

The chosen ones were Margret Reed, her four children, and her servant girl, Eliza Williams; Edward and Simon Breen, two sons from the family that had the most hides to eat; William, Eleanor, and Lovina Graves; William Murphy and his sister, Mary; Philippine Keseberg and daughter, Ada; John Denton, an English gunsmith and one of the Donners' drivers; and little Naomi Pike, who would be wrapped in a blanket and carried by John Rhoads. With the six emigrants from Alder Creek, the rescuers were prepared to bring a total of twenty-three survivors out of the Sierras. Keeping in mind the several food caches they had left along the trail, the rescuers distributed most of the remaining food in their packs to the emigrants who were left behind.

February 22 began as a "fine morning," according to Breen. He started the day by burying the body of little Caroline Pike, two days dead, in the snow.[40] Then he turned his attention to the living. He prayed for the seven members of the First Relief and the seven adults and sixteen children they were leading west toward the summit. Breen's celestial petitions might have helped, but not enough.

The First Relief, backtracking on the trail they had made a few days before, had not gone far when they were faced with a predicament. Traversing the snow was so difficult for the younger children that some of them fell behind. The problem was that fourteen of the sixteen children had no other choice except walking. The exceptions were the three-year-old girls, Naomi Pike and Ada Keseberg. John Rhoads tramped through the snow with Naomi slung over his shoulder in a blanket, and Philippine Keseberg carried her daughter as best she could while struggling through the snow.[41]

After spending so much time confined to their camps, even some older children and adults found that being back on the move was challenging. Besides being stiff and sluggish from inactivity, the emigrants were weak from starvation and hypothermia. Those who had family or friends to help fared much better than those who were alone, such as the teamster John Denton. The sickly but determined Denton, a single man with no one to offer him encouragement, relied on sheer will power to stay on his feet. On the other hand, Leanna Donner, who had such a tough time just getting from the river camp to the lake, faltered at times but somehow trudged along with help from her sister.

"I was one of the weakest in the party, and not one in the train thought I would get to the top of the first hill," Leanna later recalled. "We marched along in single file, the leader wearing snow-shoes, and the others following after, all stepping in the leader's tracks. I think my sister [Elitha] and myself were about the rear of the train, as the strongest were put in front."[42]

Others were in far worse condition than Leanna Donner. Tommy Reed, just three years old, and his sister, Patty, four days short of her ninth birthday, were completely exhausted after hiking less than two miles. As their big sister Virginia put it, they just "gave out."[43] This caused the entire procession to come to a standstill. Precious daylight travel time was being lost. Neither Margret Reed nor her other children were strong enough to carry Tommy or Patty. Aquilla Glover and Reason Tucker, the relief party's captains, quickly conferred and decided the party would continue the trek, but without Tommy and Patty.

"They were not able to stand the fatigue and it was not thought safe to allow them to proceed, so Mr. Glover informed mama that they would have to be sent back to the cabins to await the expedition," Virginia Reed later wrote. "What language can express our feelings? My mother said she would go back with her children—that we would all go back together."[44]

Glover could not allow Margret Reed to return to the camp. He realized how agonizing it was for her, but in the best interest of herself and her family, she needed to remain with her two other children, Virginia and James, and stay the course.

"Mr. Glover promised mama that as soon as they reached Bear Valley he himself would return for her children," Virginia wrote. "Finally my mother, turning to Mr. Glover said, 'Are you a Mason?' He replied that he was. 'Will you promise me on the word of a Mason that if we do not meet their father you will return and save my children?' He pledged himself that he would. My father was a member of the Mystic Tie and mama had great faith in the word of a Mason."[45] Glover looked directly into Margret's tearful eyes and said, "I thus do promise."[46] He chose Sept Moutrey to help him shepherd Tommy and Patty back to the lake camp. Then both men would return to the First Relief.

Virginia recalled that it was "a sad parting—a fearful struggle." All of the Reed children cared for each other, but Patty and Tommy were particularly close. Perhaps to reassure Margret that Tommy would be safe, Patty turned to her mother and said, "I want to see papa, but I will take good care of Tommy and I do not want you to come back [to the camp]."[47]

After hugs with Margret, Virginia, and James Jr. and just before Glover and Moutrey squatted down so their young charges could climb onto their backs, Patty hesitated. She had something more to say.

"Well, mother, if you never see me again, do the best you can." Both men turned aside, unable to hide their tears.

WHEN GLOVER AND MOUTREY returned to the camp carrying the two Reed children, the reception they received from Patrick and Peggy Breen was as frigid as the ice-covered lake. The Breens, delighted that there were five fewer hungry bodies crowded into their cabin, were still celebrating the Reed family's recent departure. Now two of them were back. The Breens were indignant. At first, Patrick Breen refused to allow Patty and Tommy to enter the cabin. Glover stayed calm. He played on the Breens' sympathy, reminding them that other relief parties would soon arrive. Finally, out of desperation, Glover said he could leave some food to help support the Reed children. The promise of extra food worked. Breen reluctantly agreed to take in the Reed children.[48]

The First Relief had advanced a mile down the trail across frozen Truckee Lake by the time Glover and Moutrey caught up with them. Camp was set up at the head of the lake. The men cut down pines and built platforms for fires. Food would be in short supply until they reached the caches. That meant each of the now twenty-eight members of the party would have to get by on just one ounce of smoked beef and a spoonful of flour twice a day.[49]

The next morning, the campers awoke to find their clothing and even their shoelaces frozen stiff. Ned Coffeemeyer, the landlocked former sailor, discovered that during the night, the rawhide thongs of his snowshoes had been poached, presumably by one of the malnourished emigrants.[50]

"At break of day we were again on the road, owing to the fact that we could make better time over the frozen snows," Virginia Reed wrote in her narrative. "The sunshine, which it would seem would have been welcome, only added to our misery. The dazzling reflection of the snow was very trying in the eyes, while its heat melted our frozen clothing, making them cling to our bodies."[51]

Ascending the pass took up a big part of the day. The going was excruciatingly slow and exhausting. Rescuers did what they could to support the emigrants, boost morale and, most important, keep them moving. That required making sure that they stayed on their feet—easier said than done, considering the large number of children negotiating the deep snow. Five-year-old James Reed Jr. was an exception. During the climb up the steep slope, he scrambled over icy boulders and followed the tracks of the men leading the way. His worried mother and sister called out encouragement and watched the boy make his way over the mountain in "snow up to his waist," as Virginia wrote. She remembered that James told her, "Every step he took was a gitting nigher to Pa and something to eat."[52]

Just before they had left camp that morning, the emigrants had been told that over the mountain pass was a cache of food the rescuers had left. After days of making do on meager rations, just the thought of food lifted their spirits. That afternoon, although they were weary from the hike, surging adrenaline quickened their stride as they approached the cache site.

When the log platform that had been built for fires came into view, the rescuers and some emigrants again picked up the pace. They knew what they would find. Their quick eyes raced across the snow to the tall pine and scaled the trunk to the high branches, where bags and bundles of meat and other vittles were safely cached, all bound tight with rawhide and suspended from the branches.

But when they reached the pine, all they found was the tree. There were no bags and bundles. What was left of the cache was strewn on the ground. Although the food had been tied high in the tree and suspended with rawhide, some clever pine martens or a wolverine had simply climbed the tree and chewed through the ties. The bags had fallen to the ground, and most of the food had been devoured.[53]

At first, the entire party stood in silent disbelief. Then many of them wept. Others were angry and stomped off, cursing their bad luck. Captain Tucker and the other six rescuers took stock of the situation. Other than the provisions that could be salvaged from the ground, combined with whatever scraps were left in the packs, there would be no more food until they reached the next cache, twenty miles ahead. That meant four long days of travel without food, and even then, they might find the next cache plundered. Tucker summed it up in the diary when he wrote "being on short allowance death stared us in the face. I made an equal divide and charged them to be careful."[54]

At first light on February 24, Moutrey, Coffeemeyer, Glover, and Daniel Rhoads—all chosen by Tucker—got a head start and slipped away from camp before the rest of the party.[55] They headed westward for Bear Valley, hoping that neither pine martens nor wolverines had discovered the next hidden store of food. If they found the cache still intact, they were to bring back as much food as they could carry. At the same time, Tucker, Sels, and John Rhoads would keep the emigrants moving and try to keep as many as possible alive.

That morning, the party had progressed only about two miles when Tucker realized that John Denton was lagging far behind. It was not the first time the amiable young Englishman had been unable to keep up with the others. From the start of the relief party's return trip, he had been one of the slower emigrants. Until then, however, he had held his own. Described by Tamzene Donner as "a useful man in camp," Denton had carved the headstone to mark the grave of Sarah Keyes at Alcove Spring. He was well liked by everyone. Although most emigrants, perhaps as a survival mechanism, gradually became callous about the well-being of others, several of them were genuinely concerned about Denton.[56]

When Denton finally caught up to the party, he collapsed in Tucker's arms. Denton—snow-blind and exhausted by starvation—could not go any farther. He realized he had become a burden to the party. True to form, Denton told Tucker that he wished to be left behind. He asked only that if they happened upon another party on the trail, to send them his way.

"He tried to keep up a hopeful and cheerful appearance, but we knew he could not live much longer," Daniel Rhoads later wrote. "We made a platform of saplings, built a fire on it, cut some boughs for him to sit upon and left him."[57] Tucker spared a smidgen of precious food for Denton. Then he fetched his coverlid and wrapped it around Denton to shield him from the cold. Cut firewood was stacked within his reach. Virginia Reed wrote that Denton, wrapped in the quilt and smoking his pipe beside a blazing fire, looked so comfortable that little James Reed wanted to stay with him.[58]

The emigrants said their good-byes and took their places in line. Tucker shook Denton's hand and joined the others. "I very unwillingly left him telling him he should soon have assistance but I am afraid he would not live to see it."[59]

The party moved on, never looking back but always watching for the pines that the rescuers had burned on their way up the Sierras as guideposts. Even though the emigrants were on the other side of the pass and descending the mountainside, it was still difficult to make any headway. Because of the afternoon sun, some men found themselves flailing in the snow when they broke through the melting crust. Every adult and child was exhausted, weak, and had a constant gnawing hunger. Many were frostbitten. All were in pitiful condition.

But on this February day—when the emigrants left one of their own to die alone—the most pathetic of the party was Philippine Keseberg, stumbling through snow with her daughter, Ada, held tightly in her arms. Devastated by the loss of her baby son in January and the earlier death of Ada's twin sister, Philippine was determined to keep Ada alive at all costs.

At first, Philippine managed to carry her little girl and keep up with the rest of the emigrants. But by the second day, Philippine was gasping for air and had to make frequent stops to catch her breath and reposition Ada in her arms. At one point, she was so depleted that she had to put Ada down to walk, but before long, the child gave out and had to be carried again.[60]

Finally, in sheer desperation, Philippine called out to the others that she would give a gold watch and twenty-five dollars to anyone willing to carry Ada.[61] Most of the rescuers were already burdened with children, such as John Rhoads carrying little Naomi Pike. The relief party managed another seven miles after leaving Denton, and Philippine somehow made it to camp with her daughter. The campers built fires on log platforms, melted snow for drinking water, and supplemented the last bits of dried meat with toasted rawhide strips for the evening repast.

During the night in the warmth of the campfire, little Ada Keseberg died in her mother's arms. Philippine became inconsolable when she awoke to find her beloved child dead. She clutched Ada to her bosom and refused to let go. When Tucker gently told her that the party was ready to leave, Philippine said she would not go on without her daughter. "I told her to give me the child and her to go on," Tucker recounted. "After she was out of sight, Rhoads and myself buried the child in the snow best we could. Her sperit went to heaven her body to the wolves."[62]

Tucker convinced Philippine to leave with the other emigrants by reminding her that she was a young woman with her whole life ahead of her. She had to go on for her own sake as well as for her husband. Numb from shock, Philippine acquiesced and walked with Tucker back to the trail. Some of the women comforted her. The party moved on five more miles before stopping for the night. There was only one item on the dinner menu that evening—roasted rawhide cut from snowshoes. "This rawhide was our sole subsistence for 3 days," Daniel Rhoads recalled.[63]

The next day, February 26, the party stopped at noon to rest and eat what Tucker described as "a small divide of shoe strings roasted."[64] The four young Donner cousins also nibbled on pieces of rawhide they had managed to tear off Tucker's tattered buckskin britches.

When the last strand of rawhide had been chewed up, the party resumed the trek. They had gone only about half a mile when two men came into view far ahead, walking toward them. They turned out to be Sept Moutrey and Ned Coffeemeyer, toting dried beef from an intact cache in Bear Valley.[65] A fire was built on the spot. The band of survivors hunkered down in the snow and feasted. By the time they had finished, the afternoon sun had softened the snow, making travel difficult. They managed one more mile and then camped.

The next day brought an even better surprise. The party's two other scouts—Aquilla Glover and Daniel Rhoads—had had an encounter of their own. Instead of all four rescuers returning to the First Relief, Glover and Rhoads had set out for the resupply camp at Mule Springs.[66] Their plan was to get more provisions and check on the whereabouts of the next relief party. They were just under way on the Bear River Trail when they saw movement in the distance. Soon, what appeared to be human figures came into view. As they drew closer, Glover and Rhoads could make out ten men, all wearing snowshoes and carrying heavy packs. As the men drew near, Glover and Rhoads greeted them. The leader of the party shook their hands and made introductions.

It was James Reed with the nine other members of the Second Relief.[67] The shouts and cheers of a dozen men echoed throughout the valley. After a round of bear hugs and backslaps, the questions flew fast and furious. Despite the commotion, Reed asked about his family. He breathed a deep sigh of relief when Glover and Rhoads assured him that all of them were very much alive and that his wife and two of his children were with the First Relief and coming this way. When Reed learned that his family was safe, he would have given any sum of gold for his fleet gray mare Glaucus, the finest horse he had ever ridden, to magically appear and carry him to his loved ones.

Unfortunately, Reed did not have even a broken-down nag to ride. Just as the First Relief was forced to do, Reed's band of rescuers had discovered that horses and mules loaded with provisions could not make their way through deep snow. Early that morning, the packs had been removed and all the animals taken back to the camp at Mule Springs. Old Caleb Greenwood admitted that he was unable go any farther on foot and returned to the resupply camp.[68] The remaining men of the relief party packed the provisions on their backs, tied on snowshoes, and proceeded through the valley to the point where they had met Glover and Rhoads.

Not all the news from the Donner Party camps was good. Less than a week before at Johnson's Ranch, Bill McCutchen had embraced his wife, Amanda, one of the recovering survivors of the Forlorn Hope. But the First Relief rescuers broke the news that McCutchen's infant daughter, Harriet, had died three weeks before while under the care of Elizabeth Graves at the lake camp.[69] Despite the great loss, McCutchen's resolve remained strong, as did his commitment to the rescue mission.

That night, after everyone else was asleep, Reed baked bread and sweet cakes, just as he had done the night before.[70] Besides dried meat, Reed wanted the starving emigrants to have fresh bread. Baking also gave him something to do besides worrying about his family. When the baking was finished, all Reed could think about was how close he was to the camp where Margret and two of his children were sleeping. Finally, out of frustration, he packed up his bedroll and roused his men earlier than usual.[71] Reed told them he wanted to get a jump on the afternoon sun and gain ground before the snow crust started to melt. The rescuers also knew the early start would hasten the reunion of Reed and his family.

The Second Relief "left camp early on a fine hard snow," Reed wrote of their departure on the morning of February 27. They had gone about four miles when they came upon "poor unfortunate starved people" scattered along the snow trail.[72] Reed instantly knew that they were members of the First Relief.

"My father was hurrying over the mountains, and met us in our hour of need with his hands full of bread," wrote Virginia Reed. "He had expected to meet us on this day, and had stayed up all night baking bread to give us. Some of his party were ahead, and when they saw us coming they called out, 'Is Mrs. Reed with you? If she is, tell her Mr. Reed is here.' We heard the call; mother knelt on the snow, while I tried to run to meet papa."[73]

Virginia tripped before she reached her father and fell into his arms. Reed asked where her mother was, and Virginia pointed to Margret, collapsed in the snow. Reed lifted up his wife and wrapped his arms around mother and daughter. In the style of a reserved Victorian gentleman, Reed controlled his emotions, unlike when he had broken down publicly while soliciting help in San Francisco. His restraint was evident in the diary entry for that day: "Here I met my wife, Mrs. Reed, and two of my little children. Two still in the mountains. I cannot describe the death-like look they all had. Bread Bread Bread Bread was the begging of every child and grown person. I gave to all what I dared and left for the scene of desolation."[74]

Reed and his party moved on to the east and into the Sierras, while the First Relief continued west. They stopped at the campsite at the head of Bear Valley where William Thompson, one of the rescuers Reed had recruited in Sonoma, was posted to dole out food from the large cache of provisions. "We camped that night and ate the bread my father had brought for us," Virginia Reed wrote.[75]

During the night, twelve-year-old William Hook, one of Jacob Donner's stepsons, was tormented by hunger. Although he had just eaten the nightly ration, all he could think about was the stockpile of food cached in a nearby tree. William shinnied up the tree and, like an insatiable wolverine, tore into the cache.[76] He ate until he was gorged and then ate more, in total disregard of the many warnings that overeating could kill a starving person.

When William was found in the morning, everything possible was done to relieve his suffering. He was given a cup of tobacco juice to drink to induce vomiting, but it was not enough. He was left behind with John Gordon, the camp keeper detached from Reed's party, and two other emigrants. They also had overeaten, but not as much as William, and they recovered quickly. Eleven-year-old William Murphy had to stay at the camp because his feet were so badly frostbitten that his shoes had to be cut off. Many years later, he recalled the ordeal and described the attempt to help William Hook.

"William Hook went out on the snow and rested on his knees and elbows. The camp-keeper [Gordon] called to him to come in. He then told me to make him come into camp. I went out and put my hand on him, speaking his name, and he fell over, being already dead. He did not die in great agony, as is usually alleged. No groan, nor signs of dying, were manifested to us. The camp-keeper and myself took the biscuits and jerked beef from his pockets, and buried him just barely under the ground, near a tree which had been fired, and from around which the snow had melted."[77]

On March 1, while the body of the Hook boy, dead from cardiac arrest, was placed in a shallow grave, the First Relief rested in a mountainside camp ten miles to the west. They stopped for the day when Margret Reed became sick, probably from one of her killer migraines.[78] Most of the party continued the next day, allowing the Reed family and some others to follow at their own pace. At the supply camp at Mule Springs, the emigrants and rescuers were surprised to find Passed Midshipman Selim Woodworth and his men, surrounded by four hundred pounds of supplies. These were the provisions that had been intended for Reed and his party to take to the Sierra camps but had been waylaid when Woodworth failed to reach the rendezvous point in time because of weather.

Four days later, Woodworth and his supplies had finally made it to Johnson's Ranch, where he reportedly declared, "I shall not return until all are safely in the camp."⁷⁹ But soon after leaving the ranch, Woodworth began to have serious misgivings that led to a change of plans. By the time he reached Mule Springs, he had decided it would be more prudent to remain there and disperse provisions to the other relief parties.

Tucker, Glover, and others who knew the importance of the supplies to the starving emigrants and rescuers took Woodworth to be deficient in courage and leadership skills. The effete naval officer did little to help. None of the new arrivals at the camp ever forgot the image of Woodworth supine on a blanket with two of his men rubbing his feet with ice to prevent frostbite while he enjoyed generous slugs of brandy from a handy keg.⁸⁰

The dauntless members of the First Relief eschewed strong drink, but according to Tucker, they settled in at their "old encampment where we met with nourishment tea and sugar which revived us a good deal."⁸¹ The next day, the Reed contingency, including Margret, reached Mule Springs. Late that afternoon, everyone was surprised to see barefooted William Murphy limp into camp along with John Gordon, the camp keeper, and the other emigrant who had overeaten but survived. Murphy told his sister, Mary, and the others crowded around him that he was inspired to walk despite the pain after having seen William Hook die.

Fortunately for Murphy and all the others, they would ride for the rest of the journey. "We were out of the snow, could see the blessed earth and green grass again," wrote Virginia Reed. "How beautiful it looked. We stayed a day or so, getting the horses and mules ready to ride. No more dragging over the snow, when we were tired, so very tired, but green grass, horses to ride, and plenty to eat."⁸²

The closer the eighteen survivors got to Johnson's Ranch, the more hopeful and optimistic they became. It was beginning to dawn on them that they were going to live after all and not waste away frozen and starved in an icy dungeon. The emigrants looked at each other in a different light.

Virginia was a very thin thirteen-year-old girl riding an ornery mule, but she was pretty and feisty enough to catch the eye of some of the young bucks escorting the emigrants out of the foothills down to the valley. One of those escorts, twenty-two-year-old Edward Pyle Jr., who had been hired along with his father to haul supplies to the Mule Creek Camp, worked up the nerve to approach Miss Virginia. He did not come a-courting but cut to the chase and asked for her hand in marriage.[83] The proposal was a bold move considering that Pyle had never spoken to Virginia before. She was not remotely contemplating marriage. She turned down the proposal by using a smile and a laugh to gently put him off without damaging his fragile male ego. Virginia and Pyle even became friends.

The relief party stopped at Johnson's Ranch for a brief rest and hot food. They also talked with some survivors of the Forlorn Hope who were still there and brought them up to date on conditions at the camps. There was little discussion about the snowshoe party's ordeal, and no one broached the subject on everyone's mind—cannibalism.

On March 4, the First Relief reached Sutter's Fort. Many of the eighteen survivors began to cry when the fort came into sight. John Sutter warmly received them, while some of his Indians helped the emigrants to dismount. Sutter provided them with every comfort they had dreamed about during many long and agonizing months. They had hot baths. Fresh clothing was issued, along with food and drink. A somewhat questionable physician whom Sutter had hired to treat the disease-plagued Indian workforce tended emigrants with physical complaints, such as William Murphy, with his severely frostbitten feet.[84]

Individuals and family members were provided with quarters or were invited to stay with families living in the area. It was the Reeds' good luck to be taken in by John Sinclair and his young wife, Mary, at their Rancho del Paso on the other side of the American River. "I really thought I had stepped over into paradise," Virginia wrote. "Mrs. Sinclair was the dearest of women. Never can I forget their kindness."[85]

Like her daughter, Margret Reed was thankful that she and her children had been given sanctuary in the Sinclair home. It pleased her to see a friendship budding between Virginia and Mary, who was only a few years older. And James Jr., on a regimen of milk, eggs, and calves' liver, was rosy cheeked and as energetic as ever.

Margret felt that she was improving physically, but when darkness descended, she felt uneasy. She had difficulty sleeping, and when she slept, it was fitful. By the end of the first week of March, the temperature had dropped again, and a cold, hard rain fell across the land. Margret thought of nothing but her husband and her two other children. After spending so much time in the Sierras, she knew the signs. If it was raining in the valley, she knew it was snowing in the mountains.[86]

SPRING CAME LATE to California in 1847. That March, a rare snow fell on San Francisco and Monterey.[87] For the first time in their lives, children from just below the foothills built snowmen and had snowball fights. Small lagoons were covered with ice, water froze in pitchers, and footlong icicles festooned roofs.

Some of the more skeptical native Californios, trying to adjust to the American conquest of their native land, theorized that "the coming of 'these Yankee devils' has completely changed the character of seasons here, the winter months especially being, it is believed, now wetter and colder than before the American advent."[88]

Members of the Donner Party looked for their own scapegoats to blame for the dangerous predicament they faced in the Sierras. A likely candidate was James Reed. After all, Reed had convinced them to take the so-called shortcut and had killed a young teamster. Maybe Lewis Keseberg was right—Reed should have been hanged instead of banished.

Still, the favorite whipping boy remained Lansford Hastings, the self-styled promoter and author of the *Emigrant's Guide*.[89] Only a year before, the emigrants had been starry-eyed and captivated by Hastings's descriptions. "Snow sometimes falls . . . especially in the vicinity of the mountains, but it seldom lies, more than two or three days."[90]

Not everything Hastings presented in his guidebook was embellished or misleading, however. Throughout the 152-page guide, he had provided a good deal of useful advice, including important suggestions that the Donner Party had failed to follow. One of the more important recommendations concerned timing. Hastings wrote:

"Emigrants should invariably, arrive at Independence, Mo., on, or before the fifteenth day of April, so as to be in readiness, to enter upon their journey, on, or before, the first day of May; after which time, they should never start, if it can, possibly, be avoided. The advantages to be derived, from setting out, at as early a day as that above suggested, are those of having an abundance of good pasturage, in passing over those desolate and thirsty plains; and being enabled to cross the mountains, before the falling of mountains of snow, or floods of rain, which usually occurs, in that region, early in October."[91] Hastings also gave a brief but ominous warning: "Unless you pass over the mountains early in the fall, you are very liable to be detained, by impassable mountains of snow, until the next spring, or, perhaps, forever."[92]

Forever. That single word offered no hope and no alternative. It came like a slap, the final word at the end of the most important sentence in Hastings's book. It meant the finality of the missing and the lost trapped in eternity. Some members of the Donner Party were already gone, but it was not too late for others. They were the ones that the members of the Second Relief, led by Reed, wanted to save.

Reed appreciated everyone on his team, especially the seasoned men who had worked as trappers and endured many mountain winters. The rescuers respected Reed. Those who knew about the killing of the teamster chose to believe Reed's version of what had happened. They understood the difficulty of making snap decisions, such as his choice to cut short his family reunion when the First and Second Relief parties met on the trail. Like Reed, the nine other rescuers were driven by the urgency to reach the mountain camps and save as many survivors as possible.

Once the Second Relief was back on the trail to the summit and the camps beyond, they stopped as little as possible except for leaving caches of food. When the hardpack snow became soft in the afternoon, John Turner, the most experienced mountaineer in the party, suggested that the rescuers sleep during daylight hours and travel at night when the crust was frozen hard and it was easier to pick out landmarks in moonlight.[93] Turner's idea worked and saved the party valuable time.

On the second night, Charles Cady, Nicholas Clark, and Charles Stone wanted to keep on moving rather than take a catnap. Reed gave them his approval. After Turner schooled them about the routing and the landmarks to look for ahead, the energetic young men were sent ahead as an advance party.

They soon made a wrong turn and were lost. After meandering through the snow for a while, they came upon a clearing and made a sad discovery—the frozen corpse of John Denton sitting against a tree trunk with his head bent forward on his chest.[94] There was evidence that some forest beast had sniffed out the body. The rescuers knew that finding Denton confirmed that they were back on the right trail.

They hurried on, crossed the summit, and were closing in on the lake camp when they saw a party of Indians. The boys did not have any firearms and were fearful that the Indians had raided the cabins and massacred the survivors. They spent the night huddled together behind a snowbank without a fire because the smoke would have given them away.

While Cady, Clark, and Stone spent a sleepless night in the snow, dreading the scene they might find in the morning at the lake camp, the rest of the Second Relief made good progress on the trail. With Tucker and young Brit Greenwood as guides, there was no risk of getting lost.

Like the advance party, the main body of rescuers also came upon Denton's body. "I found him dead. Covered him with a counterpane, and buried him in the snow, in the wildest of the wild portions of the earth," Reed wrote later to his brother-in-law, Gersham Keyes.[95]

Early on March 1, when it was just barely light enough to see, Clark, Cady, and Stone slowly inched down the trail to the emigrant camp. They scanned the treelines and snowdrifts for any sign of Indians, but there had been no massacre. The snow had started to melt, revealing the top of a cabin. Then some of the emigrants emerged. The boys went from cabin to cabin, letting people know that another relief party had come. They gave out small bits of dried meat and comforted those who appeared to be in the worst physical condition.

At the Breen cabin, the stench made the rescuers gag, but they found all five of the Breen children and Patty and Tommy Reed alive. The rescuers moved on to the other cabins. When they had made the rounds of everyone at the lake camp, Stone stayed behind while Cady and Clark hiked to the Alder Creek camp to see about those emigrants.[96]

At about noon that day, Reed and the other rescuers made it to the lake camp. They headed directly to the Breen cabin. "They saw the top of a cabin just peering above the silvery surface of the snow," Reed told J. H. Merryman for his story about the Donner Party, published in December 1847. "As they approached it, Mr. Reed beheld his youngest daughter [Patty], sitting upon the corner of the roof, her feet resting upon the snow. Nothing could exceed the joy of each, and Mr. Reed was in raptures, when on going into the cabin he found his son [Tommy] alive."[97]

At first, little Tommy did not recognize his father. But after a few minutes of hearing Reed's voice, the boy realized it was indeed his father with the beard and ruddy face tanned by wind and sun. Reed made a big pot of nourishing soup and filled Patty's aprons with biscuits. She proudly made the rounds, giving one to every person in the cabin.[98] With his children accounted for and fed, Reed talked briefly with Patrick Breen before inspecting the rest of the camp.

Breen told Reed and the others that there had been no more deaths at the lake camp in the week since the First Relief had left with a group of survivors. Breen then lowered his voice and told them that acts of cannibalism had taken place at the lake camp and he feared also at the camp on Alder Creek. Before anyone could respond, Breen assured Reed that there had been no cannibalism in the Breen cabin, and neither of Reed's children had eaten human flesh.

According to Breen, the mood in the camp had changed the day after the First Relief departed. With the two Reed children back in his cabin, Breen got it in his head that the few rations left for them and his supply of ox hides were not going to last. As much as it pained him, Breen took Towser—the only dog left in camp—for a walk. He shot the dog and dressed his flesh.[99] A short time later, Breen turned away Elizabeth Graves when she came to his cabin begging for dog meat or hides.

On February 26—Patty Reed's ninth birthday—Breen had written in his diary of "hungry times in camp." He also noted that during Levinah Murphy's recent visit to the Breen cabin, she had predicted that the wolves everyone could hear howling each night would soon dig up the dead bodies at her shanty. She also indicated that it could be in her best interest to get to the bodies before the wolves. "Mrs. Murphy said here yesterday that she thought she would commence on Milt [Milt Elliott] & eat him," Breen wrote. "I dont think that she has done so yet, it is distressing The Donnos [Donners] told the California folks [First Relief] that they would commence to eat the dead people 4 days ago, if they did not succeed that day or next in finding their cattle under ten or twelve feet of snow & did not know the spot or near it, I suppose they have done so ere this time."[100]

Reed and McCutchen hurried to the Murphy cabin and found it in far worse condition than the Breens'. "The Murphy cabin conditions passed the limits of description and almost of imagination," one historian later wrote.[101] Just outside the cabin, young Stone, who stayed behind when Cady and Clark went to Alder Creek, started a fire and was washing a pile of lice-infested clothes and bedding in a cooking pot. Reed and McCutchen stripped off their own filthy clothing to be scrubbed.

Inside the cabin, they saw that Levinah Murphy's physical and mental condition had deteriorated so much that she could no longer properly tend to the children left in her care. She had become childlike herself and alternated between laughter and tears. Her son Simon was eight years old and could take care of himself, but George Foster Jr. was only a year old, and James Eddy was three. They were hungry, dirty, and barely alive. Stone had given them some food, but Reed took a chance and gave them a little more nourishment before he and McCutchen gently bathed the little boys and wrapped them in fresh flannel bedding.[102]

Next, they cared for Lewis Keseberg, lying in pain in his own excrement and still disabled from the injury to his foot. When Reed began to bathe him, Keseberg was beside himself with humiliation. He and Reed had been constantly at odds on the trail. Now Reed was giving Keseberg comfort and assurances that everything would improve.

"When Reed's relief party left the cabins, Mr. Reed left me a half teacupful of flour, and about a half a pound of jerked beef," Keseberg later stated in an interview. "It was all he could give. Mrs. Murphy, who was left with me, because too weak and emaciated to walk, had no larger portion. Reed had no animosity toward me. He found me to weak to move. He washed me, combed my hair, and treated me kindly. When he left me, he promised to return in two weeks and carry me over the mountains."[103]

Reed told Stone to remain at the Murphy cabin to monitor the emigrants' food intake and keep them comfortable. Not far from the Murphy cabin door, Reed and McCutchen came upon the mutilated body of Milt Elliott, Reed's faithful teamster who had taken such good care of the entire Reed family. His face and head had not been touched, but the rest of Elliott's body had been dismembered.[104] Most of the flesh had been cut off his torso and limbs. Tufts of hair, small bones, and pieces of tissue were scattered about, conclusive proof that the survivors had eaten the dead.

Saddened to learn that Mrs. Murphy had carried out her plan to "commence on Milt," Reed and McCutchen made their final stop at the Graves cabin. Like all the others in camp, Elizabeth Graves and her remaining children had lost so much weight that they were hollow-eyed, skeletal, and unrecognizable. They eagerly devoured the small ration of food given to each of them and then burrowed under the blankets without uttering a sound.

Before Reed and McCutchen joined the other rescuers, who had set up camp outside to avoid sleeping in the foul and vermin-infested cabins, they took time to find the body of McCutchen's baby daughter, Harriet, in the snow. They placed her body in a shallow grave dug on a small plot of ground where the snow had melted.[105]

At his cabin, Patrick Breen wrote the final entry in the diary he had started in November. "Mond. March the 1 So fine & pleasant froze hard last night there has 10 men arrived this morning from Bear Valley with provisions there is amongst them some old they say the snow will be here until June."[106]

On the morning of March 2, Reed and three of his men headed for the tents at Alder Creek, leaving four rescuers at the lake to prepare the emigrants chosen for the return trip. At the Donner campsite, Cady and Clark, ashen-faced and somber, described to Reed what they had encountered two days before. J. Quinn Thornton included their description in his 1848 book.

> They informed him [Reed] that when they arrived at the camp, Baptiste [Jean-Baptiste Trudeau] had just left the camp of the widow of the late Jacob Donner, with the leg and thigh of Jacob Donner, for which he had been sent by George Donner, the brother of the deceased. That was given, but the boy was informed that no more could be given, Jacob Donner's body being the last they had. They had consumed four bodies, and the children were sitting upon a log, with their faces stained with blood, devouring the half-roasted liver and heart of the father, unconscious of the approach of the men, of whom they took not the slightest notice even after they came up. Mrs. Jacob Donner was in a helpless condition, without any thing whatever to eat except the body of her husband, and she declared she would die before she would eat of this. Around the fire were hair, bones, skulls, and the fragments of half-consumed limbs. Mr. Reed and party, after removing the tent to another place, and making Mrs. Donner as comfortable as possible, retired for the purpose of being relieved for a brief period from sights so terrible and revolting. They

had not gone far when they came to the snow-grave of Jacob Donner. His head was cut off, and was lying with the face up, the snow and cold having preserved all the features unaltered. His limbs and arms had been severed from the body which was cut open, the heart and liver being taken out. The leg and thigh which the boy, John Baptiste, had obtained, had been thrown back, upon the party coming up with relief. Other graves were seen, but nothing remained in them but a few fragments.[107]

Reed and his men inspected the camp. At George Donner's tent, they found the patriarch on the brink of death. He had become so weak that he could no longer lift his head or hands. Tamzene Donner—unlike her husband and their sister-in-law, Elizabeth Donner—was still strong enough to travel. Reed made note that Tamzene's three daughters—Frances, Georgia, and Eliza—were stout and hearty.[108] It was apparent that the Donner sisters' robust appearance was the result of survival cannibalism. Like their cousins, the girls had stayed alive by eating the flesh of the dead teamsters and their Uncle Jake.

Reed discreetly chose not to write about cannibalism in the relief diary. But at least one widely published newspaper story of 1847, by J. H. Merryman and based on notes provided by Reed, contained vivid and perhaps somewhat exaggerated accounts of cannibalism at both Donner Party camps.[109] In describing what he called the "deplorable condition" of the camps, Merryman wrote of Reed and his rescuers finding "the fleshless bones and half eaten bodies of the victims of famine." He referred to the human flesh and organs that the starving emigrants consumed as "their unholy feast" and recounted that some of the unfortunates were so desperately hungry, they did not bother with a cooking fire but ate the flesh and organs raw.[110]

"To Mr. Reed this was a horrid sight," wrote Merryman. "Among the bones and skulls that filled the camp kettles, he saw the remains of many an old and well-tried friend."[111]

For the rest of their lives, some Donner Party survivors, including a few from the Donner family, not only refused to discuss cannibalism but claimed that it had never occurred in the camps. Other survivors, however, did not become upset or defensive if the subject came up. Several of them freely admitted that they had eaten human flesh to stay alive.[112]

Georgia Donner, one of the three daughters of George and Tamzene, was never ashamed that as a five-year-old girl, she had survived because of the pieces of human meat she was given to eat. Thirty-two years after that terrible winter, Georgia shared some of her vivid memories in correspondence with historian C. F. McGlashan when he researched his book about the Donner Party.[113]

"My uncle's [body] was the only one they could find for some time," she wrote. "His wife expressed her wish to [un]burry the body, so that the limbs might be used. And from these food was prepared for the little ones in both camps. While eating I chanced to look up. My mother had turned away and father was crying. . . . Samuel Shoemaker is the only one that I know of being found afterward." In another letter, Georgia added a curious note about Shoemaker. "Jacob Donner's wife came down the steps one day saying to mother 'What do you think I cooked this morning?' Then answered her own question herself, 'Shoemaker's arm.' "[114]

The teenaged Jean-Baptiste Trudeau was also identified as one of those who ate human flesh, based on irrefutable eyewitness accounts of the rescuers who had seen him at the camp carrying Jake Donner's severed leg.[115] Trudeau later held forth about his cannibalism during an interview with Henry Augustus Wise, a career naval officer and author. Much of what Trudeau told Wise was included in the published work *Los Gringos*, including bogus and sensationalized accounts of the Donner Party.[116]

Before Wise's book was published, there was debate about whether Trudeau's descriptions were really the "very words" of a sixteen-year-old who has happy to be alive and no longer hungry for food but was starved for attention. Instead, were those words shaped into a distorted and embellished tale from an ambitious writer known for his fiction under the nom de plume "Harry Gringo"?[117]

There were no concerns about the other source for Wise's story of "shocking human cannibals." Identified only as "an officer of the navy in charge of the [Donner rescue] expedition," it was none other than Passed Midshipman Selim Woodworth.[118] This contentious young man not only helped Wise, he also supplied information for other Donner Party stories, such as one published in the *Monterey Californian* that claimed "mothers possessing portions of their dead companions, refused to divide it with their own children, while *alive*, and when the children died, actually devoured the bodies of their own offspring!"[119] The statement was not just an exaggeration but a barefaced lie, considering the countless examples of mothers such as Margret Reed, Peggy Breen, and others who had made sacrifices and risked their own well-being to save their children.

There was no better example of such a caring mother than Tamzene Donner at the Alder Creek camp. Reed and his men found that out. Try as they might, none of them could persuade the implacable Tamzene to leave the camp with her children and go with the rescuers. Just as she had told the First Relief, Tamzene explained that she would never abandon her husband and leave him to die alone. Instead, she and the three girls would stay and wait for the next relief party with ample provisions, led by Woodworth. If George was still alive when the rescuers came, then she would remain and allow the girls to leave.

Reed agreed, thinking that Woodworth was only a few days behind.[120] What Reed did not know was that the mercurial Woodworth had once again changed his plans. He was not en route to the camps but was waiting down the trail at a base camp he had established near Bear Valley.

Reed ended up taking only three emigrants from the Alder Creek camp—Mary Donner, two weeks away from her eighth birthday; her brother Isaac Donner, five years old; and Sol Hook, the fifteen-year-old stepson of Jacob Donner. Trudeau, disgruntled again because he had not been chosen, stayed behind at Elizabeth Donner's tent, as did her son Lewis Donner, three years old. Reed left behind rescuer Nicholas Clark to care for Elizabeth and help the others until the next relief party arrived.[121]

At the George Donner tent, Reed assigned Charles Cady to help

Tamzene care for her failing husband, the three Donner sisters, and Samuel Donner, the four-year-old son of Jacob and Elizabeth, who had been taken in by his aunt and uncle to give his declining mother some relief.

Cady and Clark were given nine pounds of jerked beef and eleven pounds of flour to carefully ration out to the nine remaining emigrants. That was thought to be enough food for a week, which surely was enough time for Woodworth to reach the camps.[122]

Before the party departed for the lake camp, Reed and Hiram Miller oversaw the sale of items from Jacob Donner's estate. Members of the rescue team bought mostly silk handkerchiefs, shawls, vests, and a variety of footwear. Nicholas Clark gave one dollar for a knife. Joseph Verrot, the rescuer from France, bought boots and clothing and paid nineteen cents for Jake's comb.[123] Reed shelled out four dollars for a pair of boots that he gave to the shoeless Keseberg that afternoon when the team returned to the lake camp.

They joined the other rescuers and the fourteen emigrants from the lake camp who had been deemed strong enough to make the long hike out of the Sierras. Those chosen were the seven members of the Breen family, five members from the Graves family, and Patty and Tommy Reed.[124] Of the total of seventeen emigrants to be evacuated by the Second Relief, only three were adults—Patrick and Margaret Breen and the bewildered Elizabeth Graves, who fretted about the security of the stash of silver and gold coins that had been cleverly concealed in the family wagon. When the emigrants had become snowbound and burned all the wagons, the coins had been removed.[125]

Five emigrants remained at Truckee Lake—Keseberg, Levinah Murphy, her son, Simon, and the young Foster and Eddy boys. Rescuer Charles Stone was put in charge of the camp with orders to minister to the infirm, especially Keseberg and Mrs. Murphy, and maintain some semblance of order.

On March 3, the Second Relief left the lake camp with seventeen emigrants. Most of the children were younger than ten, and some of them would have to be carried by the rescuers. Any adult who was not toting a child carried blankets and provisions. A few still held

326 | OUT OF TIME

on to some personal belongings. Besides the biscuits and dried beef the rescuers had doled out, the Breens had a bundle containing a few strips of beef and some coffee, tea, and sugar that they had managed to save. Elizabeth Graves entrusted her cumbersome bag of coins to one of the rescuers to carry. Unaware that her son-in-law, Jay Fosdick, had died with the snowshoe party and his body had been cannibalized, she carried the violin he had left at the lake camp.[126]

Because of all the encumbrances, the party moved slowly along the lakeshore and did not get far that first day. They camped on bare ground close to the north side of the lake. That evening as the moon rose, most of the emigrants and rescuers congregated around a fire. For the first time in a very long time, laughter could be heard. Patrick Breen took up Fosdick's fiddle and for two hours played every Irish jig and ballad he knew, much to the delight of his audience.[127] Only the seasoned mountain men noticed that the temperature was slowly but steadily dropping.

In the morning, just before the Second Relief left camp, Elizabeth Graves overheard some of the rescuers, including the one who was carrying her coins, joke about stealing the bag of money. Already concerned about her money, Elizabeth had the rescuer leave the bag with her and told Reed that she had a few chores to handle and would catch up with the party. As soon as they turned west and started up the trail, Elizabeth, with help from her older children, managed to move the bag of coins to a spot she had marked off behind a large rock. She quickly dug a hole and buried her hoard of coins. It was a nest egg to build a new life for herself and her family. When she got her family to a safe place, Elizabeth planned to return for her buried treasure.

Once she memorized the exact location of her buried cache, Elizabeth, holding her baby daughter, and her three other children moved on with some urgency to rejoin the party. It was not long before the tail end of the slow-moving Second Relief came into view. Even so, the entire Graves family was panting by the time they caught up, all of them exhausted by the accelerated pace. Soon, however, Elizabeth caught her breath. Despite prodding from Reed and McCutchen, all the emigrants tired quickly, and the party again made little progress. Reed wrote in the party diary, "Left camp early traveled on the lake 2 miles an[d] encamped under the mountain made this day about 4 miles, nothing of interest occ[urre]d."[128]

For a second night, Breen put Fosdick's violin to good use. Spirits seemed high, but the food was nearly gone, and there was no sign of Woodworth and the next relief. After breakfast the next morning, Reed had "2 Scanty meals left for all hands which would do to the following night." He sent John Turner, Matthew Dofar, and Joseph Gendreau—three experienced mountaineers—to go ahead to the first cache of food. If it had not been disturbed, they were to send back one man with food for the party while the other two proceeded to retrieve the food at the next cache.

Not long after the departure of the three mountain men, the four remaining rescuers and their seventeen tired, cold, and hungry charges broke camp. It was important to get over the summit and make up some time. Once again, the pace was slow, but by the afternoon, they finally had crossed the summit and reached a campsite that had been used by the First Relief. It was in a long alpine meadow in Summit Valley on the west slope of the Sierras near the head of the Yuba River. The men rebuilt the log platform for a fire, cut pine boughs for bedding, and gathered firewood. There was scant food and no sign of Woodworth and his party. Even the stronger rescuers were worn out.

"Here the men began to fail being for several days on half allowance," Reed wrote in his diary. "The Sky looks like snow and everything indicates a storm . . . god forbid . . . the clouds still thickening . . . terror terror . . . I feel a terrible foreboding but dare not Communicate my mind to any, death to all if our provisions do not Come in a day or two and a storm should fall on us. Very cold, a great lamentation about the Cold."

By early evening, the four remaining rescuers and seventeen emigrants were huddled around a fire. On this night, there was no fiddle serenade and no laughter. All of them stared at the fire and waited. The temperature plummeted, and the moan of the wind became a howl. Then the storm came. It was as powerful as all the others born in the Gulf of Alaska. Reed's fears were realized, as were those of Margret Reed, far away at the Sinclair ranch peering out a window at the Sierras. The ordeal was not over for the poor wretches of the Second Relief. It was the grand finale of the winter of 1847.

"My dreaded storm in now on us," Reed wrote. He called it a "perfect Hurricane." In his diary, he wrote, "The men up nearly all night making fires, some of the men began to pray. Several became [snow] blind [including Reed]. I could not see even the light of the fire when it was blazing before me."[129]

Eventually, the fire blazing on the platform built of green timber melted the snow beneath, creating a deep pit. It had already snowed more than a foot when John Breen, just fourteen, suddenly collapsed or, as he put it, "fainted or became stupid from weakness."[130] He was about to slide into the pit when one of the emigrants grabbed hold of him and dragged him to safety. Peggy Breen managed to pry open her son's clenched jaws and slip some lump sugar into his mouth, which soon revived him.

At first light the next morning, the storm was still going strong. Reed doled out the last of the food—a spoonful of flour for each person.[131] A gale-force wind and driving snow pelted the rescuers as they chopped wood and kept the fire going. None of the adult emigrants offered any help, including Patrick Breen, who appeared to be in constant prayer. The children wailed constantly from beneath their blankets. As night came on, the younger children cried themselves to sleep. Peggy Breen and Elizabeth Graves clutched their infant daughters and checked periodically to see if they were still breathing. The rest of the emigrants fell silent except for some whimpering and nightmare cries that were drowned out by the wind.

Although his snow-blind eyes still bothered him and he was physically spent, Reed took the first watch as fire tender so the others could get some sleep. He jotted in his diary, "Night Closing fast and with it the Hurricane Increases."[132]

While tending the fire, Reed became so exhausted that he collapsed and lost consciousness. The flames died down. At the same time, the logs acting as the foundation for the platform shifted, dumping much of the fire into the pit. In only a few minutes, icy air descended on the camp. The cold awakened the emigrants, and pandemonium erupted. The children screamed, and the mothers cried. Even Brit Greenwood, who had been raised in the woods, fell to his knees and joined Breen in prayer.[133]

Several if not all of the emigrants would have perished if it had not been for Bill McCutchen and Hiram Miller. Without hesitation, they sprang into action and saved many lives. "The rest of the men were disheartened, and would not use any exertion, in fact they gave up all hope and in despair, some of them commenced praying," McCutchen told a journalist in 1871. "I damned them, telling them it was not time to pray but to get up, stir themselves and get wood, for it was a matter of life or death to us in a few minutes. The fire was nearly out; the snow falling off the trees had nearly extinguished it before discovered; it was only rekindled by the exertion of Mr. Miller and myself."[134]

Once the fire was roaring again, McCutchen and Miller went to Reed's aid. They pulled him close to the fire and rubbed his feet and hands. Slowly, he began to regain his senses. When he could sit up and sip water, his two friends at last looked after themselves. Miller saw to the splayed skin of his frozen hands and fingers and, like McCutchen, stayed as close as he could to the blaze. "After we got the fire started I was so chilled that in getting warm I burned the back out of my shirt, having four on me; only discovering the mishap by the scorching of my skin," McCutchen recalled.[135]

Unfortunately, not all the emigrants survived the rampage. During the stormy night, Isaac Donner, the five-year-old son of Jacob and Elizabeth Donner, quietly died. "He was lying on the bed of pine boughs between his sister Mary and Patty Reed, and died so quietly that neither of the sleeping girls awoke," C. F. McGlashan later wrote.[136]

Mary Donner was shocked and troubled by Isaac's death. During the night while she tossed and turned in her sleep, one of her feet slipped into the fire. Her feet were so numbed by frostbite that all feeling was gone, and she did not awake when her foot was badly burned.[137] The injury prevented Mary from walking. She remained near but not too close to the fire while McCutchen and Miller placed Isaac's remains in the snow.

After two terrible nights, the storm started to slack off on the third day. The wind died down, and by about noon, the snow stopped. Reed's eyesight was fully restored, and he felt much improved. He conferred with McCutchen and announced that the relief party would take advantage of the lull in the weather and press on for Sutter's Fort.

The announcement was not received enthusiastically. The party had been without food for two days. Elizabeth Graves and her four children were so depleted that they barely had the strength to move. Margaret Breen was likely the strongest member of her family and perhaps could have walked, carrying her youngest, but she would not even think of leaving her husband and the other children behind.

Patrick Breen flat-out refused to leave camp, saying he would rather die there than out on the trail. Reed argued with Breen that if he and his family remained at the camp, they would surely perish. Breen waved him off. Out of frustration and to ensure that he would not be blamed for any more deaths, Reed summoned his men. "Then Mr. Reed called myself and others to witness, that if any of Mr. Brien's family died, their death be upon him and not upon us," McCutchen later explained. "Before leaving, we did everything in our power for those who had to remain, cutting and leaving wood enough to last several days."[138]

Mary Donner wanted to leave with Reed and promised she could hobble along and keep up. But almost as soon as she took her first few steps, she fell in the snow. Mary softly wept as she was carried back to the twelve members of the Breen and Graves families. They sat around the edge of what had become a very deep fire pit. The only food they had was the Breens' small stash of seeds and sugar. It would be several days before a relief party reached them at what would forever be called Starved Camp.

. . .

THE REMNANTS OF THE SECOND RELIEF—Reed, McCutchen, Miller, and Greenwood, who had managed to regain his courage—continued their journey along with the three young survivors. Sol Hook, distraught over the death of his stepbrother Isaac Donner and concerned about leaving his stepsister Mary Donner at Starved Camp, was a resilient fifteen-year-old strong enough to make his way unassisted. Miller, the durable teamster, grabbed up little Tommy Reed and carried him. Patty Reed refused to allow her weak and weary father to carry her. She insisted on walking.

Patty soon found that walking in the deep, soft snow into a bitterly cold wind had not become any easier since her first attempt. After a few agonizing miles, everyone but Miller was frostbitten. By then Patty, who had diligently but with much difficulty followed in her father's footprints, was slowing down and mumbling. Suddenly she cried out that before her was an incredibly beautiful scene. She was looking at a band of angels surrounded by endless stars. Reed turned in his tracks. This was not a mirage. He realized his daughter was hallucinating, a symptom of someone who was freezing to death.[139]

Reed picked her up and held her in his arms while some of the men wrapped a blanket around her and vigorously rubbed her hands and feet. "Patty thought she could walk, but gradually everything faded from her sight, and she seemed to be dying," Virginia Reed later wrote. "All other sufferings were now forgotten, and everything was done to revive the child. My father found some crumbs in the thumb of his woolen mitten; warming and moistening them between his own lips, he gave them to her and thus saved her life."[140]

The idea that a teaspoon of crumbs saved Patty's life became a favorite family story, but the massaging of her hands and feet and the comforting blanket were what raised her body temperature. When she felt better, the party moved on. Cocooned in a blanket slung like a peddler's bag over her father's back, Patty was warmed and revived by the heat from Reed's body.[141]

That day, they had made ten miles when they stopped to camp

beside the Yuba River. Hours of traversing through soft snow had left everyone thoroughly drained. A fire warded off the cold and melted snow for drinking water. The party had gone four days with no food. There was still no sight of the three fellow rescuers bearing edibles from the caches or of Woodworth with his stockpile of provisions. The members of the Second Relief did have plenty of frostbitten feet. "They could have been tracked the whole distance by their blood," Reed observed. "So severe was the pain they suffered that they forgot for a time the cravings of hunger."[142]

To combat their misery, they sat as close as possible to the fire and rubbed their cracked feet and toes with handfuls of icy snow, a common treatment for frostbite for many years.[143] It only made the wounds worse by aggravating delicate tissue and providing more moisture to the frostbite. Greenwood's feet were the worst of the lot and would end up permanently damaged. Others in the party eventually had to have toes amputated.

That night, two figures emerged from the darkness and stepped into the firelight—Charles Cady and Charles Stone, fellow members of the Second Relief.[144] Along with Nicholas Clark, they had been assigned to look after the remaining survivors at the Truckee Lake and Alder Creek camps. Cady and Stone decided to leave after determining that Clark and Jean-Baptiste Trudeau could oversee both camps on their own. Curiously, instead of each of them carrying out a child, they lugged heavy packs. They had no food, only seriously frostbitten feet. No record was left of any conversation that undoubtedly ensued when Cady and Stone sat by the fire and scoured their frozen feet with snow.

"Of what greetings were spoken and of what suspicious glances were cast askance at the packs, no one has left record," historian George R. Stewart wrote. "Probably not much was said. After all, the expedition was not under military discipline, and if Cady and Stone chose to put their own interests first, no one could well say them nay. Probably Reed and the others kept quiet. They had plenty on their minds, anyway. Freezing in the snow, you couldn't think so much about what other people did."[145]

In the case of Cady and Stone, what they did and what they did not do were nothing short of criminal. Putting their own interest first was one thing, but deserting the dying emigrants was quite another matter. Luckily for Cady and Stone, an accurate accounting of their behavior was not pieced together until much later, when their deeds were finally revealed.

They had hatched their scheme at the lake camp. James Reed and the Second Relief had not been gone long when Stone left the lake camp. He hiked to Alder Creek, where Cady and Clark had been left to care for the Donners. Clark was off hunting to supplement the few rations that were left. He had spotted bear tracks and came upon a black bear sow and her cub. Clark got off a shot and wounded the mother. Both bears escaped, and Clark continued to track the blood trail in the snow.[146]

While Clark was gone, Cady and Stone discussed the situation they faced. With scarce provisions and signs that another winter storm was headed their way, they concluded they would be much better off to leave everyone behind and strike out on their own. Tamzene Donner overheard the two men plotting their escape. "Mother, fearing that we children might not survive another storm in camp, begged Messrs. Cady and Stone to take us with them, offering them five hundred dollars in coin, to deliver us to Elitha and Leanna at Sutter's Fort," Eliza Donner wrote in her memoir.[147]

Cady and Stone accepted Tamzene's offer and promised to deliver the three Donner children—Frances, Georgia, and Eliza—to their older sisters. The men also agreed to carry the girls' keepsakes and belongings, including some silver spoons and a bundle of silk that Tamzene wanted her daughters to use as collateral or to cover expenses once they got to the settlements. She combed their hair and dressed them in linsey dresses and woolen stockings. Then Tamzene took the little girls to George Donner's deathbed so they could kiss their father good-bye.

"The men helped us up the steps and stood us up on the snow," Eliza recalled. "She [Tamzene] came, put on our cloaks and hoods, saying, as if talking to herself, 'I may never see you again, but God will take care of you.'"[148]

Soon after Cady and Stone and their young charges left the camp and a weeping Tamzene behind, they found that Frances was able to walk on her own, but the two youngest girls had to be carried. When they reached the Truckee Lake camp, their first stop was the Murphy cabin. Inside the dank and squalid cabin were Levinah Murphy, so physically and mentally depleted that she could barely care for her eight-year-old son, Simon, and one-year-old grandson, George Foster. The only other occupant was the bearded and bushy-headed Lewis Keseberg. His wild-eyed scowl frightened the little Donner girls, and they huddled like chicks in a dark corner.

Cady and Stone stayed only a few minutes. They left before dark and went to the deserted Breen cabin to sleep. That night, the same furious snowstorm that stalled the Second Relief at the Starved Camp struck the lake camp, but as Reed later wrote, "The storm did not rage with such fury on the east side of the great Chain [Sierras]."[149]

It raged enough, however, to convince Cady and Stone to leave the next day. The addition of fresh snow further convinced them how difficult it would be for them to carry even a small child over the summit and down the western slope. The sky began to clear by the afternoon, and Cady and Stone, without a second thought, turned their backs on the Murphy cabin and shuffled west through the snow. Instead of taking any children, they carried with them the silver spoons, fancy silks, and other valuables that Tamzene Donner had given to her daughters.[150]

Although frostbitten and hungry, Cady and Stone made good time. After crossing the pass, they came to a campsite where smoke curled from a hole in the ground. They peered over the edge of the pit and could make out a man and woman and several children clustered together and nearby what looked like the corpses of a woman and boy. But instead of trying to help the Breens and others who had remained at Starved Camp, Cady and Stone backed away from the pit. They resumed their journey westward and caught up with Reed and the others of the Second Relief.[151]

The next morning, the Second Relief—grown larger with the addition of Cady and Stone—returned to the trail. It was their fifth day without food. Severe frostbite and the lack of food made every step painful. Spirits were lifted when they came upon a parcel of food dangling from a tree limb, left by Matthew Dofar, one of the three mountaineers whom Reed had sent ahead several days before to search for food.

Finding that the first cache of food had been consumed by martens, Dofar, John Turner, and Joseph Gendreau pressed on but soon had to dig in when the snowstorm that had clobbered everyone in the Sierras rolled over them. They had no food and sparking a fire was difficult, but they survived and made it to the next cache. Although martens had raided that cache also, at least part of the food had been left intact. It was enough to give the three men a boost. By then, Turner was so badly frostbitten that he had to be helped along by his mates.[152]

Dofar—the healthiest of the three—backtracked a short distance and hung the cache for Reed and his party to find. He returned to Gendreau and Turner with his severely frostbitten feet, and the woodsmen continued on the trail. They carried Turner by his shoulders. They had not gone far when they encountered some members of Selim Woodworth's supply party coming from Bear Valley.

Reed and his party—many of them crippled from the cold but somewhat energized by the food Dofar had left in the cache—were not far behind. When they made camp along the Yuba, they could hear the cries and curses of long-suffering stragglers such as Brit Greenwood and Cady at Woodworth's encampment.[153] Woodworth's party sent food to the Second Relief that evening. The following morning, Reed was finally reunited with Woodworth, the naval officer whom he and many others no longer trusted, for good reason.

"At the time Reed and his companions were suffering untold horrors on the mountains, and those left at Starved Camp were perishing of starvation, Woodworth, with an abundance of supplies, was lying idle in camp at Bear Valley," historian McGlashan wrote. "That was the part that Selim E. Woodworth took in the relief of the sufferers."[154]

In a face-to-face confrontation, Reed urged Woodworth to dispatch men and supplies immediately to the emigrants at Starved

Camp and those remaining in the two camps on the other side of the Sierras. Woodworth was aghast at such a suggestion. He had absolutely no desire to go farther east after he saw the physical state of Gendreau, Dofar, and especially Turner.[155] Woodworth refused to proceed without a guide.[156]

Reed found Woodworth's behavior tantamount to a dereliction of duty by a supposed officer and gentleman. Critics of Reed from the Donner Party might have thought of him as an egotist, but no one could ever accuse him of cowardice. The same could not be said for Woodworth, who exhibited both arrogance and fear. As Reed later noted, if Woodworth had not been so headstrong and concerned for his own welfare to the detriment of others, "much suffering would have been prevented, but he relied upon his own judgment, and that judgment belonging to a man young in years and of little experience."[157]

Woodworth seemed to have forgotten his written pledge in which he had stated, "I shall not return until all the people are in camp."[158] Others who took part in the various rescues of Donner Party emigrants did not forget. Still, Woodworth often was given the benefit of the doubt and portrayed in a positive light by much of the press at the time. The *California Star* boldly declared that Woodworth "has accomplished more than could have been expected under the circumstances."[159]

In retrospect, there was a case to be made that Woodworth was judged too harshly. If his critics and detractors had probed a bit deeper and learned of his experiences when he was shipwrecked in the Indian Ocean before he joined the navy, they might have been a bit more sympathetic, at least when it came to the question of his courage. Although in some instances he had demonstrated boldness in his youth and even in later years near the close of his naval career, Woodworth's complacency and reticence to leave his base camp in the winter of 1847 were indefensible. Bernard DeVoto later wrote, "Woodworth was not coming; he never came. He was taking his comfort in camp and nourishing what, compared with the courage of the others, can only be called an ignominious cowardice. So the return of the Second Relief, which should have been the most successful, constitutes the final catastrophe of the Donner Party."[160]

If Woodworth did not fully grasp the need for urgent action, Reed certainly did. He knew more rescuers had to get to the Sierra camps as soon as possible. But he also knew that he and the Second Relief had to complete their journey and get the survivors off the western slope and back to the settlements. Woodworth was not up to the job, but fortunately, there were others in camp willing to risk their own lives to save the rest of the emigrants. To Reed's surprise, two of his California Trail companions, William Eddy and William Foster, showed up at the camp. As members of the Donner Party with sons still trapped in the Sierras, they had a vested interest in continuing the lifesaving mission.

Foster and Eddy were the only two male survivors from the Forlorn Hope, and they had eaten the flesh of the dead to stay alive. They also had their differences. Just weeks before, when they were still struggling to escape the snowy mountains, the two men were on the verge of mortal combat. Eddy vehemently disagreed with Foster's intention to kill and eat the two Indians traveling with the Forlorn Hope. Despite his protests, Eddy was unable to stop Foster from murdering Luis and Salvador. For the rest of the snowshoe party's difficult march, Eddy and Foster stayed clear of each other. But after their rescue and subsequent recovery, any animosity between them gradually vanished. They put past disagreements behind them and formed a solid bond based on a mutual goal of rescuing their sons.

Eddy had been a member of the Second Relief when it left Johnson's Ranch for the mountain camps, but he soon found that he was not physically ready. He got as far as Mule Springs and then had to return. After more convalescence, he was ready to try again, but this time he left the ranch with Foster. They rode horses as far as possible and then hiked through the snow until they caught up with Woodworth. They tried everything they could think of to get Woodworth to cross the summit, including shaming him. Probably out of humiliation and to placate Eddy and Foster, Woodworth agreed to move forward on the trail, but not very far. It was said later that Woodworth ordered his company to halt and establish camp when he grew weary from carrying his own blanket.[161]

Then along came Reed and his party. With his blessing and encouragement, Eddy and Foster were inspired to take up the gauntlet.

43. THE THIRD RELIEF

TWO FATHERS BECAME the core of the Third Relief. William Eddy and George Foster were so anxious that when they called for volunteers to join their rescue party and not a man came forward, they decided they would set out alone. Reed quashed that plan. It was folly for only two men to brave the elements and try to wrangle sick and starving emigrants over the Sierras. Instead, Reed convinced them to go back to the Bear Valley base camp and regroup.

It still proved difficult to recruit anyone, but when Selim Woodworth loosened his purse strings, the promise of pay again did the trick.[1] Hiram Miller, the Donner teamster who was already fatigued and hurting from serving with the Second Relief, joined Eddy and Foster. Charles Stone, one of the men who had deserted the emigrants and callously left the Donner girls behind, also signed on, perhaps in hopes of finding more booty. Rounding out the party were three men who had accompanied Woodworth from Mule Springs— William Thompson, Howard Oakley, and John Schull Stark, a bear-like young man said to be as strong as two men.

While the seven members of the Third Relief prepared for their mission, Reed readied his party for the final leg of their journey. Before the Second Relief left the Bear Valley camp, Patty Reed, sensing that she was safe at last and would soon be with the rest of her family, dared to reveal the tiny doll that she had kept hidden ever since the emigrants cached their personal goods months before in the Utah desert.[2] Four-inch-long Dolly, with eyes and hair painted black, had been Patty's constant companion and comforter through all the dark times.

"I took 'Dolly' out from where I had hidden her in my dress, and what a pleasant little hour we had, after all that we had gone through, but how happy we were at that camp of relief," Patty told a reporter many years later. "We knew that mama, sister and brother had plenty to eat and drink and we would see them soon."[3]

When the Second Relief was ready to leave for the west, Hiram Miller told Tommy Reed good-bye. Miller was going with the Third Relief to the Donner camps, so one of the other rescuers would have to carry the little boy. Patty climbed onto her father's back. In her hand was Dolly. Patty held Dolly close all the way down the mountain to the base camp at Mule Springs and then on to Johnson's Ranch, Sutter's Fort, and across the American River to Sinclair's Rancho del Paso. Waiting there were Margret Reed, Virginia, and James Jr. "At last my father arrived at Mr. Sinclair's with the little ones, and our family were again united," Virginia wrote. "That day's happiness repaid us for much that we had suffered; and it was spring in California."[4]

After embraces, Margret and Virginia pulled the filthy rags off Patty and Tommy. They scrubbed the children clean, dressed them in fresh clothes, and sat them down with their father to the first hot meal any of them had enjoyed in a long time. Margret spied Patty's little doll, a lock of hair from her own mother, a saltcellar, and other treasures. She was so moved that she quietly wept.[5]

James Reed was thankful. All six members of his family were safe. Not one of them had partaken of human flesh. They had persevered, and now their lives in this new and strange land were really beginning. The long hellish nightmare was over.

THE ORDEAL WAS OVER perhaps for the Reeds and other emigrants who were recuperating at Sutter's Fort and at ranches scattered throughout the Sacramento Valley. But it was not over for the emigrants and rescuers who were still engaged in a death struggle in the frigid and foreboding Sierras. The Third Relief found that out after they left the camp in Bear Valley. The weather was clear. They made good time on the crusty snow, even with fifty-pound packs of provisions procured from Woodworth's supply stockpile.

They made a slight detour on the way. Stone led them to the place where two factions of the Second Relief had come upon the frozen body of John Denton. His remains were still beneath a large tree, with more evidence that varmints had gnawed on the corpse. Unlike the other party, the rescuers took the time to search Denton and found in his pockets a small diary, a pencil and rubber eraser, and some sheets of paper. On one sheet of paper was a poem Denton had written.[6] It was not known whether the poem had been written earlier in the journey or when Denton was dying. The first stanza read:

> *O! after many roving years,*
> *How sweet it is to come*
> *Back to the dwelling place of youth,*
> *Our first and dearest home;*
> *To turn away our wearied eyes*
> *From proud ambition's towers,*
> *And wander in the summer fields,*
> *The scenes of boyhood's hours.*[7]

The relief party packed up Denton's few belongings, including the poem, and hurried on. More death waited for them up the trail when they arrived at Starved Camp the next day. Eddy and Foster were well aware of the emigrants that had been left there, and they were prepared to find most of them dead.

When the Third Relief arrived, they were somewhat surprised to see eleven survivors sitting around a fire at the bottom of a deep snow pit. J. Quinn Thornton later described the scene: "The fire at Starved Camp had melted the snow down to the ground, and the hole thus made was fifteen feet in diameter, and twenty-four feet deep. As the snow had continued to melt, they made steps by which they ascended and descended. The picture of distress was shocking indeed."[8]

The rescuers learned that Elizabeth Graves and her five-year-old son, Franklin, had died the first night after James Reed and his party had left for Johnson's Ranch. Mrs. Graves's death meant that the secret of her sack of buried coins died with her. The mangled bodies of mother and son, as well as that of Isaac Donner, had been partially eaten, the flesh roasted over the fire blazing in the deep pit. The emigrants had eaten Mrs. Graves first. Her heart and liver had been removed, and her breasts and most of the flesh from her limbs had been cut away and cooked.[9] The Breens thus had managed to keep seven children alive for five days, including two suckling infants and other children who were not their own.

John Stark, a member of the Third Relief who was known to be of immense strength and courage, volunteered to escort all eleven survivors from the camp into the Sacramento Valley. Eddy knew it was not a job for one man. He asked Howard Oakley and Charles Stone to help.

Both men saw a chance to make some money without having to continue the trek over the summit. Stone picked up one-year-old Elizabeth Graves, who was very weak and close to death. Oakley gathered up Mary Donner, with her badly burned feet. They headed back on the trail, knowing they would not only be paid three dollars per day for their service but also would collect the hefty fifty-dollar bonus for rescuing a child that was not their own.[10] This foursome made excellent time—particularly once they reached Mule Springs— and made a quick trip to Johnson's Ranch.

Stark was left with the responsibility of getting the other nine emigrants to the settlements—Jonathan and Nancy Graves and the seven Breens. He rejected a suggestion to leave most of them behind and take only the healthiest children. "I will not abandon these people," Stark promised Eddy and Foster. "I am here on a mission of mercy, and I will not half do the work. You can all go if you want to, but I shall stay by these people while they and I live."[11]

Stark made sure all the Starved Camp emigrants got out of the mountains alive. Years later, James Breen recalled being a little boy at Starved Camp. At one point, his mother thought James had stopped breathing, and she roused her husband. She was shocked when Patrick replied, "Let him die, he will be better off than any of us."[12] Peggy could not watch her son die. She massaged his chest and hands, forced him to swallow bits of sugar and snow water, and held him close to her until he opened his eyes.

Many years later, James Breen recalled the Third Relief's arrival and the heroic Stark. "Stark was finally left alone," wrote James. "To his great bodily strength, and unexcelled courage, myself and others owe their lives. There was probably no other man in California at that time, who had the intelligence, determination, and what was absolutely necessary in that emergency, the immense physical powers of John Stark. On his broad shoulders he carried the provisions, most of the blankets, and most of the time the weaker children. In regard to this, he would laughingly say that he could carry them all if there was room on his back, because they were so light from starvation."[13]

Stark pulled off this rescue feat by shuttling the children two at a time. He would carry two ahead on the trail, leave them, and return for two more. While Stark transported the children, Patrick Breen limped along, and Peggy Breen carried baby Isabella. One day, they realized all the snow was gone. They rode horses and mules from Mule Springs to Johnson's Ranch on a muddy trail.

John Breen, barely fifteen and the oldest of the seven Breen children, always remembered waking up that first morning at Johnson's Ranch. "It was long after dark when we got in the valley at Johnson's Ranch, so that the first time I saw it earlie in the morning, the weather was fine, the ground was covered with fine green grass, and there was a very fat beef hanging from the limb of an oak tree, the birds were singing from the tops of trees above our camp and the journey was over," John Breen wrote in an 1879 letter to McGlashan. "I [kept] looking at the scene and could scarcely believe I was alive. The scene that I saw that morning seems to be photographed on my mind; most of the incidents are gone from my memory through the lapse of years, but I can always see the camp near Johnson's Ranch."[14]

Thanks to Stark, every member of the Breen family and the two Graves children reached the safety of the settlements. The same could not be said for little Elizabeth Graves. Stone managed to get the baby, known as Elizabeth Jr., to Sutter's Fort, but she died on April 1.[15] Nonetheless, Stone was pleased to collect his fifty-dollar bonus.

At the fort, there was concern about the health and recovery of many of the emigrants. James Breen looked like a skeleton, and his frozen feet and burns were so worrisome that there was talk of amputating one of his legs. But he fully recovered and became a prominent attorney and superior-court judge who died in 1899.[16]

Although there had been criticism of the Second Relief for leaving the Breens and others behind at Starved Camp, the mature James Breen defended the decision. "No one can attach blame to those who voted to leave part of the emigrants," he wrote. "It was a desperate case. Their idea was to save as many as possible, and they honestly believed that by attempting to save all, all would be lost."[17]

That was the same attitude adopted by Eddy, Foster, Miller, and Thompson of the Third Relief when they crossed to the eastern slope of the High Sierras and made their way to Truckee Lake. They planned to save as many emigrants as possible, but only those who had a strong chance of surviving the return trip. Eddy and Foster prayed that their sons were not only alive but in good enough physical condition to travel.

On March 13, they reached the lake and went to the Murphy cabin, where they had last seen their sons alive in mid-December. They called out for their boys. "They [the rescuers] came in like they were most wild," Frances Donner recalled. "We were frightened at first."[18]

In the dim light, Eddy and Foster could make out figures huddled together and lying on makeshift beds. Foster recognized his mother-in-law, Levinah Murphy, and called out her name.[19] Nearly blind and feebleminded, she turned just as Foster and Eddy excitedly asked for the whereabouts of their sons. Her one-word reply staggered them.

"Dead," Mrs. Murphy told them. Three-year-old James Eddy and two-year-old William Foster had died only a few days before, and both of their bodies had been cannibalized.[20] Members of the Second Relief had told Eddy and Foster that based on what they had seen at the camp in February, the chances of the boys' surviving were poor, but the news was still staggering.

As the two fathers sought to regain their composure, Levinah Murphy delivered a second stunning blow. Ironically one of the first of the emigrants to eat human flesh, she pointed an accusatory finger at Lewis Keseberg, cowering in a dark corner.[21] She claimed that Keseberg had grown so impatient for little George Foster to die that he took the boy to bed with him to keep warm and strangled him during the night.[22] Keseberg vehemently denied the charge and said the boy had died from natural causes. He freely admitted to butchering the bodies of both boys but emphatically stressed that he did not hasten their deaths.

Eddy and Foster were outraged. If Foster had still carried the rifle he had used to kill the Indian guides, he probably would have used it. But Foster realized his mother-in-law was not stable.[23] Eddy, wondering if Keseberg might have had a hand in his son's death, was so outraged that he resolved to kill him if they ever met again.

In her correspondence with C. F. McGlashan in 1879, Georgia Donner provided her memories as a five-year-old of the death of the Foster boy. She remembered Keseberg taking the child to bed with him but had no memory of anything out of the ordinary that evening. "In the morning the child was dead," Georgia wrote. "Mrs. Murphy took it, sat down near the bed where my sister and myself were lying, laid the little one on her lap, and made remarks to other persons, accusing Keseberg of killing it. After a while he [Keseberg] came in, took it from her, and hung it up in sight, inside the cabin, on the wall."[24]

In another letter to McGlashan, Georgia provided further details of the scene at the cabin. "The dead child that Keseberg hung on the wall was not eaten by him alone. A part was given to my sisters and myself, and Simon Murphy [Levinah's young son] whom I remember kindly cut a piece, laid it on the coals, cooked and ate it."[25]

Even though Eddy suspected that Keseberg had killed both his son and the Foster boy, he made another horrible discovery that morning at the lake camp. Eddy learned that like his son, his wife and daughter had been cannibalized.[26] Facing the fact that his entire family was gone, Eddy willed himself to focus on the party's mission. He turned his attention to the emigrants who were still living and had a chance.

Levinah Murphy was only thirty-seven years old, but because of all she had been through trying to keep her family alive, she looked at least twice that age.[27] Her end was approaching fast, and she was not chosen to leave with the Third Relief. Neither was Keseberg. The cloud of suspicion that hung over him, coupled with his foul disposition and bad behavior during the overland journey, did not serve him well. But Keseberg's injured foot prevented him from making the difficult hike.

That left the three Donner sisters—Frances, Georgia, and Eliza—and Levinah's son Simon Murphy, who would turn nine the next day, March 14. It was decided that with some help from the rescuers, all four of them were strong enough to make the return trip. All that remained was to determine the status of the emigrants at Alder Creek.

Amazingly, almost as if on cue, a dazed and confused Tamzene Donner wandered into the Murphy cabin and was immediately swarmed by her three daughters. She had trudged through the snow from Alder Creek out of concern for the girls after finding out that they were still at the lake camp and had not been rescued as promised by Cady and Stone. Tamzene had discovered this betrayal of trust after Nicholas Clark, the only Second Relief rescuer who remained to care for the Donners, visited the lake camp and discovered that the sisters had been left there by his two supposed comrades. As if the news that her daughters had not made it out of the Sierras was not enough, Tamzene became even more upset when told that Keseberg was talking about killing the girls for food.[28]

Once the Third Relief members calmed the Donner girls and unwound their arms from their mother's neck, Tamzene related all that had taken place since the Reed rescue party had departed. Just as the big storm that swept over the Sierras was lifting, her nephew Lewis Donner, three-year-old son of Jacob and Elizabeth, had died. His grief-stricken mother Elizabeth—Aunt Betsy—had made her way to the other tent and laid the dead child in Tamzene's lap. With Clark's help, Tamzene buried the lad in the hard snow. Soon after, the emotionally and physically drained Elizabeth quietly passed away and was laid in a snowy grave by Clark and Jean-Baptiste Trudeau.[29]

Clark was finally successful at hunting bear. He had shot and killed the elusive bear cub after trapping it in a cave. The fresh animal meat lasted a bit longer than the rations left by the Second Relief.

Once the bear meat was gone, the survivors returned to eating flesh taken from the corpses of Aunt Betsy and others stored in the snow.[30]

Finally, just the day before, when Tamzene learned of her daughters' predicament, she had decided to go to the lake camp. She left Clark and Trudeau at her tent to look after young Samuel Donner and her husband, George.

When she finished telling her story to the rescuers, Tamzene beseeched Eddy and Foster to go back with her to Alder Creek to see about those waiting there. Perhaps they could take little Sammie with them when they left or do something about George's gangrenous arm. Eddy sympathized but told her they saw no need to go to Alder Creek. Time was of the essence, and they had to leave.

Tamzene reminded them of Clark and Trudeau, who were still healthy and could be rescued. Growing more desperate, she asked the rescuers to wait while she returned to her camp to alert the two men there so they could leave and carry out Sammie. Mostly, she pleaded for her daughters and purportedly offered Eddy a large sum of money to rescue her children.[31]

Eddy told her to keep her money. He said he would "save her children or die in the effort."[32] He told Tamzene that Clark and Trudeau could make it out of the Sierras on their own, and it was much too late to help the others. The rescue party had not brought extra provisions and could not risk being stranded by another storm. Eddy noted that Tamzene still looked healthy enough to travel and should join her daughters and return with the Third Relief.

For the third time with as many relief parties, Tamzene refused to leave. As before, she again explained that as long as George Donner drew breath, she would remain with him. That was her final decision. This meant that once again, Tamzene had to bid her daughters farewell. It might have been more painful than the first time for her, recognizing that most likely she would never see them or the other family members again.

"Now, she was about to confide us to the care of a party whose leader swore either to save us or die with us on the trail," Eliza Donner later recalled of that day at Truckee Lake. "We listened to the sound of her voice, felt her good-bye kisses, and watched her hasten away to father, over the snow through the pines, and out of sight, and knew we must not follow."[33] When Tamzene turned and walked away, she did not look back.

The rescuers helped the Donner girls and the Murphy boy gather their few belongings and don the warmest clothing available. The men brought firewood to the cabin and told Mrs. Murphy good-bye. They ignored Keseberg.

"As we were ready to start, Mrs. Murphy walked to her bed, laid down turned her face to the wall," Georgia Donner later wrote. "One of the men gave her a handful of dried meat. She seemed to realize that we were leaving her, that her work was finished."[34]

The Third Relief left the camp at noon. They had been there no more than two hours. Each rescuer was assigned a child. Eddy carried Georgia Donner; Foster toted his young brother-in-law, Simon Murphy; Thompson took charge of Frances Donner; and Hiram Miller carried Eliza, the youngest of the children and the only one of the four that had to be carried all the way.

"Our first stop was the mountain-side overlooking the lake, where we were given a light meal of bread and meat and a little water," was how Eliza recalled the start of the journey. "When we reached the head of the lake, we overtook Nicholas Clark and John Baptiste who had deserted my father in his tent and were hurrying toward the settlement. Our coming was a surprise to them, yet they were glad to join the party. . . . After our evening allowance of food we were stowed snugly between blankets in a snow trench near the summit of the Sierras, but were so hungry that we could hardly get to sleep, even after being told that more food would do us harm."[35]

When Clark and Trudeau surprisingly appeared on the trail, Eddy and the others could not help but notice that Clark was lugging a heavy sack that turned out to be filled with more Donner family spoils and a pair of Jacob Donner's guns. Clark claimed that Tamzene had given him the valuables for safekeeping. That explanation was suspicious because Clark and Trudeau obviously had left Alder Creek before Tamzene returned from the lake camp.

Eddy and his men also thought it disturbing that instead of carrying out little Samuel Donner, Clark chose to take the sack of loot. When pressed about it, Clark shot back that baby Samuel had expired before they left Alder Creek. Only later did Eddy and the rescuers find out that Samuel Donner had not died that day but on March 20, a full week later.[36] They remained wary of Clark and Trudeau but allowed them to travel with the party to Johnson's Ranch.

Compared with the earlier rescue return trips, the Third Relief had a relatively easy time. The weather was much improved, and the party made good time. A few days out, one of the rescuers came upon a bundle alongside the trail. It was part of the Donner loot that Cady and Stone had taken but had to leave behind when Cady's feet swelled from frostbite. William Thompson—earning a fifty-dollar bonus for carrying Frances Donner—turned out to be handy with a needle and thread. He pulled the fine silk dresses from the pack and turned them into cloaks for the three girls.[37] They proudly wore them all the rest of the way.

The Third Relief caught up with some of the refugees whom Stark was still bringing out of Starved Camp. Then all of them crossed the snow line and came to Mule Springs, where they would rest for a few days. From there, they rode horseback to Johnson's Ranch. The local women who were waiting for them took away the girls' silk robes and dressed them in calico, much to the sisters' displeasure.[38]

"We went from Johnson's Ranch to Sinclair's house, where Mrs. [Margret] Reed was staying," Frances Donner wrote years later to her sister Eliza. "It was late in the day when we stopped, they were not prepared to accommodate us but could not send us on to the Fort. Mrs. Reed suggested that the corner of the carpet be ripped up and folded over us as a covering that night so we slept. We reached Sutter's Fort the next night and were given over to the care of our young half sisters Elitha and Leanna. They had worked for different parties while waiting our arrival and had bought material for clothing and also shoes."[39]

Soon after the Third Relief completed their mission, there were plans to return to the Sierras and rescue whoever might still be alive.

Some of the men from the three rescue parties, including a few who had been on at least two of the missions, were game to go once more. In late March, another party set out. Again, the weather turned bad, and an onslaught of storms stopped them before they could pass through Bear Valley.

After another attempt failed to come together, it seemed that many of the well-intended rescuers began to question whether they should muster a new team. Probably George Donner and his nephew Samuel Donner were dead at Alder Creek, and Levinah Murphy likely had perished at the lake camp. That meant if there were any survivors, they were Lewis Keseberg and Tamzene Donner. No one thought Keseberg was worth risking their lives for, and Tamzene had turned down three opportunities to leave.

44. THE FOURTH RELIEF

IN APRIL 1847, when the weather cleared and winter finally turned to spring, a Fourth Relief was organized. It was not a rescue party but a salvage party that would recover belongings and anything of value at Truckee Lake and Alder Creek. Alcalde John Sinclair drew up an agreement stipulating how everything recovered would be divided among survivors, heirs, and salvagers. Half of what was recovered would go to the estates of the Donner brothers and the other half to the salvage party as payment for their services.[1] If they found a survivor to bring back, that would be a bonus.

A burly mountain man named William O. Fallon was chosen to lead the Fourth Relief.[2] The six men whom Fallon would lead into the Sierras were seasoned veterans who knew the terrain.[3]

On April 10, 1847, just three days before the Fourth Relief began their mission, the *California Star* published a lurid and greatly exaggerated account of the conditions at the emigrant camps. The metaphorical references to the popular principle of Manifest Destiny that appeared in the story, filled with outrageous lies and factual errors, forever shaped the public perception of the Donner Party. Instead of presenting the besieged emigrants as the foot soldiers of Manifest Destiny, they were contorted into unworthy failures who proved themselves incapable of upholding the key themes of America's divine right to expand across the continent. The Donner Party was seen as being inept and unable to control their own actions and behavior, thus making it impossible for them to control the wilderness they sought to conquer and civilize.[4]

The *California Star* account set the stage for how future generations would view the Donner Party, but a barrage of stories followed that ensured the curtain would never come down on this drama of human struggle. One of the more sensationalized published reports was based on a written log that was never found, supposedly written by Fallon, the leader of the Fourth Relief. It is unlikely that Fallon wrote the words that ended up in print. Most likely, a ghostwriter handled the chore.

The Fourth Relief left Johnson's Ranch on April 13 and reached the lake cabins four days later. There were no signs of life, but there was abundant evidence of death.[5] Scattered about were dismembered corpses, limbs stripped of flesh, and skulls, most of them split open. While they reconnoitered the site, three Indians suddenly bolted from a hiding place and fled into the trees, never to be seen again.

After spending at least two hours searching the lake camp for survivors and any valuables or personal effects worth salvaging, the party made their way to the Alder Creek camp. On the way, they came upon fresh footprints in the snow that were not made by moccasins but by boots. But when they got to the camp, they again could not find any survivors. It was another ghastly scene. All sorts of personal items, including books, bolts of calico, shoes, tools, and broken furniture, were strewn about. The melting snow revealed the carcasses of an ox and a horse.

As at the lake camp, there were body parts everywhere. Outside a tent, they found human flesh inside a large iron kettle. They guessed that it had come from George Donner, whose body was nearby, wrapped in a sheet, most likely by Tamzene.[6] The body had been butchered and the head split open and brains removed. The men continued to search, but there was no trace of Tamzene.[7]

They camped there and the next day resumed the work of gathering anything that might have some value. There was no sign of the money they had been told would be waiting for them. Frustrated but determined, some of the party remained at Alder Creek and continued to rummage through belongings and dig in the snow for jewelry and money. The rest of the team headed back to Truckee Lake.[8]

When they arrived, they found Keseberg in the old Breen cabin. He was shivering and looked dazed, all wound up in a blanket on the floor surrounded by human bones. Next to him was a pan full of water and what appeared to be fresh human liver and lungs. Someone asked him where he had been. It turned out that when the party first got to the camp, Keseberg was off scavenging, left the trail, and was lost for a while before he got back to the cabin.[9]

The rescuers moved closer to Keseberg and began to interrogate him. They asked how he had managed to stay alive, as if they held it against him. He told them straight out that he had survived by eating the meat of the dead. Then they demanded to know what had happened to Tamzene Donner. He looked up at their angry faces and told them what they already knew—she was dead. Keseberg told them about her final days, when they were the only two survivors left, after Levinah Murphy and George Donner had died. He said that Mrs. Murphy lingered only a few days after the Third Relief left the camp.[10] He remained in the cabin, living off the flesh of the dead and listening to the wolves scratching at the cabin door.

Then one night, Tamzene—soaking wet and cold—came to the cabin and told Keseberg about the deaths of her nephew Sammie and her beloved George. He recalled that she was chilled and dazed and could not stop crying. She spoke of her daughters and how she longed to see them. Keseberg said he had tried to keep her calm. He wrapped her in a blanket and put her to bed. He told her to sleep. In the morning, he checked on her and found that she was dead.[11]

Tamzene had wanted to see her children and her grandchildren not yet born. She had wanted to cross to the other side of the mountains. She had wanted to open her school and walk through fields of flowers and smell the sea. Instead, she died in an icy hovel, and her dreams died with her.

Keseberg admitted that he had eaten Tamzene's body, and none of her remains could be found.[12] The rescuers accused Keseberg of murdering Tamzene and stealing the Donners' money and valuables. He denied their accusations, but they continued to pressure him to admit his guilt. When Fallon, an intimidating figure, grew weary of the denials, he threatened to hang Keseberg unless he told them where he had hidden the money.[13] Keseberg gave in and told them where he had hidden some money that he said Tamzene had given him to take to her children. When the money was counted, it totaled $273, a pittance compared to what the rescuers thought they would recover.[14]

On April 21, the Fourth Relief left the camp bearing packs that weighed at least one hundred pounds each. With them, Keseberg—able to walk with only a little pain—made his way, wearing the boots that James Reed had given to him. During a rest stop along the Yuba River, a piece of cloth in the snow caught Keseberg's eye. When he gave the cloth a tug, he found the body of his baby daughter, Ada, who had perished on the return trip with a rescue party.[15] Until then, Keseberg had believed that his wife and daughter had survived.

For the rest of what turned out to be a miserable life, Keseberg was branded as a "human cannibal" and a ghoulish thief and killer. Members of the Fourth Relief, especially Fallon, spread shocking tales about Keseberg and the atrocities they swore he had committed.

On April 29, 1847, a little more than a year after the original Donner-Reed Party had departed from Springfield, Illinois, Keseberg—the last surviving member—arrived at Sutter's Fort. At last, the journey was over.

AFTERMATH

It had taken four relief parties and more than two months to rescue the Donner Party survivors. In the end, forty-one people died, and forty-six survived. Five perished before reaching the Sierra Nevadas, thirty-five died at the camps or trying to cross the mountains, and one died just after reaching the valley.

Many of the survivors lost toes to frostbite and suffered from chronic physical and psychological disorders, but some learned to deal with the emotional and mental complications that plagued them for the rest of their lives. The death toll was highest among the very young and the oldest. Surprisingly, children and teenagers between five and nineteen fared far better than adults in their prime.

Not only did males succumb at a higher rate than females, they also died sooner. This was in large part because of the maternal role of the women, which made them fight to stay alive to care for their families. Women also did not have to take part in much of the backbreaking work that the men faced throughout the journey. Men were bigger and more active. They required more sustenance than females, who had less muscle but more fat reserves.

All four Donner adults—the original couples, George and Tamzene and Jacob and Elizabeth—died. The Reeds and Breens were the only two families without a single loss of life. Family ties had helped to preserve those who survived the catastrophe. These groups naturally formed strong support networks, saving food for their own members and not sharing provisions with those outside their group, especially the single males.

Although tales of cannibalism among the Donner Party were always highly exaggerated, there was no doubt that the vast majority of the men, women, and children had resorted to eating human meat. Most were careful to not eat from the bodies of their own kinfolk. The Reeds were considered to be the only family not to have engaged in the consumption of human beings. Unlike Lewis Keseberg and a few others, most of the survivors never spoke publicly about the cannibalism.

Cannibalism and a doomed wagon train made good copy and even better headlines. The story of the Donner Party disaster quickly spread across the country and entered the popular culture. The hideousness of the ordeal passed from truth to legend. Myths abounded, and inflated newspaper accounts exaggerated the truth. Much of the distortion and lies went unchecked for years. Newspapers printed every word of all the letters and diaries, including some diaries that were forged. They also reported absolutely wild tales of people feasting on human flesh not to survive but out of pure pleasure.

The primary focus of the more scurrilous stories was Lewis Keseberg, an easy target who had been accused of many crimes, ranging from stealing valuables from the dead and dying to outright murder of men, women, and children. Vilified as a notorious "man-eater," Keseberg remained the most infamous member of the Donner Party. He was never charged with any crimes and finally filed suit to stop the spread of scandalous stories about him. He won, but the court awarded him only one dollar.

Keseberg and his wife had lost two children in the Donner Party tragedy and one earlier but later had eight more children. He outlived his wife by twenty years, and all but one of his children preceded him in death. All his business ventures failed, and his quick temper got him into trouble with the law. By the late 1890s, Keseberg was penniless and homeless. He died in a hospital for the poor. Many people chose to believe the outrageous tales and blatant lies told about the Donner Party and especially about Keseberg, who was definitely not the only cannibal in the camps.

What made the Donner Party so distinctive was that this group of people had originally set out to civilize what they saw as a barbaric land. The acts of survival cannibalism refigured their story with a cruel twist—the civilizers themselves became savages.

For a time, emigration to California fell off, but in January 1848, gold was discovered in John Sutter's creek. By 1849, more than one hundred thousand treasure hunters had rushed to California to prospect the streams and canyons where the Donner Party had suffered. In 1850, California entered the Union as the thirty-first state.

Lansford Hastings, who had always been the main culprit for the plight of the Donner Party, received death threats because of his recommendation of the Hastings Cutoff. He eventually moved to San Francisco and practiced law but was unable to make a go of it. During the Civil War, he proposed leading an army of southerners west to seize Arizona Territory for the Confederacy. After the war, he published *The Emigrant's Guide to Brazil.* He died in Brazil in 1870 trying to establish a colony of former Confederate soldiers.

Most of the survivors of the Donner Party were absorbed into the growing population of California. Some became recluses. Most of the families seldom saw each other after they were rescued.

Mary Graves, a survivor of the Forlorn Hope, found a husband and was married in May 1847, before the snow had even melted in the passes.

The Breen family settled in San Juan Batista, where Patrick became a prominent rancher. Of the six infants in the Donner Party, Isabella Breen was the only one to survive to adulthood. She was also the last survivor of the entire Donner-Reed Party to die. Her passing in 1935 in Hollister, California, at the age of ninety was widely reported.

William Eddy remarried and started a new family in California. It was said that he did try to find Keseberg and murder the man who had cannibalized his family, but James Reed talked him out of it.

The orphaned Donner and Graves children did not fare as well as most. Some of the younger Donners were adopted by various families. The older girls, including one who was just fourteen, quickly found husbands for financial support. The eldest of the Donner family survivors, Elitha, died in 1923 at the age of ninety. She had spent her last fifty years on a ranch near Sacramento. She never talked about what had happened at her family's camp, but every year when a nearby school studied the mandatory unit on the Donner Party, she would sit in the classroom, listening silently from the back row.

In death and for years to come, Tamzene Eustis Donner became widely regarded as a heroine. She attained almost a cult status because of her courageous acts, especially her refusal to leave her dying husband, which ultimately cost her her life. Several novels, many poems, and even a ballet have focused on Tamzene.

For James Reed, the luck of the Irish returned. He settled his family in San Jose, made a fortune in real estate and gold, and became one of the new state's leading citizens. He never spoke in public of the killing of John Snyder. His wife, Margret, went on to live a peaceful life and never again suffered from migraines. When eight-year-old Patty Reed arrived in California, she still had the bundle with her special things hidden in her ragged dress. She treasured the lock of her grandmother's hair, taken when the old woman became the first of the party to die on the trail, and the little wooden doll that many years later ended up on display in a museum at Sutter's Fort. Patty was ninety-three when she died in 1931.

Patty's big sister, Virginia, had died ten years earlier at the age of eighty-seven. Until the day she died, Virginia—like Frances Donner—always made sure she had cookies or candy with her at all times. Long before, when she was thirteen and had just been rescued from the mountains, Virginia vowed that she would never again be caught without food. That was also when she wrote a cousin back in Illinois to tell her that the ordeal was over and she and her family were safe. Some of her final words from that letter serve as a fitting benediction for the Donner Party story:

"We have left everything, but I don't care for that. We have got through with our lives. Don't let this letter dishearten anybody. Remember, never take no cutoffs and hurry along as fast as you can."

DONNER PARTY MEMBERS AND AFFILIATION WITH GROUP

NAME	AGE	AFFILIATION	DISPOSITION
Antonio	23	Cattle herder *Comment: Cannibalized*	Died in the Sierras
Breen, Edward	13	Second child of Patrick and Peggy Breen	Survived
Breen, Isabella Margaret	1	Seventh child of Patrick and Peggy Breen	Survived
Breen, James	5	Fifth child of Patrick and Peggy Breen	Survived
Breen, John	14	Eldest child of Patrick and Peggy Breen	Survived
Breen, Margaret (Peggy) Bulger	40	Wife of Patrick Breen	Survived
Breen, Patrick	51	Husband/father of Breen family *Comment: Wrote the only account of the Donner Party during the winter of 1846–1847*	Survived

NAME	AGE	AFFILIATION	DISPOSITION
Breen, Patrick, Jr.	9–11	Third child of Patrick and Peggy Breen	Survived
Breen, Peter	3	Sixth child of Patrick and Peggy Breen	Survived
Breen, Simon Preston	7–9	Fourth child of Patrick and Peggy Breen	Survived
Burger, Karl (Dutch Charley)	30	Teamster for Lewis Keseberg *Comment: Died in Lewis Keseberg's lean-to tent*	Died in the Sierras
Denton, John	28–30	Walker with Donner train	Died in the Sierras
Dolan, John Patrick	30–40	Teamster for Donner *Comment: Cannibalized*	Died in the Sierras
Donner, Elitha Cumi	13	Child of George and Mary Blue Tenant Donner	Survived
Donner, Eliza Poor	3	Youngest child of George and Tamzene Donner	Survived
Donner, Elizabeth Blue Hook	40–45	Wife of Jacob Donner	Died in the Sierras
Donner, Frances Eustis	6	Child of George and Tamzene Donner	Survived

NAME	AGE	AFFILIATION	DISPOSITION
Donner, George, Jr.	62	Husband/father of George Donner family *Comment: Farmer from Springfield, Illinois; wagon master; stricken with an arm infection; cannibalized*	Died in the Sierras
Donner, George	9	Son of Jacob and Elizabeth Donner	Survived
Donner, Georgia	4	Child of George and Tamzene Donner	Survived
Donner, Isaac	5	Third child of Jacob and Elizabeth Donner *Comment: Cannibalized*	Died in the Sierras
Donner, Jacob (Jake)	56	Younger brother of George Donner *Comment: Cannibalized*	Died in the Sierras
Donner, Leanna Charity	11–12	Child of George and Mary Blue Tenant Donner	Survived
Donner, Lewis	3	Fifth child of Jacob and Elizabeth Donner	Died in the Sierras
Donner, Mary	7	Second child of Jacob and Elizabeth Donner	Survived
Donner, Samuel	4	Fourth child of Jacob and Elizabeth Donner *Comment: Cannibalized*	Died in the Sierras
Donner, Tamzene Eustis Dozier	45	Wife of George Donner *Comment: Cannibalized*	Died in the Sierras

NAME	AGE	AFFILIATION	DISPOSITION
Eddy, Eleanor Priscilla	25	Wife of William Eddy	Died in the Sierras
Eddy, James (Jimmy)	3	Son of William and Eleanor Eddy *Comment: Cannibalized*	Killed in the Sierras
Eddy, Margaret	1	Daughter of Willliam and Eleanor Eddy	Died in the Sierras
Eddy, William Henry	28–30	Teamster for Donner *Comment: Carriage maker; skilled hunter*	Survived
Elliott, Milford (Milt)	28	Teamster for Reed *Comment: Cannibalized*	Died in the Sierras
Fosdick, Jay	23	Son-in-law of Franklin Graves; husband of Sarah *Comment: Cannibalized; died during the Forlorn Hope expedition that left via snowshoe to seek help*	Died in the Sierras
Fosdick, Sarah Graves	21	First child of Franklin and Elizabeth Graves; wife of Jay Fosdick	Survived
Foster, (Jeremiah) George	4	Son of William and Sarah Foster; Levinah Murphy grandson *Comment: Cannibalized*	Died in the Sierras
Foster, Sarah Murphy	19	Wife of William Foster and daughter of Levinah Murphy	Survived

NAME	AGE	AFFILIATION	DISPOSITION
Foster, William McFadden	28–30	Husband of Sarah Murphy Foster	Survived
Graves, Eleanor (Ellen)	14–15	Fourth child of Franklin and Elizabeth Graves	Survived
Graves, Elizabeth	1	Ninth child of Franklin and Elizabeth Graves *Comment: Cannibalized*	Died in the Sierras
Graves, Elizabeth Cooper	45–47	Wife of Franklin Ward Graves	Died in the Sierras
Graves, Franklin Ward	57	Husband of Elizabeth Graves; head of Graves family *Comment: Cannibalized; made the snowshoes for the Forlorn Hope expedition*	Died in the Sierras
Graves, Franklin Ward, Jr.	5	Eighth child of Franklin and Elizabeth Graves *Comment: Cannibalized*	Died in the Sierras
Graves, Jonathon	6-7	Seventh child of Franklin and Elizabeth Graves	Survived
Graves, Lovina	12	Fifth child of Franklin and Elizabeth Graves	Survived
Graves, Mary Ann	19–20	Second child of Franklin and Elizabeth Graves	Survived
Graves, Nancy	9	Sixth child of Franklin and Elizabeth Graves	Survived

NAME	AGE	AFFILIATION	DISPOSITION
Graves, William Cooper	17	Third child of Franklin and Elizabeth Graves	Survived
Halloran, Luke	25	Storekeeper from St. Joseph, Missouri; joined Donners en route *Comment: Joined Donner train at Bridger's Fort; died of tuber-culosis; buried in the salt flats of the Great Salt Lake Desert*	Died on the trail
Hardcoop	60	Traveled with Lewis Keseberg *Comment: Belgian; suffering dehydration, "gave out" and left behind in western Nevada desert*	Died on the trail
Herron, Walter	27	Teamster for Reed	Survived
Hook, Solomon Elijah	14	Son of Elizabeth Blue Hook Donner by first husband	Survived
Hook, William	12	Son of Elizabeth Blue Hook Donner by first husband	Died in the Sierras
James, Noah	16–20	Teamster for Jacob Donner	Survived
Keseberg, Ada	3	Daughter of Lewis and Philippine Keseberg	Died in the Sierras
Keseberg, (Elisabeth) Philippine	23	Wife of Lewis Keseberg	Survived

NAME	AGE	AFFILIATION	DISPOSITION
Keseberg, Lewis (Johann)	32	Husband of Philippine Keseberg	Survived
Keseberg, Lewis, Jr.	1	Born on the trail; only son of Lewis and Philippine Keseberg	Died on the trail
Keyes, Sarah	70	Mother of Margret Reed; mother-in-law of James Reed *Comment: First train member to die; died of natural causes early in the journey; buried in Kansas*	Died on the trail
Luis	18–20?	Miwok Indian vaquero sent by Captain Sutter as a guide *Comment: Cannibalized; slain by William Foster while a member of the Forlorn Hope expedition*	Murdered in the Sierras
McCutchen, Amanda Henderson	25	Wife of William McCutchen; mother of Harriet	Survived
McCutchen, Harriet	1	Only daughter of William and Amanda McCutchen	Died in the Sierras
McCutchen, William	30	Husband of Amanda; father of Harriet	Survived

NAME	AGE	AFFILIATION	DISPOSITION
Miller, Hiram O.	30	Teamster for Donner family *Comment: Left the Donner party on July 2, 1846, at Fort Laramie to join another train*	Survived
Murphy, John Landrum	16	Second child of Levinah Murphy	Died in the Sierras
Murphy, Levinah W. Jackson	36	Widow with five children; matriarch of the Murphy family *Comment: Cannibalized*	Died in the Sierras
Murphy, Lemuel B.	12–13	Fourth child of Levinah Murphy *Comment: Cannibalized*	Died in the Sierras
Murphy, Meriam (Mary M.)	14	Third child of Levinah Murphy	Survived
Murphy, Simon Peter	8	Sixth child of Levinah Murphy	Survived
Murphy, William Green	10	Fifth child of Levinah Murphy	Survived
Pike, Catherine	1	Younger daughter of William and Harriet Murphy Pike	Died in the Sierras
Pike, Harriet Frances Murphy	18–21	Eldest child of Levinah Murphy; wife/widow of William Pike	Survived
Pike, Naomi Levinah	2–3	Elder daughter of William and Harriet Murphy Pike	Survived

NAME	AGE	AFFILIATION	DISPOSITION
Pike, William	25–32	Husband of Harriet Pike; son-in-law of Levinah Murphy *Comment: Accidentally shot by William Foster in October 1846*	Killed in the Sierras
Reed, James Frazier (Francis)	45–46	Husband of Margret (Peggy) Reed; father of Reed family *Comment: Banished from the train after stabbing and killing John Snyder; member of the Second Relief Party*	Survived
Reed, James Frazier (Francis), Jr.	5–6	Second child of James and Margret Reed	Survived
Reed, Margret (Peggy) Keyes Backenstoe	32	Wife of James Reed *Comment: Daughter of Sarah Keyes, the first train member to die*	Survived
Reed, Martha Jane (Patty)	8–9	First child of James and Margret Reed	Survived
Reed, Thomas Keyes (Tommy)	3–4	Third child of James and Margret Reed	Survived
Reed, Virginia Elizabeth Backenstoe	13	Child of Margret Backenstoe Reed with former husband	Survived

NAME	AGE	AFFILIATION	DISPOSITION
Reinhardt, Joseph	30	Associate of Jacob Wolfinger and Gus Spitzer; traveled with Keseberg *Comment: Aided Spitzer to murder Wolfinger along the trail*	Died in the Sierras
Salvador	30	Miwok Indian sent by Sutter as a guide *Comment: Cannibalized; killed by William Foster; sent with Luis to help rescue the survivors*	Murdered in the Sierras
Shoemaker, Samuel	25	Walker/teamster for Jacob Donner *Comment: Cannibalized*	Died in the Sierras
Smith, James	25	Teamster for Reed family	Died in the Sierras
Snyder, John	25	Teamster for Graves family *Comment: Killed by James Reed in a trail altercation at Pauta Pass*	Killed on the trail
Spitzer, Augustus	30	Provided general help for Donner train; traveled with Kesebergs *Comment: Involved in the killing of Wolfinger*	Died in the Sierras
Stanton, Charles	35	Traveled with Donners	Died in the Sierras

NAME	AGE	AFFILIATION	DISPOSITION
Trudeau, Jean-Baptiste	16–23	Traveled with George Donner family *Comment: Trudeau claimed to have knowledge of Indian languages*	Survived
Williams, Baylis	24	Handyman for the Reeds; half brother of Eliza Williams *Comment: First to die at the lake camp on December 14, 1846*	Died in the Sierras
Williams, Eliza	31	Cook/servant for Reeds; half sister of Baylis Williams	Survived
Wolfinger, Doris	20	Wife/widow of Jacob Wolfinger	Survived
Wolfinger, Jacob Karl	26	Merchant traveling with Keseberg family *Comment: Killed in October 1846 by Reinhardt and Spitzer*	Murdered on the trail

RELIEF TEAMS AND DONNER PARTY SURVIVORS/DEATHS

PARTY OF FORLORN HOPE
SURVIVORS, DECEMBER 1846

Eddy, William
Fosdick, Sarah Graves
Foster, Sarah Murphy
Foster, William
Graves, Mary
McCutchen, Amanda Henderson
Pike, Harriet Murphy

PARTY OF FORLORN HOPE DEATHS,
DECEMBER 1846

Antonio
Dolan, Patrick
Fosdick, Jay
Graves, Franklin
Luis
Murphy, Lemuel
Salvador
Stanton, Charles (leader)

FIRST RELIEF VOLUNTEERS,
FEBRUARY 1847

Brueheim, Adolph (a.k.a. "Greasy
    Jim")
Coffeemeyer, Edward (Ned)
Coon, Billy
Curtis, Jotham
Eddy, William
Glover, Aquila (coleader)
Moutrey, Riley Septimus
Rhoads, Daniel
Rhoads, John
Ritchie, Colonel Matthew D.
Sell, Joseph (a.k.a. Joe Foster)
Tucker, John
Tucker, Reason P. (Dan) (coleader)

FIRST RELIEF SURVIVORS

Breen, Edward
Breen, Simon
Donner, Elitha
Donner, George, Jr.
Donner, Leanna
Graves, Eleanor
Graves, Lovina
Graves, William
James, Noah
Keseberg, Philippine
Murphy, Mary
Murphy, Willliam
Pike, Naomi
Reed, James, Jr.
Reed, Margret
Reed, Virginia
Williams, Eliza
Wolfinger, Doris

FIRST RELIEF DEATHS

Denton, John
Foster, George
Hook, William
Keseberg, Ada

SECOND RELIEF VOLUNTEERS,
EARLY MARCH 1847

Cady, Charles L.
Clark, Nicholas
Dofar, Matthew
Dunn, Patrick H.
Gendreau, Joseph
Greenwood, Brittain
McCutchen, William
Miller, Hiram Owens
Reed, James Frazier (leader)
Stone, Charles
Turner, John
Woodworth, Selim Edward

SECOND RELIEF SURVIVORS

Breen, Isabella
Breen, James
Breen, John
Breen, Margaret
Breen, Patrick
Breen, Patrick, Jr.
Breen, Peter
Donner, Mary
Graves, Jonathon
Graves, Nancy
Hook, Solomon
Reed, Patty
Reed, Thomas

SECOND RELIEF DEATHS

Donner, Isaac
Donner, Lewis
Graves, Elizabeth (at Sutter's Fort)
Graves, Elizabeth Cooper
Graves, Franklin Ward, Jr.

THIRD RELIEF VOLUNTEERS,
MID-MARCH 1847

Eddy, William
Foster, William F.
Oakley, Howard
Stark, John Schull
Thompson, William

THIRD RELIEF SURVIVORS

Donner, Eliza
Donner, Frances
Donner, Georgia
Murphy, Simon
Trudeau, Jean-Baptiste

THIRD RELIEF DEATHS

(none)

FOURTH RELIEF VOLUNTEERS,
MID-MARCH 1847

Coffeemeyer, Edward (Ned)
Fallon, William O. (leader)
Foster, William M.
Keyser, Sebastian
Rhoads, John
Sels, Joseph
Tucker, Reason (Dan)

FOURTH RELIEF SURVIVORS

Keseberg, Lewis

FOURTH RELIEF DEATHS

(none)

ACKNOWLEDGMENTS

THE SEEDS FOR this book were planted years ago during a discussion with Philip Marino, associate editor and marketing director for Liveright Publishing, a division of W. W. Norton. My longtime editor and friend, Robert Weil, executive editor at Norton and editor-in-chief and publishing director of the Liveright imprint, mentored Phil. As *Publisher's Weekly* wisely noted, "By any measure, Weil is not only a good editor but a great one." Phil Marino has followed in Weil's footsteps. With the thoughtful input of my diligent literary agent, James Fitzgerald, a book proposal was crafted and accepted, and I began my journey—literally and figuratively—with the Donner Party.

I am grateful for the consistent guidance and input of my agent and editor and the others at Norton who helped to ensure that this book became a reality. That includes editorial assistant Gina Iaquinta and copy editor Fred Weimer. Thanks to Kathy King for her assistance early on in the book's development. To get the job done there were others who stepped up in my behalf. I am forever grateful to Casey Fuetsch and Rowena Mills for their invaluable assistance. They were always there for me, helping to hone and shape this book and offer their wise counsel.

Pat Holl, Hierpub LLC, deserves a standing ovation for her help with research and securing permissions for photographs as well as directing the creation of the map showing the route of the Donner Party. A tip of my author's hat to Rebecca Irons Perry for providing a "must have" photo.

Steve Gerkin, a fellow author and dear friend, assisted with research and along with his wife, Sue, cheered me on during the arduous writing process and was always there for me. So was Allen "Storm" Strider, a true and worthy compadre, who has helped see me through the creation of many books. Semper Fi to you.

I again dedicated this book, like most of my previous works, to my wife and life partner, Suzanne Fitzgerald Wallis. Clearly, I owe her so much for being by my side through the good and bad times. Suzanne had a hand in every aspect of this book's creation. She was with me on research field trips, rummaging through countless archives and libraries, during many interviews, and last but certainly not least, locating and helping secure the images that illustrate the book. She was backed up by our fine gentlemen felines—Juniper and Martini— my beloved literary muses.

The help I received from Donner family descendants was enormous. William A. Springer, a sixth-generation Donner descendant, was absolutely essential to me during the long research phase and well beyond. Bill was relentless in his efforts to ferret out the true story of his ancestors and the others who accompanied them on the westward trek from Illinois to California. He continually kept me on track and pointed me in the right direction, and he provided a tremendous amount of research material from the collection he and his late brother, Donald Donner Springer, have assembled over many years. Thanks also to Douglas Donner Springer, Donald's son and Bill's nephew, and to Bill's brother, Phil M. Springer, who continues to farm Donner land near Springfield, Illinois.

A host of other individuals and entities also deserve my thanks. They include:

Illinois: Tom Huber, map librarian, Illinois State Library, Springfield; Thomas J. Wood, university archivist, Brookens Library, University of Illinois at Springfield; Kathryn M. Harris, library services director, Cheryl Schnirring, manuscripts manager, and Debbie S. Hamm, library associate, Manuscript Section, Abraham Lincoln Presidential Library, Springfield; Jeff McLinden, general manager, President Abraham Lincoln Hotel, Springfield; Curtis Mann, manager, Sangamon Valley Collection, Lincoln Library, Springfield; William Furry, executive director, Illinois Historical Society,

Springfield; Cathy S. Mosley, Springfield; Prairie Archives Bookstore, Springfield; Lincoln Home National Historic Site, National Park Service, Springfield; Illinois State Archives, Springfield; Nancy L. Spinner Collection, Sherman; Buz Waldmire, Rochester; Fred Puglia, Decatur; Mickey Robinson, executive director, Coal County Chamber of Commerce, Gillespie; Galena–Jo Daviess County Historical Society, Galena.

Missouri: The Mark Twain Boyhood Home & Museum, Hannibal; Missouri State Archives, Jefferson City; Lexington Historical Museum, Lexington; Richard Edwards, curator of education, Merrill Mattes Library, National Frontier Trails Museum, Independence; Kathy Conway, National Frontier Trails Museum, Independence; Mormon Visitors Center, Independence; Jackson County Historical Society, Independence; Rice-Tremonti Historic Home & Aunt Sophie's Cabin, Raytown; Trailside Museum, Kansas City; Missouri History Museum, St. Louis; State Historical Society of Missouri, Columbia.

California: Donner Memorial State Park, Truckee; Norm Sayler Collection, Donner Summit Historical Society, Soda Springs; Lee Anne Titangos and Susan E. Snyder, Bancroft Library, University of California, Berkeley; Peter E. Hanff and Anne Chadwick Williams, the *Sacramento Bee*, Sacramento; Annie R. Mitchell History Room, Tulare County Library, Visalia; Clyde Arbuckle Photograph Collection, San Jose Public Library; the California Pioneer Heritage Foundation, Placerville.

And gratitude also goes to the Jon B. Lovelace Collection of California Photographs, Carol M. Highsmith's America Project, Library of Congress, Prints and Photographs Division, Washington, D.C.; Yale Collection of Western Americana, Beinecke Rare Book and Manuscript Library, Yale University, New Haven, Connecticut; Robert McCubbin, Robert M. McCubbin Collection, Santa Fe, New Mexico; Utah State Historical Society, Salt Lake City; Tom Perry Special Collections, Harold B. Lee Library, Brigham Young University, Provo, Utah; the Scotts Bluff National Monument, National Park Service, Gering, Nebraska; Chimney Rock State Historic Site,

Bayard, Nebraska; the Nevada State Museum, Carson City; Sharon Von Aschwege, Kearney, Nebraska; the Great Platte River Road Archway Monument, Kearney, Nebraska; Fort Laramie Historic Site, Fort Laramie, Wyoming; North Wind Picture Archive, Alfred, Maine; the Walters Art Museum, Baltimore, Maryland.

NOTES

CHAPTER I: A MIGRATING PEOPLE

1. http://www.fmoran.com/danner.htm. In 2000, the National Society Daughters of the American Revolution accepted the Revolutionary War service record of George Donner Sr.

2. *Portrait and Biographical Album of DeWitt and Piatt Counties, Illinois* (Chicago: Chapman Brothers Publishing Co., 1891), 657. The cannonball story is attributed to the descendants of Tobias Donner, one of the sons of George Donner Sr. Tobias farmed and raised stock in DeWitt County before moving to Menard County, where he died in 1856.

3. Donner-Springer Family Collection. Many published works and other sources fail to mention Ann Mary Donner, believed to be the eldest child of George Sr. and his wife, Mary Huff Donner. Donner family files show that Ann Mary was born in 1778 in North Carolina and died in 1847 in Sangamon County, Illinois.

4. Sources often claim that Jacob Donner, son of George Donner Sr. and Mary Huff Donner, was older than his brother George Jr. However, Donner family records state that George Jr. was born in "about 1786" and Jacob was born in "about 1790."

5. Donner descendants believe that Samuel Donner, one of Jacob's four sons, possibly went west to Kentucky much earlier than his brother George Sr.

6. Donner-Springer Family Collection.

7. Ibid. According to Donner family records that Jo Ann Brant Schmidt secured from the Kentucky State Archives, George Donner Jr. wed Susannah Holloway just after she gave birth to their first child. Included in the files, in which the name Donner is variously spelled Danner and Tanner as well as Donner, a deposition dated April 8, 1811, states, "William Hunter, a longtime neighbor of George Davidson, deposes saying Susannah Holloway lived with George Davidson between fifteen and twenty years. She attended school, but made small progress. . . . He further states nine or ten months before Susannah married George Tanner [Donner], Mr. Davidson came to him and requested Susannah live with him for she was in a state of Pregnancy and as Mrs. Davidson was in the same situation it would be most inconvenient for her to stay at his house. Susannah stayed with William Hunter about eight months. Davidson furnished her with materials to make fifty yards of cloth, which she had sold. Sometime after Susannah was delivered of her child she left William's house and married Mr. Tanner [Donner] who William Hunter always understood was the father of the child."

8. Sam K. Swope, "From Lycoming County, Pennsylvania, to Parke County,

Indiana: Recollections of Andrew TenBrook, 1786–1823," *Indiana Magazine of History*, Vol. LXI, No. 1 (Bloomington: Indiana University, 1965), 2.

9. Ibid.

10. Jo Ann Brant Schmidt, "Who Was Captain George Donner?" *Donner Party Bulletin*, Issue No. 3, January-February 1998. Retrieved from www.utahcrossroads .org/donnerpartybulletin.htm.

CHAPTER 2: THE BEST LAND UNDER HEAVEN

1. Neil Harris and Michael Conzen, *Illinois: A Descriptive and Historical Guide* (Chicago: A. C. McClurg & Co., 1939), 27.

2. Donner-Springer Family Collection.

3. John Mack Faragher, *Sugar Creek: Life on the Illinois Prairie* (New Haven and London: Yale University Press, 1988), 59. Visitors to the area often pronounced the word San-ga-MON, while locals prefer a slurred SANG-uh-min.

4. Donner-Springer Family Collection; Barbara Wilder Politano, ed., *Their Courage Is Our Legacy: Donner Family History Compiled for the George Donner Family Reunion*, 1996.

5. Wayne G. Broeh Jr., *John Deere's Company: A History of Deere & Company and Its Time* (New York: Doubleday & Co., 1984), 41–42.

6. Ibid., 45–46.

7. Donner-Springer Family Collection; John Carroll Power, *History of the Early Settlers of Sangamon County, Illinois* (Springfield: Edwin A. Wilson & Co., 1876), 1022.

8. Carol A. Lipscomb, "Karankawa Indians," *Handbook of Texas Online*, http://www .tshaonline.org/handbook/online/articles/bmk05, published by the Texas State Historical Association.

9. Donner-Springer Family Collection.

10. Ibid.

11. Ibid.

12. C. F. McGlashan, *History of the Donner Party: A Tragedy of the Sierra* (San Francisco: A. L. Bancroft & Co., Printers, 1881), 138.

13. Henry F. Waters, *New England Historical and Genealogical Register*, Vol. 32 (Boston: David Clapp & Son, 1878), 211; Kristin Johnson, *New Light on the Donner Party*, http://www.utahcrossroads.org/DonnerParty, Utah Crossroads Chapter, Oregon-California Trails Association. Tamsen is the spelling most often used in the literature of the Donner Party, but she herself spelled it Tamzene.

14. Waters, ibid. William and his second wife had no children of their own. Hannah died in 1821, and William died in 1843.

15. Donner-Springer Family Collection, Tamzene Donner Letters File.

16. Gabrielle Burton, *Searching for Tamsen Donner* (Lincoln: University of Nebraska Press, 2009), 22.

17. Donner-Springer Family Collection.

18. Ibid.

19. Ibid.

20. Ibid.

21. Ibid.

22. McGlashan, *History*, 141.

23. Donner-Springer Family Collection.

CHAPTER 3: GRAY GOLD

1. C. F. McGlashan, *History of the Donner Party: A Tragedy of the Sierra* (Sacramento: H. S. Crocker Co., Printers, 1902), 42; John Carroll Power, *History of the Early Settlers of Sangamon County, Illinois* (Springfield: Edwin A. Wilson & Co., 1876), 600; James D. Lodesky, *Polish Pioneers in Illinois, 1818–1850* (Bloomington, IN: Exlibris Corporation, 2010), 152.
2. Power, *History of the Early Settlers of Sangamon County.*
3. Kristin Johnson, "The Reed Family," *New Light on the Donner Party*, http:// www .utahcrossroads.org/DonnerParty, Utah Crossroads Chapter, Oregon-California Trails Association; William Frazier to James Frazier Reed, Spared & Shared 2, http://sparedandshared2.wordpress.com/letters/1846-william-frazier-to-james-frazier-reed, 1846 letter.
4. "Galena and its Mines," *Harper's New Monthly Magazine*, Vol. 32 (New York: Harper & Brothers, 1866), 692–693. The village was named Galena in 1827, but it was not until 1829 that the name of the post office was changed to Galena, Jo-Daviess County, Illinois, with Galena as the county seat.
5. Lodesky, *Polish Pioneers*, 151.
6. Henry E. Legler, *Life in the Diggins* (Milwaukee: Sentinel Co., 1898), 165–168.
7. James Lewis, "The Black Hawk War of 1832," http://lincoln.lib.niu.edu/black-hawk/. This project presents searchable primary-source materials describing the Black Hawk War of 1832. It is part of the larger Abraham Lincoln Historical Digitization Project, Northern Illinois University Libraries.
8. Abraham Lincoln Timeline, http://www.historynet.com/abraham-lincoln-timeline.
9. Johnson, "The Reed Family," *New Light on the Donner Party*. Others of prominence who served in the Black Hawk War included future U.S. President Zachary Taylor; famous generals Winfield Scott, Albert Sidney Johnston, and Joseph E. Johnston; William Hamilton, son of Alexander Hamilton; and Jefferson Davis, president of the Confederate States of America.
10. Evelyn Dameier, "Kellogg's Grove," http://gis.hpa.state.il.us/hargis/ PDFs/200106.pdf, National Register of Historic Places Nomination Form, January 18, 1978, HARGIS Database, Illinois Historic Preservation Agency.
11. Sangamon County Illinois Archives, Military Records, Captain Jacob M. Early's Co., http://files.usgwarchives.net/il/sangamon/military/otherwar/rosters/ unindepend293gmt.tx.
12. Notice published in the *Illinois Weekly State Journal* (Springfield), 1832, 3.
13. *Laws of the State of Illinois* (Vandalia, IL: William Walters Public Printer, 1837), 63; notice published in the *Illinois Weekly State Journal*, 1833, 2.
14. Johnson, "The Reed Family," *New Light on the Donner Party.*
15. John Carroll Power, *History of the Early Settlers of Sangamon County, Illinois* (Springfield, IL: Edwin A. Wilson & Co., 1876), 427–428.
16. Ibid.
17. Power, *History*, 428.
18. Erika Holst, "Lincoln and the Donner Party," *Lincoln Footnotes*, 2010, http:// www.lincolnfootnotes.com/1/category/donner%20party/1.html.
19. *History of Sangamon County, Illinois* (Chicago: Interstate Publishing Co., 1881), 853–854.
20. Johnson, "The Reed Family," *New Light on the Donner Party.*
21. Sangamon County Historical Society, Sangamon Link, Northern Cross Rail-

road, http://sangamoncountyhistory.org/wp?p=1608. It is believed that state representative Abraham Lincoln voted in support of the Internal Improvements Act in a trade for other legislators' votes to move the state capital to Springfield.

22. Village of Riverton, "A Short History of the Village of Riverton," 2007, http://voril.com/History/history.htm.

23. *Illinois Weekly State Journal*, July 11, 1835, 1.

CHAPTER 4: SNAKE HEADS

1. H. J. Stratton, "The Northern Cross Railroad," *Journal of the Illinois State Historical Society (1908–1984)*, Vol. 28, No. 2 (1935), 5.

2. History and Development of the Enos Park Area/Enos Park Neighborhood Improvement Association, http://www.epnia.com/history-and-development -of-the-enos-park-area/#early.

3. Ibid.

4. Bruce Alexander Campbell, *The Sangamon Saga* (Springfield, IL: Phillips Brothers, 1976), 56.

5. Paul M. Angle, *"Here I Have Lived": A History of Lincoln's Springfield* (Chicago and New Salem, IL: Abraham Lincoln Book Shop, 1971), 99–100, 145. It was said that when Lincoln learned that his fiancée had enjoyed the train ride, he wrote, "God be praised for that." Lincoln and Mary Todd wed in Springfield, Illinois, on November 4, 1842.

6. Ibid., 145.

7. Ibid., 147.

8. *Lewiston Evening Journal*, May 13, 1893, 4.

9. *History of Sangamon County, Illinois* (Chicago: Interstate Publishing Co., 1881), 985.

10. Nancy Spinner Collection.

11. Ibid.

12. John Carroll Power, *History of the Early Settlers of Sangamon County, Illinois* (Springfield, IL: Edwin A. Wilson & Co., 1876), 761. Weber was quartermaster in the last expedition of the Mormon War of 1846. During the Gold Rush of 1849, he took his family to California. They returned to Illinois in 1851, where Weber farmed and was elected sheriff and tax collector of Sangamon County, serving from 1854 to 1856.

13. "Wanted" notice in the *Illinois Weekly State Journal*, 1841, 4.

14. Sangamon County Historical Society, SangamonLink, Northern Cross Railroad, http://sangamoncountyhistory.org/wp?p=1608.

15. Ibid.

16. Ibid.

17. Ibid.

18. Harry E. Pratt, "Abraham Lincoln's First Murder Trial," *Journal of the Illinois State Historical Society (1908–1984)*, Vol. 37, No. 3 (September 1944), 242–249.

19. Pratt, "Abraham Lincoln's First Murder Trial," 245.

20. Ibid., 247.

21. Ibid., 248–249.

22. United States House of Representatives, *House Documents*, Vol. 28 (Washington, D.C.: U.S. Government Printing Office, 1846), 164; article in *Illinois Weekly State Journal*, 1845, 3.

23. Notice in the *Illinois Weekly State Journal*, 1846, 4.

CHAPTER 5: CALIFORNIA DREAMING

1. Bernard DeVoto, *The Year of Decision, 1846* (Boston: Little, Brown & Company, 1942). This is the penultimate book of a trilogy, which includes *Across the Wide Missouri* and *The Course of Empire*, covering the expansion of the western frontier.

2. Michael Wallis, *The Wild West 365* (New York: Abrams, 2011), 66.

3. Lyman Beecher, *A Plea for the West* (Cincinnati: Truman & Smith; New York: Leavitt, Lord & Co., 1835), 190. A leader in the Second Great Awakening of the United States, Beecher was notorious for his anti-Catholic stance and writings such as this nativist tract.

4. William E. Channing, *Letter to the Honorable Henry Clay, On the Annexation of Texas to the United States* (Boston: James Munroe & Co., 1837).

5. *Illinois Weekly State Journal*, March 25, 1845, Donner-Springer Family Collection. Although Illinois was a "free" state, a form of slavery persisted under the guise of a system of indentured servitude. Some landowners rented out indentured servants as laborers. The indentured girl that Gersham Keyes sought was Clarissa Milsted.

6. John Carroll Power, *History of the Early Settlers of Sangamon County, Illinois* (Springfield, Illinois: Edwin A. Wilson & Co., 1876), 428, 716.

7. William B. Ide, "From our Oregon Correspondent," *Illinois Weekly State Journal*, September 4, 1845, 4.

8. George R. Stewart, *The California Trail* (Lincoln and London: University of Nebraska Press, 1962), 57–58, 90.

9. Wallis, *The Wild West*, 8.

10. Olive Newell, *Trail of the Elephant: The Emigrating Experience on the Truckee Route of the California Trail, 1844–1852* (Nevada City, CA: Nevada County Historical Society, 1997), 33.

11. Ibid.; Stewart, *The California Trail*, 33.

12. Louis W. Flanders, Simeon Ide, and Edith F. Dunbar, *A Genealogy of the Ide Family* (Rutland, VT: Tuttle Co., 1931), 30.

13. Dale Morgan, *Overland in 1846: Diaries and Letters of the California-Oregon Trail*, Vol. 2 (Lincoln and London: University of Nebraska Press, 1993), 750, n. 62.

14. Abraham Lincoln Presidential Library, Springfield, Illinois, SC 1868, Folder 5, James W. Keyes.

15. *Illinois Weekly State Journal*, February 26, 1845, Donner-Springer Family Collection. This advertisement was published in the newspaper continuously through the March 5, 1846, edition.

16. Nancy Spinner Collection.

17. Brian R. Dirck, *Lincoln the Lawyer* (Champaign: University of Illinois Press, 2008), 76.

18. Ibid., 77.

CHAPTER 6: THE BOLD PLUNGE

1. John Carroll Power, *History of the Early Settlers of Sangamon County, Illinois* (Springfield, IL: Edwin A. Wilson & Co., 1876), 608.

2. Ibid., 707.

3. Richard E. Hart, *Lincoln's Springfield*, http://lincolnsspringfield.blogspot.com/2007/03/lincolns-springfield-1838-richard-e.html.

4. Edwin Allen Sherman, *Fifty Years of Masonry in California*, Vol. II (San Francisco:

George Spaulding & Co., 1898), 14. Reed was initiated into Springfield (Illinois) Lodge No. 4 on July 5, 1839.

5. Reed Papers, Sutter's Fort Historical Monument Collection; Dale Morgan, *Overland in 1846: Diaries and Letters of the California-Oregon Trail*, Vol. II (Lincoln and London: University of Nebraska Press, 1963), 474–475.

6. Ibid., 485–486.

7. Michael Wallis, *The Wild West 365* (New York: Abrams, 2011), 70.

8. William Montgomery Meigs, *The Life of Thomas Hart Benton* (Philadelphia and London: J. B. Lippincott Co., 1904), 309.

9. Wallis, *The Wild West*, 70.

10. Eliza P. Donner Houghton, *The Expedition of the Donner Party and Its Tragic Fate* (Chicago: A. C. McClung, 1911), 5–6.

11. John C. Frémont, *Report of the Exploring Expedition to the Rocky Mountains in the Year 1842 and to Oregon and North California in the Years 1843–1844* (Washington, D.C.: Gals and Seaton, 1845), 241–242.

12. Houghton, *The Expedition*, 6.

13. *Sangamo Journal* (Springfield), March 26, 1846. The same notice appeared in the issue of April 2, 1846.

14. Wallis, *The Wild West*, 126.

15. Dee Brown, *The American West* (New York: Simon & Schuster, 1994), 32.

16. Houghton, *The Expedition*, 5.

17. Virginia Reed Murphy, *Across the Plains in the Donner Party: A Personal Narrative of the Overland Trip to California 1846–47* (Golden, CO: Outbooks, 1980), 11. This narrative of the journey originally appeared in *The Century Magazine*, Vol. 42, 1891.

CHAPTER 7: WAGONS HO! APRIL 1846

1. Nancy Spinner Collection.

2. Abraham Lincoln Presidential Library and Museum, Springfield, Illinois, Manuscript Department, James F. Reed file, SC 1251.

3. Margaret R. Koch, "The Gold Gulch Letters of James Frazier Reed," *Santa Cruz County History Journal*, Issue No. 2 (1995), 26.

4. Dale Morgan, *Overland in 1846: Diaries and Letters of the California-Oregon Trail*, Vol. 1 (Lincoln and London: University of Nebraska Press, 1963), 248.

5. Edwin A. Sherman, "Gives Details of Reed-Donner Trip," *Illinois Weekly State Journal*, September 21, 1910, 2.

6. "Newly Discovered Lincoln Document Traveled with the Donner Party to California," *Illinois Heritage*, Vol. 13, No. 5 (September-October 2010), 9.

7. Eliza P. Donner Houghton, *The Expedition of the Donner Party and its Tragic Fate* (Chicago: A. C. McClung, 1911), 6.

8. Morgan, *Overland in 1846*, Vol. II, 481–482. The list appeared in the *Sangamo Journal*, March 5, 1846.

9. Virginia Reed Murphy, *Across the Plains in the Donner Party: A Personal Narrative of the Overland Trip to California 1846–47* (Golden, CO: Outbooks, 1980), 12.

10. Evelyn Vancil Lowdermilk-Ball, "A New Colonial History: Lines of Lowdermilk Brown Hudson and Moore Vancil Donner" (Okmulgee, OK, 1977), 175. This document is available at the Illinois State Historical Library, Springfield.

11. Murphy, *Across the Plains*, 12.

CHAPTER 8: FAREWELL, APRIL 14–15, 1846

1. Kristin Johnson, "The Reed Family," *New Light on the Donner Party*, http://www .utahcrossroads.org/DonnerParty/Briefmyths.htm, Utah Crossroads Chapter, Oregon-California Trails Association. The exact date of departure of the Donner-Reed Party depends on which family is to be believed. The Reed family maintained that the party left Springfield on April 14, 1846, but Eliza Donner Houghton, writing in her memoir, stated that it was "Thursday, April 15, 1846." This date not only contradicts the Reeds, but it also contradicts itself. That year, April 15 fell on Wednesday, not Thursday. It is not clear whether Eliza meant Wednesday, April 15, or Thursday, April 16. Most historians have chosen to believe that she meant the former.

2. Virginia Reed Murphy, *Across the Plains*, 14–15.

3. Ibid., 14–15.

4. Ibid., 15.

5. Eliza P. Donner Houghton, *The Expedition of the Donner Party and its Tragic Fate* (Chicago: A. C. McClung, 1911), 7.

6. Departure Point of the Donner Party Historical Marker, mounted on a kiosk in the pedestrian mall adjacent to the Old State Capitol in downtown Springfield, Illinois.

7. Editor's Column, "Abe Lincoln of San Jose," *San Jose Evening News*, June 28, 1919, 6. Martha Jane (Patty) Reed married Frank Lewis in 1856 and had eight children. Evelyn Wells interviewed her for a series of articles entitled "The Tragedy of Donner Lake," published in June and July 1919 in the *San Francisco Morning Call*. Based on her conversations with Patty Reed Lewis, Wells conjectured that Lincoln seriously considered joining the Donner-Reed Party.

8. "History Minutes: Abraham Lincoln and Oregon," Oregon Historical Society, http://www.ohs.org/education/history-minutes-abraham-lincoln-and-oregon .cfm. In 1849, President Zachary Taylor appointed Lincoln secretary of Oregon Territory, with the possibility of a governorship. Despite encouragement from his political allies to accept the post, Lincoln declined, primarily because of opposition from his wife, who did not wish to move to unsettled country with small children and, more important, because she believed the move would derail her husband's political future.

9. Richard E. Hart, "Lincoln's Springfield: Photography of Historic Mather Residence," *For the People: A Newsletter of the Abraham Lincoln Association*, Vol. 12, No. 3 (Summer 2010), 1, 3. A descendant of Cotton Mather and early Harvard College President Increase Mather, Thomas Mather, in 1836, purchased the property where the Donner-Reed Party camped. He lived there until his death in 1853.

10. Ibid. The Mather property and surrounding area became the site for the new state capitol, constructed between 1867 and 1887. Although the hill was altered, the slightly elevated site gave the capitol a sweeping view of the entire city.

11. Houghton, *The Expedition*, 8.

12. Homer Croy, *Wheels West* (New York: Hastings House Publishers, 1955), 13.

13. Ibid.

14. Houghton, *The Expedition*, 8.

15. *History and Improvements of Oak Ridge Cemetery* (Springfield: Phillips Brothers, State Printer, 1901, revised and adopted 1902), 14–15. John Hutchinson, an undertaker and cabinetmaker, established Hutchinson Cemetery in 1846. By

1857, more than one thousand people had been buried there, including Abraham Lincoln's son Edward, who died of pulmonary tuberculosis before his fourth birthday in 1850.

16. Nancy Spinner Collection.
17. Murphy, *Across the Plains*, 12, 14.
18. Yiannis G. Papakosta et al., "Horse Madness (Hippomania) and Hippophobia," *History of Psychiatry* (London; Thousand Oaks, CA; New Delhi: AGE Publications, December 2005), 467–471. From the abstract: "Anthropophagic horses have been described in classical mythology. From a current perspective, two such instances are worth mentioning and describing: Glaucus of Potniae, King of Efyra, and Diomedes, King of Thrace, who were both devoured by their horses. In both cases, the horses' extreme aggression and their subsequent anthropophagic behavior were attributed to their madness (hippomania) induced by the custom of feeding them flesh."

CHAPTER 9: INDEPENDENCE BOUND,
APRIL 15–MAY 10, 1846

1. Peter R. Limburg, *Deceived: The Story of the Donner Party* (Pacifica, CA: IPS Books, 1998), 21; Jared Diamond and James A. Robinson, eds., *Natural Experiments of History* (Cambridge, MA: Harvard University Press, 2010), 69. Although the American-coined designation *immigrant* was in common usage by 1820 and the name *pioneer* in the western sense first appeared in 1817, names such as *mover*, *settler*, and *emigrant* seemed to have been preferred.
2. Murphy, *Across the Plains*, 5.
3. C. F. McGlashan, *History of the Donner Party: A Tragedy of the Sierra* (Sacramento: H. S. Crocker Co., 1902), 24.
4. Evelyn Vancil Lowdermilk-Ball, "A New Colonial History: Lines of Lowdermilk Brown Hudson and Moore Vancil Donner" (Okmulgee, OK, 1977), 174–175.
5. Ibid., 176–177.
6. Bernard DeVoto, *The Year of Decision, 1846* (Boston: Little, Brown & Co., 1943), 125–126.
7. Murphy, *Across the Plains*, 5.
8. The Potawatomi Trail of Death Historical Marker, mounted on a kiosk in the pedestrian mall adjacent to the Old State Capitol in downtown Springfield, Illinois, was erected in 2000 by the Pokagon Potawatomi Tribal Council.
9. The Bancroft Library, University of California, Berkeley, California, Charles Fayette McGlashan Letters and Papers, Virginia Reed Murphy cover letter and 14-page memoir document sent to C. F. McGlashan, June 8, 1879. Bancroft MSGB 570, Carton 1, Folder 100. Some chroniclers of the Donner-Reed journey maintain that the party crossed the Mississippi upstream at Quincy, Illinois, and others claim they entered Missouri at St. Louis, but based on the writing of Virginia Reed, the crossing clearly took place at Hannibal, Missouri.
10. Ibid.

CHAPTER 10: QUEEN CITY OF THE TRAILS, MAY 10–12, 1846

1. Floyd C. Shoemaker, ed., *Missouri Historical Review*, Vol. 10 (Columbia: State Historical Society of Missouri, 1916), 225. In 1930, the American Historical Society, Inc., published a book by Shoemaker and Walter Williams, *Missouri: Mother of the West*.

2. Kristin Johnson, ed., *Crossroads*, Vol. 8, No.1 (Winter 1997), Utah Crossroads Chapter of the Oregon-California Trails Association, http://user.xmission .com/-octsa/newsv8n1.htm. The original letter is in the James W. Keyes Papers, Illinois State Historical Library, Springfield.

3. Kristin Johnson, ed., *"Unfortunate Emigrants": Narratives of the Donner Party* (Logan: Utah State University Press, 1996), 15. This book contains a wide selection of early accounts of the 1846 journey of the Donner Party taken from journals, diaries, and other historic documents.

4. Ibid., 6.

5. Ibid., 15.

6. "Kansas Before 1854: A Revised Annals," Part Fifteen, 1846, compiled by Louise Barry, *The Kansas Historical Quarterly*, Vol. 30, No. 3 (Autumn 1964), 349.

7. Michael Wallis, *The Wild West 365* (New York: Harry N. Abrams, 2011), 678.

8. Kenneth L. Holmes, ed., *Covered Wagon Women*, Vol. 1: *Diaries & Letters from the Western Trails, 1840–1849* (Lincoln and London: University of Nebraska Press, 1995).

9. Carroll D. Hall, ed., *Donner Miscellany: 41 Diaries and Documents* (San Francisco: Book Club of San Francisco, 1947), 11.

10. Houghton, *The Expedition*, 10.

CHAPTER 11: INDIAN COUNTRY, MAY 12–18, 1846

1. National Historic Trails, Audio Tour Route Interpretive Guide, Western Missouri to Northeastern Kansas (Salt Lake City: National Park Service, National Trails System Intermountain Region, 2005), 12–14. Protected vestiges of the swales exist today, covered with grass on prairie hillsides and in public parks in the Independence and Kansas City, Missouri, area.

2. Carroll D. Hall, ed., *Donner Miscellany: 41 Diaries and Documents* (San Francisco: Book Club of California, 1947), 11. In 1946, a descendant of Patty Reed Lewis donated a collection of family documents and memorabilia to Sutter's Fort. The Miller-Reed diary was among those items. In 1947, Carroll D. Hall, curator of Sutter's Fort, published the Miller-Reed diary, along with other documents and papers from the Reed collection. Despite allegations of inauthenticity and other questions raised by a few skeptics, leading scholars, including the highly regarded historian Dale L. Morgan, defended the diary and its contents. After a thorough analysis of the diary, Morgan called it "the most staggering historical find in years." Kristin Johnson, ed., *Donner Party Bulletin*, Issue No. 5, May-June 1998. Retrieved from http://user.xmission.com/~octa/DonnerParty/Bulletin05 .htm. In this issue, Johnson provides a full account of what is now known as the Miller-Reed diary. Hiram O. Miller, an original member of the Donner-Reed Party, recorded the wagon train's journey from May 12, 1846, the day the party left Independence, Missouri, until July 2, when Miller left the group to join the Bryant-Russell Party. At that time, James F. Reed took over writing the entries and continued to do so until October 4, 1846. The original leather-bound journal is at Sutter's Fort in Sacramento, California, now a state historic fort holding one of the world's largest collections of material related to the Donner Party.

3. Douglas V. Meed, *The Mexican War 1846–1848* (Oxford, U.K.: Osprey Publishing, 2002), 8.

4. Hall, *Donner Miscellany*, 11.

5. New Santa Fe Historical Society, http://www.newsantafe.org/.

6. United States Senate, Committee on Territories, *Affairs in the Indian Territory* (Washington, D.C.: U.S. Government Printing Office, 1879), 307.

7. Martyn J. Bowden, "The Great American Desert and the American Frontier, 1800–1882, Popular Images of the Plains," in *Anonymous American: Explorations in Nineteenth-Century Social History*, Tamara K. Hareven, ed., (Englewood Cliffs, NJ: Prentice-Hall, 1971), 48–79.

8. Houghton, *The Expedition*, 11–12.

9. Gregory M. Franzwa, *The Oregon Trail Revisited* (Tucson: Patrice Press, 1972), 131–132. According to Franzwa, "The Lone Elm itself was about three feet thick at the trunk, but by 1844 it was nearly stripped of its branches and bark. The emigrants needed firewood and they took it wherever they could find it. By the close of the decade they had burned the whole tree."

CHAPTER 12: SOLDIER CREEK, MAY 19, 1846

1. *The Mexican-American War and the Media, 1845–1848*, Virginia Tech, Department of History, www.history.vt.edu/MxAmWar/newspapers/RW/RW846Jan-June.htm; Jeffrey Rogers Hummel, "The American Militia and the Origin of Conscription: A Reassessment," *Journal of Libertarian Studies*, Vol. 15, No. 4 (Fall 2001), 29–77.

2. Merrill J. Mattes, *Fort Laramie Park History, 1834–1977* (Denver: Rocky Mountain Regional Office, National Park Service, 1980), 18.

3. Murphy, *Across the Plains*, 11.

4. Ibid., 15–16.

5. "Kansas Before 1854: A Revised Annals," Part Fifteen, 1846, compiled by Louise Barry, *Kansas Historical Quarterly*, Vol. 30, No. 3 (Autumn 1964), 353.

6. Edwin Bryant, *What I Saw in California* (New York: D. Appleton; Philadelphia: G. Appleton, 1848), 46. Bryant was dubious of reports of soldiers dumping so much contraband whiskey into the stream that the fish were poisoned.

7. Frank Mullen Jr., *The Donner Party Chronicles* (Reno: Halcyon Imprint of the Nevada Humanities Committee, 1997), 44–45. William Henry Russell was sometimes confused with a contemporary, William Hepburn Russell, an emigrant to Missouri who, along with Alexander Majors and William B. Waddell, founded and operated the short-lived Pony Express.

8. William Henry Russell (1802–1873), http://genforum.geneaology.com/Russell/messages/ 11998.html. Posted by William Anderson LaBach (1938–2013), a Georgetown, Kentucky, attorney and descendant of several well-known Kentuckians.

9. Bernard DeVoto, *The Year of Decision, 1846* (Boston: Little, Brown & Co., 1942), 122.

10. William Henry Russell, http://www.usgwarchives.net/copyright.htm, submitted by William LaBach; U.S. Marshals Service, History of Western District of Missouri, http:www.usmarshals.gov/ district/mo-w/general/history.htm. William Henry Harrison was the ninth president of the United States and the first president to die in office. His term of office began on March 4, 1841, and on April 4, exactly one month later, he died of pneumonia. His appointment of Owl Russell as U.S. Marshal for the Western District of Missouri was recorded on April 13, 1841, nine days after Harrison died, during a congressional recess. Russell served until March 29, 1843.

11. Morgan, *Overland in 1846*, Vol. I, 237. Morgan goes on to write in the several pages (237–244) he devotes to the Jefferson map, "No trace of Jefferson's visit to

California has been found, other than his map. It is assumed that he returned east by sea, sometime in 1847 or 1848."

12. Dorothy Sloan—Rare Books Auction 15, Lots 131 & 132, www.dsloan.com/ Auctions/A15/ A15Web132-133.htm.

13. Shirley Ann Wilson Moore, *Sweet Freedom's Plains: African Americans on the Overland Trails, 1841–1869*, for the National Park Service, National Trails Intermountain Region, Salt Lake City and Santa Fe, January 31, 2012, 83–88. Moore writes, "The Fremont expeditions and the experiences of other overland travelers produced maps and guides that gained acceptance with potential migrants. However, another lesser known but intriguing map and trail guide also emerged during the dawning era of overland emigration. It was the work of an African American, T. H. Jefferson, who was likely the son of the slave Sally Hemings and her owner, President Thomas Jefferson of Virginia, [who] created a remarkable map and guide from his own experiences on the overland trail. . . . T. H. Jefferson would have been the couple's eldest son, Thomas (Tom), who was a teenager when Meriwether Lewis spent some time as a guest at Monticello before President Jefferson sent the Lewis and Clark Expedition to explore the West. . . . T. H. Jefferson's life and lineage remain wrapped in mystery and debate."

14. Daniel M. Rosen, *The Donner Party*, "Log Entries for May 1846," http://www .donnerpartydiary.com/may46.htm. The original letter is in the James W. Keyes Papers, Illinois State Historical Library, Springfield.

15. Edwin Bryant, *What I Saw in California* (New York: D. Appleton; Philadelphia: G. Appleton, 1848), 46.

16. Houghton, *The Expedition*, 12–13.

CHAPTER 13: THE OTHERS, MAY 20, 1846

1. Edwin Bryant, *What I Saw in California* (New York: D. Appleton; Philadelphia: G. Appleton, 1848), 48.

2. Daniel M. Rosen, "Log Entries for May 1846," http://www.donnerpartydiary .com/may46.htm.

3. Robert Nelson, *Enemy of the Saints: The Biography of Governor Lilburn Boggs of Missouri* (Baltimore: PublishAmerica, 2011), 134–136.

4. "Kansas Before 1854: A Revised Annals," Part Fifteen, 1846, compiled by Louise Barry, *The Kansas Historical Quarterly*, Vol. 30, No. 3 (Autumn 1964), 349.

5. Houghton, *The Expedition*, 13.

6. Ibn Khaldun, *The Muqaddimah*, trans. Franz Rosenthal, ed. N. J. Dawood (Princeton, NJ: Princeton University Press, 2005), 209.

7. Thomas D. Clark, Introduction, in Edwin Bryant, *What I Saw in California* (Lincoln and London: University of Nebraska Press, 1985), viii.

8. Lois Chambers Taylor, "Andrew Jackson Grayson," in *The Condor*, Vol. 51, No. 2 (March-April 1949), 49.

9. Margaret C. S. Christman, *1846: Portrait of the Nation* (Washington, D.C., and London: Smithsonian Institution Press for the National Portrait Gallery, 1996), 96, 98.

10. Historical and Biographical Notes; Lilburn Williams Boggs, 1836–1843; Office of Governor, Record Group 3.6; Missouri State Archives, Jefferson City, Missouri. Boggs had two sons with his first wife, Julia Ann Bent, and ten children with his second wife, Panthea Grant Boone, daughter of Jesse Boone, Daniel Boone's son.

11. Wallis, *The Wild West*, 20.
12. Monte B. McLaws, "The Attempted Assassination of Missouri's Ex-Governor, Lilburn W. Boggs," *Missouri Historical Review*, Vol. 60, Issue 1 (October 1965), 51.
13. D. Michael Quinn, "The Culture of Violence in Joseph Smith's Mormonism," *Sunstone: Mormon Experience, Scholarship, Issues & Art*, Issue 164 (October 2011), 25.
14. Ibid.
15. Houghton, *The Expedition*, 13–14.
16. Ibid.

CHAPTER 14: PEOPLE OF THE SOUTH WIND, MAY 21–24, 1846

1. Frank Mullen Jr., *The Donner Party Chronicles* (Reno: Nevada Humanities Committee, 1997), 46.
2. Edwin Bryant, *What I Saw in California* (New York: D. Appleton; Philadelphia: G. Appleton, 1848), 49.
3. Ibid.
4. Morgan, *Overland in 1846*, Vol. I, 547.
5. Bryant, *What I Saw*, 49.
6. Ibid.
7. Ibid.
8. Ibid., 50.
9. Morgan, *Overland in 1846*, Vol. I, 199–200.
10. Ibid., 200.
11. George H. Himes, "History of the Press of Oregon, 1839–1850," *Quarterly of the Oregon Historical Society*, Vol. III (March 1902–December 1902), 349.
12. Howard M. Corning, *Dictionary of Oregon History* (Portland, OR: Binfords & Mort Publishing, 1989), 68.
13. Morgan, *Overland in 1846*, Vol. II, 461.
14. Ibid., 540.
15. Ibid., 530.
16. Francis Parkman, *The Oregon Trail* (Garden City, NY: Doubleday & Co., 1946), 55.
17. Richard E. Jensen, "The Pawnee Mission, 1834–1846," *Nebraska History* 75 (1994), 301–310. The *Daily Missouri Republican*, October 31, 1848, published a letter written by a soldier at Fort Kearny, Nebraska, that stated, "The Missionaries turned their attention to these fellows [the Pawnee] some time ago; but after laboring ten years without making a single convert, and having most of their small things stolen, they retired from the field with disgust leaving the Pawnees to work out their own salvation."
18. Bryant, *What I Saw*, 50.
19. Ronald D. Parks, *The Darkest Period: The Kanza Indians and Their Last Homeland, 1846–1873* (Norman: University of Oklahoma Press, 2014), 55. Hard Chief's Kaw (or Kanza) name was spelled differently by various Indian agents and traders.
20. Ibid., 56.
21. Bryant, *What I Saw*, 544.
22. Ibid.
23. Houghton, *The Expedition*, 16.

24. Cora Miranda Baggerly Older, *Love Stories of Old California* (Freeport, NY: Books for Libraries Press, 1940), 187.
25. Bryant, *What I Saw*, 54.
26. Ibid., 56.
27. Ibid., 57.

CHAPTER 15: ALCOVE SPRING, MAY 25–29, 1846

1. Virginia Reed Murphy, *Across the Plains in the Donner Party: A Personal Narrative of the Overland Trip to California 1846–47* (Golden, CO: Outbooks, 1980), 16.
2. Houghton, *The Expedition*, 15–16.
3. Morgan, *Overland in 1846*, Vol. I, 207.
4. Bryant, *What I Saw*, 58.
5. Ibid.
6. Ibid., 134.
7. Morgan, *Overland in 1846*, Vol. I, 208.
8. Bryant, *What I Saw*, 60.
9. J. Quinn Thornton, *Oregon and California in 1848*, Vol. I (New York: Harper & Brothers Publishers, 1849), 48.
10. Bryant, *What I Saw*, 61.
11. Ibid.
12. Ibid.
13. Thornton, *Oregon and California*, Vol. I, 54. Thornton also noted that once again, "The hunters and fishermen returned unsuccessful."
14. Bryant, 61.
15. National Register of Historic Places. James Reed more than likely carved his entire surname into the rock, but over time, some letters were worn away, leaving only the initials "J.F.R." Thornton, 54.
16. Murphy, *Across the Plains*, 16.
17. Bryant, *What I Saw*, 64.
18. Gregory M. Franzwa, *The Oregon Trail Revisited* (Tucson, Arizona: The Patrice Press, 1972), 163.
19. Morgan, *Overland in 1846*, Vol. I, 209.
20. Murphy, *Across the Plains*, 16.
21. Katherine Wakeman Cooper, "Patty Reed," *Overland Monthly* (January-June 1917), 517–520. Patty Reed never forgot the death of her grandmother at Alcove Spring. For many years, she tried to locate the gravesite and bring Sarah Keyes's remains to California. She had no success and ultimately was forced to abandon her plans.

CHAPTER 16: THE RHETORIC OF FEAR, MAY 30–JUNE 2, 1846

1. Bryant, *What I Saw*, 65.
2. Ibid.
3. Murphy, *Across the Plains*, 16.
4. J. Quinn Thornton, *Oregon and California in 1848*, Vol. I (New York: Harper & Brothers, 1849), 58.
5. Ibid.
6. Ibid., 67-68.
7. Antonio B. Rabbeson, *Growth of Towns: Olympia, Tumwater, Portland, and San Francisco*, Bancroft MS PB-17, Bancroft Library, University of California–Berkeley.

8. Bryant, *What I Saw*, 69.
9. Houghton, *The Expedition*, 22.
10. Morgan, *Overland in 1846*, Vol. II, 555.
11. Bryant, *What I Saw*, 70.
12. Wallis, *The Wild West*, 174. Torture of captured foes and removal of scalps for trophies were not peculiar to Indians. Scalping had been practiced in many cultures in Europe as far back as ancient Greece, although the more common custom was to display the severed heads of enemy combatants. Early settlers in America paid bounties for Indian scalps and other body parts. Some sources believe the origin of the word *redskin* lies in the collecting of bloody Indian scalps.
13. Ibid., 84.

CHAPTER 17: EBB AND FLOW, JUNE 3–7, 1846

1. Bryant, *What I Saw*, 71.
2. Ibid.
3. Morgan, *Overland in 1846*, Vol. 1, 406, n. 42.
4. Germany Births and Baptisms, 1558–1898, Index, FamilySearch, Johann Ludwig Keseberg, 01 Jun 1814, citing FHL microfilm 923182.
5. Germany Marriages, 1558–1929, Index, FamilySearch, Johann Ludwig Keseberg and Elisabeth Philippine Zimmermann, 22 Jul 1842; citing Evangelisch, Berleburg Stadt, Westfalen, Prussia, FHL microfilm 591331.
6. Germany Births and Baptisms, 1558–1898.
7. Johnson, *"Unfortunate Emigrants."*
8. Frank Mullen Jr., *The Donner Party Chronicles* (Reno: Nevada Humanities Committee, 1997), 63.
9. Johnson, *"Unfortunate Emigrants."*
10. Morgan, *Overland in 1846*, Vol. I, 406, n. 42.
11. Bryant, *What I Saw*, 72–73.
12. Ibid., 72.
13. Ibid., 76.
14. Mullen, *The Donner Party Chronicles*, 64.
15. Bryant, *What I Saw*, 76–77.
16. Ibid., 77.

CHAPTER 18: ON THE PLATTE, JUNE 8–10, 1846

1. Merrill J. Mattes, *The Great Platte River Road: The Covered Wagon Mainline via Fort Kearny to Fort Laramie* (Lincoln and London: University of Nebraska Press, 1987), 6. Originally published by the Nebraska State Historical Society in 1969, Merrill's book is considered the basic primer of the overland trails from the Missouri River to Fort Laramie during the 1840s and 1850s.
2. Morgan, *Overland in 1846*, Vol. II, 556.
3. Bryant, *What I Saw*, 77.
4. Morgan, *Overland in 1846*, Vol. II, 556.
5. Lawrence C. Allin, "'A Mile Wide and an Inch Deep': Attempts to Navigate the Platte River," *Nebraska History*, Vol. 63 (Spring 1982), 1.
6. Francis Parkman, *The Oregon Trail* (Garden City, NY: Doubleday & Co. 1946), 53–54.
7. Bryant, *What I Saw*, 98.
8. Ibid., 79.

9. Ibid.

10. Mullen, *The Donner Party Chronicles*, 66.

CHAPTER 19: LIFE GOES ON, JUNE 10–15, 1846

1. David J. Wishart, ed., *Encyclopedia of the Great Plains* (Lincoln and London: University of Nebraska Press, 2004), 279.

2. Merrill J. Mattes, *The Great Platte River Road: The Covered Wagon Mainline via Fort Kearny to Fort Laramie* (Lincoln and London: University of Nebraska Press, 1987), 57.

3. Gary L. Krapu, Kenneth J. Reinecke, and Charles R. Frith, "Sandhill Cranes and the Platte River," USGS Northern Prairie Wildlife Research Center, Paper 87, 1982, 542.

4. Morgan, *Overland in 1846*, Vol. II, 553–554.

5. Bryant, *What I Saw*, 61.

6. Ibid., 82–83.

7. Robert Nelson, *Enemy of the Saints: The Biography of Governor Lilburn W. Boggs of Missouri* (Baltimore, MD: PublishAmerica, 2011), 148. It is believed that young William Boggs and not his father, the former governor of Missouri, accompanied Andrew Grayson on the hunting trip.

8. Bryant, *What I Saw*, 84–85.

9. Ibid., 85.

10. Ibid.

11. Morgan, *Overland in 1846*, Vol. II, 560.

12. Ibid., Vol. I, 274.

13. Ibid., 275–276.

14. Ibid., 276–277.

15. Bryant, *What I Saw*, 86–87.

16. Ibid., 88; James Tompkins, ed., "Reminiscences of A. H. Garrison: His Early Life, Across the Plains and of Oregon from 1846 to 1903," *Overland Journal*, Vol. 11, No. 2 (1993), 10–31.

17. J. Quinn Thornton, *Oregon and California in 1848*, Vol. I (New York: Harper & Brothers Publishers, 1849), 76–77.

18. Bryant, *What I Saw*, 88.

19. Morgan, *Overland in 1846*, Vol. I, 152.

20. Bryant, *What I Saw*, 89.

21. Tompkins, "Reminiscences."

22. Thornton, *Oregon and California*, 77–78.

23. Bryant, *What I Saw*, 90.

24. Ibid.

25. Thornton, *Oregon and California*, 79.

26. Bryant, *What I Saw*, 91.

27. Tompkins, "Reminiscences."

28. Bryant, *What I Saw*, 91.

CHAPTER 20: A LETTER FROM TAMZENE DONNER, JUNE 16, 1846

1. Eliza P. Donner Houghton, *The Expedition of the Donner Party and its Tragic Fate* (Chicago: A. C. McClung, 1911), 24–25. This letter written by Tamzene Donner to a friend in Springfield, Illinois, was originally published in the *Sangamo Journal*, Springfield, Illinois, on July 23, 1846.

CHAPTER 21: CHANGE OF COMMAND, JUNE 16–19, 1846

1. Morgan, *Overland in 1846*, Vol. II, 563.
2. Ibid., 564.
3. Ibid., 560.
4. Ibid., 557–559.
5. Ibid.
6. Bryant, *What I Saw*, 79–80.
7. Houghton, *The Expedition*, 22–23.
8. Morgan, *Overland in 1846*, Vol. I, 759, 599. In a news report published on July 21, 1846, in the *Jefferson Inquirer*, Jefferson City, Missouri, it was stated that the Palmer Party brought six hundred to seven hundred letters to St. Joseph, Missouri.
9. Ibid., 759. On June 21, 1846, the rest of Palmer's men who had not been present at the Russell Party's campground caught up with the main party. After Palmer arrived in St. Joseph, Missouri, on July 7, 1846, the newspaper later reported eighteen men in his party. Palmer returned to his home in Indiana. The next year, he published a popular guidebook and returned to Oregon with his wife and children. Soon after settling there, he served as commissary general of volunteers in the war with the Cayuse Indians. Later, he spent time in the California gold fields, returned to cofound Dayton, Oregon, and in 1853, was appointed superintendent of Indian affairs for the Oregon Territory by President Franklin Pierce. Palmer went on to serve as speaker of the state House of Representatives and as a state senator. He narrowly lost the 1870 gubernatorial race. Palmer died in Dayton, Oregon, in 1881.
10. Ibid., 557.
11. Ibid., 759.
12. Ibid., 566. Owl Russell and most wagon-train leaders made a rule for the emigrants concerning privacy when the need to relieve oneself arose. Men were told to go to one side of the trail and women to the other. If the terrain was flat and barren, as was often the case, women would spread their ankle-length dresses to form a screen. The first toilet paper did not appear in the United States until the late 1850s and was not commonly used for many more years. On the trail, rags that could be washed and reused served this purpose. Rags also were used as menstrual pads.
13. Murphy, *Across the Plains*, 16.
14. Ibid., 17.
15. Ibid., 17–18.
16. Ibid.

CHAPTER 22: CHASING MIRAGES, JUNE 19–25, 1846

1. John C. Roberts, "Traveling the Great Platte River Road," *Caxtonian*, Journal of the Caxton Club, Vol. XVII, No. 10 (October 2009), 4.
2. Ibid. The hill that marked the entrance into Ash Hollow became known as Windlass Hill, but at the time the Boggs Party made the difficult descent, that name was not used. The exact origin of the name is unknown. A popular legend claims that there was a windlass or hand-cranked winch on the summit of the hill to lower wagons, but none of the emigrant diaries or letters mentions the device or calls the hill by that name.

3. Morgan, *Overland in 1846*, Vol. II, 577–578; Vol. I, 153, 213, 383, n. 15. Stanton was referring to the burial of Eli Griggery, a young man headed to the Oregon Country with Nicolas Carriger's caravan. Only a few days earlier, Griggery, who suffered from heart disease, had been examined by Edwin Bryant when he was summoned to examine a boy's leg injury that ultimately caused the boy's death. A short time later, Bryant conferred with Griggery and told him there was nothing he could do for his heart problem. Griggery was buried below a bluff at the side of the trail. Just two days later, the wife of Redwood Easton—another member of the Carriger Party whom Bryant had seen—died and was buried near the trail.

4. Rudolph E. Umland, *Nebraska: A Guide to the Cornhusker State*, Federal Writers' Project (New York: Hastings House, 1939), 383.

5. Morgan, *Overland in 1846*, Vol. I., 172, 213, 409, n. 57.

6. William Willis, *Genealogy of the McKinstry Family* (Boston: Henry W. Dutton, Printers, 1858), 24. George McKinstry was born in Hudson, New York, on September 15, 1810, and his sister Susan was born there on June 1, 1814. She married their first cousin, Justus McKinstry, younger brother of James P. McKinstry, the career naval officer who served with Selim Woodworth.

7. Bryant, *What I Saw*, 79–80.

8. Ibid., 76.

9. Roberts, "Traveling," 4.

10. Carroll D. Hall, ed., *Donner Miscellany: 41 Diaries and Documents* (San Francisco: Book Club of California, 1947), 15.

11. Bryant, *What I Saw*, 102–103.

12. Julie Fanselow, *The Traveler's Guide to the Oregon Trail* (Helena, Montana: Falcon Press Publishing Co., 1992), 75–77.

13. Morgan, *Overland in 1846*, Vol. I, 258.

CHAPTER 23: SAGE ADVICE, JUNE 26–27, 1846

1. Douglas Pappas and Lester C. Hunt, *Wyoming, A Guide to Its History, Highways, and People*, Federal Writers' Project (New York: Oxford University Press, 1941), 6, 72. The federal government established Wyoming Territory on July 25, 1868. It was admitted to the Union as the forty-fourth state on July 10, 1890.

2. Julie Fanselow, *The Traveler's Guide to the Oregon Trail* (Helena, MT: Falcon Press Publishing Co., 1992), 87–90.

3. David Walker Lupton, "Fort Bernard on the Oregon Trail," *Nebraska History*, Vol. 60, No. 1 (1979), 24.

4. John D. Unruh Jr., *The Plains Across: The Overland Emigrants and the Trans-Mississippi West, 1840–1860* (Urbana, Chicago, London: University of Illinois Press, 1979), 251.

5. Ibid.

6. Morgan, *Overland in 1846*, Vol. II, 574–575. George Curry, using his pen name, Laon, drafted the dispatch at Fort Bernard on June 25, 1846. He added a postscript the next day. It was published in the *St. Louis Weekly Reveille* on August 10, 1846.

7. Bryant, *What I Saw*, 113.

8. Ibid.

9. Bernard DeVoto, *The Year of Decision, 1846* (Boston: Little, Brown & Co., 1942), 168.

10. Bryant, *What I Saw*, 113–114.
11. George Donner's letter was written at Fort Bernard on June 27, 1846, and published in the *Sangamo Journal* on August 19, 1846. It appeared on page 2 with an editor's note: "The following letter from an old neighbor has been politely communicated to us for publication."
12. Houghton, *The Expedition*, 27–28.
13. DeVoto, *The Year of Decision*, 181.
14. Lupton, "Fort Bernard," 30.
15. Parkman, *The Oregon Trail*, 108.
16. Ibid., 108–109.
17. Ibid., 108.
18. DeVoto, *The Year of Decision*, 181.
19. Ibid., 183–184.
20. Kristin Johnson, "The Reed Family," *New Light on the Donner Party*, http://www .utahcrossroads.org/DonnerParty, Utah Crossroads Chapter, Oregon-California Trails Association.
21. DeVoto, *The Year of Decision*, 54–55, 58.
22. Ibid., 116–117.
23. Charles L. Camp, ed., *James Clyman, American Frontiersman, 1792–1881: The Adventures of a Trapper and Covered Wagon Emigrant as Told in His Own Reminiscences and Diaries* (San Francisco: California Historical Society, 1928), 228.
24. DeVoto, *The Year of Decision*, 184.
25. Lansford W. Hastings, *The Emigrants' Guide to Oregon and California* (Cincinnati, OH: George Conclin, 1845), 137–138.
26. Camp, *James Clyman*, 229.
27. Ibid.

CHAPTER 24: A SENSE OF URGENCY,
JUNE 28–JULY 12, 1846

1. David Walker Lupton, "Fort Bernard on the Oregon Trail," *Nebraska History*, Vol. 60, No. 1 (1979), 31.
2. Bryant, *What I Saw*, 114–115.
3. Lupton, "Fort Bernard," 32.
4. Houghton, *The Expedition*, 28–29.
5. Murphy, *Across the Plains*, 18–19.
6. Morgan, *Overland in 1846*, Vol. II, 582–583. Charles Stanton's letter to his brother, Sidney Stanton, was written on July 5, 1846, and was published in the *New York Herald* on October 25, 1846.
7. Ibid., 583.
8. Ibid., 584.
9. Houghton, *The Expedition*, 24–25.
10. J. Quinn Thornton, *Oregon and California in 1848*, Vol. I (New York: Harper & Brothers Publishers, 1849), 114.
11. Bryant, *What I Saw*, 118.
12. Hall, *Donner Miscellany*, 16.
13. Bryant, *What I Saw*, 120.
14. Murphy, *Across the Plains*, 18.
15. Bryant, *What I Saw*, 120–121.

16. Thornton, *Oregon and California*, 119–120.
17. Hall, *Donner Miscellany*, 16.
18. Murphy, *Across the Plains*, 18–19.
19. Ibid., 19.
20. Morgan, *Overland in 1846*, Vol. II, 612.
21. Ibid.
22. Ibid., 613.
23. Hall, *Donner Miscellany*, 16.
24. Morgan, *Overland in 1846*, Vol. I, 278–279.

CHAPTER 25: PARTING OF THE WAYS,
JULY 13–19, 1846

1. Morgan, *Overland in 1846*, Vol. II, 614.
2. Ibid., 771–772.
3. Bryant, *What I Saw*, 127, 133–134. Bonney hid by day to avoid Indian hunters or war parties. He made it back to his home in Oxford, Ohio, where he remained for the rest of his life. He died in Oxford on June 10, 1887, two weeks before his eightieth birthday.
4. Ibid.
5. Morgan, *Overland in 1846*, Vol. II, 616.
6. Ibid.
7. Ibid., 618.
8. Ibid.
9. Morgan, *Overland in 1846*, Vol. II, 615.
10. Ibid., 619.
11. Ibid.
12. Hall, *Donner Miscellany*, 17.
13. Frank Mullen Jr., *The Donner Party Chronicles* (Reno: Nevada Humanities Committee, 1997), 101.
14. Hall, *Donner Miscellany*, 17.
15. Thornton, *Oregon and California*, 142–143.

CHAPTER 26: THE DONNER PARTY, JULY 20–28, 1846

1. Robert Nelson, *Enemy of the Saints: The Biography of Governor Lilburn W. Boggs of Missouri* (Baltimore: PublishAmerica, 2011), 154–155.
2. Guy L. Dorius, "Crossroads in the West: The Intersections of the Donner Party and the Mormons," *Nauvoo Journal*, Vol. 9, No. 1 (1997), 18. Levinah (pronounced luh-VINE-uh) was sometimes spelled Lavinia or Levina, but the correct spelling is Levinah. Her two oldest daughters were married in a double ceremony on December 29, 1842, in Clark County, Missouri.
3. Orson Pratt Brown, "The Life & Times of Orson Pratt Brown," www.orson prattbrown.com/murphy-dfraper/jeremiah-and-levina-jackson-murphy.html. Raised as Baptists in South Carolina, Jeremiah and Levinah Murphy joined the Mormon Church in 1836 while living in Tennessee.
4. Joseph A. King, *Winter of Entrapment: A New Look at the Donner Party* (Toronto: P. D. Meany, 1992), 18.
5. Ibid., 5–6.
6. Ibid., 6.

7. Ibid., 11–12.
8. Ibid.
9. Ibid., 16.
10. Thornton, *Oregon and California*, Vol. I, 142–143.
11. Hall, *Donner Miscellany*, 18.
12. Ibid.

CHAPTER 27: BETRAYED, JULY 28–31, 1846

1. Bryant, *What I Saw*, 145.
2. Ibid., 135, 136, 141.
3. G. B. Dobson, "Wyoming Tales and Trails," www.wyomingtalesandtrails.com/bridger.html.
4. Wallis, *The Wild West*, 16.
5. Bryant, *What I Saw*, 143.
6. Ibid., 142.
7. Ibid., 144.
8. Ibid.
9. Ibid.
10. Ibid., 621, 763. Joe Walker left Fort Bridger on about July 25, 1846.
11. Peter R. Limburg, *Deceived: The Story of the Donner Party* (Pacifica, CA: IPS Books, 1998), 54.
12. Bryant, *What I Saw*, 145.
13. Morgan, *Overland in 1846*, Vol. I, 415, n. 18.
14. Ibid., 414, n. 3.
15. Shirley Ann Wilson Moore, *Sweet Freedom's Plains: African Americans on the Overland Trails, 1841–1869*, for the National Park Service, National Trails Intermountain Region, Salt Lake City and Santa Fe, January 31, 2012, 83–88.
16. Morgan, *Overland in 1846*, Vol. 1, 415–416.
17. Ibid., Vol. II, 775.
18. Bryant, *What I Saw*, 144. Bryant wrote in his journal, "I heard of an instance of a pint of miserable whiskey being sold for a pair of buckskin pantaloons, valued at ten dollars. I saw two dollars in money paid for half a pint."
19. Morgan, *Overland in 1846*, Vol. I, 263, 434. Some historians referred to Halloran as a "waif," but he was a merchant in St. Joseph, Missouri, whose store at the corner of Main and Jules streets carried a variety of spices, condiments, cutlery, and tools as well as everything from hip boots and hats to padlocks and Norfolk thumb latches for securing doors and gates.
20. Houghton, *The Expedition*, 33.
21. Kelly J. Dixon, Julie M. Schablitsky, and Shannon A. Novak, eds., *An Archaeology of Desperation: Exploring the Donner Party's Alder Creek Camp* (Norman: University of Oklahoma Press, 2011), 35.
22. Kristin Johnson, "Teamsters and Others," *New Light on the Donner Party*, http://www.utahcrossroads.org/DonnerParty/Teamsters.htm, Utah Crossroads Chapter, Oregon-California Trails Association.
23. DeVoto, *The Year of Decision*, 318–319.
24. Morgan, *Overland in 1846*, Vol. I, 279–280.
25. Ibid.

CHAPTER 28: THE HASTINGS CUTOFF,
AUGUST 1–22, 1846

1. Houghton, *The Expedition*, 34.
2. Hall, *Donner Miscellany*, 19.
3. Ibid.
4. Joseph A. King, *Winter of Entrapment: A New Look at the Donner Party* (Toronto: P. D. Meany, 1992), 25.
5. Ibid.
6. Ibid., 25–26.
7. DeVoto, *The Year of Decision*, 319–320.
8. Morgan, *Overland in 1846*, Vol. II, 620.
9. Michael Wallis and Michael S. Wiliamson, *The Lincoln Highway: Coast to Coast from Times Square to the Golden Gate* (New York and London: W. W. Norton & Co., 2007), 226.
10. Murphy, *Across the Plains*, 20.
11. Mullen, *The Donner Party Chronicles*, 114.
12. W. W. Allen and R. B. Avery, *California Gold Book: First Nugget, Its Discovery and Discoverers and Some of the Results Proceeding Therefrom* (San Francisco and Chicago: Donohue & Hennebery, 1893), 63. This book was written primarily to document the authenticity of the first piece of gold discovered at Sutter's Fort. The authors also discussed some of the early travelers on the California Trail, including the Harlan-Young Party of 1846.
13. The Harlan Family in America, *History of George Harlan*, Recollections of his daughter, Mary Ann Harlan Smith, http://www.harlanfamily.org/GeorgeH852 .htm. The Harlan Family in America is a nonprofit association formed in 1987 to perpetuate and promote the Harlan family heritage and genealogy. The family genealogy is documented in *The History and Genealogy of the Harlan Family* by Alpheus Harlan, originally published in 1914.
14. Murphy, *Across the Plains*, 20–21.
15. Mullen, *The Donner Party Chronicles*, 118.
16. Gary Topping, "Overland Emigration, the California Trail, and the Hastings Cutoff," *Utah Historical Quarterly*, Vol. 56, No. 2 (1988), 121.
17. J. Roderic Korns, *West from Fort Bridger: The Pioneering of the Immigrant Trails across Utah, 1846–1850* (Salt Lake City: Utah State Historical Society, 1951), 198.
18. Topping, "Overland Emigration," 121.
19. Hall, *Donner Miscellany*, 20.
20. Murphy, *Across the Plains*, 21.
21. Kristin Johnson, ed., *"Unfortunate Emigrants": Narratives of the Donner Party* (Logan: Utah State University Press, 1996), 213, 214, 216.
22. George R. Stewart, *Ordeal by Hunger: The Story of the Donner Party* (Boston and New York: Houghton Mifflin Co., 1963), 36.
23. Lee Kreutzer, National Historic Trails Audio Tour Route Interpretive Guide, *Utah—Crossroads of the West* (Salt Lake City: National Park Service, National Trails—Intermountain Region, 2010), 14.
24. Hall, *Donner Miscellany*, 21.

CHAPTER 29: THE FEARFUL LONG DRIVE,
AUGUST 23–SEPTEMBER 10, 1846

1. Murphy, *Across the Plains*, 21.
2. "Salt Lake Desert," *The American Southwest*, http://www.americansouthwest.net/utah/salt_lake_desert/.
3. Morgan, *Overland in 1846*, Vol. I, 289.
4. J. Roderic Korns, *West from Fort Bridger: The Pioneering of the Immigrant Trails across Utah, 1846–1850* (Salt Lake City: Utah Historical Society, 1951), 207.
5. Houghton, *The Expedition*, 36. Eliza Donner, a little girl at the time of Halloran's death in Utah, recalled that instead of his body being put in a coffin, it was "wrapped in sheets and carefully enclosed in a buffalo robe, then reverently laid to rest in a grave on the shore of Great Salt Lake, near that of a stranger, who had been buried by the Hastings party a few weeks earlier." Her statement is only partly correct. Halloran was not buried wrapped in a bison robe but was laid to rest in a coffin built of wooden boards taken from one of the emigrant wagons.
6. Korns, *West from Fort Bridger*, 141.
7. Ibid., 207.
8. Ibid.
9. Ethan Rarick, *Desperate Passage: The Donner Party's Perilous Journey West* (New York: Oxford University Press, 2008), 33–34.
10. "Behold, I will do a new thing; now it shall spring forth; shall ye not know it? I will even make a way in the wilderness, *and* rivers in the desert," Isaiah 43:19, King James Version.
11. Brian Butko, *Greetings from the Lincoln Highway: America's First Coast-to-Coast Road* (Mechanicsburg, PA: Stackpole Books, 2005), 217.
12. David M. Rosen, *The Donner Party*, "Log Entries for August 1846," http://www.donnerpartydiary.com/Aug46.htm.
13. Houghton, *The Expedition*, 39–40.
14. Ibid., 40.
15. Rush Spedden, "The Fearful Long Drive," *Overland Journal*, Vol. 12, No. 2 (1994), 11.
16. Bryant, *What I Saw*, 238, 243.
17. Mullen, *The Donner Party Chronicles*, 136.
18. Murphy, *Across the Plains*, 22.
19. Eddy Breen, recovering from his broken leg, and Philippine Keseberg with her nursing baby boy were unable to walk and rode in wagons. William Baylis, the Reeds' albino handyman, rode in a wagon during the day but more than likely walked at night.
20. Mullen, *The Donner Party Chronicles*, 138.
21. Houghton, *The Expedition*, 41.
22. Ibid.
23. J. Quinn Thornton, *Oregon and California in 1848*, Vol. I (New York: Harper & Brothers, 1849), 105–106.
24. Korns, *West from Fort Bridger*, 210.
25. Mullen, *The Donner Party Chronicles*, 140.
26. Murphy, *Across the Plains*, 22, 24.
27. Ibid., 14.
28. Mullen, *The Donner Party Chronicles*, 142.
29. David M. Rosen, *The Donner Party*, "Log Entries for September 1846," http://

www.donnerpartydiary.com/sep46.htm. A few of the many myths about the Donner Party concern the famous Reed family wagon that is still often referred to as the "Pioneer Palace Car" or the "Palace Wagon." Neither of these names was ever used when the Donner Party was on the California Trail. The name first appeared in an 1891 memoir written by Virginia Reed Murphy. Another myth claims that the family wagon was not only left in the salt desert but was buried there, but that is not true. Only the feather bed and cookstove from the large family wagon were abandoned in the desert. The wagon was neither buried nor left in the desert. In his diary entries and elsewhere, James Reed makes reference to this wagon, such as his entry dated Wednesday, September 9, 1846, in which he describes accepting borrowed cattle from Graves, Pike, and Breen so he could "bring his family waggon along."

30. Ibid.
31. Eliza W. Farnham, *California In-door and Out* (New York: Edwards & Co., 1856), 399.

CHAPTER 30: RACE AGAINST TIME, SEPTEMBER 11–OCTOBER 4, 1846

1. Korns, *West from Fort Bridger*, 214–215.
2. Rosen, "Log Entries for September 1846," http://www.donnerpartydiary.com/sep46.htm. James Reed's account of McCutchen and Stanton volunteering to ride ahead to California first appeared in an 1871 article in the *Pacific Rural Press*. In an article published in the *Century Illustrated Monthly Magazine* in 1891, Virginia Reed also wrote about C. T. Stanton and William McCutchen and how they "bravely offered their services and started on bearing letters from the company to Captain Sutter asking for relief."
3. Korns, *West from Fort Bridger*, 216.
4. Bryant, *What I Saw*, 190.
5. Ibid. Bryant did not identify the two members of the party who were brandishing rifles during the altercation. He did comment in his journal that the "ebullition of anger was soon allayed" and the mule team commenced the day's march on time.
6. Korns, *West from Fort Bridger*, 216.
7. Ibid.
8. Ibid., 218.
9. Rosen, "Log Entries for September 1846."
10. Lee Kreutzer, National Historic Trails Audio Tour Route Interpretive Guide, *Across Nevada* (Salt Lake City: National Park Service, National Trails—Intermountain Region, 2012), 18–19.
11. Ibid., 2, 4. Frémont named the river for the German botanist Alexander von Humboldt. Western Historian Dale Morgan called the Humboldt "the most necessary river of America, and the most hated."
12. Ibid., 18.
13. Allan Lonnberg, "The Digger Indian Stereotype in California," *Journal of California and Great Basin Anthropology*, Vol. 3, No. 2 (1981), 215–216. In this article, the author includes a quote from George C. Yount (1794–1865), the first U.S. citizen to be ceded a Spanish land grant in the Napa Valley (1836). On Yount's lavish tombstone in Yountville, California, the inscription reads in part ". . . he was the true embodiment of the finest qualities of an advancing civilization blending

with the existing primitive culture." The quote from Yount's pioneer diary reads: "In their wanderings for a place of encampment, the party first encountered that species of Red Man peculiar to California and the Sierra Nevada Range. From their mode of living on roots and reptiles, insects and vermin, they have been called Diggers. In fact, they almost burrow into the ground like the mole and are almost as blind to everything comely. At the time our trappers supposed they had found the lowest dregs of humanity. But . . . they were in error. They were destined to find a race lower than these."

14. Korns, *West from Fort Bridger*, 218.
15. Ibid., 220.
16. Ibid.
17. Rosen, "Log Entries for September 1846."
18. Ibid.

CHAPTER 31: BLOOD RAGE, OCTOBER 5–20, 1846

1. Laura Engelhardt, "The Problem with Eyewitness Testimony," *Stanford Journal of Legal Studies*, Vol. 1, Issue 1 (1999), 27–28. This journal article was based on a talk by Barbara Tversky, professor of psychology, and George Fisher, professor of law, sponsored by the *Stanford Journal of Legal Studies*. "Once witnesses state facts in a particular way or identify a particular person as the perpetrator, they are unwilling or even unable—due to the reconstruction of their memory—to reconsider their initial understanding. . . . Although juries and decision-makers place great reliance on eyewitness identification, they are often unaware of the danger of false memories," 27. "Bias creeps into memory without our knowledge, without our awareness. While confidence and accuracy are generally correlated, when misleading information is given, witness confidence is often higher for the incorrect information than for the correct information. This leads many to question the competence of the average person to determine credibility issues," 28.
2. Korns, *West from Fort Bridger*, 221. "That Reed was interrupted in the middle of this entry and never completed it, is one of the fascinating features of the [James Reed] diary. It seems likely that on October 4 the detachment of the company with which Reed was traveling moved down the river from 10 to 15 miles to encamp for the night in the vicinity of Redhouse."
3. Houghton, *The Expedition*, 47. In her account of the activities of October 5, 1846, this Donner daughter mistakenly places the scene at Gravelly Ford, a common error and one of the oldest myths in the Donner Party story. As was often the case, some of the primary sources who perpetuated such misinformation were members of the company who in their later years relied on faulty memories. Although the Gravelly Ford location was discredited by most reputable researchers by 1960, the misinformation persisted for many more years.
4. Ibid.
5. Murphy, "Across the Plains in the Donner Party: A Personal Narrative of the Overland Trip to California," as printed in *The Century Illustrated Monthly Magazine*, Vol. 42, New Series Vol. 20, May 1891–October 1891 (New York: The Century Co., 1891), 418. Like Eliza Donner did in her memoir, the adult Virginia Reed mistakenly placed the October 5, 1846, confrontation between her father and John Snyder at Gravelly Ford.
6. Mullen, *The Donner Party Chronicles*, 168–169.

7. George R. Stewart, *Ordeal by Hunger: The Story of the Donner Party* (Boston and New York: Houghton Mifflin Co., 1963), 64.

8. Murphy, *Across the Plains*, 418–419.

9. Stewart, *The California Trail*, 64–65.

10. Lee Kreutzer, National Historic Trails Audio Tour Route Interpretive Guide, *Across Nevada* (Salt Lake City: National Park Service, National Trails—Intermountain Region, 2012), 28.

11. Murphy, *Across the Plains*, 419.

12. Kristin Johnson, Donner Blog, "John Snyder's Grave," May 27, 2013, http://donnerblog.blogspot.com/. As is the case with so many aspects of the Donner Party story, there has been much discussion about the precise location of the confrontation between Snyder and Reed and Snyder's burial site. The majority of trail historians, such as Johnson, accept a site near what is today called Iron Point, Nevada, and not the Gravelly Ford site.

13. Murphy, *Across the Plains*, 420.

14. Daniel James Brown, *The Indifferent Stars Above* (New York: HarperCollins Publishers, 2010), 109–110.

15. Rosen, "Log Entries for October 1846," http://www.donnerpartydiary.com/oct46.htm.

16. Murphy, *Across the Plains*, 420.

17. Mullen, *The Donner Party Chronicles*, 170.

18. Rosen, "Log Entries for October 1846."

19. Murphy, *Across the Plains*, 420.

20. Rosen, "Log Entries for October 1846."

21. Mullen, *The Donner Party Chronicles*.

22. Family Tales, Benjamin Lippincott letter to John Stephens, February 6, 1847, http://www.familytales.org/results.php?collection=55.

23. Ibid. It is not known whether the Donner Party respectfully reinterred Sallee's bones or did nothing and simply rode on. Although there is no known record of when it took place, Sallee's remains were eventually collected and brought back to Callaway County, Missouri, where he was given a proper funeral and buried with many members of the Sallee family in the Richland Baptist Cemetery near Kingdom City, Missouri.

24. Houghton, *The Expedition*, 52. In her memoir, Eliza recalled that her father, George Donner, listened thoughtfully to the accounts of Hardcoop's abandonment. She added that "he could not but feel deeply the bitterness of such a fate."

25. Brown, *The Indifferent Stars*, 106.

26. Stewart, *Ordeal by Hunger*, 70.

27. Mullen, *The Donner Party Chronicles*, 174.

28. Ibid.

29. Ibid.

30. Ibid.

31. Kreutzer, *Across Nevada*, 36.

32. Peter R. Limburg, *Deceived: The Story of the Donner Party* (Pacifica, California: IOPS Books, 1998), 96.

33. Rosen, "Log Entries for October 1846."

34. Brown, The *Indifferent Stars*, 108.

35. Kreutzer, *Across Nevada*, 43. When the Donner Party reached Truckee Meadows,

it was the land of the Washoe tribe, the Wa She Shu, who called the meadow Welgonuh. Today Truckee Meadows is the site of Reno, Nevada.

CHAPTER 32: PERSEVERANCE, OCTOBER 21–30, 1846

1. Eliza W. Farnham, *California In-door and Out* (New York: Edwards & Co., 1856), 401. The Breens were among the most vocal advocates of not camping in Truckee Meadow but pushing on before big snowfalls occurred.
2. James Frazier Reed, "Narrative of the Sufferings of a Company of Emigrants in the Mountains of California in the Winter of '46 and '47," *Illinois Journal* (Springfield), December 9, 1847.
3. James Frazier Reed, "The Snow-Bound, Starved Emigrants of 1846," *Pacific Rural Press* (San Francisco), March 25, April 1, 1871.
4. Ibid.
5. John D. Unruh Jr., *The Plains Across: The Overland Emigrants and the Trans-Mississippi West, 1840–60* (Urbana: University of Illinois Press, 1979), 365.
6. Ibid.
7. Albert L. Hurtado, *John Sutter: A Life on the North American Frontier* (Norman: University of Oklahoma Press, 2006), 205.
8. Scott Lankford, *Tahoe Beneath the Surface: The Hidden Stories of America's Largest Mountain Lake* (Berkeley, CA: Heyday and Sierra College Press, 2010), 82; Donald L. Hardesty, *The Archaeology of the Donner Party* (Reno: University of Nevada Press, 1997), 134, n. 6. Some sources claim that the Miwok names of Luis and Salvador were Eema Ochej and Queyuen, respectively.
9. Hurtado, *John Sutter*, 38–39. The origins of the Indian boy remain unknown. Because Carson and the mountain man who sold the boy to Sutter traveled throughout the West, the boy could have come from any of several tribes.
10. Lankford, *Tahoe*, 82–84.
11. Ibid., 84.
12. Rosen, "Log Entries for October 1846," http://www.donnerpartydiary.com/oct46.htm.
13. Guy L. Dorius, "Crossroads in the West: The Intersections of the Donner Party and the Mormons," *Nauvoo Journal*, Vol. 9, No.1 (Spring 1997), 18. Levinah Murphy's son William Murphy was a small boy when his two older sisters met and wed their husbands. He spoke of the nuptials in an address he delivered in Truckee, California, on February 8, 1896. Some of his remarks were included in the Dorius article: "[The] river closed with ice for the winter—a long dreary winter it was indeed. And yet to some it was not without its romance; as the two elder children, girls, were married on the boat that winter, one to the Mate, and the other to the Engineer; and with early spring, the released boat acted as a wedding barge, and reached St. Louis safe but not overly sound."
14. Ibid., 19.
15. Ibid. Other varying accounts state that prior to his death, Pike lingered from twenty minutes to two hours. All of them make mention of the young man's pain and great suffering.
16. Mary A. M. Murphy, letter written May 25, 1847, California Territory, www.rootsweb.ancestry.com/~tnweakle/3Murphy_Letters.htm.
17. Mullen, *The Donner Party Chronicles*, 186.
18. Farnham, *California*, 401.
19. Ibid.

20. Virginia Reed Murphy, "Across the Plains in the Donner Party: A Personal Narrative of the Overland Trip to California," as printed in *The Century Illustrated Monthly Magazine*, Vol. 42, New Series Vol. 20, May 1891–October 1891 (New York: The Century Co., 1891), 421.

21. Ibid.

22. J. Quinn Thornton, *The California Tragedy*, California Centennial Edition, copyright by Joseph A. Sullivan (Oakland: Biobooks, 1945), 27.

23. Houghton, *The Expedition*, 58–59. When Eliza Donner wrote her book that was published in 1911, she relied on many accounts told to her by older siblings and members of the company because she was only three years old in 1846. One of her sources was her half sister Elitha Donner, ten years older than Eliza. In her account, which appeared in Eliza's book, Elitha described the wagon accident in detail, including the rescue of the two young Donner daughters. "Father and uncle, in great alarm, rushed to your rescue. Georgia was soon hauled out safely through the opening in the back of the wagon sheets, but you were nowhere in sight, and father was sure you were smothering because you did not answer his call. They worked breathlessly getting things out, and finally uncle came to your limp form. You could not have lasted much longer, they said."

24. Ibid.

CHAPTER 33: SNOWBOUND, NOVEMBER 1846

1. Mullen, *The Donner Party Chronicles*, 188.

2. Mark McLaughlin, *The Donner Party: Weathering the Storm* (Carnelian Bay, CA: Mic Mac Publishing, 2007), vii. Weather and cultural historian Mark McLaughlin has lived in the Lake Tahoe, Nevada, area since 1978. He has taught at Sierra College, Rocklin, California, in the foothills of the Sierra Nevadas.

3. Ibid., 7.

4. Frederick J. Teggart, editor and curator of the Academy of Pacific Coast History, *Diary of Patrick Breen—One of the Donner Party* (Dillon, CO: VistaBooks, 1991), 5.

5. Farnham, *California*, 403.

6. Ibid., 404.

7. Ibid., 404–405.

8. Ibid., 405.

9. Ethan Rarick, *Desperate Passage: The Donner Party's Perilous Journey West* (New York: Oxford University Press, 2008), 108.

10. C. F. McGlashan, *History of the Donner Party: A Tragedy of the Sierra* (Truckee, CA: Crowley & McGlashan, 1879), 207.

11. Mullen, *The Donner Party Chronicles*, 192.

12. Limburg, *Deceived*, 108–109.

13. McGlashan, *History*, 58.

14. Ibid., 209.

15. Ibid.

16. Murphy, "Across the Plains," 421.

17. McGlashan, *History*, 209.

18. Lansford W. Hastings, *The Emigrants' Guide to Oregon and California* (Cincinnati, Ohio: George Conclin, stereotyped by Shepherd & Co., 1845), 144.

19. Kelly J. Dixon, Julie M. Schablitsky, and Shannon A. Novak, *An Archaeology of*

Desperation: Exploring the Donner Party's Alder Creek Camp (Norman: University of Oklahoma Press, 2011), 38.

20. Ibid.

21. Marshall Fey, "The Alder Creek Trail," *Donner Summit Heirloom*, Issue 45 (May 2012), 8. The exact site of the Donner camp, often referred to as the lower camp or river camp, has always been the subject of dispute. According to Fey, "Fortunately, many early trail researchers were able to examine the beginning of the trail at the future site of the Prosser House before the area was hidden under the waters of Prosser Reservoir in the mid 1960s. John Markle's 1849 diary . . . was the early proof of the Donner Family campsite." In his diary, Markle stated that the "Donner camp site could be seen from a high point near the junction of these two creeks [Prosser and Alder]. And this was the only place one could stand and look toward the head of Alder Creek Valley and see the two [Donner] tree stumps. Cut at snow level, the more than 12 foot high stumps could be viewed 2 miles away."

22. David M. Rosen, *The Donner Party*, "Log Entries for November 1846," http://www.donnerpartydiary.com/nov46.htm. Trudeau's remarks were published in the *San Francisco Call* on October 11, 1891, from an earlier interview he had given to a correspondent from the *St. Louis Republic*.

23. Ibid.

24. Dixon, Schablitsky, and Novak, *An Archaeology of Desperation*, 40. In her 1911 book, George Donner's daughter Eliza Donner Houghton claimed that the three single men with the party and a fourth from the lake camp who later joined them built a hut, but there is no evidence of its existence. Three other Donner daughters all wrote that the single men lived in their family tent.

25. Houghton, *The Expedition*, 64–65.

26. Donald L. Hardesty, *The Archaeology of the Donner Party* (Reno: University of Nevada Press, 1997), 49.

27. Rosen, "Log Entries for November 1846."

28. Ibid.

29. Kristin Johnson, *New Light on the Donner Party*, http://user.xmission.com/~octa/DonnerParty/Statistics.htm.

CHAPTER 34: DESPERATE TIMES, DESPERATE MEASURES, NOVEMBER–DECEMBER 1846

1. Bryant, *What I Saw*, 346–347.

2. Fred Blackburn Rogers, *William Brown Ide, Bear Flagger* (San Francisco, California: John Howell Books, 1962), 44.

3. John Carroll Power, *Early Settlers of Sangamon County, Illinois* (Springfield: Edwin A. Wilson, 1876), 428.

4. Ibid., 35.

5. Ibid., 45. Todd's initial rendering of a grizzly bear was said to have looked more like a hog. The priceless memento of the Bear Flag Revolt was destroyed in the 1906 San Francisco earthquake.

6. Bryant, *What I Saw*, 347.

7. James K. Polk, *The Diary of James K. Polk during His Presidency, 1845–1849*, Vol. 1, edited and annotated by Milo Milton Quaife (Chicago: A. C. McClung & Co., 1910), 413, n. 36. The diary was first printed from the original manuscript in the collections of the Chicago Historical Society. Along with a mass of letters and mis-

cellaneous papers preserved by Polk, the diary remained in the possession of the Polk family until 1901, when it was purchased by the Chicago Historical Society.

8. Bryant, *What I Saw*. Edward Meyer Kern, a topographer for John C. Frémont's third expedition in 1845, was placed in command of Sutter's Fort, also known as New Helvetia and Fort Sacramento, during the Bear Flag Revolt.

9. Kristin Johnson, ed., *"Unfortunate Emigrants": Narratives of the Donner Party* (Logan: Utah State University Press, 1996), 193.

10. Richard F. Kaufman, *Saving the Donner Party and Forlorn Hope* (Bloomington, IN: Archway Publishing, 2014), 28.

11. Mullen, *The Donner Party Chronicles*, 190.

12. Johnson, *Unfortunate Emigrants*, 193.

13. Morgan, *Overland in 1846*, Vol. I, 447, n. 115.

14. Johnson, *"Unfortunate Emigrants,"* 194.

15. Ibid.

16. Ibid., 195.

17. Daniel James Brown, *The Indifferent Stars Above* (New York: HarperCollins Publishers, 2010), 126.

18. DeVoto, *The Year of Decision*, 356.

19. Brown, *The Indifferent Stars*, 126–127.

20. Mullen, *The Donner Party Chronicles*, 198.

21. DeVoto, *The Year of Decision*, 356.

22. Hardesty, *The Archaeology*, 47, 111. In 1980, Hardesty, a University of Nevada anthropology professor, led a team that excavated the site of the Murphy-Eddy cabin at Donner Lake. They tested burned bones that proved to be from a bear, most likely a grizzly that had been roasted.

23. Mullen, *The Donner Party Chronicles*, 202.

24. Frederick J. Teggart, editor and curator of the Academy of Pacific Coast History, *Diary of Patrick Breen One of the Donner Party* (Dillon, CO: VistaBooks, 1991), 3–5. Breen gave the diary to George McKinstry, who in 1871 gave it to historian and publisher Hubert Howe Bancroft. In summarizing the Donner Party's experience in the Sierras, Bancroft described the diary as "the most precious and fascinating record of these events." He also considered it "one of the most highly prized treasures of my library." In 1905, Bancroft gave the diary to the University of California as part of the Bancroft Collection, where it remains in the special collections of the Bancroft Library at the University of California–Berkeley.

25. Ibid., 5.

26. Johnson, *"Unfortunate Emigrants,"* 221.

27. Teggart, *Diary of Patrick Breen*, 5.

28. Rosen, "Log Entries for November 1846," http://www.donnerpartydiary.com/nov46.htm.

29. Proclamation of Thanksgiving by Abraham Lincoln, www.abrahamlincoln online.org/lincoln/speeches/thanks.htm. Sarah Hale, author and editor of *Godey's Lady's Book* for more than forty years, launched a letter-writing campaign in November 1846 in an effort to make the last Thursday in November a national holiday called Thanksgiving Day. Seventeen years later, her goal was achieved when on October 3, 1863, President Abraham Lincoln issued the official Proclamation of Thanksgiving. George Washington was the first president to proclaim a day of thanksgiving, issuing his proclamation on October 3, 1789,

exactly seventy-four years before Lincoln issued his. Hale, a prolific author, also wrote or cowrote the famous "Mary Had a Little Lamb," published in 1830.

30. Hall, *Donner Miscellany*, 36.
31. Teggart, *Diary of Patrick Breen*, 5–6.
32. Mullen, *The Donner Party Chronicles*, 220.
33. Rosen, "Log Entries for November 1846."
34. Mullen, *The Donner Party Chronicles*, 22.
35. Houghton, *The Expedition*, 64–65.

CHAPTER 35: THE FORLORN HOPE, DECEMBER 1846

1. Richard F. Kaufman, *Saving the Donner Party and Forlorn Hope* (Bloomington, Indiana: Archway Publishing, 2014), 62.
2. Teggart, *Diary of Patrick Breen*, 7. The December 17, 1846, entry in Patrick Breen's diary states, "Bealis [sic] died night before last," making his death date December 15. Credible sources agree with that date. However, other equally credible sources maintain that Baylis Williams died on December 14.
3. Murphy, "Across the Plains," 423.
4. John Carroll Power, *History of the Early Settlers of Sangamon County, Illinois* (Springfield, Illinois: Edwin A. Wilson & Co., 1876), 1022.
5. C. F. McGlashan, *History of the Donner Party: A Tragedy of the Sierra* (Truckee, CA: Crowley & McGlashan, 1879), 95.
6. Houghton, *The Expedition*, 69.
7. McGlashan, *History*, 95.
8. Houghton, *The Expedition*, 69.
9. Ibid.
10. Hall, *Donner Miscellany*, 10.
11. Johnson, *"Unfortunate Emigrants,"* 40, n. 54.
12. Houghton, *The Expedition*, 69.
13. Ibid.
14. Ibid., 70.
15. Robyn Fivush, "Children's Recollections of Traumatic and Nontraumatic Events," *Development and Psychopathology*, Vol. 10, Issue 4 (Cambridge, U.K.: Cambridge University Press, 1998), 699, 700, 702. When various books and articles about the Donner Party began to emerge, including those written by members of the emigrant company, the veracity of anyone who had been a child at the time was often called into question. Frequently it was suggested that a small child could not possibly recall any details. Although it was true that there were discrepancies in dates and names, some incidents were altered, and details were unknowingly or intentionally omitted, not all of the children's memories, including traumatic experiences, were repressed or forgotten. According to the report cited here by Robyn Fivush, a psychologist from Emory University, there are "striking similarities in the development of young children's ability to recall traumatic and nontraumatic events. From about age 3 years on, children can give reasonably coherent accounts of their past experiences and can retain these memories over long durations." The report went on to state that it is "abundantly clear that even quite young children have well-organized, accurate memories of their past experience" and can recall those memories much later in their lives. It was also noted that even traumatic incidents that might have been

repressed are often "recoverable" in later years. Other studies of children's recall of stress shows that in many instances, children not only retain memories of stressful situations but continue to be emotionally affected by events experienced in early childhood. In some cases, the highly traumatic events experienced in childhood might have long-term consequences for later psychological well-being.

16. Houghton, *The Expedition*, 70.
17. Ibid., 70–71.
18. Teggart, *Diary of Patrick Breen*, 7.
19. Stewart, *Ordeal by Hunger*, 119–120.
20. Mullen, *The Donner Party Chronicles*, 228.
21. Ibid.
22. Brown, *The Indifferent Stars*, 144.
23. Mark McLaughlin, *The Donner Party: Weathering the Storm* (Carnelian Bay, CA: Mic Mac Publishing, 2007), 49–50.
24. Kaufman, *Saving the Donner Party*, 65.
25. Ibid.
26. McGlashan, *History*, 71–72.
27. *Oxford Dictionaries* (Oxford University Press, 2015), http://www.oxforddiction aries.com/us/definition/english/forlorn-hope.
28. McLaughlin, *The Donner Party*, 51–52.
29. McGlashan, *History*, 73.
30. Morgan, *Overland in 1846*, Vol. II, 466–467. After Stanton's death, George McKinstry wrote to Philip Stanton, who replied in a letter dated February 14, 1848, which chronicled Charles Stanton's life.
31. McGlashan, *History*, 76–77.

CHAPTER 36: CAMP OF DEATH, DECEMBER 1846

1. Kaufman, *Saving the Donner Party*, 50.
2. Stephen A. McCurdy, "Epidemiology of Disaster: The Donner Party (1846–1847), *Western Journal of Medicine*, Vol. 160, No. 4 (April 1994), 340–342. Dr. McCurdy examined the pattern of mortality in the Donner Party, focusing on the epidemiologic aspects of their entrapment in the Sierras and how elements such as sex, age, and social support were key factors in survival.
3. Teggart, *Diary of Patrick Breen*, 8.
4. Ibid.
5. Ibid.
6. Department of the Army, *U.S. Army Survival Field Manual: FM 21-76*, June 1992, 7.
7. Ibid., 11.
8. DeVoto, *The Year of Decision*, 398–399.
9. McGlashan, *History*, 79.
10. MLHS Online Academy, Mountain Lakes, New Jersey, http://www.mtlakes.org/hs/acad/tech/hunger/starvation.htm.
11. Ibid.
12. Stewart, *Ordeal by Hunger*, 127.
13. Henry Guly, "History of Accidental Hypothermia," *European Resuscitation Journal*, Vol. 82, No. 1 (January 2011), 122–125. Death from exposure to cold has

been recognized for thousands of years, but the word *hypothermia* was first used in the late nineteenth century. Hypothermia was not generally recognized as a clinical condition until the mid-twentieth century, and then only in extreme conditions such as immersion in cold water or snow.

14. Stewart, *Ordeal by Hunger*, 127–128.

15. Ibid., 128.

16. Ibid., 128–129.

17. McGlashan, *History*, 80–81.

18. Eliza W. Farnham, *California In-door and Out* (New York: Edwards & Co., 1856), 412–413.

19. McGlashan, *History*, 81–82.

20. DeVoto, *The Year of Decision*, 61, 400. DeVoto wrote of the winter of 1823–1824, when James Clyman and fellow mountain man William Sublette almost froze to death during a blizzard in the Wind River Mountains. According to DeVoto, "There was no wood and but little sage; their fire was blown away. They pulled their robes over them and the gale battered them till morning."

21. McGlashan, *History*, 82–83.

22. Bertil Wedin, Leif Vanggard, and Jorma Hirvonen, "'Paradoxical Undressing' in Fatal Hypothermia," *Journal of Forensic Science*, Vol. 24, No. 3 (July 1979), 543. Known as "paradoxical undressing," this bizarre act occurs while the victim of hypothermia is probably in a state of mental confusion when the body temperature is low. The phenomenon seems to be a terminal event in some fatal cases of hypothermia.

23. DeVoto, *The Year of Decision*, 400.

24. Ibid.

25. Stewart, *Ordeal by Hunger*, 132.

26. Ibid., 132–133.

27. Elizabeth Culotta, "Neanderthals Were Cannibals, Bones Show," *Science Magazine*, Vol. 286, No. 5437 (October 1999), 18–19; Tom Mueller, "CSI: Italian Renaissance," *Smithsonian*, July-August 2013, 52. Smithsonian anthropologists found evidence of cannibalism at Virginia's Jamestown Colony, probably from the winter of 1609. Cut marks on the skull and tibia of a newly exhumed fourteen-year-old girl's remains indicated that her brain, tongue, cheeks, and leg muscles had been removed after death.

28. Cormac Ó Gráda, "Carleton and Others on Famine's Darkest Secret," keynote address at the Carleton Summer School, Clogher, Ireland, August 6, 2012. A chronicler of the tragic Great Irish Famine of the 1840s, Ó Gráda wrote, "Cannibalism is famine's darkest secret, a taboo topic. It is not a feature of all famines but it is, I think, more common than lots of people care to imagine. It is a measure of how unimaginably horrific famines are." Ó Gráda's primary focus was cannibalism during life-threatening food shortages such as the Great Irish Famine and not the ceremonial or ritual consumption of human flesh in non-emergency situations.

29. McGlashan, *History*, 85.

30. Brown, *The Indifferent Stars*, 174.

31. Ibid., 175.

32. McGlashan, *History*, 85.

CHAPTER 37: THE STARVING TIME,
JANUARY 1847

1. Stewart, *Ordeal by Hunger*, 133.
2. Kaufman, *Saving the Donner Party*, 79.
3. Stewart, *Ordeal by Hunger*, 135.
4. Teggart, *Diary of Patrick Breen*, 8.
5. Houghton, *The Expedition*, 71.
6. Teggart, *Diary of Patrick Breen*, 8.
7. Rosen, "Log Entries for December 1846," http://www.donnerpartydiary.com/dec46.htm.
8. Murphy, "Across the Plains," 422.
9. Teggart, *Diary of Patrick Breen*, 9.
10. Murphy, "Across the Plains," 422.
11. Donner-Springer Family Collection, Bill Springer, curator; Stewart, *Ordeal by Hunger*, 168. The Reed family started their journey from Illinois with five dogs—Barney, Tracker, Tyler, Trailer, and the little terrier named Cash. All the dogs except Cash died along the trail.
12. Morgan, *Overland in 1846*, Vol. II, 285.
13. Ibid.
14. Ibid.
15. Stewart, *Ordeal by Hunger*, 138; Houghton, *The Expedition*, 70.
16. Kaufman, *Saving the Donner Party*, 81.
17. Charles F. Hohn and James A. Glynn, *California's Social Problems* (Newbury Park, California: Pine Forge Press, 2002).
18. Mullen, *The Donner Party Chronicles*, 250; Kristin Johnson, "Some Donner Party Myths and Mysteries in Brief," http://www.utahcrossroads.org/DonnerParty/Briefmyths.htm. Some authors have questioned the veracity of Eddy's deer-hunting story. Mullen writes, "Historians will debate the deer tale because Eddy is the only survivor who mentions the incident. Mary Ann Graves, who later wrote an account of the escape, is frank about cannibalism but omits the deer story." Johnson, however, does not discount the deer story as fiction made up by Eddy, who was known to exaggerate. Johnson writes that "the episode as described by J. Quinn Thornton in *Oregon and California in 1848* is melodramatic and perhaps not entirely accurate." She also wrote that just because Mary Ann Graves did not mention the deer hunt in a letter she wrote does not mean the incident did not occur.
19. Stewart, *Ordeal by Hunger*, 141.
20. C. F. McGlashan, *History of the Donner Party: A Tragedy of the Sierra* (Truckee, CA: Crowley & McGlashan, 1879), 87; Stewart, *Ordeal by Hunger*, 142. Both authors write that Sarah Foster was the primary butcher of Jay Fosdick's body. Stewart suggests that Sarah Foster acted alone, and McGlashan writes, "This was the first time that women's hands had used the knife, but by the act a life was saved."
21. Mullen, *The Donner Party Chronicles*, 250.
22. Thornton, *Oregon and California*, 149.
23. Stewart, *Ordeal by Hunger*, 145–146.
24. Mary Stuckey, "The Donner Party and the Rhetoric of Western Expansion," *Communications Faculty Publications* (Atlanta: Georgia State University, 2011), 237. Stuckey writes, "By far, the most significant role played by indigenous people in

the Donner Party story is that of two Miwoks, Luis and Salvador, sent from Fort Sutter as part of the first relief party. . . . These American Indians were robbed of their names, replaced with those of their conqueror's choosing. In addition, they were never given a voice. Even in the fictionalized versions of the story, they are rendered mute."

25. McGlashan, *History*, 106; Stewart, *Ordeal by Hunger*, 146.
26. Mullen, *The Donner Party Chronicles*, 254.
27. California Department of Parks and Recreation, "The Miwok People," http://www.parks.ca.gov/?page_Id=22538.
28. Stewart, *Ordeal by Hunger*, 147–148. Ritchie is sometimes spelled Ritchey.

CHAPTER 38: IN DIRE STRAITS,
JANUARY–FEBRUARY 1847

1. Samuel López De Victoria, "Beware of She-Wolves," Psych Central Web, February 11, 2014, http://psychcentral.com/blog/archives/2014/02/11/beware-of-she-wolves/. López claims that a woman "becomes a she-wolf out of necessity to survive in the recreational jungle of life" because she "feels that there is no other way to make it through life successfully . . . just like a wolf in the wild, they will destroy their prey and devour them should the opportunity arise."
2. Stewart, *Ordeal by Hunger*, 171.
3. Ibid, 171. In his book about the Donner Party, originally published ninety years after their ordeal in the Sierras, Stewart mildly chided young Virginia when he wrote, "So impressed was Virginia Reed with his [Breen's] piety that she swore to become a Catholic if rescued, in childish lack of logic forgetting that her own mother and many others were praying just as fervently and probably just as efficaciously in the Protestant fashion."
4. Re emigrants' reading: ibid., 172; Samuel Kirkham, *English Grammar in Familiar Lectures* (Rochester, NY: William Alling, 1845). The book was originally published in 1823. The Reed family's copy of Kirkham's *Grammar*, as it was commonly called (the full title of the book contained forty words), is the forty-fifth edition, published in 1845. It is unknown whether the book was purchased by the family or was a gift. The book was so popular that it went through more than one hundred printings in the nineteenth century; Larry Bishop, preparer, *Researcher's Guide to Sutter's Fort's Collection of Donner Party Material*, Box 8-14-308, Folder 4, Sutter's Fort State Historic Park (Sacramento: State Museum Resource Center, 2005), 21. Abraham Lincoln mastered Kirkham's *Grammar* as part of his intensive self-improvement program. He was known to have recommended the book to friends and associates. He presented his copy to Ann Rutledge, his first true love, shortly before she died of typhoid fever.
5. Sidney Babcock, *The Flock of Sheep; or Familiar Explanations of Simple Facts* (New Haven, CT: S. Babcock, 1840), 1–16.
6. Teggart, *Diary of Patrick Breen*, 10–11. Breen spelled Sutter's phonetically as Siuters, the way people pronounced the name of the fort at that time.
7. Kristin Johnson, "Some Donner Party Myths and Mysteries in Brief," *New Light on the Donner Party*, http://www.utahcrossroads.org/DonnerParty/Briefmyths.htm.
8. McGlashan, *History*, 91–92.
9. Ibid., 102.
10. Houghton, *The Expedition*, 74.

11. Teggart, *Diary of Patrick Breen*, 11.
12. Ibid.
13. Ibid.
14. Stewart, *Ordeal by Hunger*, 174.
15. McGlashan, *History*, 102–103. McGlashan contends that the boy was not able to eat the small piece of meat. Murphy family sources, including Landrum's siblings, state that he did eat the meat and then died.
16. Joseph A. King, "William G. Murphy's Lecture and Two Letters to Mrs. Houghton," *Dogtown Territorial Quarterly*, Summer Issue No. 26, 49. In 1896, to mark the fiftieth anniversary of the entrapment of the Donner Party, William Green Murphy delivered a lecture at Truckee, California, about the ordeal that had occurred when he was eleven years old. His lecture was subsequently published in the *Marysville Appeal* on February 9, 1896.
17. Ethan Rarick, *Desperate Passage: The Donner Party's Perilous Journey West* (New York: Oxford University Press, 2008), 155.
18. Teggart, *Diary of Patrick Breen*, 13.
19. Limburg, *Deceived*, 148.
20. Teggart, *Diary of Patrick Breen*, 13.
21. Murphy, "Across the Plains," 424–425.
22. Ibid., 423.

CHAPTER 39: MAN ON A MISSION,
JANUARY–FEBRUARY 1847

1. William Gilpin, *Mission of the North American People, Geographical, Social, and Political* (Philadelphia: J. B. Lippincott U.S. Navy Lieutenant & Co., 1874), 130 (from an 1846 letter).
2. Mullen, *The Donner Party Chronicles*, 188.
3. Harry Laurenz Wells, *History of Nevada County, California* (Oakland: Thompson & West, 1880), 89–90. By late 1847, the Reverend Dunleavy apparently had taken up strong drink, and he "retrograded rapidly." By 1849, his addiction to alcohol and attraction to the newly discovered deposits of gold in the Sierra Nevadas resulted in his leaving the ministry. He and his wife moved to Rough and Ready, a small community in Nevada County, California, where he opened the first saloon in town and later built a tenpin alley for the miners' amusement. "His [Dunleavy's] success as a saloon-keeper was of course death to his moral nature—and the finale of his career, after a year or two of deepening degradation, was a wretched death among strangers at Mazatlan," Wells wrote in his book.
4. San Francisco Board of Supervisors, *San Francisco Municipal Reports for the Fiscal Year* (San Francisco: Neal Publishing Co., 1911), 1285–1286. On January 30, 1847, U.S. Navy Lieutenant Washington Bartlett, the first chief magistrate, or alcalde, of San Francisco under the United States flag issued the proclamation changing the name of Yerba Buena to San Francisco. Bartlett soon returned to active duty, and Edwin Bryant was appointed in his place and sworn into office on February 22, 1847. The city and the rest of Alta California officially became a United States military territory in 1848 by the terms of the Treaty of Guadalupe Hidalgo, which ended the Mexican-American War.
5. Mullen, *The Donner Party Chronicles*.
6. Lewis R. Hamersly, *The Records of Living Officers of the U.S. Navy and Marine*

Corps (Philadelphia: J. B. Lippincott & Co., 1878), 76. Although most books about the Donner Party list Hull as a commodore in 1847, he was a commander and had been since 1841. Hull was commissioned as captain in 1855 and was made a commodore in 1862 during his service in the Civil War.

7. Hall, *Donner Miscellany*, 35.

8. Johnson, *"Unfortunate Emigrants,"* 195. Located in San Francisco, the *Pacific Rural Press* published Reed's memories of the Donner Party's experiences in two installments, on March 25 and April 1, 1871.

9. Bryant, *What I Saw*, 316–317.

10. Limburg, *Deceived*, 156. Reed's $10,000 in 1847 would have been worth about $300,000 in 2015.

11. John E. Richards, "A Future Supreme Court Justice Looks Back," *California Supreme Court Historical Society Newsletter*, Spring-Summer 2010, 10.

12. Ibid. Richards served as associate justice of the California Supreme Court, 1924–1932, and previously on the Court of Appeals, First District, 1913–1924. His article first appeared in Oscar Tully Shuck's 1901 *History of the Bench and Bar in California* under the title "The Early Bench and Bar of San Jose."

13. Ibid. The name *calaboose* originated in the late eighteenth century from the Creole French *calaboose* and the Spanish *calabozo*, or dungeon.

14. Johnson, *"Unfortunate Emigrants,"* 193.

15. F. J. Ryan, "The City of Stockton," *Californian Illustrated Magazine*, Vol. 4, 723; Ilka Stoffregen Hartman, *The Youth of Charles M. Weber: Founder of Stockton*, Issue 8 of Monograph, Holt-Atherton Pacific Center for Western Studies (Stockton, CA: University of the Pacific, 1979). This 54-page monograph offers more detail about the life of the man born Karl David Weber, who changed his name and is remembered for having founded Stockton, California.

16. Cora Baggerly Older, *When San Jose Was Young*, No. 152, "How Reed Saved the Donner Party" (San Jose: *Evening News*, April 10, 1917). The *Evening News* was a weekly newspaper published in San Jose from January 1, 1898, through December 30, 1922. In 1916–1917, the newspaper published a series of 340 articles called *When San Jose Was Young*. The articles were written by Cora Baggerly Older, a prolific author of plays, novels, and several nonfiction books. She was married to San Francisco journalist Fremont Older; *The History Bandits*, "When San Jose Was Young": A Study in Historical Representation, http://the historybandits.com/2015/01/15/when-san-jose-was-young-a-study-in-historical-representation/. This blog publication contends that the series was written by a group of writers for the *Evening News*. According to the blog author, using the pseudonym Etta Place, the series "served the sensational and the romantic. . . . The Evening News writers viewed history as an intoxicating wine, but were unable to realize that they themselves were intoxicated by their own biases and limitations."

17. Stewart, *Ordeal by Hunger*, 154.

18. *The West, Its History and Romance*, Anderson Galleries Auction Catalogue, November 28, 1921, Vol. 26, No. 106. Report by R. F. Pinckney, Commanding U.S. Forces at Pueblo San José, certifying that he has discharged Jonathan (Jotham) Curtis from military service because Curtis, while subject to the orders of James F. Reed, had been insubordinate and abusive [Pueblo de San José, January 29, 1847]; Hubert Howe Bancroft, *History of California, 1846–1849*, Vol. V (San Francisco: History Co., 1886), 539.

19. Douglas V. Meed, *The Mexican War, 1846–1848* (Oxford, U.K.: Osprey Publishing, 2002), 71.
20. Alissandra Dramov, *Carmel by-the-Sea, The Early Years (1903–1913)* (Bloomington, IN: AuthorHouse, 2012), 39–40.
21. Reverend Walter Colton, *Three Years in California* (New York and Cincinnati: A. S. Barnes, H. W. Derby & Co., 1850), 158–159.
22. William F. James and George H. McMurry, *History of San Jose, California: Narrative and Biographical* (San Jose, CA: A. H. Cawston, 1933), 64.
23. Dorothy F. Regnery, *The Battle of Santa Clara* (San Jose: Smith and McKay Printing Co., 1978), 24, 28–29.
24. Ibid., 24.
25. George Henry Tinkham, *California Men and Events* (Stockton, CA: Record Publishing Co., 1915), 52.
26. Regnery, *The Battle of Santa Clara*, 97.
27. "Battle of Santa Clara," *California Star* (Yerba Buena), February 6, 1847. Early Franciscan padres sprinkled mustard seeds along the Camino Real and other trails to mark them with the big yellow blossoms. Some rancheros reportedly used the mustard plants for cattle forage.
28. *California Star,* February 6, 1847, 3.
29. Edwin A. Sherman, "An Unpublished Account of the Battle of Santa Clara, Written by John [sic] Frazier Reed Using his Saddle Horn as a Desk," *San Francisco Chronicle*, September 4, 1910, 2.
30. Zoeth Skinner Eldridge, *The Beginnings of San Francisco, from the Expedition of Anza, 1774, to the City Charter of April 15, 1850* (New York: John C. Rankin Co., 1912), 265.
31. Hall, *Donner Miscellany*, 46.
32. Damian Bacich, "The Zacatecan Franciscans in Alta California: A Misunderstood Legacy," *Bolítin: Journal of the California Mission Studies Association*, Vol. 28, Nos. 1–2, 68–69.
33. Hall, *Donner Miscellany*, 42.
34. Ibid., 47.
35. Bill Anderson and Penny Anderson, eds., *Dogtown Territorial Quarterly*, No. 26 (Summer 1996), 10.

CHAPTER 40: TO THE RESCUE, FEBRUARY 1847

1. The Virtual Museum of San Francisco, http://www.sfmuseum.org/hist/name.html. The official proclamation reads: "AN ORDINANCE WHEREAS, the local name of Yerba Buena, as applied to the settlement or town of San Francisco, is unknown beyond the district; and has been applied from the local name on the cove, on which the town is built: Therefore, to prevent confusion and mistakes in public documents, and that the town may have the advantage of the name given on the public map. IT IS HEREBY ORDAINED, that the name of SAN FRANCISCO shall hereafter be used in all official communications and public documents, or records appertaining to the town." It was signed by Washington Bartlett, chief magistrate, and dated January 30, 1847. Although the name change became official on that date, many people accustomed to the name of Yerba Buena continued to call the town by that name for several months.
2. Mark McLaughlin, *The Donner Party: Weathering the Storm* (Carnelian Bay, California: Mic Mac Publishing, 2007), 79. Reed was right about the "false spring." In

his diary for February 2–6, 1847, Patrick Breen writes of the continuous snow that fell as a result of a powerful storm system that had developed in the Gulf of Alaska.

3. American Indians in the Federal Decennial Census, 1790–1930, http://www .archives.gov/research/census/native-americans/1790-1930.html. Prior to 1900, few Indians were included in the federal census. Indians are not identified in the censuses of 1790 through 1840. In 1848, Indians in California still outnumbered whites by ten to one.

4. Martha J. (Patty) Reed Lewis Collection, Various Citizens to R. F. Stockton, January 1847; Collected Correspondence November 1, 1831, to September 8, 1851; undated, Box 8-4-308, Folder 132, Sutter's Fort State Historic Park, Sacramento, California.

5. Morgan, *Overland in 1846*, Vol. II, 793, n. 184.

6. Ibid., 337.

7. McLaughlin, *The Donner Party*, 80.

8. Stewart, *Ordeal by Hunger*, 155.

9. Zoeth Skinner Eldredge, *The Beginnings of San Francisco, from the Expedition of Anza, 1774, to the City Charter of April 15, 1850* (New York: John C. Rankin Co., 1912), 563; H. H. Bancroft, *California Pioneer Register and Index, 1542–1848* (Baltimore: Regional Publishing Co., 1964), 68. Historian and ethnologist Hubert Howe Bancroft, who moved to California in 1852, had this to say about Sam Brannan: "He probably did more for [San Francisco] and for other places than was effected by the combined efforts of scores of better men; and indeed, in many respects he was not a bad man, being as a rule straightforward as well as shrewd in his dealings, as famous for his acts of charity and open-handed liberality as for in enterprise, giving also frequently proofs of personal bravery."

10. Andrew Jackson Grayson Papers, Biography, BANC MSS C-B 514, Bancroft Library, University of California–Berkeley. Soon after arriving in California in October 1846, Grayson joined the California Battalion, attaining the rank of colonel. When his service was completed, he moved his family to San Francisco. He purchased property there and in other parts of the Bay Area. After gold was discovered in California in 1848, Grayson acquired a stake and then launched a merchandising enterprise that made him one of the wealthiest men in San Francisco by 1851. After 1853, Grayson devoted his life to travel throughout the western wilderness, studying and painting birds.

11. Stewart, *Ordeal by Hunger*, 156.

12. Thornton, *Oregon and California*, Vol. I, 160.

13. Ibid., 161.

14. Morgan, *Overland in 1846*, Vol. II, 700–701, quoting the *California Star*, February 6, 1847.

15. McLaughlin, *The Donner Party*, 81.

16. Limburg, *Deceived*, 157; Albert L. Hurtado, *John Sutter: A Life on the North American Frontier* (Norman: University of Oklahoma Press, 2006), 44, 78, 203.

17. Johnson, *"Unfortunate Emigrants."*

CHAPTER 41: THE FIRST RELIEF

1. Morgan, *Overland in 1846*, Vol. I, 324. The partial quote was taken from a lengthy 1879 narrative written by George W. Tucker for C. F. McGlashan, an early chronicler of the Donner Party. It was based on Tucker's recollections

of 1846–1847, when he traveled with his family as overland emigrants at about the same time as the Donner Party. When Tucker was fifteen, he served as an auxiliary, or helper, for the First Relief, the first rescue team to reach the trapped members of the Donner Party.

2. Stewart, *Ordeal by Hunger*, 150–151. Regarding the delivery of the letter to John Sinclair, Stewart writes, "An Indian runner took the letter, for the recent rains had made the valley half lake and half quagmire, and a horse would have bogged down in the first sink hole." This is one of several references that contradict the statements of George Tucker, who claimed in his 1879 memoir that John Rhoads (Tucker misspelled his name as Rhodes) delivered the Eddy letter written at Johnson's Ranch to the Sinclair Ranch. In addition, Daniel Rhoads, younger brother of John, wrote in 1873 that an Indian runner carried the Eddy letter. Rhoads also digresses to explain that the use of Indians as messengers was a common practice in California at the time. "Sometimes these mail carriers received a small reward and sometimes not; but I never heard of a letter failing to reach the person to whom it was sent." The Statement of Daniel Rhoads of Kingston, Fresno County, 1873, is contained in the Rhoads Family Papers in the Bancroft Library, University of California–Berkeley.

3. Stewart, *Ordeal by Hunger*, 151.

4. "Pay of the Army," *Niles National Register*, Volume 70, Whole No. 1815 (July 11, 1846), 293. During the Mexican War, more often than not, disease and primitive medical treatment took more lives than enemy bullets. Of the many hardships that had to be endured, not getting paid on a regular basis contributed greatly to dissatisfaction and low morale among the troops.

5. Stewart, *Ordeal by Hunger*.

6. Ibid.

7. DeVoto, *The Year of Decision*, 424; Stewart, *Ordeal by Hunger*, 151.

8. Ibid., 151, 153.

9. Mullen, *The Donner Party Chronicles*, 266.

10. Bill Anderson and Penny Anderson, eds., *Dogtown Territorial Quarterly*, No. 26 (Summer 1996), 8, 9, 44; J. Kenneth Davies, "Thomas Rhoads, Forgotten Mormon Pioneer of 1846," *Nebraska History*, Vol. 64 (1983), 83, 86; Gale R. Rhoades and Kerry Ross, *Footprints in the Wilderness: A History of the Lost Rhoades Mines* (Salt Lake City: Dream Garden Press, 1980), 126–137.

11. Bill Anderson and Penny Anderson, eds., *Dogtown Territorial Quarterly*, No. 26, 45.

12. Hall, *Donner Miscellany*, 55. At the end of the First Relief diary (the Ritchie-Tucker diary), in handwriting attributed to John Sinclair, is the following statement: "Mr. Sinclair arrived at Mr. Johnson's [ranch on Bear Creek] Sunday the thirty first of January having left his residence the day previous on foot." This appears to be a discrepancy. It does not seem possible that Sinclair could hike forty miles from his ranch to Johnson's ranch in such a short amount of time. It took the band of volunteers traveling on horseback from Sutter's Fort to Johnson's ranch two full days and nights.

13. McLaughlin, *The Donner Party*, 87.

14. Morgan, *Overland in 1846*, Vol. I, 325–326.

15. Kaufman, *Saving the Donner Party*, 94.

16. Stewart, *Ordeal by Hunger*, 177, 182, 202. Stewart uses Coon's name three times in his book.

17. Morgan, *Overland in 1846*, Vol. II, 177–178; Stewart, *Ordeal by Hunger*, 177. In various diaries, Coffeemeyer appears as Caffemeyer, Coffemire, and Copymier.
18. Thornton, *Oregon and California*, Vol. I, 167, 180.
19. John Charles Frémont, *Memoirs of my Life* (Chicago: Belford, Clarke & Co., 1886), 169.
20. Hall, *Donner Miscellany*, 51, 55–56. The First Relief Party diary—entitled "Notes Kept by M. D. Ritchie on the Journey to Assist the Emigrants"—includes entries from two members of the team, Matthew Ritchie and Reason Tucker. It states that the First Relief departed Johnson's Ranch on February 5, 1847. Several sources, including historians and researchers, have accepted this date. Other credible sources, however, believe the First Relief left on its mission on February 4. In his book *Ordeal by Hunger: The Story of the Donner Party*, historian George R. Stewart states that diarist Ritchie might have been confused and was a day off when he wrote February 5 instead of February 4.
21. Hall, *Donner Miscellany*, 56.
22. Ibid.
23. Ibid., 52.
24. C. F. McGlashan, *History of the Donner Party: A Tragedy of the Sierra* (San Francisco: A. L. Bancroft & Company, Printers, 1881, 1902), 116.
25. Ibid. 116–117.
26. Ibid., 117. George Tucker had nothing good to say about his companion Billy Coon, whom Tucker claimed "was partially insane, and was no company at all."
27. Morgan, *Overland in 1846*, Vol. I, 328.
28. Ibid., 327.
29. Hall, *Donner Miscellany*, 52. Most accounts support the diary entry of Matthew Ritchie, who wrote, "On the 12th moved camp about two miles and stopped to make snow shoes tried them on and found them of no benefit cast them away."
30. Ibid.
31. Morgan, *Overland in 1846*, Vol. I, 452, n. 5. Stewart called wolverines the "unrelenting enemy of the relief parties in 1847." Once plentiful in California, wolverines—the largest member of the weasel family—were almost completely eradicated because of unregulated trapping and poisoning campaigns. In 1922, the last wolverine was seen in the Sierra Nevadas of California until 2008, when a wolverine was photographed and the sighting was confirmed. Since then, there have been more sightings, and it is hoped that someday wolverines will return to the Sierras.
32. Hall, *Donner Miscellany*, 52–53.
33. Ibid., 53.
34. McLaughlin, *The Donner Party*, 90.
35. Morgan, *Overland in 1846*, Vol. I, 326.
36. Hall, *Donner Miscellany*, 53. The diary entry was incorrectly dated February 18, the date the relief party arrived at Truckee Lake and made contact with some of the survivors.
37. Morgan, *Overland in 1846*, Vol. I, 328.

CHAPTER 42: THE SECOND RELIEF

1. Hall, *Donner Miscellany*, 50. McCutchen wrote the letter on January 27, 1847, while he and Caleb Greenwood were guests at the Yount Ranch.
2. DeVoto, *The Year of Decision*, 426.

3. Hall, *Donner Miscellany*, 62–63.
4. Morgan, *Overland in 1846*, Vol. II, 702–705.
5. Ibid., Vol. I., 201–202.
6. Ibid., Vol. II, 702–703.
7. Ibid., 704–705.
8. Newspaper quotation re McKinstry: ibid., 702. Hall, *Donner Miscellany*, 63.
9. Morgan, *Overland in 1846*, Vol. I, 338.
10. Ibid.
11. Hall, *Donner Miscellany*, 48–49.
12. Ibid.
13. Hall, *Donner Miscellany*, 64.
14. David J. Wishart, ed., *Encyclopedia of the Great Plains* (Lincoln and London: University of Nebraska Press, 2004), 813. The hides of bull buffalo were commonly used in the making of bullboats, hence the name.
15. Ric Hornor and Jody Hornor, *The Golden Hub—Sacramento* (Pilot Hill, CA: Electric Canvas/19th Century Books, 2008), 61–62.
16. McLaughlin, *The Donner Party*, 94.
17. Morgan, *Overland in 1846*, Vol. I, 338.
18. McLaughlin, *The Donner Party*, 94; Robert Hendrickson, *The Facts on File Encyclopedia of Word and Phrase Origins* (New York: Checkmark Books, 2004), 341. The use of the phrase *hell-bent-for-leather* in America dates to the first half of the nineteenth century. It was used to describe someone riding a horse fast and recklessly.
19. Morgan, *Overland in 1846*, Vol. I, 338–339.
20. Robert Glass Cleland, *This Reckless Breed of Men: The Trappers and Fur Traders of the Southwest* (Albuquerque: University of New Mexico Press, 1976), 114, 332; Bryant, *What I Saw*, 356. After arriving in California, Edwin Bryant was en route to Sonoma when he came upon a hunter's camp that "looked like a butcher's stall." It was there that Bryant met Caleb Greenwood and three of his sons, including one named Governor Boggs Greenwood after the former governor of Missouri. He also met John Turner, whose physique and coarse language left a lasting impression on Bryant. He later wrote, "The swearing of Turner, a man of immense frame and muscular power, during our evening's conversation, was almost terrific. I had heard mountain swearing before, but his went far beyond all former examples. He could do all swearing for our army in Mexico, and then have a surplus."
21. Hurtado, *John Sutter*, 200–201.
22. Stewart, *Ordeal by Hunger*, 209–210.
23. DeVoto, *The Year of Decision*, 433.
24. Stewart, *Ordeal by Hunger*, 208.
25. Brown, *The Indifferent Stars*, 211; Hall, *Donner Miscellany*, 53.
26. Murphy, "Across the Plains," 423.
27. Ibid. 424.
28. Morgan, *Overland in 1846*, Vol. I, 328.
29. Kristin Johnson, "Donner Party Cannibalism: Did They or Didn't They?" *Wild West*, Vol. 26, No. 4 (December 2013), 31.
30. Morgan, *Overland in 1846*, Vol. I, 329.
31. McGlashan, *History*, 144–145.
32. Teggart, *Diary of Patrick Breen*, 14–15.

33. Hall, *Donner Miscellany*, 53.
34. Volney Steele, *Bleed, Blister, and Purge: A History of Medicine on the American Frontier*, (Missoula, MT: Mountain Press Publishing Co., 2005), 118–120.
35. Houghton, *The Expedition*, 101.
36. Ibid., 343.
37. DeVoto, *The Year of Decision*, 430.
38. Houghton, *The Expedition*, 75, 103; DeVoto, ibid. DeVoto wrote, "Tamsen [sic] said staunchly that if food did not come by the time it [the food that remained in camp] used up, they would began eating what they had refrained from eating."
39. Kelly J. Dixon, Julie M. Schablitsky, and Shannon A. Novak, eds., *An Archaeology of Desperation: Exploring the Donner Party's Alder Creek Camp* (Norman: University of Oklahoma Press, 2011), 46.
40. Teggart, *Diary of Patrick Breen*, 15.
41. Stewart, *Ordeal by Hunger*, 195.
42. McGlashan, *History*, 146–147.
43. Murphy, *Across the Plains*, 425.
44. Ibid.
45. Ibid.
46. Stewart, *Ordeal by Hunger*, 198.
47. Murphy, *Across the Plains*, 425.
48. Stewart, *Ordeal by Hunger*, 198; Teggart, *Diary of Patrick Breen*, 15.
49. McGlashan, *History*, 199.
50. Stewart, *Ordeal by Hunger*, 199.
51. Murphy, *Across the Plains*, 425.
52. Morgan, *Overland in 1846*, Vol. I, 286. From a letter that Virginia Reed wrote to her cousin, Mary C. Keyes, dated May 16, 1847.
53. Hall, *Donner Miscellany*, 53. In his diary, Tucker blames a bear for destroying the cache of food. At least one Donner author claimed the culprit was a mountain lion. It is more likely, however, that the cache was raided by the smaller pine marten or by a wolverine.
54. Ibid.
55. DeVoto, *The Year of Decision*, 431.
56. McGlashan, *History*, 148. "Death had become fearfully common, and his victims were little heeded by the perishing company," McGlashan wrote after describing the death of an emigrant.
57. Morgan, *Overland in 1846*, Vol. I, 329.
58. Murphy, *History*, 425.
59. Hall, *Donner Miscellany*, 54.
60. Limburg, *Deceived*, 169.
61. McGlashan, *History*, 148. It is not clear whether anyone took up Philippine Keseberg on her offer of money and a watch to carry her daughter. Most sources do not indicate whether she was successful. One source states only that "she found a taker," and another source claims that John Rhoads carried Ada, a seemingly difficult feat because Rhoads carried Naomi Pike during the entire journey.
62. Letter from Reason Tucker to McGlashan, 1879, Folder 53, McGlashan Papers, Bancroft Library, University of California–Berkeley.
63. Morgan, *Overland in 1846*, Vol. I, 330.
64. Hall, *Donner Miscellany*, 54.

65. DeVoto, *The Year of Decision*, 432.
66. Kaufman, *Saving the Donner Party*, 104.
67. Ibid.
68. DeVoto, *The Year of Decision*, 433.
69. Ibid.
70. Morgan, *Overland in 1846*, Vol. I, 345.
71. Ibid.
72. Ibid.
73. Murphy, *Across the Plains*, 425.
74. Morgan, *Overland in 1846*, Vol. I, 345.
75. Mullen, *The Donner Party Chronicles*, 295.
76. McGlashan, *History*, 155.
77. Ibid., 155–156.
78. Mullen, *The Donner Party Chronicles*, 296.
79. Morgan, *Overland in 1846*, Vol. II, 708. Woodworth made this statement in a letter to George McKinstry Jr., dated February 28, 1847.
80. Stewart, *Ordeal by Hunger*, 205.
81. Morgan, *Overland in 1846*, Vol. I, 334.
82. Mullen, *The Donner Party Chronicles*, 295.
83. Kristin Johnson, *New Light on the Donner Party*, "Rescuers and Others," http://www.utahcrossroads.org/DonnerParty/Rescuers.htm, Utah Crossroads Chapter, Oregon-California Trails Association; DeVoto, *The Year of Decision*, 433.
84. Hurtado, *John Sutter*, 210–211. Hurtado described the physician hired by Sutter as "a shadowy character known only to history as Dr. Bates." Although Bates was said to have "worked hard to cure Sutter's Indians," he seldom had much success. Sutter questioned whether Bates's practice of bleeding his patients, one of the customary medical treatments at the time, did more harm than good. During a measles epidemic, Sutter's Indians died by the score, making it difficult for Sutter to bring in his wheat. Even Bates got sick but eventually recovered.
85. Murphy, *Across the Plains*, 426.
86. Stewart, *Ordeal by Hunger*, 206.
87. McLaughlin, *The Donner Party*, 161.
88. Frank Soulé, John H. Gihon, and James Nisbet, *The Annals of San Francisco* (New York: D. Appleton & Company, 1855), 514.
89. Hastings, *The Emigrants' Guide*, 152.
90. Ibid., 84.
91. Ibid., 147.
92. Ibid., 144.
93. Kaufman, *Saving the Donner Party*, 113.
94. Stewart, *Ordeal by Hunger*, 211; McGlashan, *History*, 157. McGlashan, based on information provided by Charles Cady, mistakenly states that Cady and his two fellow rescuers, Clark and Stone, came across the frozen corpse of Charles Stanton and not John Denton. The frozen body of Stanton was found at least fifteen miles from that location.
95. Morgan, *Overland in 1846*, Vol. I, 304. Reed's statement correctly identifying the body he came upon as Denton and not Stanton, as others suggested, appeared in a letter Reed sent from Napa Valley to Gersham Keyes in Springfield, Illinois, dated July 2, 1847. The letter was reprinted in Springfield's *Illinois Journal* on December 23, 1847.

96. DeVoto, *The Year of Decision*, 434.

97. Morgan, *Overland in 1846*, Vol. I, 297–298. Titled "Narrative of Sufferings of a Company of Emigrants in the Mountains of California, in the Winter of '46 and '47 by J. F. Reed, Late of Sangamon County, Illinois," Merryman's story was first published in the *Illinois State Register* on December 3, 1847, followed by publication in the *Illinois Journal* in Springfield on December 9, 1847.

98. Murphy, *Across the Plains*, 425.

99. Teggart, *Diary of Patrick Breen*, 15.

100. Ibid.

101. Stewart, *Ordeal by Hunger*, 212.

102. Limburg, *Deceived*, 176.

103. McGlashan, *History*, 210. Keseberg made this statement during an April 4, 1879, interview with McGlashan.

104. Stewart, *Ordeal by Hunger*, 214.

105. Brown, *The Indifferent Stars*, 219.

106. Teggart, *Diary of Patrick Breen*, 16.

107. Thornton, *Oregon and California*, Vol. I, 199–200.

108. Morgan, *Overland in 1846*, Vol. I, 346. Reed referred to George and Tamzene Donner's daughters as "3 Stout harty children" in the March 1 entry of the Second Relief diary.

109. Ibid., 289, 447, n. 109.

110. Ibid., 98.

111. Ibid.

112. Kristin Johnson, "Donner Party Cannibalism: Did They or Didn't They?" *Wild West*, Vol. 26, No. 4, December 2013 (Leesburg, VA: Weider History Group, 2013), 35.

113. John Grebenkemper and Kristin Johnson, "Forensic Canine Search for the Donner Family Winter Camps at Alder Creek," *Overland Journal*, Vol. 33, No. 2 (Summer 2015), 64–89.

114. Ibid., 68–69.

115. Stewart, *Ordeal by Hunger*, 215.

116. H. A. Wise, *Los Gringo; or, An Inside View of Mexico and California, with Wanderings in Peru, Chili, and Polynesia* (New York: Baker & Scribner, 1849), 74–75.

117. Johnson, *"Unfortunate Emigrants,"* 132.

118. Ibid.

119. Ibid., 133; Morgan, *Overland in 1846*, Vol. II, 721. In the April 24, 1847, edition of the *Californian*, an editorial note states, "We conversed freely with Mr. Woodworth and with some of the men who accompanied him to the Mountain for the relief of the suffering people."

120. Morgan, *Overland in 1846*, Vol. I, 346. In his diary, Reed wrote that Tamzene Donner was "able to travel but preferred to stay with her husband until provisions should arrive, which was confidently expected by Comd. Woodworth."

121. Joseph A. King, *Winter of Entrapment: A New Look at the Donner Party* (Toronto: P. D. Meany Publishers, 1992), 81.

122. Stewart, *Ordeal by Hunger*, 219.

123. Rarick, *Desperate Passage*, 194; Hall, *Donner Miscellany*, 80–81. No money changed hands at the sale. Hiram recorded each purchase, and the buyers were told to settle up when the party reached Sutter's Fort. A total of $118.81 was raised and given to Jacob Donner's blood kin.

124. McGlashan, *History*, 161.

125. Ibid., 161–162.

126. Stewart, *Ordeal by Hunger*, 220.

127. Ibid., 222.

128. Morgan, *Overland in 1846*, Vol. I, 347.

129. Ibid., 348.

130. Rarick, *Desperate Passage*, 199.

131. Stewart, *Ordeal by Hunger*, 225.

132. Morgan, *Overland in 1846*, Vol. I, 348.

133. Stewart, *Ordeal by Hunger*, 226.

134. Johnson, *"Unfortunate Emigrants,"* 202, 205. This account from McCutchen was originally published by the *Pacific Rural Press* on April 1, 1871.

135. Ibid., 205.

136. McGlashan, *History*, 177.

137. Stewart, *Ordeal by Hunger*, 226.

138. Johnson, *"Unfortunate Emigrants,"* 206.

139. Limburg, *Deceived*, 187. The symptoms for moderate hypothermia include the cessation of shivering, sleepiness, and seeing things that are not there.

140. Murphy, *Across the Plains*, 426.

141. Stewart, *Ordeal by Hunger*, 229.

142. Morgan, *Overland in 1846*, Vol. I, 300.

143. DeVoto, *The Year of Decision*, 437.

144. Limburg, *Deceived*, 188.

145. Stewart, *Ordeal by Hunger*, 235.

146. Limburg, *Deceived*, 189.

147. Houghton, *The Expedition*, 107.

148. Ibid., 108.

149. Morgan, *Overland in 1846*, Vol. I, 350.

150. Stewart, *Ordeal by Hunger*, 235.

151. McLaughlin, *The Donner Party*, 112.

152. Stewart, *Ordeal by Hunger*, 240. When Turner, so well known for his herculean strength, finally arrived at Johnson's Ranch after the rescue, he was totally incapacitated from frostbite and unable to walk. Not long after surviving the Sierra trek, he was killed when he accidentally shot himself in the leg while cleaning his rifle.

153. Limburg, *Deceived*, 192.

154. McGlashan, *History*, 180–181.

155. DeVoto, *The Year of Decision*, 438.

156. Morgan, *Overland in 1846*, Vol. I, 300–301.

157. Ibid., 296, 448, n. 119. In this footnote, the author notes, "Reed is more outspoken about Woodworth in this letter than in any other document relating to the Donner tragedy."

158. Ibid., 352.

159. *California Star*, San Francisco, April 3, 1847, quoted in Morgan, *Overland in 1846*, Vol. II, 715.

160. DeVoto, *The Year of Decision*, 416.

161. Morgan, *Overland in 1846*, Vol. I, 353.

CHAPTER 43: THE THIRD RELIEF

1. DeVoto, *The Year of Decision*, 438.
2. McGlashan, *History*, 182.
3. Mullen, *The Donner Party Chronicles*, 305.
4. Murphy, *Across the Plains*, 426.
5. McGlashan, *History*, 182.
6. Joseph A. King, "William G. Murphy's Lecture and Two Letters to Mrs. Houghton," *Dogtown Territorial Quarterly*, Summer Issue No. 26, 89.
7. Ibid.; Morgan, *Overland in 1846*, Vol. I, 796, n. 204. Denton's poem was published in full in the *California Star* on April 10, 1847. The journal that was supposedly taken from his pocket was never found. According to Dale Morgan, "If it is true that Denton kept a journal, what happened to it is unknown." Morgan also pointed out that the *Star* did not specifically state that Denton composed the poem while waiting for death to come. Some people have surmised that the detail about the Englishman writing the poem as he lay dying in the snow was added for emotional appeal.
8. Thornton, *Oregon and California*, 220. Thornton based his description of the Starved Camp on conversations with Eddy.
9. Stewart, *Ordeal by Hunger*, 244–245.
10. King, *Winter of Entrapment*, 91–92.
11. McGlashan, *History*, 196.
12. Ibid., 185.
13. King, *Winter of Entrapment*, 92.
14. Joseph A. King, "The Real Breens versus Persistent Donner Party Mythology: Critiquing the Chroniclers," *The Californians*, Vol. 10, No. 1 (July-August 1992), 14.
15. King, *Winter of Entrapment*, 120; Donald L. Hardesty, *The Archaeology of the Donner Party* (Reno and Las Vegas: University of Nevada Press, 1997), 126.
16. King, *Winter of Entrapment*, 120.
17. McGlashan, *History*, 198.
18. Rarick, *Desperate Passage*, 217.
19. Stewart, *History*, 247.
20. Kristin Johnson, *New Light on the Donner Party*, "The Murphy Family," http://www.utahcrossroads.org/DonnerParty/Murphy.htm, Utah Crossroads Chapter, Oregon-California Trails Association. According to Murphy family records, George Foster's full name was Jeremiah George Foster, but he was referred to as George. There is also much confusion about the boy's true age. Some sources refer to him as a nursing infant, while others state that he was four years old when he died. Family records show that he was born on August 25, 1844, in St. Louis, Missouri. He was one year old when his family set out on the California Trail but had turned two by the time of his death.
21. McGlashan, *History*, 200.
22. Ibid.
23. Kaufman, *Saving the Donner Party*, 139–140.
24. McGlashan, *History*, 200.
25. Stewart, *Ordeal by Hunger*, 312.
26. Kaufman, *Saving the Donner Party*, 140.
27. Ibid., 139–140.
28. Dixon, Schablitsky, and Novak, *An Archaeology of Desperation*, 52.

29. Ibid.
30. Ibid., 325, 327.
31. Thornton, *Oregon and California*, 117; Stewart, *Ordeal by Hunger*, 249. Both sources claim that Eddy refused to take $1,500 in silver offered by Tamzene Donner if he would save the lives of her daughters. According to Stewart, Eddy told her that "he would not burden himself of even a hundred dollars of that weight, but that he would take the children out or die with them on the trail."
32. Ibid.
33. Houghton, *The Expedition*, 121.
34. Stewart, *Ordeal by Hunger*, 311.
35. Houghton, *The Expedition*, 124.
36. Kaufman, *Saving the Donner Party*, 142–147. The author devoted five pages to what he called "The Eddy and Nicholas Clark Controversy." Morgan, *Overland in 1846*, Vol. I, 357; DeVoto, *The Year of Decision*, 441.
37. Houghton, *The Expedition*, 126–127.
38. Ibid., 130–131.
39. Bill Anderson and Penny Anderson, eds., *Dogtown Territorial Quarterly*, No. 26, 20–21.

CHAPTER 44: THE FOURTH RELIEF

1. McLaughlin, *The Donner Party*, 121.
2. Ibid.; Stewart, *Ordeal by Hunger*, 256–257.
3. Limburg, *Deceived*, 205.
4. *California Star*, April 10, 1847.
5. DeVoto, *The Year of Decision*, 443.
6. Ibid.
7. Stewart, *Ordeal by Hunger*, 260.
8. Ibid.
9. Ibid., 261.
10. Ibid.
11. Ibid., 262.
12. Ibid.
13. DeVoto, *The Year of Decision*, 443.
14. Limburg, *Deceived*, 209.
15. Ibid., 211.

BIBLIOGRAPHY

PRIVATE COLLECTIONS

Donner-Springer Family Collection

Nancy Spinner Collection

ARCHIVES, MUSEUMS, LIBRARIES, AND HISTORICAL SOCIETIES

Abraham Lincoln Presidential Library and Museum, Springfield, Illinois, Manuscript Department.

Bancroft Library, University of California–Berkeley.

Lowdermilk-Ball, Evelyn Vancil. "A New Colonial History: Lines of Lowdermilk Brown Hudson and Moore Vancil Donner." Okmulgee, OK, 1977, 175. Illinois State Historical Library, Springfield.

Martha J. (Patty) Reed Lewis Collection, Various Citizens to R. F. Stockton, January 1847; Collected Correspondence November 1, 1831, to September 8, 1851; undated, Box 8-4-308, Folder 132, Sutter's Fort State Historic Park, Sacramento, California.

Missouri State Archives, Jefferson City, Missouri.

Rabbeson, Antonio B. *Growth of Towns: Olympia, Tumwater, Portland, and San Francisco.* Bancroft MS PB-17, Bancroft Library, University of California–Berkeley.

Sutter's Fort Historical Monument Collection.

MICROFILM

Germany Births and Baptisms, 1558–1898, Index, FamilySearch, Johann Ludwig Keseberg, 01 Jun 1814, citing FHL microfilm 923182.

Germany Marriages, 1558–1929, Index, FamilySearch, Johann Ludwig Keseberg and Elisabeth Philippine Zimmermann, 22 Jul 1842; citing Evangelisch, Berleburg Stadt, Westfalen, Prussia, FHL microfilm 591331.

BOOKS

Allen, W. W., and R. B. Avery. *California Gold Book: First Nugget, Its Discovery and Discoverers and Some of the Results Proceeding Therefrom.* San Francisco and Chicago: Donohue & Hennebery, 1893.

Angle, Paul M. *"Here I Have Lived": A History of Lincoln's Springfield.* Chicago and New Salem, IL: Abraham Lincoln Book Shop, 1971.

Babcock, Sidney. *The Flock of Sheep; or Familiar Explanations of Simple Facts.* New Haven, CT: S. Babcock, 1840.

Bancroft, H. H. *California Pioneer Register and Index, 1542–1848.* Baltimore: Regional Publishing Co., 1964.

Bancroft, Hubert Howe. *History of California, 1846–1849*, Vol. V. San Francisco: History Co., 1886.

Beecher, Lyman. *A Plea for the West*. Cincinnati: Truman & Smith; New York: Leavitt, Lord & Co., 1835.

Bowden, Martyn J. "The Great American Desert and the American Frontier, 1800–1882, Popular Images of the Plains," in *Anonymous American: Explorations in Nineteenth-Century Social History*, Tamara K. Hareven, ed. Englewood Cliffs, NJ: Prentice-Hall, 1971.

Broeh, Wayne G. Jr., *John Deere's Company: A History of Deere & Company and Its Time*. New York: Doubleday & Co., 1984.

Brown, Daniel James. *The Indifferent Stars Above*. New York: HarperCollins, 2010.

Brown, Dee. *The American West*. New York: Simon & Schuster, 1994.

Bryant, Edwin. *What I Saw in California*. New York: D. Appleton; Philadelphia: G. Appleton, 1848.

Burton, Gabrielle. *Searching for Tamsen Donner*. Lincoln: University of Nebraska Press, 2009.

Butko, Brian. *Greetings from the Lincoln Highway: America's First Coast-to-Coast Road*. Mechanicsburg, PA: Stackpole Books, 2005.

Camp, Charles L., ed. *James Clyman, American Frontiersman, 1792–1881: The Adventures of a Trapper and Covered Wagon Emigrant as Told in His Own Reminiscences and Diaries*. San Francisco: California Historical Society, 1928.

Campbell, Bruce Alexander. *The Sangamon Saga*. Springfield, IL: Phillips Brothers, 1976.

Channing, William E. *Letter to the Honorable Henry Clay, On the Annexation of Texas to the United States*. Boston: James Munroe & Co., 1837.

Christman, Margaret C. S. *1846, Portrait of the Nation*. Washington, D.C., and London: Smithsonian Institution Press for the National Portrait Gallery, 1996.

Clark, Thomas D. Introduction, in Edwin Bryant, *What I Saw in California*. Lincoln and London: University of Nebraska Press, 1985.

Cleland, Robert Glass. *This Reckless Breed of Men: The Trappers and Fur Traders of the Southwest*. Albuquerque: University of New Mexico Press, 1976.

Colton, Reverend Walter. *Three Years in California*. New York and Cincinnati: A. S. Barnes, H. W. Derby & Co., 1850.

Corning, Howard M. *Dictionary of Oregon History*. Portland, OR: Binford & Mort Publishing, 1989.

Croy, Homer. *Wheels West*. New York: Hastings House Publishers, 1955.

DeVoto, Bernard. *The Year of Decision, 1846*. Boston: Little, Brown & Co., 1942.

Diamond, Jared, and James A. Robinson, eds. *Natural Experiments of History*. Cambridge, MA: Harvard University Press, 2010.

Dirck, Brian R. *Lincoln the Lawyer*. Champaign: University of Illinois Press, 2008.

Dixon, Kelly J., Julie M. Schablitsky, and Shannon A. Novak. *An Archaeology of Desperation: Exploring the Donner Party's Alder Creek Camp*. Norman: University of Oklahoma Press, 2011.

Dorothy Sloan—Books. Catalog, Auction 15, Lots 131 and 132. Austin, Texas, n.d.

Dramov, Alissandra. *Carmel-by-the-Sea: The Early Years (1903–1913)*. Bloomington, IN: AuthorHouse, 2012.

Eldredge, Zoeth Skinner. *The Beginnings of San Francisco, from the Expedition of Anza, 1774, to the City Charter of April 15, 1850*. New York: John C. Rankin Co., 1912.

Fanselow, Julie. *The Traveler's Guide to the Oregon Trail*. Helena, MT: Falcon Press Publishing Co., 1992.

Faragher, John Mack. *Sugar Creek: Life on the Illinois Prairie*. New Haven and London: Yale University Press, 1988.

Farnham, Eliza W. *California In-door and Out*. New York: Edwards & Co., 1856.

Flanders, Louis W., Simeon Ide, and Edith F. Dunbar. *A Genealogy of the Ide Family*. Rutland, VT: Tuttle Co., 1931.

Franzwa, Gregory M. *The Oregon Trail Revisited*. Tucson, AZ: Patrice Press, 1972.

Frémont, John Charles. *Memoirs of My Life*. Chicago: Belford, Clarke & Co., 1886.

Frémont, John C. Report of the Exploring Expedition to the Rocky Mountains in the Year 1842 and to Oregon and North California in the Years 1843–1844. Washington, D.C.: Gals and Seaton, 1845.

Gilpin, William. *Mission of the North American People, Geographical, Social, and Political*. Philadelphia: J. B. Lippincott U.S. Navy Lieutenant & Co., 1874.

Hall, Carroll D., ed. *Donner Miscellany: 41 Diaries and Documents*. San Francisco: Book Club of San Francisco, 1947.

Hamersly, Lewis R. *The Records of Living Officers of the U.S. Navy and Marine Corps*. Philadelphia: J. B. Lippincott & Co., 1878.

Hardesty, Donald L. *The Archaeology of the Donner Party*. Reno and Las Vegas: University of Nevada Press, 1997.

Harris, Neil, and Michael Conzen. *Illinois: A Descriptive and Historical Guide*. Chicago: A. C. McClurg & Co., 1939.

Hartman, Ilka Stoffregen. *The Youth of Charles M. Weber: Founder of Stockton*, Issue 8 of Monograph, Holt-Atherton Pacific Center for Western Studies. Stockton, CA: University of the Pacific, 1979.

Hastings, Lansford W. *The Emigrants' Guide to Oregon and California*. Cincinnati, OH: George Conclin, stereotyped by Shepherd & Co., 1845.

Hendrickson, Robert. *The Facts on File Encyclopedia of Word and Phrase Origins*. New York: Checkmark Books, 2004.

History and Improvements of Oak Ridge Cemetery. Springfield, IL: Phillips Brothers, State Printer, 1901, revised and adopted 1902.

History of Sangamon County, Illinois. Chicago: Interstate Publishing Co., 1881.

Hohn, Charles F., and James A. Glynn. *California's Social Problems*. Newbury Park, CA: Pine Forge Press, 2002.

Holmes, Kenneth L., ed., *Covered Wagon Women*, Vol. 1: *Diaries & Letters from the Western Trails, 1840–1849*. Lincoln and London: University of Nebraska Press, 1995.

Hornor, Ric, and Jody Hornor. *The Golden Hub—Sacramento*. Pilot Hill, CA: Electric Canvas/19th Century Books, 2008.

Houghton, Eliza P. Donner. *The Expedition of the Donner Party and Its Tragic Fate*. Chicago: A. C. McClung, 1911.

Hurtado, Albert L. *John Sutter: A Life on the North American Frontier*. Norman: University of Oklahoma Press, 2006.

James, William F., and George H. McMurry. *History of San Jose, California: Narrative and Biographical*. San Jose, CA: A. H. Cawston, 1933.

Johnson, Kristin, ed. *"Unfortunate Emigrants": Narratives of the Donner Party*. Logan: Utah State University Press, 1996.

Kaufman, Richard F. *Saving the Donner Party and Forlorn Hope*. Bloomington, IN: Archway Publishing, 2014.

Khaldun, Ibn. *The Muqaddimah*. Trans. Franz Rosenthal, ed. N. J. Dawood. Princeton, NJ: Princeton University Press, 2005.

King, Joseph A. *Winter of Entrapment: A New Look at the Donner Party*. Toronto: P. D. Meany, 1992.

Kirkham, Samuel. *English Grammar in Familiar Lectures*. Rochester, NY: William Alling, 1845. The book was originally published in 1823.

Korns, J. Roderic. *West from Fort Bridger: The Pioneering of the Immigrant Trails across Utah, 1846–1850*. Salt Lake City: Utah State Historical Society, 1951.

Lankford, Scott. *Tahoe Beneath the Surface: The Hidden Stories of America's Largest Mountain Lake*. Berkeley: Heyday and Sierra College Press, 2010.

Legler, Henry E. *Life in the Diggins*. Milwaukee: Sentinel Co., 1898.

Limburg, Peter R. *Deceived: The Story of the Donner Party*. Pacifica, CA: IPS Books, 1998.

Lodesky, James D. *Polish Pioneers in Illinois, 1818–1850*. Bloomington, IN: Exlibris Corp., 2010.

Mattes, Merrill J. *The Great Platte River Road: The Covered Wagon Mainline via Fort Kearny to Fort Laramie*. Lincoln and London: University of Nebraska Press, 1987. Originally published by Nebraska State Historical Society in 1969.

McGlashan, C. F. *History of the Donner Party: A Tragedy of the Sierra*. Sacramento: H. S. Crocker Co., Printers, 1902.

McGlashan, C. F. *History of the Donner Party: A Tragedy of the Sierra*. San Francisco: A. L. Bancroft & Co., Printers, 1881.

McGlashan, C. F. *History of the Donner Party: A Tragedy of the Sierra*. Truckee, CA: Crowley & McGlashan, 1879.

McLaughlin, Mark. *The Donner Party: Weathering the Storm*. Carnelian Bay, CA: Mic Mac Publishing, 2007.

Meed, Douglas V. *The Mexican War, 1846–1848*. Oxford, U.K.: Osprey Publishing, 2002.

Meigs, William Montgomery. *The Life of Thomas Hart Benton*. Philadelphia and London: J. B. Lippincott Co., 1904.

Morgan, Dale. *Overland in 1846: Diaries and Letters of the California-Oregon Trail*, Vol. I. Lincoln and London: University of Nebraska Press, 1963.

Morgan, Dale. *Overland in 1846: Diaries and Letters of the California-Oregon Trail*, Vol. II. Lincoln and London: University of Nebraska Press, 1963.

Mullen, Frank Jr., *The Donner Party Chronicles*. Reno: Nevada Humanities Committee, 1997.

Murphy, Virginia Reed. "Across the Plains in the Donner Party: A Personal Narrative of the Overland Trip to California," as printed in *The Century Illustrated Monthly Magazine*, Vol. 42, New Series Vol. 20, May 1891–October 1891. New York: Century Co., 1891.

Murphy, Virginia Reed. *Across the Plains in the Donner Party: A Personal Narrative of the Overland Trip to California 1846–47*. Golden, CO.: Outbooks, 1980.

Nelson, Robert. *Enemy of the Saints: The Biography of Governor Lilburn Boggs of Missouri*. Baltimore: PublishAmerica, 2011.

Newell, Olive. *Trail of the Elephant: The Emigrating Experience on the Truckee Route of the California Trail, 1844–1852*. Nevada City, CA: Nevada County Historical Society, 1997.

Older, Cora Miranda Baggerly. *Love Stories of Old California*. Freeport, NY: Books for Libraries Press, 1940.

Pappas, Douglas, and Lester C. Hunt. *Wyoming: A Guide to Its History, Highways, and People*. Federal Writer's Project. New York: Oxford University Press, 1941.

Parkman, Francis. *The Oregon Trail*. Garden City, NY: Doubleday & Co., 1946.

Parks, Ronald D. *The Darkest Period: The Kanza Indians and Their Last Homeland, 1846–1873*. Norman: University of Oklahoma Press, 2014.

Politano, Barbara Wilder, ed. *Their Courage Is Our Legacy: Donner Family History Compiled for the George Donner Family Reunion*. 1996.

Polk, James K. *The Diary of James K. Polk during His Presidency, 1845–1849*, Vol. 1. Edited and annotated by Milo Milton Quaife. Chicago: A. C. McClung & Co., 1910.

Portrait and Biographical Album of DeWitt and Piatt Counties, Illinois. Chicago: Chapman Brothers Publishing Co., 1891.

Power, John Carroll. *History of the Early Settlers of Sangamon County, Illinois*. Springfield, IL: Edwin A. Wilson & Co., 1876.

Rarick, Ethan. *Desperate Passage: The Donner Party's Perilous Journey West*. New York: Oxford University Press, 2008.

Regnery, Dorothy F. *The Battle of Santa Clara*. San Jose: Smith & McKay Printing Co., 1978.

Rhoades, Gale R., and Kerry Ross. *Footprints in the Wilderness: A History of the Lost Rhoades Mines*. Salt Lake City, UT: Dream Garden Press, 1980.

Rogers, Fred Blackburn. *William Brown Ide, Bear Flagger*. San Francisco, CA: John Howell Books, 1962.

San Francisco Board of Supervisors. *San Francisco Municipal Reports for the Fiscal Year*. San Francisco: Neal Publishing Co., 1911.

Sherman, Edwin Allen. *Fifty Years of Masonry in California*, Vol. II. San Francisco: George Spaulding & Co., 1898.

Shoemaker, Floyd C., ed., *Missouri Historical Review*, Vol. 10. Columbia: State Historical Society of Missouri, 1916.

Soulé, Frank, John H. Gihon, and James Nisbet, *The Annals of San Francisco*. New York: D. Appleton & Co., 1855.

Steele, Volney. *Bleed, Blister, and Purge: A History of Medicine on the American Frontier*. Missoula, MT: Mountain Press Publishing Co., 2005.

Stewart, George R. *The California Trail*. Lincoln and London: University of Nebraska Press, 1962.

Stewart, George R. *Ordeal by Hunger: The Story of the Donner Party*. Boston and New York: Houghton Mifflin Co., 1963.

Stuckey, Mary. "The Donner Party and the Rhetoric of Western Expansion," in *Communications Faculty Publications*. Atlanta: Georgia State University, 2011.

Teggart, Frederick J., editor and curator of the Academy of Pacific Coast History. *Diary of Patrick Breen—One of the Donner Party*. Dillon, CO: VistaBooks, 1991.

Thornton, J. Quinn. *Oregon and California in 1848*, Vol. I. New York: Harper & Brothers, 1849.

Thornton, J. Quinn. *The California Tragedy*. California Centennial Edition, copyright by Joseph A. Sullivan. Oakland: Biobooks, 1945.

Tinkham, George Henry. *California Men and Events*. Stockton, CA: Record Publishing Co., 1915.

Twain, Mark. *Life on the Mississippi*. New York: Harper & Brothers, 1902.

Umland, Rudolph E. *Nebraska: A Guide to the Cornhusker State*. Federal Writers' Project. New York: Hastings House, 1939.

Unruh, John D., Jr. *The Plains Across: The Overland Emigrants and the Trans-Mississippi West, 1840–1860.* Urbana, Chicago, and London: University of Illinois Press, 1979.

Wallis, Michael. *The Wild West 365.* New York: Harry N. Abrams, 2011.

Wallis, Michael, and Michael S. Williamson. *The Lincoln Highway: Coast to Coast from Times Square to the Golden Gate.* New York and London: W. W. Norton & Co., 2007.

Waters, Henry F. *New England Historical and Genealogical Register,* Vol. 32. Boston: David Clapp & Son, 1878.

Wells, Harry Laurenz. *History of Nevada County, California.* Oakland: Thompson & West, 1880.

The West, Its History and Romance. Anderson Galleries Auction Catalogue, November 28, 1921, Vol. 26, No. 106.

Willis, William. *Genealogy of the McKinstry Family.* Boston: Henry W. Dutton, Printers, 1858.

Wise, H. A. *Los Gringos; or, An Inside View of Mexico and California, with Wanderings in Peru, Chili, and Polynesia.* New York: Baker & Scribner, 1849.

Wishart, David J., ed. *Encyclopedia of the Great Plains.* Lincoln and London: University of Nebraska Press, 2004.

PERIODICALS, NEWSPAPERS, AND JOURNALS

Allin, Lawrence C. "'A Mile Wide and an Inch Deep': Attempts to Navigate the Platte River." *Nebraska History,* Vol. 63 (Spring 1982).

Anderson, Bill, and Penny Anderson, eds. *Dogtown Territorial Quarterly,* No. 26 (Summer 1996).

Bacich, Damian. "The Zacatecan Franciscans in Alta California: A Misunderstood Legacy." *Bolítin: Journal of the California Mission Studies Association,* Vol. 28, Nos. 1–2.

"Battle of Santa Clara." *California Star* (Yerba Buena), February 6, 1847.

California Star, February 6, 1847; April 10, 1847.

Cooper, Katherine Wakeman. "Patty Reed." *Overland Monthly* (January-June 1917).

Culotta, Elizabeth. "Neanderthals Were Cannibals, Bones Show." *Science Magazine,* Vol. 286, No. 5437 (October 1999).

Daily Missouri Republican, October 31, 1848.

Davies, J. Kenneth. "Thomas Rhoads, Forgotten Mormon Pioneer of 1846." *Nebraska History,* Vol. 64 (1983).

Dorius, Guy L. "Crossroads in the West: The Intersections of the Donner Party and the Mormons." *Nauvoo Journal,* Vol. 9, No.1 (Spring 1997).

Editor's Column, "Abe Lincoln of San Jose." *San Jose Evening News,* June 28, 1919.

Engelhardt, Laura. "The Problem with Eyewitness Testimony." *Stanford Journal of Legal Studies,* Vol. 1, No. 1 (1999).

Fey, Marshall. "The Alder Creek Trail." *Donner Summit Heirloom,* No. 45 (May 2012).

Fivush, Robyn. "Children's Recollections of Traumatic and Nontraumatic Events." *Development and Psychopathology,* Vol. 10, No. 4 (Cambridge, U.K.: Cambridge University Press, 1998).

"Galena and its Mines." *Harper's New Monthly Magazine,* Vol. 32 (1866).

Grebenkemper, John, and Kristin Johnson. "Forensic Canine Search for the Donner Family Winter Camps at Alder Creek." *Overland Journal,* Vol. 33, No. 2 (Summer 2015).

Guly, Henry. "History of Accidental Hypothermia." *European Resuscitation Journal*, Vol. 82, No. 1 (January 2011).

Hart, Richard E. "Lincoln's Springfield: Photography of Historic Mather Residence." *For the People: A Newsletter of the Abraham Lincoln Association*, Vol. 12, No. 3 (Summer 2010).

Himes, George H. "History of the Press of Oregon, 1839–1850." *Quarterly of the Oregon Historical Society*, Vol. III (March 1902–December 1902).

Hummel, Jeffrey Rogers. "The American Militia and the Origin of Conscription: A Reassessment." *Journal of Libertarian Studies*, Vol. 15, No. 4 (Fall 2001).

Ide, William B. "From Our Oregon Correspondent." *Illinois Weekly State Journal*, September 4, 1845.

Illinois Weekly State Journal, February 26, 1845, Donner-Springer Family Collection.

Illinois Weekly State Journal, July 11, 1835.

Illinois Weekly State Journal, March 25, 1845, Donner-Springer Family Collection.

Jefferson Inquirer, Jefferson City, Missouri, July 21, 1846.

Jensen, Richard E. "The Pawnee Mission, 1834–1846." *Nebraska History* 75 (1994).

Johnson, Kristin. "Donner Party Cannibalism: Did They or Didn't They?" *Wild West*, Vol. 26, No. 4 (December 2013).

"Kansas Before 1854: A Revised Annals," Part Fifteen, 1846, compiled by Louise Barry. *Kansas Historical Quarterly*, Vol. 30, No. 3 (Autumn 1964).

King, Joseph A. "The Real Breens versus Persistent Donner Party Mythology: Critiquing the Chroniclers." *The Californians*, Vol. 10, No. 1 (July-August 1992).

King, Joseph A. "William G. Murphy's Lecture and Two Letters to Mrs. Houghton." *Dogtown Territorial Quarterly*, Summer Issue No. 26.

Koch, Margaret R. "The Gold Gulch Letters of James Frazier Reed." *Santa Cruz County History Journal*, Issue No. 2 (1995).

Lewiston Evening Journal, May 13, 1893.

Lonnberg, Allan. "The Digger Indian Stereotype in California." *Journal of California and Great Basin Anthropology*, Vol. 3, No. 2 (1981).

Lupton, David Walker. "Fort Bernard on the Oregon Trail." *Nebraska History*, Vol. 60, No. 1 (1979).

McCurdy, Stephen A. "Epidemiology of Disaster: The Donner Party (1846–1847)." *Western Journal of Medicine*, Vol. 160, No. 4 (April 1994).

McLaws, Monte B. "The Attempted Assassination of Missouri's Ex-Governor, Lilburn W. Boggs." *Missouri Historical Review*, Vol. 60, No. 1 (October 1965).

Mueller, Tom. "CSI: Italian Renaissance," *Smithsonian*, July-August 2013.

"Newly Discovered Lincoln Document Traveled with the Donner Party to California." *Illinois Heritage*, Vol. 13, No. 5 (September-October 2010).

Older, Cora Baggerly. *When San Jose Was Young*, No. 152, "How Reed Saved the Donner Party." San Jose: *Evening News*, April 10, 1917.

Papakostas, Yiannis G., et al. Horse Madness (Hippomania) and Hippophobia." *History of Psychiatry*. London, Thousand Oaks, CA, and New Delhi: AGE Publications, December 2005.

"Pay of the Army." *Niles National Register*, Vol. 70, Whole No. 1815 (July 11, 1846).

Pratt, Harry E. "Abraham Lincoln's First Murder Trial." *Journal of the Illinois State Historical Society (1908–1984)*, Vol. 37, No. 3 (September 1944).

Quinn, D. Michael. "The Culture of Violence in Joseph Smith's Mormonism." *Sunstone: Mormon Experience, Scholarship, Issues & Art*, No. 164 (October 2011).

Reed, James Frazier. "Narrative of the Sufferings of a Company of Emigrants in the

Mountains of California in the Winter of '46 and '47." *Illinois Journal* (Springfield), December 9, 1847.

Reed, James Frazier. "The Snow-Bound, Starved Emigrants of 1846." *Pacific Rural Press* (San Francisco), March 25, April 1, 1871.

Richards, John E. "A Future Supreme Court Justice Looks Back." *California Supreme Court Historical Society Newsletter,* Spring-Summer 2010.

Roberts, John C. "Traveling the Great Platte River Road." *Caxtonian,* Journal of the Caxton Club, Vol. XVII, No. 10 (October 2009).

Ryan, F. J. "The City of Stockton." *Californian Illustrated Magazine,* Vol. 4.

Sangamo Journal, August 19, 1846.

Sangamo Journal (Springfield), March 26, 1846. The same notice appeared in the issue of April 2, 1846.

Sherman, Edwin A. "Gives Details of Reed-Donner Trip." *Illinois Weekly State Journal,* September 21, 1910.

Sherman, Edwin A. "An Unpublished Account of the Battle of Santa Clara, Written by John [sic] Frazier Reed Using his Saddle Horn as a Desk." *San Francisco Chronicle,* September 4, 1910.

Spedden, Rush. "The Fearful Long Drive." *Overland Journal,* Vol. 12, No. 2 (1994).

Stratton, H. J. "The Northern Cross Railroad." *Journal of the Illinois State Historical Society (1908–1984),* Vol. 28, No. 2 (1935).

Swope, Sam K. "From Lycoming County, Pennsylvania, to Parke County, Indiana: Recollections of Andrew TenBrook, 1786–1823." *Indiana Magazine of History,* Vol. LXI, No. 1 (1965).

Taylor, Lois Chambers. "Andrew Jackson Grayson." *The Condor,* Vol. 51, No. 2 (March-April 1949).

Tompkins, James, ed., "Reminiscences of A. H. Garrison: His Early Life, Across the Plains and of Oregon from 1846 to 1903." *Overland Journal,* Vol. 11, No. 2 (1993).

Topping, Gary. "Overland Emigration, the California Trail, and the Hastings Cutoff." *Utah Historical Quarterly,* Vol. 56, No. 2 (1988).

Wedin, Bertil, Leif Vanggard, and Jorma Hirvonen, "'Paradoxical Undressing' in Fatal Hypothermia," *Journal of Forensic Science,* Vol. 24, No. 3 (July 1979).

ELECTRONIC DOCUMENTS AND SOURCES

Abraham Lincoln Timeline, http://www.historynet.com/abraham-lincoln-timeline.

Brown, Orson Pratt. "The Life & Times of Orson Pratt Brown," www.orsonpratt-brown.com/ murphy-dfraper/jeremiah-and-levina-jackson-murphy.html.

California Department of Parks and Recreation. "The Miwok People," http://www. parks.ca.gov/?page_Id=22538.

Dameier, Evelyn. "Kellogg's Grove," http://gis.hpa.state.il.us/hargis/PDFs/200106. pdf, National Register of Historic Places Nomination Form, January 18, 1978, HARGIS Database, Illinois Historic Preservation Agency.

Dobson, G. B. "Wyoming Tales and Trails," www.wyomingtalesandtrails.com/ bridger.html.

Family Tales, Benjamin Lippincott letter to John Stephens, February 6, 1847, http:// www.familytales.org/results.php?collection=55.

Frazier, William, to James Frazier Reed. Spared & Shared 2, http://sparedandshared2 .wordpress.com/letters/1846-william-frazier-to-james-frazier-reed; 1846 letter.

The Harlan Family in America, *History of George Harlan,* Recollections of his daughter, Mary Ann Harlan Smith, http://www.harlanfamily.org/GeorgeH852.htm.

Hart, Richard E. *Lincoln's Springfield*, http://lincolnsspringfield.blogspot.com/2007/03/lincolns-springfield-1838-richard-e.html.

History and Development of the Enos Park Area/Enos Park Neighborhood Improvement Association, http://www.epnia.com/history-and-development-of-the-enos-park-area/#early.

The History Bandits, "When San Jose Was Young": A Study in Historical Representation, http://the history bandits.com/2015/01/15/when-san-jose-was-young-a-study-in-historicalrepresentation/.

"History Minutes: Abraham Lincoln and Oregon." Oregon Historical Society, http://www.ohs.org/education/history-minutes-abraham-lincoln-and-oregon.cfm.

Holst, Erika. "Lincoln and the Donner Party." *Lincoln Footnotes*, 2010, http://www.lincolnfootnotes.com/1/category/donner%20party/1.html.

http://www.fmoran.com/danner.htm.

Johnson, Kristin. Donner Blog, "John Snyder's Grave," May 27, 2013, http://donnerblog,blogspot.com/.

Johnson, Kristin. *New Light on the Donner Party*, "Some Donner Party Myths and Mysteries in Brief," http://www.utahcrossroads.org/DonnerParty/Briefmyths.htm; "Teamsters and Others"; "The Reed Family," http:// www.utahcrossroads.org/DonnerParty, Utah Crossroads Chapter, Oregon-California Trails Association; "Rescuers and Others"; "The Murphy Family."

Johnson, Kristin, ed. *Crossroads*, Vol. 8, No. 1 (Winter 1997), Utah Crossroads Chapter of the Oregon-California Trails Association, http://user.xmission.com/-octsa/newsv8n1.htm.

Johnson, Kristin, ed. *Donner Party Bulletin*, No. 5 (May-June 1998). Retrieved from http://user.xmission.com/~octa/DonnerParty/Bulletin05.htm.

Lewis, James. "The Black Hawk War of 1832," http://lincoln.lib.niu.edu/blackhawk/.

Lipscomb, Carol A. "Karankawa Indians," *Handbook of Texas Online*, http://www.tshaonline.org/handbook/online/articles/bmk05, published by the Texas State Historical Association.

López De Victoria, Samuel. "Beware of She-Wolves." Psych Central Web, February 11, 2014, http://psychcentral.com/blog/archives/2014/02/11/beware-of-she-wolves/.

The Mexican-American War and the Media, 1845–1848, Virginia Tech, Department of History, www.history.vt.edu/MxAmWar/newspapers/RW/RW846JanJune.htm.

MLHS Online Academy, Mountain Lakes, New Jersey, http://www.mtlakes.org/hs/acad/tech/hunger/starvation.htm.

Murphy, Mary A. M. Letter written May 25, 1847, California Territory, www.rootsweb.ancestry.com/~tnweakle/3Murphy_Letters.htm.

New Santa Fe Historical Society, http://www.newsantafe.org/.

Oxford Dictionaries (Oxford University Press, 2015), http://www.oxforddictionaries.com/us/definition/english/forlorn-hope.

Proclamation of Thanksgiving by Abraham Lincoln, www.abrahamlincolnonline.org/lincoln/speeches/thanks.htm.

Rosen, Daniel M. *The Donner Party*, "Log Entries for May 1846," http://www.donnerpartydiary.com/may46.htm. The original letter is in the James W. Keyes Papers, Illinois State Historical Library, Springfield; "Log Entries for August 1846"; "Log Entries for September 1846"; "Log Entries for October 1846," http://www.donnerpartydiary.com/oct46.htm; "Log Entries for November 1846"; "Log Entries for December 1846," http://www.donnerpartydiary.com/dec46.htm.

"Salt Lake Desert." *The American Southwest,* http://www.americansouthwest.net/utah/salt_lake_desert/.

Sangamon County Historical Society, Sangamon Link, Northern Cross Railroad, http://sangamoncountyhistory.org/wp?p=1608.

Schmidt, Jo Ann Brant. "Who Was Captain George Donner?" *Donner Party Bulletin,* No. 3 (January-February 1998). Retrieved from www.utahcrossroads.org/donnerpartybulletin.htm.

U.S. Marshals Service, History of Western District of Missouri, http:www.usmarshals.gov/district/mo-w/general/history.htm.

Village of Riverton, "A Short History of the Village of Riverton," 2007, http://voril.com/History/history.htm.

Virtual Museum of San Francisco, http://www.sfmuseum.org/hist/name.html.

William Henry Russell (1802–1873), http://genforum.geneaology.com/Russell/messages/11998.html, submitted by William LaBach.

William Henry Russell, http://www.usgwarchives.net/copyright.htm, submitted by William LaBach.

GOVERNMENT DOCUMENTS

American Indians in the Federal Decennial Census, 1790–1930. National Archives.

Department of the Army. *U.S. Army Survival Field Manual: FM 21-76,* June 1992.

Krapu, Gary L., Kenneth J. Reinecke, and Charles R. Frith. "Sandhill Cranes and the Platte River." USGS Northern Prairie Wildlife Research Center, Paper 87, 1982.

Kreutzer, Lee. National Historic Trails Audio Tour Route Interpretive Guide, *Across Nevada.* Salt Lake City: National Park Service, National Trails—Intermountain Region, 2012.

Kreutzer, Lee. National Historic Trails Audio Tour Route Interpretive Guide, *Utah—Crossroads of the West.* Salt Lake City: National Park Service, National Trails—Intermountain Region, 2010.

Laws of the State of Illinois. Vandalia, IL: William Walters Public Printer, 1837.

Mattes, Merrill J. *Fort Laramie Park History, 1834–1977.* Denver: Rocky Mountain Regional Office, National Park Service, 1980.

Moore, Shirley Ann Wilson. *Sweet Freedom's Plains: African Americans on the Overland Trails, 1841–1869,* for the National Park Service, National Trails Intermountain Region, Salt Lake City and Santa Fe, January 31, 2012.

National Historic Trails, Audio Tour Route Interpretive Guide, Western Missouri to Northeastern Kansas. Salt Lake City: National Park Service, National Trails System Intermountain Region, 2005.

National Register of Historic Places.

Sangamon County Illinois Archives, Military Records, Captain Jacob M. Early's Co.

United States House of Representatives, *House Documents,* Vol. 28. Washington, D.C.: U.S. Government Printing Office, 1846.

United States Senate, Committee on Territories. *Affairs in the Indian Territory.* Washington, D.C.: U.S. Government Printing Office, 1879.

UNPUBLISHED WORKS

Ó Gráda, Cormac. "Carleton and Others on Famine's Darkest Secret," keynote address at the Carleton Summer School, Clogher, Ireland, August 6, 2012.

INDEX

Page numbers in *italics* refer to illustrations.
Page numbers beginning with 379 refer to endnotes.

abolitionists, 56
acorns, 260
Adobe Rock, 160
aguardiente (fiery water), 128, 274
Alcove Spring, 85–86, 92, 100, 122,
    140, 166, 307
Alder Creek, 212, 213, 216, 226–31,
    241, 251–52, 256, 262, 264–65,
    300–301, 302, 318, 319, 321–22,
    324–25, 332, 346, 351, 352
Alta California, xv, 29–30, 217, 272,
    276
altitude sickness, 290
American Fur Company, 126
American Revolution, 5
American River, 285
American Tract Society, 59
amputation, 108–9
Anderson, Robert, 18
Antelope Hills, 144
antelopes, 97–98
Antonio (cattle herder), 154, 215, 236,
    244–45, 246, 250, 359
    death of, 245
Appalachian Mountains, 6
Arizona, xvi
Arizona Territory, 357
Army, U.S., 65
Ash Hollow, 122–23, 394
"Ash Hollow Hotel," 123
Ashland plantation, 72

Auburn, Ill., 14
Austria, 16

Backenstoe, Lloyd Carter, 20
Bancroft, Hubert Howe, 407, 416
Barbour, James, 62
Barney (dog), 75
Barry, Ill., 51
Bartlett, Washington, 270, 275, 279,
    280, 284
Bates, Dr., 421
Bear Flag Republic, 217–18
Bear Flag Revolt, 218–19, 272–73
Bear River, 153, 157–58, 209, 219, 287,
    296, 297
Bear River Trail, 309
Bear Valley, 195–96, 289, 290, 311, 339
Beaver Creek, 137
beaver-fur trade, 126
Becknell, William, 52, 63
Beecher, Lyman, 27
Belleville, Ill., 99
Bent, Silas, 73
Bent, Charles, 73
Bent, William, 73
Benton, Thomas Hart, 35, 56
Bent's Fort, 73
Big Blue River, 61, 74, 83, 86, 89–90,
    148
Big Meadows, 189
Big Mountain, 160

Big River Rover, 89
Big Sandy Creek, 145, 149
Billy (pony), 47, 66, 82, 135, 138–39, 173, 254
bison, 34, 78, 80, 98, 102, 103, 104–6, 114, 118, 120, 126, 136, 139
bison manure, 103; see also "buffalo chips"; "Plains oak"
Black Hawk (Sauk war leader), 18
Black Hawk War, 18–19, 25, 40, 130
Black Paint Creek, 78
Black's Fork, 151
bluestem grass, 8
Boggs, Julia Ann Bent, 73
Boggs, Lilburn W., 73–74, 76, 83, 84, 85, 93, 96, 117, 120, 126, 127, 131, 133, 141, 142, 143, 147, 148, 217, 253, 272
    attempted assassination of, 73
Boggs, Panthea Boone, 72–73, 76
Boggs, Sonora Hicklin, 73–74
Boggs, William, 73–74, 105, 139
Boggs Party, 121, 122–25, 128, 143, 145, 149, 394
    Bryant mule riders leaving of, 138
    Clyman's advice to, 130–32
    at Fort Bernard, 126–32
    Fourth of July celebrated by, 137–38
    hunting by, 139
    increasing factionalism in, 136–37
    pace of, 123
    Sioux encountered by, 134–35, 138–39
    slowness of, 133, 139
    splitting of, 141–46
    urgency felt by, 133–40
Boiling Springs, 191
Bonney, Wales B., 142
Boone, Alphonso D., 76, 78, 139, 147
Boone, Chloe Donnelly, 78
Boone, Daniel, 6, 73, 76, 263
Boyle, Emmet D., xviii
Brannan, Sam, 279, 293, 416
Breen, Edward, 161, 180, 192, 222, 225, 252, 302, 359, 400
    compound fracture of, 157–58
Breen, Isabella Margaret, 343, 357, 359
Breen, James, 180, 342–44, 359
Breen, John, 174, 175, 180, 183, 194, 200, 206–7, 208, 252, 267, 328, 343, 359
Breen, Margaret Bulger "Peggy," 148–49, 157, 158, 161, 180, 192, 262–63, 266, 267, 304–5, 324, 325, 328, 330, 342, 343, 359
Breen, Patrick, 148–49, 157, 164, 174, 188, 190, 206, 208, 235, 252, 263–64, 265, 299, 300, 304–5, 318–19, 325, 326, 327, 328, 330, 342, 343, 357, 359
    diary of, 224, 226, 227, 241, 251, 253, 264, 319–20, 321, 407
Breen, Patrick, Jr., 360
Breen, Peter, 360
Breen, Simon Preston, 302, 360
Breen family, 199, 201, 215, 255
Breen Party, 149
Bridger, Jim, 149, 150–51, 152, 153–54, 155
Brown, W. B., 76
Brueheim, Adolph "Greasy Jim," 286, 289–90
Bryant, Edwin, 69, 72, 75–76, 77, 78–79, 80–81, 83, 84, 89, 90–91, 95–96, 100, 105–11, 117, 118, 123, 124, 125, 127, 128, 131, 133–34, 138, 150–51, 154, 176, 217, 270, 272, 398, 419
    Alcove Spring found by, 85–86
    antelope described by, 97–98
    Bear Flag Revolt and, 218–19
    broken wagon of, 99
    Fourth of July celebrated by, 137–38
    medical training of, 107
    Platte River described by, 101–2
    on Sarah Keyes's death, 87
    on Walker, 151–52
    warning about Hastings Cutoff given by, 152, 154, 155
Bryant, William Cullen, 72
Bryant-Russell pack train, 150, 152, 154, 159, 176, 194
Bryant-Russell Party, 168
Buckley, Spencer, 118
buffalo, see bison
"buffalo chips," 103, 104, 112
buffalo-robe trade, 126
bullboats, 295

bullwhackers, 37
Burger, Charles, 96, 215, 236, 237, 360
  death of, 253
Burnt Spring, 166
Burton, John, 271–72, 276–77
Butler, William, 32

cabin fever, 17
Cache Cave, 159
Cache Creek, 294
Cady, Charles, 296, 317–18, 319, 321–
  22, 324–25, 332–34, 346, 349, 421
California, xvi, 34, 36, 76, 179, 218,
  274, 357
  increasing immigration to, 71–72
California Battalion, 218–19
California Bear Republic flag, 218
California Crossing, 119
California Star, 277, 279, 293, 336,
  351–52
California Trail, 34, 55, 63–64, 131,
  168, 176, 177, 196, 207
Californios, 273–74, 275, 276, 279,
  315
Camino Real, 415
Camp of Strife, 259
cannibalism, xvi–xvii, 243–44, 246,
  248, 250–51, 259, 280, 293, 314,
  318–19, 320, 322–23, 342, 344,
  355–56, 410, 411
Carriger, Nicolas, 395
Carson, Kit, 63, 125, 197
Cash (dog), 58, 75, 254
Cayuse Indians, 394
Cedar Bluffs, 122
Cedar Mountains, 168
Channing, William Ellery, 28
Cheyenne Indians, 136
Chihuahua, Mexico, 57, 60
Chimney Rock, 124–25
cholera epidemics, xv
  of 1833, 20
City Hotel, 279
Civil War, U.S., 18, 357
Clark, Nicholas, 296, 317–18, 319,
  321–22, 324–25, 332, 346–47,
  348–49, 421
Clay, Henry, 28, 67, 72
Clear Lake Township, 11

Clyman, James, 18, 130–32, 133, 141,
  147, 191, 197, 246
Coffeemeyer, Edward "Ned," 286, 305,
  306, 309
Colton, Walter, 274
Columbia Plateau, 159
Congress, U.S., 45, 61, 65
conscription, 65
constipation, 243
consumption, 87, 154
continental divide, 141, 144
Coon, William, 285, 288
Cornwall, Josephus Adamson, 87, 107,
  109
cotton, 51
Courthouse Rock, 124
Crows, 128
Crusoe, Robinson, 179
Crystal Peak, 201
Cumberland Gap, 6
curlews, 104
Curry, George Law, 77, 104, 117, 123,
  127
Curtis, Jotham, 220, 221, 273, 286,
  288, 289–90

Daniels, William, 276
Deere, John, 9
dehydration, 242
Delaware Indians, 7, 80
Democratic Review, xv
Denton, John, 42, 87, 113, 230, 265,
  302, 303, 308, 341, 360, 421
  abandonment of, 307
  death of, 317
  poem written by, 341, 424
Derusha, Frederic, 108
Devil's Gate, 143
DeVoto, Bernard, xv, 27, 36, 336–37,
  410, 420
diarrhea, 243
Dickerson, Gallant D., 123–24
Digger Indians, 179, 401–2
Diomedes, king of Thrace, 386
Dofar, Matthew, 296, 327, 335, 336
Dog Valley, 201
Dolan, John Patrick, 148–49, 199–200,
  201, 215, 222, 236, 243, 244, 250,
  360

Dolan, John Patrick (*continued*)
  cannibalizing of, 247–48
  death of, 246–47
Donner, Ann Mary, 5, 379
Donner, Elitha Cumi, 9, 42, 300, 301, 303, 333, 349, 357, 360, 405
Donner, Elizabeth Blue Hook "Betsy" (Jacob's wife), 9, 33, 42, 231, 233, 300–301, 321, 322, 324, 355, 360
  death of, 346
Donner, Elizabeth (George Jr's daughter), 6, 346
Donner, Elizabeth (George Jr.'s sister), 5
Donner, Elizabeth Hunter (William's wife), 9
Donner, Eliza Poor, 15, 35, 38, 40, 42, 44, 45, 46, 69, 71, 74, 80, 82, 92, 118, 128–29, 134, 154, 157, 165, 167, 168, 169–70, 201–2, 214–15, 228–29, 230, 232, 233–35, 251–52, 256, 264–65, 301, 322, 333, 347–48, 360, 400, 405
  on departure from Independence, 59
  on Indian Country, 62–63
  Jacob's death and, 231
Donner, Frances Eustis, 15, 42, 212, 234, 322, 333, 334, 344, 346, 348, 349, 360
Donner, George, Jr., 5–6, 7, 8, 9, 10, 11, 14–15, 28, 33, 41, 42, 44, 56, 62, 83, 90, 121, 128, 131, 144, 145–46, 148, 150, 153, 166, 167, 173, 185, 186, 199, 201, 213, 226–27, 230, 265, 279, 300, 301, 321, 322, 324–25, 333, 347, 350, 352, 353, 355, 361, 379
  first marriage of, 6
  hand injury of, 202, 212, 214, 228, 233
  Illinois farm of, 33
  Jacob's death and, 231
  missing horses of, 177
  overturned wagon of, 201–2
  and Reinhardt's confession, 232–33
  sale of farm by, 30–31, 36
  second marriage of, 42, 213
  third marriage of, 15

Donner, George, Sr., 5, 6, 7, 8, 84, 113
Donner, George (son of Jacob), 9, 42, 361
Donner, George T. (William's son), 10
Donner, Georgia Ann, 15, 42, 201, 234, 322, 323, 333, 345, 346, 348, 361
Donner, Isaac, 9, 42, 324, 331, 342, 361
  death of, 329
Donner, Jacob "Jake," 5–10, 28, 30, 31, 33, 40, 42, 56, 90, 131, 144–46, 148, 171–72, 199, 201, 202, 212–13, 218, 227, 228, 241, 279, 300, 321, 323, 325, 355, 361
  camp of, 214
  death of, 230–31
Donner, John, 5
Donner, Leanna Charity, 9, 42, 213, 232, 300, 301, 303, 333, 349, 361
Donner, Lewis, 9, 42, 324, 361
  death of, 346
Donner, Lydia (George Jr.'s daughter), 6
Donner, Lydia (George Jr.'s sister), 5
Donner, Mary Blue Tenant (George Jr.'s second wife), 9, 10
Donner, Mary (Jacob's daughter), 9, 42, 324, 329–30, 331, 342, 361
Donner, Mary Margaret Huff (George Sr.'s wife), 5
Donner, Mary "Polly" (George Jr.'s daughter), 6
Donner, Samuel, 9, 42, 325, 347, 349, 350, 353, 361
Donner, Sarah, 6
Donner, Susannah (George Jr.'s daughter), 6
Donner, Susannah Holloway (George Jr.'s first wife), 6, 7, 379
Donner, Tamzene Eustis Dozier (George Jr.'s third wife), 11–15, 30–31, 33, 41, 42, 44, 85, 92–93, 117, 122, 128, 136, 140, 146, 147, 149, 154, 161, 165, 167, 202, 212, 214, 228–29, 233, 265, 300, 301, 307, 322, 324–25, 333, 334, 346–48, 350, 352, 355, 358, 362, 422, 425

botanical specimens gathered by, 62, 70–71, 79–80
correspondence of, 57–58
as correspondent for *Sangamo Journal*, 46
death and cannibalization of, 353
in decision to leave Illinois, 31
drawings by, 49, 80
education of, 11–12
first marriage of, 12–13
goods packed by, 35
letter from, 112–14
rumored "lost journal" of, 49
teaching of, 14
writings of, 49
Donner, Tobias, 5, 7, 9
Donner, William, 6, 9, 10, 47, 59
Donner Hill, 163
Donner Lake (Truckee Lake), xix, 205–7, 211–12, 215, 251, 252–53, 262, 287, 291, 292, 297, 302, 325, 332, 334, 344, 351, 352
Donner Party Archaeology Project, xvi
Donner-Reed Party, xv, 147–49, 150, 181, 278, 279, 355–58
advertisement for teamsters for, 36–37
advice sought by, 33–36
Alder Creek camp of, 212, 213, 216, 226–31, 241, 251–52, 256, 262, 264–65, 300–301, 302, 318, 319, 321–22, 324–25, 332, 346, 351, 352
attempts at crossing Frémont Pass made by, 208–11
Bear River camp of, 157–58
Big Blue River crossing by, 61
cabins built by, 215–16
Cady's and Stone's desertion of, 332–34
cannibalism practiced by, xvi–xvii, 243–44, 246, 248, 250–51, 259, 280, 293, 314, 318–19, 320, 322–23, 342, 344, 355–56, 410, 411
cash carried by, 40
as cautionary tale, xvii
Christmas Day at Truckee Lake for, 252–53

death of livestock of, 227
departure of, 39–41, 42–47, 385
depleted food stores of, 175, 181
disconnection and loss of identity for, 262
Donner cabin built by, 213–14
Donner Lake camp of, xix, 205–7, 211–12, 215, 251, 252–53, 262, 287, 291, 292, 297, 302, 325, 332, 334, 344, 351, 352
at Emigration Canyon, 162–63
first camp of, 45–47
first death in, 87
First Relief Party in, 282–91, 295, 297–309
food supplies of, 222–23
Forlorn Hope Party of, 230–39, 240–49, 250–51, 257–61, 277, 280
at Fort Bridger, 150–56
Fourth Relief Party for, 351–54
George Donner elected head of, 145–46
at Great Salt Lake, 164–65
in Great Salt Lake Desert, 168–74
Hardcoop abandoned by, 187–88, 189
Hastings Cutoff taken by, 143, 145–46, 157–63
histories of, xvi–xvii
Humboldt River reached by, 177–80
at Humboldt Sink, 190
hunting by, 177, 223–24
in Independence, 55–59
Indian encounters of, 66–67, 178–79
Indian Territory entered by, 62–63, 66
in journey to Independence, 48–52
joined by Graves family, 162
Kaw River crossed by, 66–67
in Little Santa Fe, 61–62
livestock of, 47
at Lone Elm, 63
McKinstry's critique of, 293–94
at "Mad Woman Camp," 176
members of, 42–43, 359–69
oxen poisoned by alkali in, 144–45
oxen slaughtered by, 222–23
Paiute attacks on, 187, 189–90

Donner-Reed Party (*continued*)
  personal motives of, xvii
  preparations of, 33–38
  provisions of, 58
  published accounts of, xvi
  Reed family wagon in, 58, 401
  Reed's banishment from, 184–86
  Reed's route taken by, 161–62
  in retreat to Truckee Lake, 211–12
  Russell Party joined by, 67–69
  on Santa Fe Trail, 60–64
  scapegoats for, 315–16
  second attempt at Frémont Pass,
    223
  Second Relief Party in, 292–338
  sensational reporting on, 351–52
  sense of community lost by, 186–87,
    199
  separation into three groups of,
    199
  snowshoe trek of, 235–36
  in snowstorm at Pilot Peak, 174
  snowstorms endured by, 205–16,
    226–27, 265
  Snyder-Reed fight in, 182–83
  speed of, 60–61, 63
  supplies of, 40–41, 112–13
  Stanton's resupply of, 200–201
  stolen livestock of, 179
  teamsters in, 42–43
  Third Relief Party in, 339–50
  Thornton's account of, 74
  time of departure of, 34
  at Truckee Meadows, 198–99
  Truckee Meadows reached by, 193,
    194
  on Truckee Route, 191–92
  wagons abandoned by, 187, 189,
    190–91
  Walker encountered by, 152
  weaponry for, 34, 37–38
  at Weber Canyon, 159–60, 163
"dope" (axle grease), 62
Douglas, Stephen A., 18, 25, 56
Dozier, Tully B., 12–13
draft, 65
draft horses, 37
Dry Sandy Creek, 144, 149

Dunleavy, James G. T., 68, 270, 279–
  80, 283, 413
dysentery, 126

Early, Jacob M., 18, 25, 40
Echo Canyon, 158
Eddy, Eleanor Priscilla, 99, 190, 192,
  236, 362
  death of, 267, 287
Eddy, James P. "Jimmy," 99, 190, 319–
  20, 325, 344, 362
Eddy, Margaret, 99, 190, 192, 362
  death of, 267, 287
Eddy, William Henry, 99, 170, 179,
  184, 187, 188, 190–92, 201, 215,
  222, 223, 226, 232, 236, 238–39,
  242–45, 247, 251, 257–61, 277,
  280, 286–88, 291, 337, 357, 362,
  425
  bear shot by, 223–24
  letter dictated by, 280, 282–83, 284,
    417
  Third Relief Party and, 339–50
Eddy family, 171, 199, 208
Eighth Judicial Circuit, 45
Elizabeth City, N.C., 12
Elliott, Milford "Milt," 43, 50, 58, 170,
  182, 184, 185–86, 188, 226, 233,
  235, 236, 238, 241, 255, 256, 319,
  362
  cannibalizing of, 320
  death of, 267
Emigrant Gap, 220, 273
Emigrant's Guide to Oregon and California
  (Hastings), 36, 92, 130, 315–16,
  357
Emigration Canyon, 162–63
English Grammar in Familiar Lectures
  (Kirkham), 263, 412
Eustis, Hannah Coggswell, 11
Eustis, Tamesin, 11
Eustis, William, 11
Eustis, William, Jr., 14
Ewing, Robert, 85, 123
Expedition, The (Houghton), 405

Fallon, William O., 351–54
Fanny (saddle horse), 44

Fever River, 17
firewood, 227, 253
First Episcopal Methodist Church
    (Springfield, Ill.), 33
First Relief Party, 282–91, 295, 297–
    309, 310, 311–13, 319, 324, 327
Flock of Sheep, The; or Familiar
    Explanations of Simple Facts, 263
Florence, Ill., 51
Ford, Thomas, 40
Forlorn Hope Party, 230–39, 240–49,
    250–51, 257–61, 277, 280, 298–99,
    310, 314, 337, 357
Fort Bernard, 126–32, 133, 134, 137
Fort Bridger, 142, 145, 146, 150,
    151–53, 157
Fort Hall, 29, 132, 145, 146, 147, 151
Fort Laramie, 29, 76, 112, 117, 118,
    123, 125, 126, 127, 130, 134, 149
Fort Sonoma, 292–93
Fort Sumter, 18
Fosdick, Jay, 222, 235, 247, 257, 258–
    59, 326, 362
    death of, 258
Fosdick, Sarah Graves, 235, 245–46,
    257, 258–59, 362
Foster, George (Jeremiah), 325, 362,
    424
    Third Relief Party and, 339–50
Foster, George, Jr.(one year old), 319–
    20, 325, 334
Foster, Sarah Murphy, 198, 223, 236,
    248, 249, 250, 258–59, 363
Foster, William McFadden, 198–99,
    215, 223, 227, 236, 237, 244, 247,
    250, 258–59, 337, 363
    death of, 344–45
    erratic behavior of, 259–60
    plan to kill Miwok guides by, 257
Fourth Relief Party, 351–54
Francis, Allen, 46, 49
Francis, Simeon, 46
Franklin, Mo., 52
Frazier, James Anderson, 16
Freemasons, 33–34
Frémont, Jessie Benton, 35
Frémont, John C., 34–36, 63, 86, 125,
    178, 221, 286, 296, 389

Bear Flag Revolt and, 218–19
    as symbol of Manifest Destiny, 35
Frémont Pass, 205–6, 209
Frémont Springs, 125
"French-Indians," 66
"French leave," 283
frostbite, 242, 251, 257, 332
Fugate Township, 7
Fulton, Mo., 67
fur trade, 151
fur trappers, 55, 80

Galena, Ill., 17
galena (ore), 17
Galena River, 17
gangrene, 107
Garrison, Abraham, 109
Garrison, Enoch, 107–9, 110, 158
Garrison, Henry, 107, 110
Garrison, Margaret Ellison, 107
Gazette, 119
Gendreau, Joseph, 296, 327, 335, 336
German Prairie, Ill., 11, 19
Gilpin, William, 269–70
Glaucus (Greek mythology), 47
Glaucus (horse), 47, 60, 68, 82, 101,
    106, 159, 170, 182, 185, 186,
    194–96, 310
Glaucus of Potniae, king of Efyra,
    386
Glover, Aquilla, 283, 285, 286, 290,
    303, 304–5, 306, 309, 310, 313
gluten paste, 19
gnats, 98
gold, 357
Gold Rush of 1849, 382
Goode, John B., 91
Gordon, John, 312, 313
Gordon, William, 294
Grand Island, 101
Gravelly Ford, 179
Graves, Eleanor (Ellen), 302, 363
Graves, Elizabeth, 342, 343, 363
Graves, Elizabeth Cooper, 162, 189,
    192, 235, 266, 310, 319, 320, 325,
    326, 328, 330, 363
    cans buried by, 326
    death of, 341–42

Graves, Franklin Ward, 162, 179, 183, 187, 208, 215, 222, 223, 224, 225, 228, 235, 237, 238, 244, 363
death of, 245–46
Graves, Franklin Ward, Jr., 341, 363
Graves, Jonathan, 342–43, 363
Graves, Lovina, 266, 302, 363
Graves, Mary Ann, 215, 223, 235, 237, 239, 242–43, 245–46, 258, 259, 357, 363, 411
Graves, Nancy, 342–43, 364
Graves, William Cooper, 183, 188, 206, 208, 225, 230, 250, 302, 364
Graves family, 181–82, 199, 200, 208, 255
Grayback Hills, 168
Grayson, Andrew Jackson, 72, 80, 85, 98, 102, 105, 153, 189, 217, 218, 279, 416
Grayson, Edward, 72
Grayson, Frances, 72, 85
"Great American Desert," 62
Great Basin, 35, 158–59
Great Blue Earth River, see Big Blue River
Great Britain, 27
Great Irish Famine, 410
Great Plains, 27, 62
Great Platte River Road, 100
Great Salt Lake, 160, 164–65
Great Salt Lake Desert, 165, 168–74
Great Salt Lake Valley, 164
Greek mythology, 248
Greeley, Horace, 56
Green River, 149, 151
Greenwood, Boggs, 419
Greenwood, Britton, 296, 317, 329, 332
Greenwood, Caleb, 29–30, 153, 292–93, 294, 295, 310, 419
Greenwood Cutoff, 153
Griggery, Eli, 395
Guadalupe Hidalgo, Treaty of, 413

Hadley Creek, 51
Hale, Sarah, 407–8
Halloran, Luke, 154, 161, 364, 398
death of, 165–66, 400
hallucinations, 331

Hannibal, Mo., 51
Hard Chief (Kaw leader), 78–79
Hardcoop, 96, 187–88, 189, 190, 364
Hargrave, John, 165
Harlan-Young Party, 152, 153, 158, 159, 160, 161, 165
Harper's Ferry, Va., 34
Harrison, William Henry, 67, 388
Hart Grove Creek, 61
Hastings, Lansford Warren, 36, 38, 92, 130–31, 133, 141, 142, 145, 146, 149, 150, 151–52, 153, 154, 159, 160, 161, 165, 167, 168, 176, 211, 315–16, 357
Hastings Cutoff, 142–43, 147, 151, 154–56, 157–63, 164, 165, 175, 177, 211, 269, 279, 357
Hastings Pass, 168
Hawaiian Islands, 40
Hemings, Sally, 68, 389
hemp, 51
Herndon, William H., 42
Herron, Walter, 43, 170, 171, 186, 197–98, 217, 364
in ride to Sutter's Fort, 194–96
hippomania, 386
Holloway, Susannah, 47
Hook, Solomon Elijah, 9, 42, 301, 324, 331, 364
Hook, William, 9, 42, 301, 313, 364
death of, 311–12
Hope Springs, 167
Hoppe, Jacob D., 153
Hoppe Party, 153
Houghton, Eliza P. Donner, xviii, xx, 385, 406, see also Donner, Eliza Poor
House of Representatives, U.S., 67
Hudspeth, James, 150, 151–52, 159
Hull, Joseph B., 270–71, 278–79, 292, 295
Humboldt River, 131, 158, 168, 176, 177–78
Humboldt Sink, 177, 190, 232
Hutchinson Cemetery, 46
hypothermia, 244, 246–47, 303, 410

Idaho, 29
Ide, William Brown, 29–30, 218

Illinois, xv, 8–9, 17, 18, 28
  cholera epidemic in, 20
  lead mining in, 16–17
  Mormon exodus from, 94
  railroad brought to, 21, 22–24
Illinois College, 50
Illinois prairie, 62
Illinois River, 50–51
Illinois State Journal, 46
incest, 248
Independence, Mo., 34, 47, 48, 55–59,
    71, 72, 316
  Donner Party arrival in, 55
  Donner Party departure from, 59
  Mexican trading caravans in, 57
  Public Square in, 56, 57
  springs near, 57
Independence Crossing, 83, 86
Independence Rock, 137, 139–40, 141
Indiana, 7
Indian Creek, 72
"Indian problem," 62
Indian Queen (sloop), 295–96
Indian Removal Act of 1830, 50
Indians, xv, xvii, 7, 28, 35, 36, 65–66,
    82, 91, 95, 102, 113, 120, 187, 260
  Donner-Reed Party's encounter
    with, 66–67, 178–79
  Russell Party encounters with,
    78–79, 93
  stereotypes of, 178–79
  trade with, 34, 41
  see also specific Indians
Indian Territory, 62
inflammatory rheumatism, 109
influenza epidemic, 13
Internal Improvements Act, 21
Internal Improvement System, 22
Ireland, 16
  potato famine in, xvi
Isaiah, Prophet, 166

Jackson, Andrew, 50
Jackson County, Mo., 155
Jacksonville, Ill., 23, 50
Jacksonville Road, 47, 50
James, Noah, 42, 114, 233, 235, 264–
    65, 301, 364
Jamestown, Ill., 21, 22, 24–25

Jamestown colony, 248, 410
Jefferson, Thomas, 27, 68, 389
Jefferson, Thomas H., 68, 153, 168,
    181, 389
Johnson, John Calhoun, 168
Johnson, Kristin, xvi–xvii, 411
Johnson, William, 285, 296
Johnson's Ranch, 209, 236, 261, 277,
    280, 281, 282, 284–85, 288, 294,
    296, 310, 312, 314, 337, 340, 343,
    349, 423
Jordan River, 164
Juzgado (San José), 272

Kansas, 62, 63, 70–71
Kansas City, Mo., 55
Kanza Indians, 78
Karankawa Indians, 10
Kaw Indians, 78–79, 80
Kaw (Kansas) River, 57, 64, 66–67
Kearny, Stephen W., 276
Kentucky, 6, 67
Kern, Edward Meyer, 219, 271, 283–
    84, 285
Keseberg, Elisabeth Philippine
    Zimmerman, 96, 166, 193, 208,
    265, 302, 308–9, 364, 368, 400,
    420
Keseberg, Johann Ludwig Christian
    "Lewis," 96–97, 136, 173, 187–88,
    210, 225, 253, 265–66, 315, 320,
    325, 334, 346, 348, 350, 352–54,
    356, 357, 365
  in attempt at crossing Frémont Pass,
    210, 211
  and death of William Foster, 344–45
  dislike of, 166
  foot wound of, 208, 215
  Reed loathed by, 184
  temper of, 96–97
Keseberg, Juliane Karoline "Ada," 96,
    302, 308, 354, 364, 420
  death of, 308
Keseberg, Lewis, Jr., 166, 265, 365
Keseberg, Mathilde Elise, 96
Keseberg family, 199, 255
Keyes, Elizabeth, 19–20
Keyes, Gershom, 47, 58–59, 317
Keyes, Humphrey, 19, 31

Keyes, James, 19–20, 47, 68, 70
Keyes, Mary C., 140
Keyes, Robert Caden, 29–30, 38, 218
Keyes, Sarah Handley, 19, 20, 22, 28,
    43–44, 47, 58, 65–66, 82, 89, 107,
    140, 166, 173, 187, 218, 307, 365
  death of, 87–88
  health of, 70
  wagon of, 38
Kinderhook, Ill., 51
Kirkendall, William Henry, 95, 105,
    123
Kirkham, Samuel, 263, 412

Lafitte, Jean, 10
land ownership, 71
Landrum, John, 264
Laramie Peak, 126
Lard, Mary Lucy, 110
La Salle (steamship), 198
laudanum, 108
Lavely, William, 39
lead (mineral), 16, 17
Lewis, Martha Jane Reed "Patty," *see*
    Reed, Martha Jane "Patty"
Lewis, Meriwether, 389
Lewis and Clark Expedition (1804),
    55, 389
Lexington, Mo., 51–52
lice, 266
Lienhard, Heinrich, 96–97, 153
"lighthouses" (bars), 17
Lincoln, Abraham, xvi, 18, 19, 21, 23,
    28–29, 39, 40, 42, 44–45, 46, 56,
    65, 130, 219, 274, 385, 407–8
  first major trial of, 25
Lincoln, Mary Todd, 23, 29, 44–45,
    49, 218
Lippincott, Benjamin S., 123, 189, 217,
    218
Little Blue River, 98, 100
Little Sandy Creek, 149, 279
Little Santa Fe, Mo., 61–62
Lone Elm, 63
Long Island, N.Y., 270
Los Angeles, Calif., 218
Los Gringos (Wise), 323–24
Louisiana, 65

Luis (Miwok Indian guide), 196–97,
    200, 208, 209, 210, 216, 226, 236,
    241, 247, 257, 258, 337, 365
  murder and cannibalization of,
    259–60

"Mad Woman Camp," 176
malnutrition, 230
Manifest Destiny, xv, xvii, 33, 48, 61,
    269–70, 351
  Benton on, 35
  critics of, 28
  origin of phrase, 27
  religious underpinnings of, 27–28
Margaret (saddle horse), 44, 177
Marines, U.S., 275
Mather, Thomas, 45
Maxey, James M., 33–34, 55–56
McCoon, Perry, 295, 296
McCutchen, Amanda Henderson, 155,
    176, 215–16, 235, 258, 259, 266,
    310, 365
McCutchen, Harriet, 155, 176, 235,
    310, 321, 365
  death of, 266
McCutchen, William, 155, 175–76,
    177, 179, 184, 186, 191, 193, 196,
    197, 219–21, 235, 264, 266, 269,
    270, 273, 286, 289, 292, 293,
    295–96, 310, 319, 320–21, 329,
    330, 365
McFarlan's Castle, 124
McGlashan, Charles F., 209–10, 231,
    238, 245, 246, 323, 329, 335, 343,
    345, 421
McKinstry, George W., 77, 84, 85, 86,
    97, 123, 127, 217, 272, 293–94
Meredosia, Ill., 22, 23
Merryman, J. H., 318, 322
Mexican-American War, xvi, 61, 65,
    272–76, 283, 293
Mexicans, 36
Mexico, xvii, 28, 61, 65, 217, 272, 273,
    276
  U.S. war with, xvi, 61, 65, 272–76,
    283, 293
Miami Indians, 7
Miller, Hiram Owens, 42–43, 60–61,

106, 113–14, 137, 138, 154, 297, 325, 329, 330, 331, 339–50, 366
mirages, 124, 169–70
Mission San José, 276–77
Mississippi River, 50, 51, 386
Missouri, 55
  as pro-slavery, 56
Missouri River, 51, 101
  as epicenter of western migration, 55–56
Missouri Statesman, 118
Miwok Indians, 196–97, 225, 260–61
Mojave Desert, 159
Monterey, Calif., 30, 218, 274, 315
Monterey Californian, 324
Montgomery, John B., 274
Morgan, Dale E., 68
Mormons, 73, 93–94, 95, 117, 142, 148
Mormon War of 1846, 382
mosquitoes, 98
Moutrey, Mary Lucy Lard, 284
Moutrey, Riley Septimus "Sept," 110, 283–84, 300, 304, 306, 309
Mule Creek Camp, 314
mules, 37, 133–34
Mule Springs, 288, 290, 297, 309, 310, 312–13, 337, 340, 349
Murphy, Jeremiah, 148
Murphy, John Landrum, 265–66, 366
Murphy, Lemuel B., 235, 237, 250, 252, 264, 366
  death of, 248–49
Murphy, Levinah W. Jackson, 147–48, 198, 236, 252, 264–66, 299, 319–20, 325, 334, 344–46, 348, 350, 353, 366
Murphy, Meriam "Mary M.," 198, 302, 313, 366
Murphy, Simon Peter, 265, 319, 325, 334, 345, 346, 348, 366
Murphy, Virginia Reed, *see* Reed, Virginia Elizabeth Backenstoe
Murphy, William Green, 235, 237, 252, 265, 266, 302, 312, 313, 314, 366, 404

Napoleon I, emperor of France, 28
Native Sons of the Golden West, xix

Navy, U.S., 123, 282
Neanderthals, 248
Nevada, xvi, 158, 175
Nevada County, Calif., 413
New Mexico, xvi
New Orleans Picayune, 65
New Purchase, 7
North Carolina, 5
Northern Cross Railroad, 21, 22–24, 45
North Platte River, 101, 119, 122, 126, 139

Oakley, Howard, 339–50
Old City Graveyard (Springfield, Ill.), 46
"Olden Oaken Bucket, The" (Woodworth), 123
Older, Cora Baggerly, 414
opium, 126
Oregon Territory, 27, 29, 35, 36, 44–45, 56, 71
Oregon Trail, 34, 35, 55, 57, 63–64
Oregon Trail, The: Sketches of Prairie and Rocky Mountain Life (Parkman), 57
Organ, Micajah, 9
Organ, Susannah Donner, 5, 9
O'Sullivan, John L., xv, 27
Otoe Indians, 101
oxbows, 177
oxen, 34, 37, 47, 209

Pacific Spring, 144
Pacific Squadron, 123
Paiute Indians, 178, 179, 187, 189–90, 191, 193
Palmer, Joel, 118–19, 394
Palmyra, Mo., 56
Panic of 1837, xv, 10, 22, 28
Parkman, Francis, 57, 63, 78, 101, 126–27, 129–30, 134
Pasquotank River, 12
Pauta Pass, 181
Pawnee Indians, 78, 90–91, 93, 118, 122, 390
pepperbox (handgun), 198
Permanent Indian Frontier (Indian Territory), 62

Pike, Caroline, 302
Pike, Catherine, 264, 366
    death of, 299–300
Pike, Harriet Frances Murphy, 198–99,
    235–36, 248, 299, 366
Pike, Naomi Levinah, 299, 302, 308,
    366, 420
Pike, William, 159–60, 162, 182, 187,
    198–99, 236, 367, 404
Pilot Peak, 169, 170–71, 172, 174
Pinkney, Robert F., 276
Pioneer Monument, *xviii*, xix–xx
"Pioneer Prairie Palace" (wagon), 38,
    41, 401
Plains Indians, 120
"Plains oak" (bison manure), 103
Platte River, 80, 93, 99, 100–102,
    103–4, 112, 113
plovers, 104
plows, prairie-breaking, 9
Poland, 16
Polk, James K., xvi, 61, 218
Poor, Elizabeth Eustis "Betsey," 12, 13,
    57–58
potato famine, xvi
Potawatomi Indians, 9, 50, 51
Potawatomi Trail of Death, 50
prairie, 8, 70–71, 79–80, 100, 113
prairie breaking, 9
Prairie Christian Church (German
    Prairie, Ill.), 33
prairie dogs, 104
prairie peas, 85
"prairie potato," 79
prairie schooners, 63
prairie wolf (coyote), 223
Prince Darco (greyhound), 56
"Problem with Eyewitness Testimony,
    The," 402
Proclamation of Thanksgiving,
    407–8
Prosser Creek, 212
Prussia, 16
Putnam, Charles, 119
Putnam, Nathan, 119
Pyle, Edward, Jr., 314

Quincy, Ill., 56

railroads, construction of, 23
Rancho del Paso, 314, 340
Redlum Spring, 168
Reed, Gershom Francis, 28, 31, 46
Reed, James Frazier (Francis), 16–21,
    22, 28–29, 33, 43, 56, 58, 60, 68,
    71, 82, 83, 84, 86, 87, 90, 97, 101,
    105, 117, 130, 131, 135, 137, 144,
    145, 148, 153, 155, 157, 159–61,
    163, 165–66, 170, 173, 179, 180,
    181, 197–98, 211, 216, 219, 221,
    254, 264, 269–74, 282, 286, 289,
    298, 309–10, 315, 340, 357, 358,
    367, 401
    advice sought by, 33–34
    arrogance of, 106, 269
    banishment of, 184–86
    bankruptcy of, 39
    in Battle of Santa Clara, 275
    bison hunting by, 106
    in Black Hawk War, 18–19
    Butler lawsuit against, 32
    California property bought by,
        270–72
    Clyman's advice to, 131–32
    collapse on Second Relief of, 328–
        29
    correspondence of, 70
    and death of youngest child, 31
    in decision to leave Illinois, 28–30,
        31
    diary of, 402, 422
    as entrepreneur, 19, 21
    in failed attempt to reach Donner-
        Reed Party, 219–20
    financial troubles of, 24–26, 31–32,
        39–40
    at Fort Bridger, 150
    Grandma Keyes's wagon and, 38
    at Independence Rock, 141
    as Indian agent, 40
    legal challenges of, 38
    letters of introduction carried by, 40,
        68
    lieutenant commission of, 272–73
    Lincoln friendship of, 25
    marriage to Margret Keyes
        Backenstoe of, 20

Masonic membership of, 33–34, 40
mill of, 21, 22, 24–25, 43, 50
Mission San José controlled by, 276–77
as pension agent, 25
plan to get supplies from Sutter of, 175–76
railroad contract of, 21, 22–24
rescue party formed by, 278–81
in ride to Sutter's Fort, 194–96
in San Francisco, 278–79
Second Relief Party and, 292–338
secret money stash of, 219
self-confidence of, 31
Snyder's attack on, 182–83, 403
as standard bearer for Manifest Destiny, 269–70
at Sutter's Fort, 217–19, 270
on Vasquez and Bridger, 155–56
Reed, James Frazier, Jr. (Francis), 20, 43, 201, 255, 304, 305, 307, 315, 340, 367
Reed, Margret Wilson Keyes Backenstoe "Peggy," 20, 22, 28, 31, 43, 46, 58, 70, 87, 128, 135, 161, 171, 183, 185, 188, 199, 200, 216, 228, 253–55, 265, 267, 302, 303–4, 311, 312, 313, 314–15, 324, 328, 340, 349, 358, 367
attempt to cross Sierras made by, 255–56
in Breen cabin, 256
dog killed by, 254
migraines of, 57, 90, 222
oxen bought by, 222
Reed, Martha Frazier, 16
Reed, Martha Jane "Patty," *xviii*, xx, 20, 43–44, 82, 88, 173, 201, 209, 215, 255, 266, 303, 304, 318–19, 325, 329, 358, 367
doll of, 173, 263, 339–40
hallucination of, 331
Reed, Thomas Keyes "Tommy," 20, 43, 201, 255, 303, 318–19, 325, 331, 340, 367
Reed, Virginia Elizabeth Backenstoe, 20, 22, 28, 38, 41, 43–44, 47, 48, 50, 51, 75, 82, 87, 119–20, 134–35,

138–39, 140, 157, 159, 161, 164, 168–69, 171–72, 173, 182–83, 185–87, 200–201, 210, 230, 252, 253, 254, 255, 256, 262–63, 267, 268, 269, 303, 304, 305, 307, 311, 313–14, 331, 340, 358, 367, 401, 412
on Big Blue crossing, 89
conversion of, 263, 298
fear of Indians of, 65–66
marriage proposal to, 314
Reinhardt, Joseph, 97, 191, 193, 214, 228, 368, 369
confession of, 241
death of, 231–32
Report of the Exploring Expedition to the Rocky Mountains in the Year 1842 (Frémont), 35–36
Republican Party, 25
Rhoads, Amanda, 284
Rhoads, Daniel, 284, 288–89, 290–91, 299, 306, 307, 309, 310
Rhoads, John, 285, 300, 302, 306, 308, 417, 420
Rhoads, Thomas Foster, 284
Ritchie, Harriet, 261, 286
Ritchie, Matthew Dill, 261, 286, 289, 290, 418
Ritchie, William Dill, 286
Roberts, John, 25
Rockwell, Orrin Porter, 73, 142
Rocky Mountains, 101, 126, 130
Rough and Ready, Calif., 413
Round Grove, *see* Lone Elm
Ruby Mountains, 176, 177
Ruby Valley, 168
Russell, William Henry "Owl," 67–69, 71, 72, 83, 85, 113, 117–18, 119, 129, 131, 145, 217, 272, 279, 388, 394
resignation of as emigrant leader, 120
Russell, Zanette Freeland, 67
Russell Party, 67, 70, 74, 75–81, 82–83, 86, 91, 117, 124, 129, 145, 148, 152, 189, 217, 270, 394
at Big Blue River, 83–88
Big Blue River crossed by, 89–90

Russell Party (*continued*)
  bison herds encountered by, 105–6
  bylaws and regulations governing,
    84–85
  children of, 119
  command change of, 120–21
  Curry's chronicling of, 77–78
  disagreements in, 91
  discontent with regulations of, 85
  diversity of members of, 71–72
  fear of Mormons and, 93–94
  fights among, 90
  German contingency of, 96–97
  governing of, 71
  human skull found by, 102
  hunting by, 97–98, 103–6, 112,
    117–18
  Indian encounters of, 78–79, 93
  markmanship practice by, 76
  Oregon emigrants' departure from,
    91–92
  overturned wagon of, 95–96
  Palmer party met by, 118–19
  on Platte River, 100–102, 103–4,
    112–14
  sickness in, 93, 98, 117–18
  slow pace of, 77, 81, 118
  South Platte crossed by, 119–20
  splitting of, 77
  violence in, 95
  "Young Men" faction of, 85
  see also Boggs Party; Donner-Reed
    Party
Russia, 16

Sacramento (launch), 280
Sacramento River, 270
Sacramento Valley, 282
St. Charles, Mo., 55
St. Joseph, Mo., 55, 71
St. Louis, Mo., 51, 55, 124
St. Louis Reveille, 104, 117
St. Louis Weekly Reveille, 77, 127
Sallee, William Pierre, 189, 403
salt flats, 168–69
Salt Lake, 131, 132, 142, 152
Salt Lake Valley, 162–63
Salvador (Miwoke Indian guide), 196–

97, 200, 208, 209, 210, 216, 226,
    236, 241, 247, 257, 258, 337, 368
  murder and cannibalism of, 259–60
Sanchez, Don Francisco, 275
sandhill cranes, 104
Sandwich Islands, 40
San Francisco, Calif., 132, 221, 270,
    277, 278–79, 281, 282, 315, 413,
    415
Sangamo Journal, 36–37, 39, 46, 49
Sangamon County, Ill., 9, 11, 18, 28
Sangamon River, 9, 21
San José, Calif., 271–72, 358
San Juan Batista, 357
Santa Barbara, Calif., 218
Santa Clara, Battle of, 275–76
Santa Clara de Asis, 275
Santa Fe, N.Mex., 60, 63
Santa Fe Trail, 34, 52, 55, 57, 60–64, 73
scalping, 93, 392
Schallenberger, Moses, 207, 215
Scott, Hiram, 125
Scotts Bluff, 125
Second Great Awakening, 27
Second Relief Party, 292–338, 339, 344
Sels, Joseph, 284, 286, 306
Senate, U.S., 35, 67
Shakespeare, William, 248
Shawnee Indians, 66, 93
Shoemaker, Samuel, 42, 228, 323, 368
  death of, 231–32
Shoshone Indians, 177, 178
Sierra Nevada Mountains, xvi, xix, 30,
    35–36, 132, 158–59, 182, 193, 194,
    199, 207
  1846–1847 snowstorms in, 205–16
Sinclair, John, 280–81, 282, 284, 287,
    314–15, 340, 349, 351, 417
Sinclair, Mary, 282–83, 314–15
Sioux Indians, 122, 127, 128–29, 134–
    35, 136, 138–39
Six Mile Ranch, 168
Skull Valley, 166, 168
slaves, slavery, xv, xvi, 27, 51, 56
slave trade, 197
Smith, James, 43, 228, 368
  death of, 231–32
Smith, Joseph, 73, 93

snake heads, 23
Snake Indians, 29
Snake River, 147
snow blindness, 238, 264
snowshoes, 228, 257, 289, 291
Snyder, John, 162, 181–82, 184, 185, 189, 216, 358, 368, 403
Soldier Creek, 67–68, 69, 70
South Pass, 141, 144
South Platte River, 101, 119
Spanish missions, 276
Spitzer, Augustus, 97, 191, 193, 215, 228, 232–33, 241, 253, 368
    death of, 267
Spottswood, Henry, 25
Spottswood, James, 25
Spring Creek, 45
Springfield, Ill., xv, xvi, 9, 18, 22–23, 44, 57, 148
    earliest burial site in, 46
    reading society of, 46
Springfield Lodge No. 4, A.F. & A.M. (Springfield, Ill.), 33–34
"Spy Company," 18–19
"squaw man," 29
Stansbury Mountains, 166
Stanton, Charles Tyler, 92–93, 100, 101, 122, 135–36, 139, 141–42, 143, 144, 154, 158, 159–60, 162, 177, 179, 184, 186, 191, 193, 196, 197–98, 200, 208, 209–10, 216, 223, 225–26, 227, 228, 233, 235, 236, 238, 240, 368, 421
    death of, 239
    poem written by, 239
    in ride to Sutter's Fort for supplies, 176
Stanton, Philip, 239
Stanton, Sidney, 100
starch, 19
Stark, John, 276
Stark, John Schull, 339–50
starvation, 246, 303
    symptoms of, 243
Starved Camp, 327–30, 334, 335–36, 341, 342, 344, 349
State School for the Deaf and Dumb (Jacksonville, Ill.), 50

Steep Hollow Creek, 287–88
Stephens, W. D., *xviii*
Stevens-Townsen-Murphy Party, 207
Stewart, George R., 332, 412, 417
Stockton, Robert F., 278
Stone, Charles, 296, 317–18, 319, 320, 325, 332–34, 339–50, 421
Stone, Theophilus, 51
Stone, William S., 55–56
"stone duels," 17
Suarez del Real, José María, 277
Sugar Creek, Ill., 11, 14
Summit Valley, 327
Sutter, John A., 29, 30, 168, 175, 186, 196, 197, 200, 210, 217, 219, 225, 226, 270, 275, 277, 280, 284, 288, 314, 357, 421
    slave trading by, 197, 200
Sutter's Fort, 29, 30, 36, 176, 194–95, 205–6, 219, 269, 270, 279, 282, 283, 293, 340, 349, 399
    First Relief's arrival at, 314
Sweetwater River, 139, 141
Switzler, William F., 118

Taos Lightning, 128
Taylor, John, 21, 24–25
Taylor, Zachary, 61, 385
teamsters, 38, 42–43
    duties of, 37
Texas, 10, 27, 61, 65, 273
    annexation of, xvi
Thanksgiving Day, 226
Third Relief Party, 339–50
Thirty-Two Mile Creek, 100
Thompson, William, 311, 339–50
Thornton, Jessy Quinn, 56–57, 64, 74, 80, 84, 85, 89, 91, 107–8, 109–10, 124, 129, 131, 136, 137, 138, 145, 146, 147, 170, 201, 259, 280, 321–22, 341
Thornton, Nancy, 74, 80, 91, 109, 110, 129, 137, 145, 147
tobacco, 51, 136
Todd, William Levi, 29–30, 49, 218
toilet paper, 394
Tooele Valley, 160
Towser (dog), 319

Tracker (dog), 75
trade goods, 34, 41
traders, 55
Trailer (dog), 75
transcontinental railroad, 100
Truckee, Calif., xix
Truckee Lake, *see* Donner Lake
Truckee Meadows, 193, 194, 198–99
Truckee River, 36, 192–93, 194, 201
Truckee Route, 191–92, 207
Trudeau, Jean-Baptiste, 154, 212, 213, 214, 225, 233, 264–65, 301, 321, 323–24, 332, 346, 347, 348, 349, 369
Truett, Henry B., 25
Tucker, George W., 285, 287–88, 417
Tucker, Reason Penelope, 285, 286, 290, 291, 298, 300–301, 303, 306, 307, 308–9, 313, 317, 418
Turner, John, 296, 317, 327, 335, 336, 419, 423
Tversky, Barbara, 402
Twenty Wells, 166
Tyler (dog), 75

United States Magazine and Democratic Review, 27
urbanization, xv
U.S. Model 1841, 34
Utah, xvi, 158

Vallejo, Mariano, 292
Vasquez, Pierre Luis "Louis," 149, 150–51, 152, 153–54, 155
Vermillion Creek, 82–83
Verrot, Joseph, 286, 288, 325
Virginia, 16
voyageur, 286

Wabash Railroad, 24
wagon trains:
    dangers of, 72
    departure times for, 55, 316
    governing of, 71
    illness on, 107–9
    letters exchanged by, 118
    marriages on, 109–10
    privacy on, 119
    speed of, 60
    stream fording by, 61, 76
    troublemakers weeded out by, 68
    women on, 82
    see also specific wagon trains
Wakarusa River, 64
Walker, Joseph R., 151, 153
Wall, J. B., 118
War of 1812, 7, 16, 130
Warren (sloop), 275
Wasatch Mountains, 131, 158–59, 160, 162–63, 164
Washington, George, 130
Washoe Indians, 227
weapons, 34, 37–38, 41
Weber, John R., 24
Weber, Joseph María, 272, 274–75, 277
Weber Canyon, 159–60
Weber River, 293
Westport, Mo., 55
Whig Party, xvi, 25, 65, 130
whiskey, 62, 398
Wilder, Frances Donner, *xviii*, xx, *see also* Donner, Frances Eustis
Wilderness Road, 6
wild rose, 79
wild tulip, 79
Williams, Baylis, 46, 70, 75, 170, 188, 228, 253, 369, 400
    albinism of, 43
    death of, 230
Williams, Eliza, 43, 119, 228, 255, 265, 302, 369
Wind River Range, 143, 144
Wisconsin, 18
Wise, Henry Augustus, 323–24
Wolfinger, Dorthea (Doris), 97, 190–91, 193, 199, 201, 213, 232–33, 301, 369
Wolfinger, Jacob Karl, 97, 190–91, 241, 267, 369
    death of, 193, 232–33
wolverines, 289, 418
Wood River, 101
Woodworth, Samuel, 123

Woodworth, Selim Edward, 123, 294–95, 297, 312–13, 324, 325, 327, 332, 335–36, 337–38, 339
  cowardice of, 336–37
Wyoming Territory, 76, 102, 126

Yerba Buena, *see* San Francisco, Calif.
Young, Brigham, 93–94
Young, Samuel, 155
Yount, George C., 293, 401–2
Yuba River, 290–91, 327, 332

ABOUT THE AUTHOR

A best-selling author and award-winning reporter, Michael Wallis is a historian and biographer of the American West who has gained national prominence for a body of work beginning in 1988 with *Oil Man*, his biography of Frank Phillips.

His fifteen other books include *Route 66: The Mother Road*, credited with sparking the resurgence of interest in the highway, as well as *The Real Wild West: The 101 Ranch and the Creation of the American West*, *Mankiller: A Chief and Her People*, *Way Down Yonder in the Indian Nation: Writings from America's Heartland*, *Pretty Boy: The Life and Times of Charles Arthur Floyd*, *Billy the Kid: The Endless Ride*, and *David Crockett: The Lion of the West*. His work has appeared in hundreds of national and international magazines and newspapers, including *Time, Life, People, Smithsonian, The New Yorker,* and the *New York Times*.

Wallis has won many prestigious awards and honors. They include the Will Rogers Spirit Award, the Western Heritage Award from the National Cowboy & Western Heritage Museum, the Oklahoma Book Award from the Oklahoma Center for the Book, and the Best Western Nonfiction Award from the Western Writers of America.

He was inducted into the Writers Hall of Fame of America and the Oklahoma Professional Writers Hall of Fame and was the first inductee into the Oklahoma Route 66 Hall of Fame. He received the Arrell Gibson Lifetime Achievement Award from the Oklahoma Center for the Book, as well as the Lynn Riggs Award and the first John Steinbeck Award.

A charismatic speaker who has lectured extensively throughout the United States, Wallis was featured as the voice of the Sheriff in *Cars*, an animated feature film from Pixar Studios.

Wallis and his wife, Suzanne Fitzgerald Wallis, make their home in Tulsa, Oklahoma.